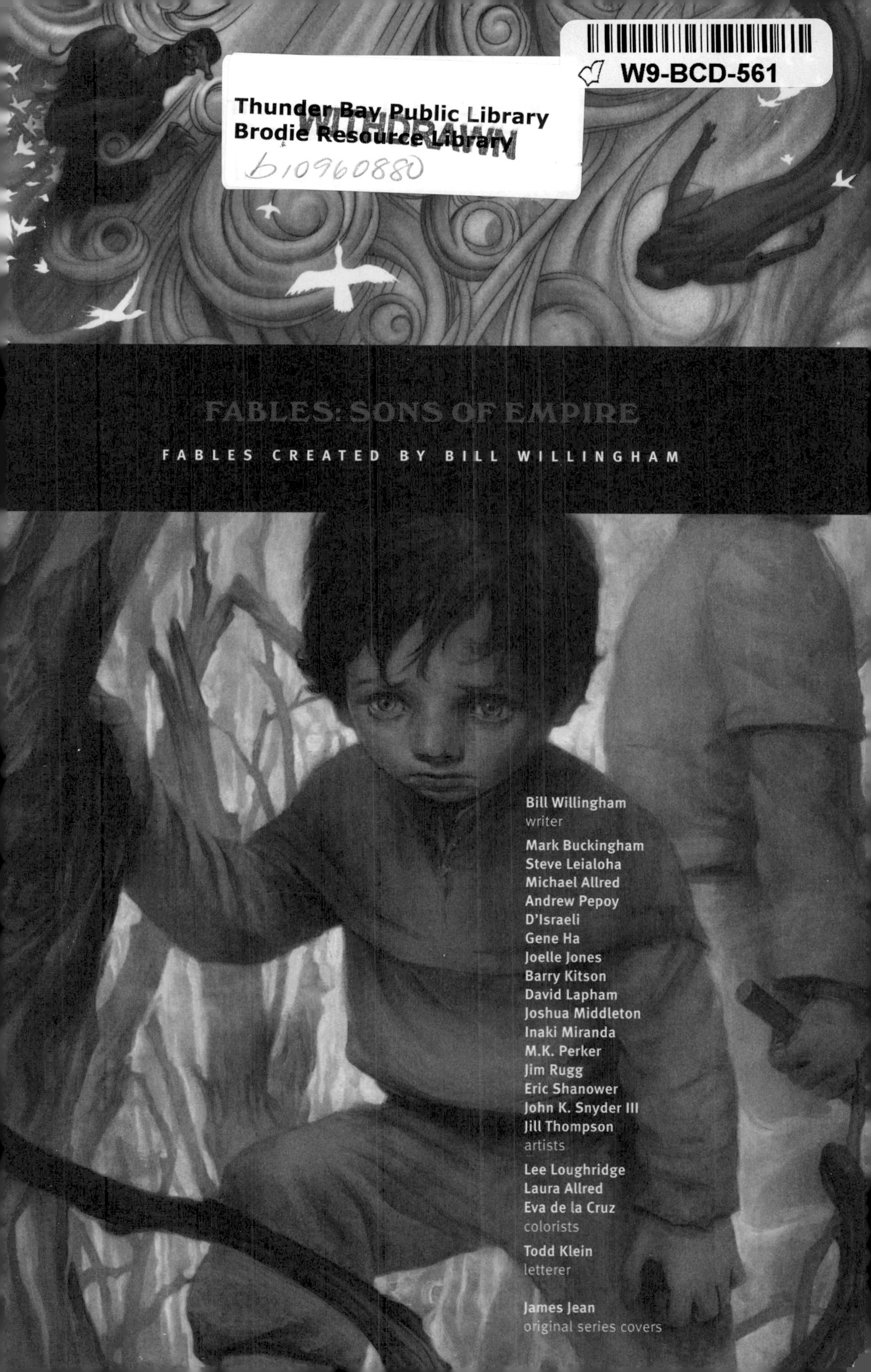

FABLES: SONS OF EMPIRE

FABLES CREATED BY BILL WILLINGHAM

Bill Willingham
writer

Mark Buckingham
Steve Leialoha
Michael Allred
Andrew Pepoy
D'Israeli
Gene Ha
Joelle Jones
Barry Kitson
David Lapham
Joshua Middleton
Inaki Miranda
M.K. Perker
Jim Rugg
Eric Shanower
John K. Snyder III
Jill Thompson
artists

Lee Loughridge
Laura Allred
Eva de la Cruz
colorists

Todd Klein
letterer

James Jean
original series covers

KAREN BERGER Senior VP-Executive Editor **SHELLY BOND** Editor-original series **ANGELA RUFINO** Assistant Editor-original series
SCOTT NYBAKKEN Editor-collected edition **ROBBIN BROSTERMAN** Senior Art Director **PAUL LEVITZ** President & Publisher
GEORG BREWER VP-Design & DC Direct Creative **RICHARD BRUNING** Senior VP-Creative Director
PATRICK CALDON Executive VP-Finance & Operations **CHRIS CARAMALIS** VP-Finance **TERRI CUNNINGHAM** VP-Managing Editor
ALISON GILL VP-Manufacturing **HANK KANALZ** VP-General Manager, WildStorm **JIM LEE** Editorial Director-WildStorm
PAULA LOWITT Senior VP-Business & Legal Affairs **MARYELLEN MCLAUGHLIN** VP-Advertising & Custom Publishing
JOHN NEE VP-Business Development **GREGORY NOVECK** Senior VP-Creative Affairs **SUE POHJA** VP-Book Trade Sales
CHERYL RUBIN Senior VP-Brand Management **JEFF TROJAN** VP-Business Development, DC Direct **BOB WAYNE** VP-Sales

Cover illustration by James Jean.
Logo design by Brainchild Studios/NYC

F A B L E S :   S O N S   O F   E M P I R E

DC Comics, 1700 Broadway, New York, NY 10019
A Warner Bros. Entertainment Company
Printed in Canada. First Printing.
ISBN: 1-4012-1316-2
ISBN: 978-1-4012-1316-9

*This volume marks my 20th anniversary as a professional comic artist, which seems like the perfect moment to thank those who
were with me at the beginning. My old Stoke gang: Dribbs, Yok, Drew, Chris Ski and especially Shane Oakley and Matt Brooker.
The Best of Friends. The Best of Times. This is also for Neil Gaiman. The Best of Best Men.*

— *Mark Buckingham*

This volume is dedicated to Steve Graves, treasured old ghost.

— *Bill Willingham*

Table of Contents

Who's Who in Fabletown 4

Sons of Empire, Chapter One:
Some Ideas Toward the Prospect of a Final Solution for Fabletown 7
Pencils by Mark Buckingham • Inks by Steve Leialoha • Colors by Lee Loughridge

Hair 27
Art by Gene Ha • Colors by Lee Loughridge

Sons of Empire, Chapter Two:
The Four Plagues 30
Pencils by Mark Buckingham • Inks by Steve Leialoha and Andrew Pepoy • Colors by Lee Loughridge

Porky Pine Pie 50
Art by Joshua Middleton

Sons of Empire, Chapter Three:
The Burning Times 53
Pencils by Mark Buckingham • Inks by Steve Leialoha and Andrew Pepoy • Colors by Lee Loughridge

A Thorn In Their Side? 73
Art by Michael Allred • Colors by Laura Allred

Sons of Empire, Chapter Four:
Over There 76
Pencils by Mark Buckingham • Inks by Steve Leialoha anc Andrew Pepoy • Colors by Lee Loughridge

The Road to Paradise 96
Art by Inaki Miranda • Colors by Eva de la Cruz

Jiminy Christmas 99
Pencils by Mark Buckingham • Inks by Steve Leialoha, Andrew Pepoy and Mark Buckingham
Colors by Lee Loughridge

Father and Son, Chapter One:
A Man's Home Is His Castle 132
Art by Michael Allred • Colors by Laura Allred

Father and Son, Chapter Two:
Big Scary Monsters! 155
Art by Michael Allred • Colors by Laura Allred

Burning Questions 179

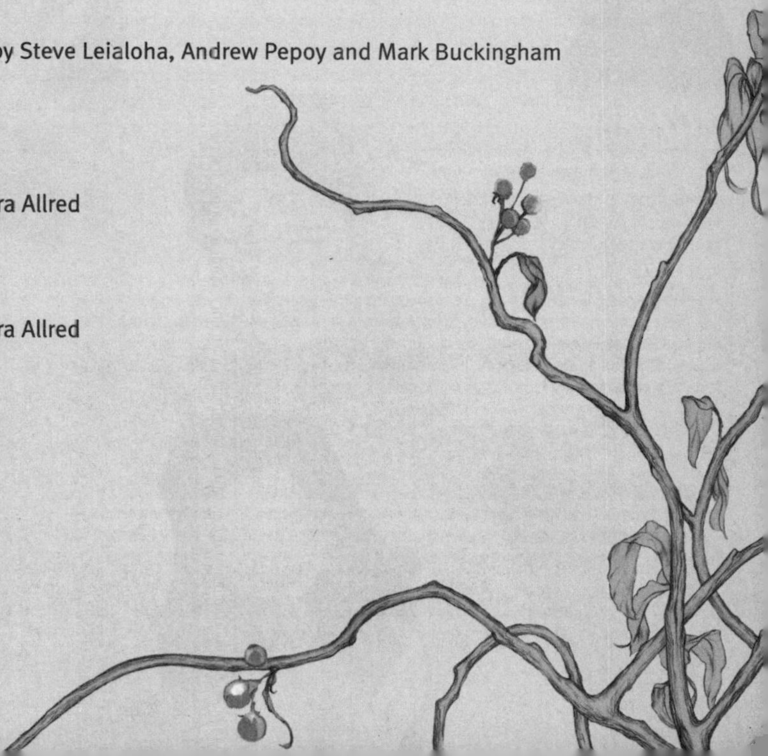

WHO'S WHO IN FABLETOWN

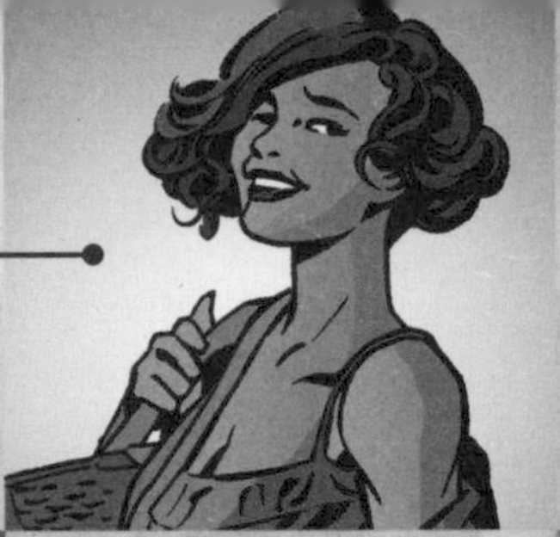

RED RIDING HOOD

The newest arrival from the Homelands, she turned out not to be Boy Blue's true love — but why is she hanging around Flycatcher so often?

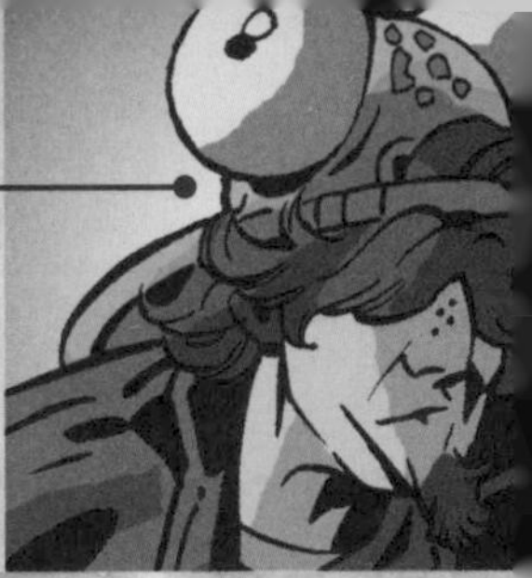

FLYCATCHER

Prince Ambrose, the legendary Frog Prince. A nice and unassuming fellow who keeps the Woodland Building clean.

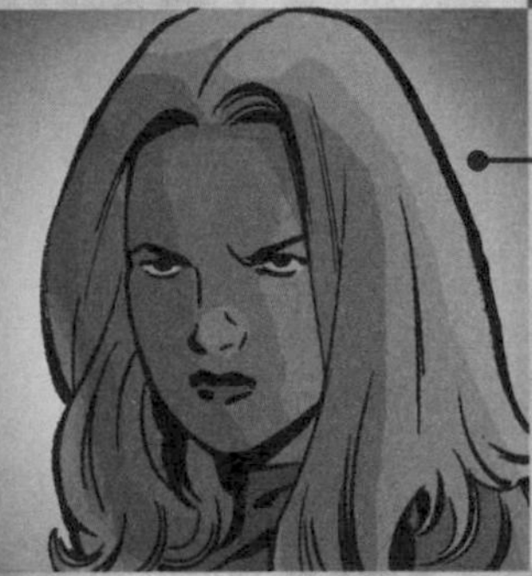

BEAUTY

She's still married to Beast after all these years, and now she's the deputy mayor of Fabletown.

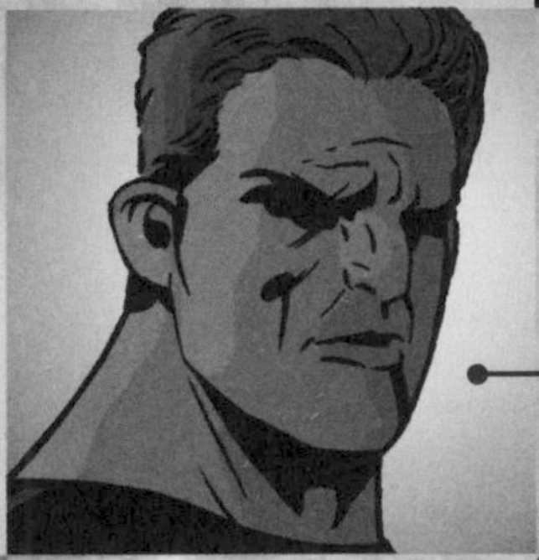

BEAST

Beauty's husband and the sheriff of Fabletown.

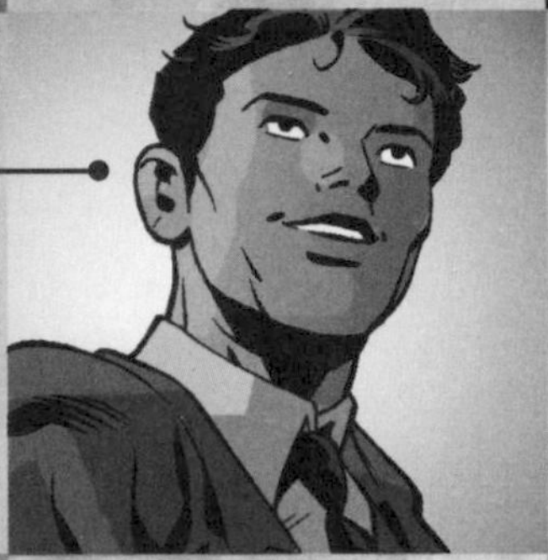

PRINCE CHARMING

The mayor of Fabletown and a womanizing rake of some repute.

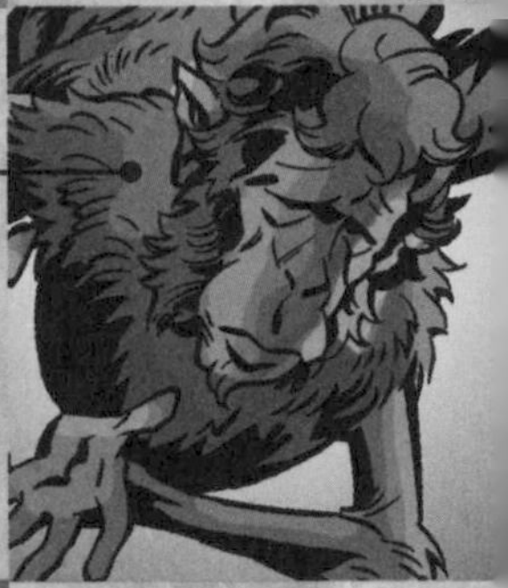

BUFKIN

A flying monkey who works in the Woodland's business office. Sometimes he drinks too much and sometimes he sees too much.

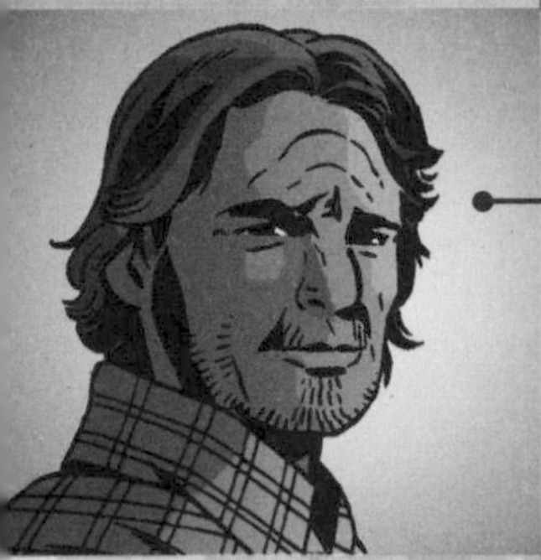

BIGBY WOLF

He's married to Snow White now and lives with her and their cubs in Wolf Valley, just east of The Farm.

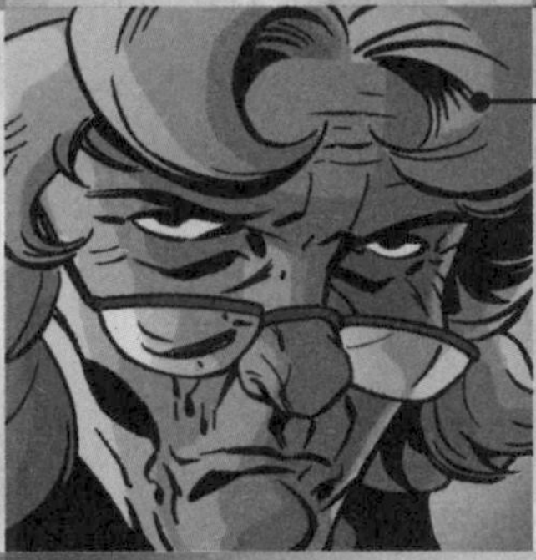

FRAU TOTENKINI

The legendary Black Forest W
She's up to something — something she has not yet revealed to her fellow Fable

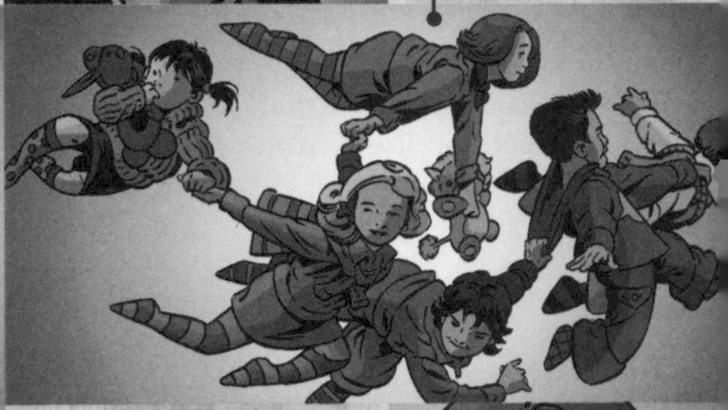

THE CUBS

Darien, Ambrose, Blossom, Winter, Therese and Conner. They're growing like weeds.

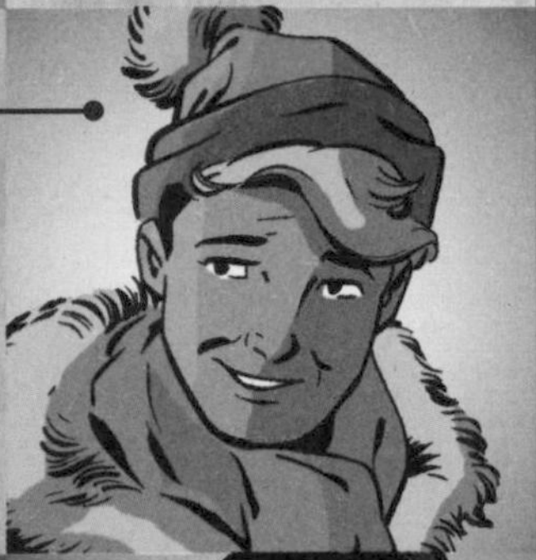

BOY BLUE

Once a hero and once a clerk, now he's up at the Farm, working off a debt to Fabletown society.

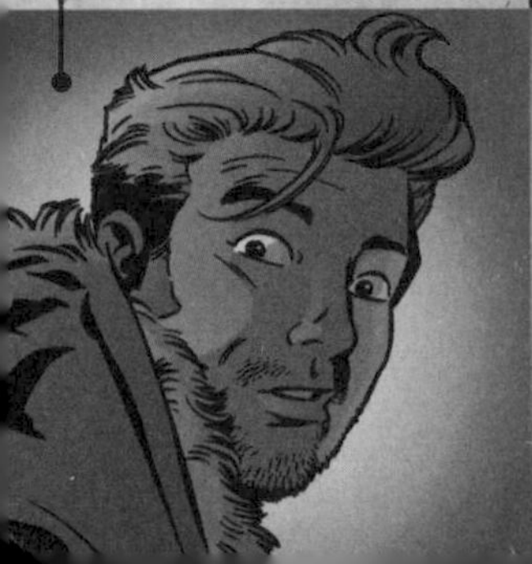

JACK HORNER

A con man and trickster. He was booted out of Fabletown forever years ago.

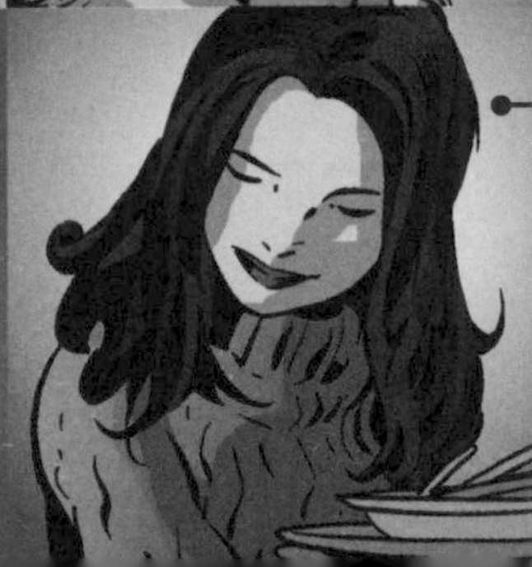

SNOW WHITE

The former deputy mayor of Fabletown, she's now raising her children with Bigby in Wolf Valley.

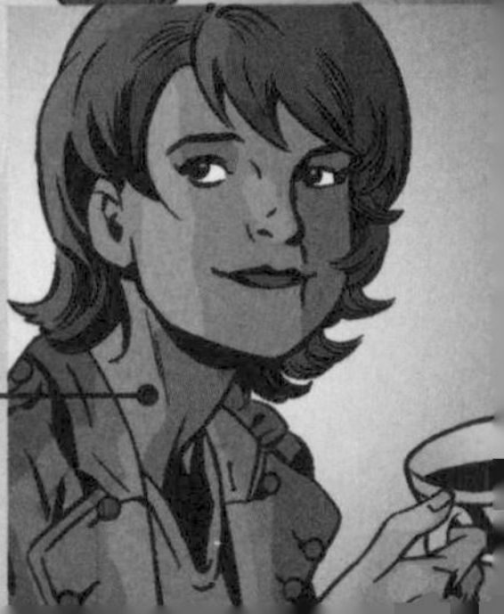

ROSE RED

Snow White's twin sister. She used to be the bad girl, but now she runs the Farm.

WHO'S WHO OUTSIDE OF FABLETOWN

GEPPETTO

The bloody-handed Adversary, conqueror of the Homelands and the real power behind the throne of the Empire.

PINOCCHIO

As the first-carved, he's Geppetto's most beloved son — but he's also a bit of a brat.

THE EMPEROR

Another of Geppetto's carved magic puppets, he's the Empire's figurehead.

MUDDLECOCK

A humble clerk in the vast Imperial bureaucracy, blessed with above average intellect and deductive skills.

THE SNOW QUEEN

Her friends can call her Lumi. She's a wicked sorceress and one of Geppetto's chief lieutenants and enforcers.

SIR RODNEY GREENWOOD

Once a wooden soldier, now he's real flesh and blood — and one of the Empire's spies in Fabletown.

KEVIN THORN

He's just a normal mundane human, right? Then why is he able to see things others can't?

THE GIANTS OF THE CLOUD KINGDOMS

New allies of Fabletown in an alliance against the Empire.

MR. NORTH

He's the mighty North Wind as well as Bigby's father and beloved grandfather to the cubs.

MISTRAL

A minor wind, one of Mr. North's many attendants.

THE STORY SO FAR

In retribution for the Adversary's attack against them (documented in FABLES VOL. 4: MARCH OF THE WOODEN SOLDIERS), the citizens of Fabletown have finally struck back at the Homelands Empire, destroying the magic grove of trees from which Geppetto's animated puppet children are carved. Has an all-out war been started or averted as a result? No one can say just yet, but in the meantime Fabletown is enjoying a rare time of peace. Bigby and Snow were finally married, and moved with their cubs into a new home in the recently christened Wolf Valley, just east of the Farm. All seems well.

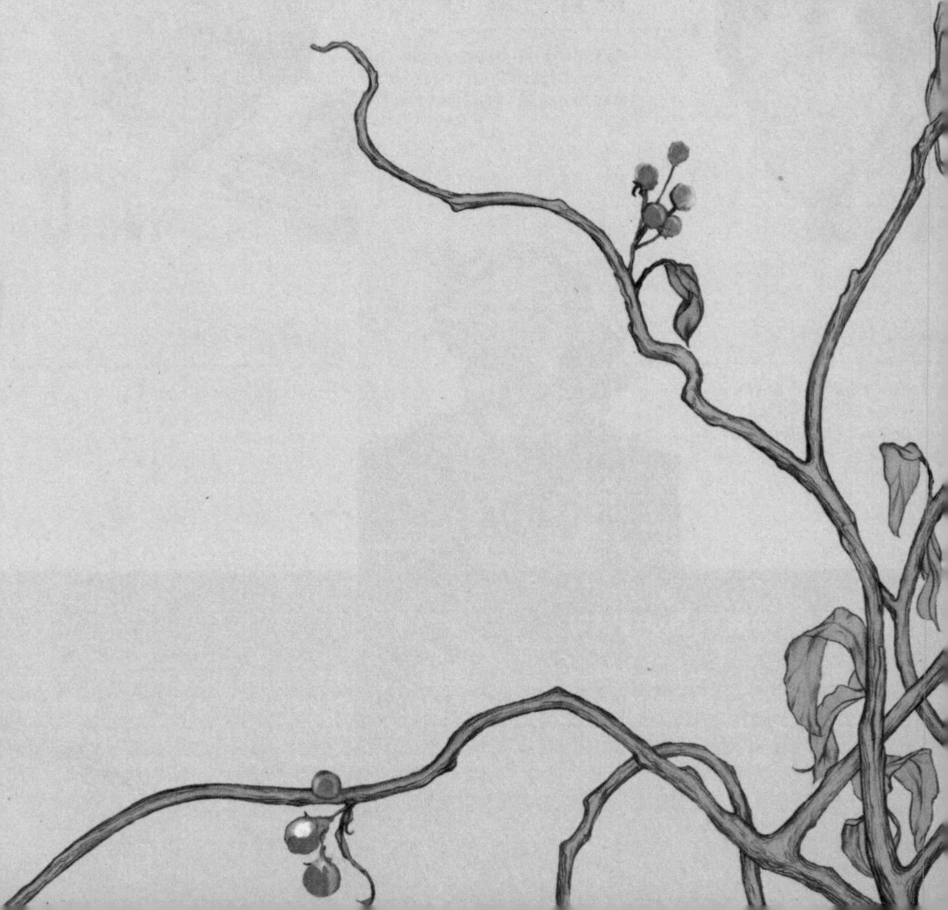

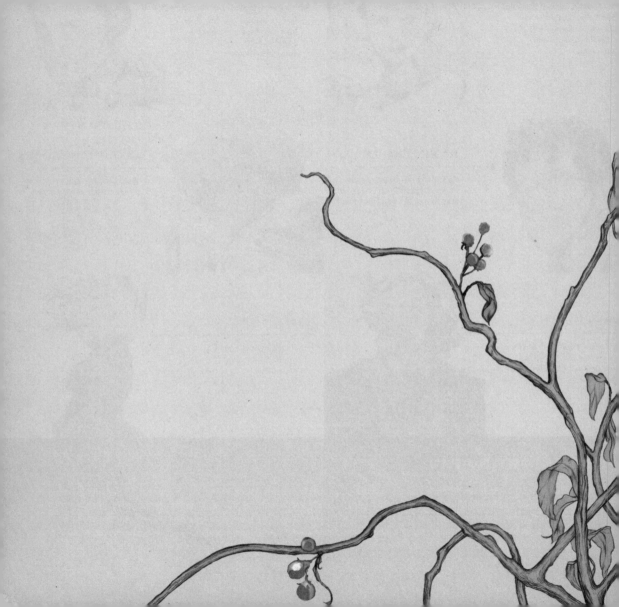

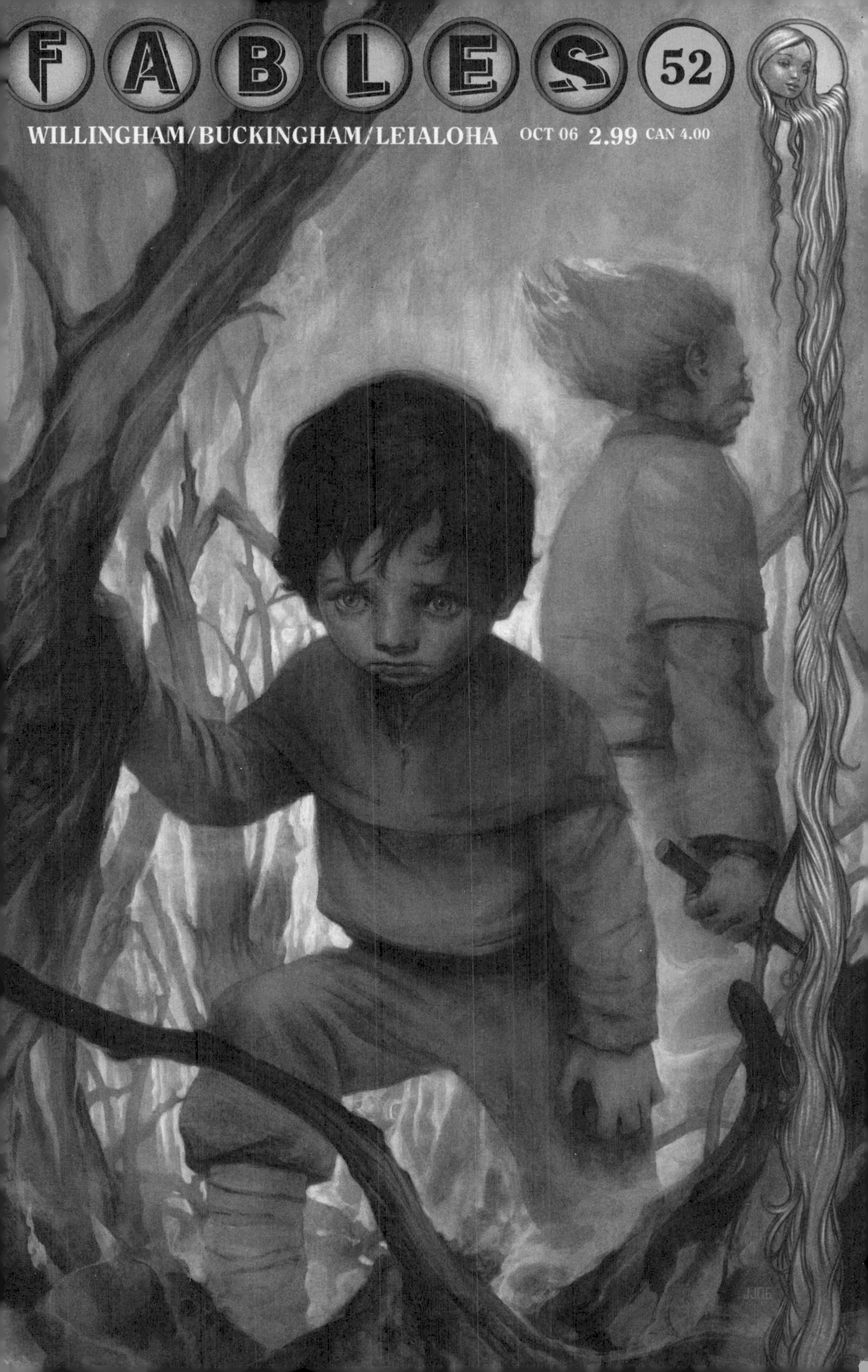
FABLES
52
WILLINGHAM/BUCKINGHAM/LEIALOHA
OCT 06 2.99 CAN 4.00

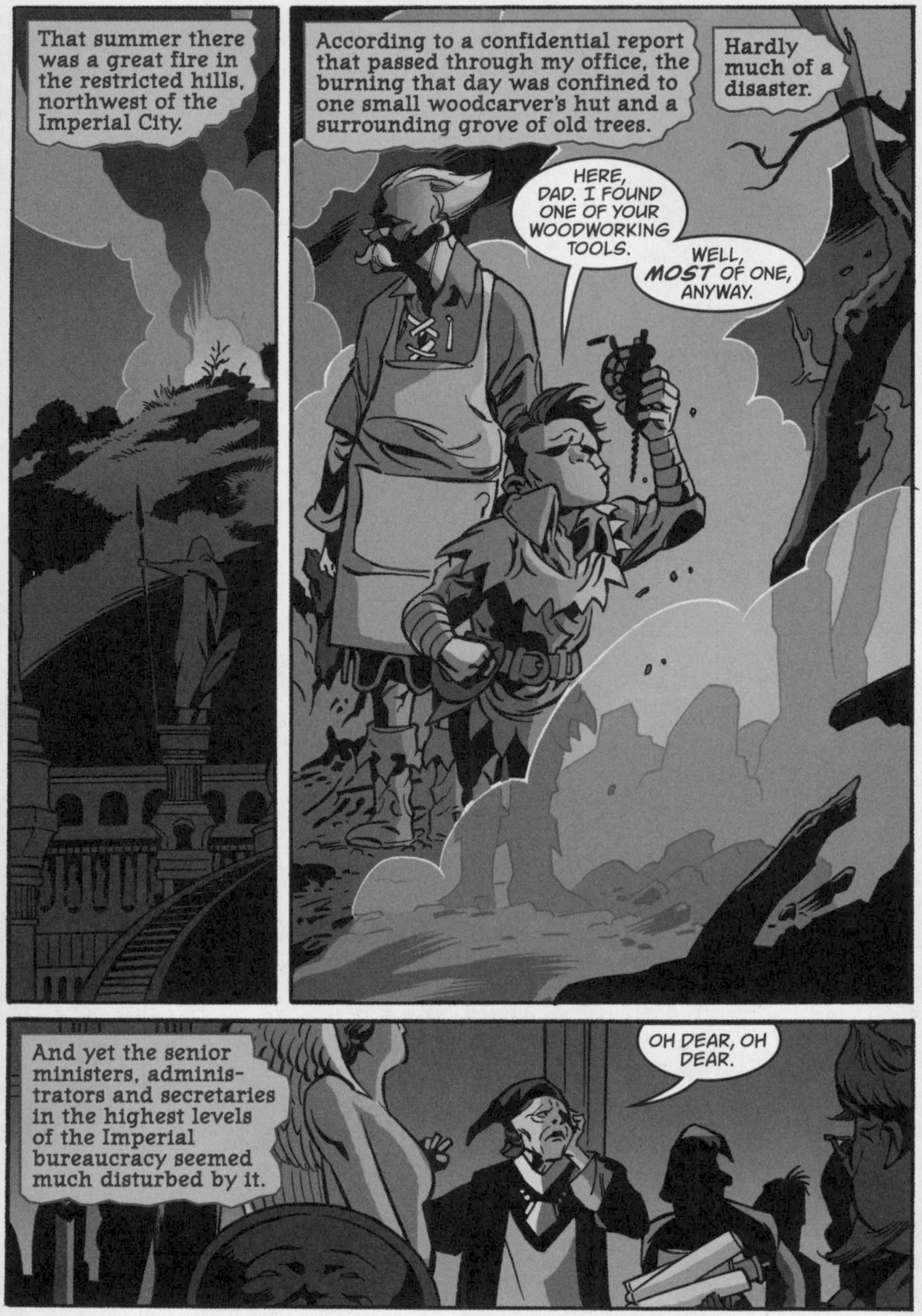

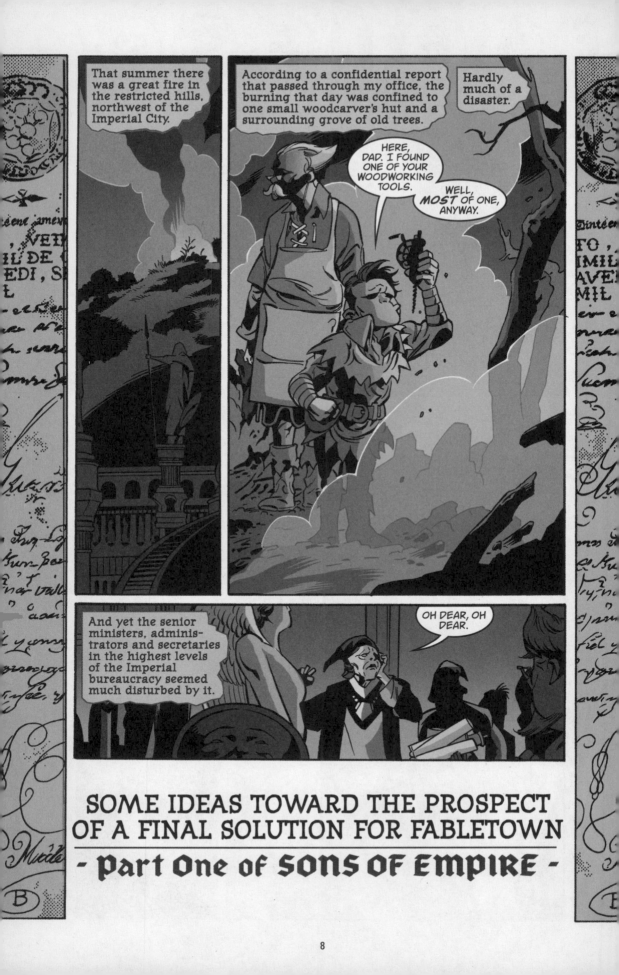

That summer there was a great fire in the restricted hills, northwest of the Imperial City.
According to a confidential report that passed through my office, the burning that day was confined to one small woodcarver's hut and a surrounding grove of old trees.
Hardly much of a disaster.
HERE, DAD. I FOUND ONE OF YOUR WOODWORKING TOOLS.
WELL, MOST OF ONE, ANYWAY.
And yet the senior ministers, administrators and secretaries in the highest levels of the Imperial bureaucracy seemed much disturbed by it.
OH DEAR, OH DEAR.

SOME IDEAS TOWARD THE PROSPECT OF A FINAL SOLUTION FOR FABLETOWN

- Part One of SONS OF EMPIRE -

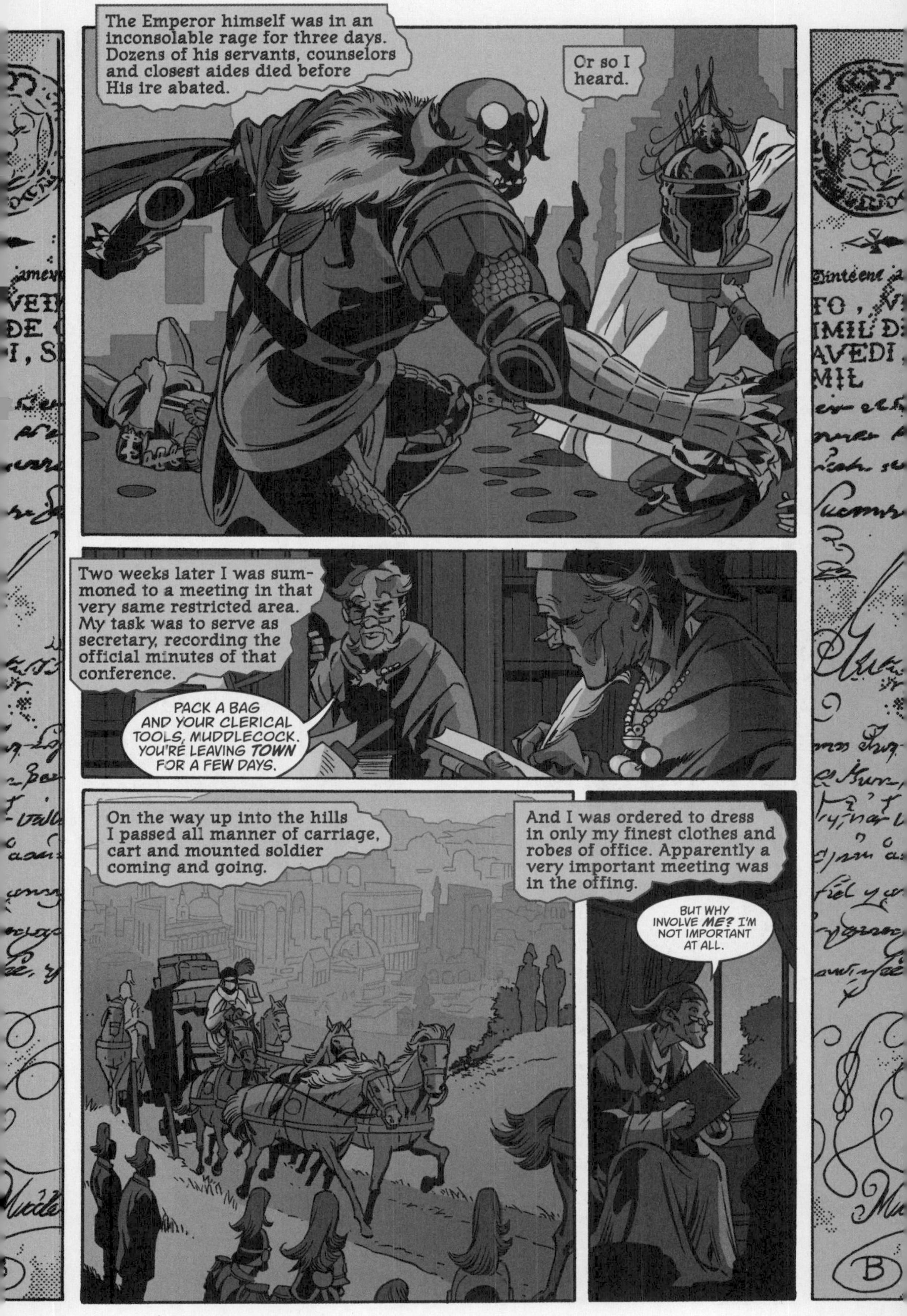
The Emperor himself was in an inconsolable rage for three days. Dozens of his servants, counselors and closest aides died before His ire abated.
Or so I heard.
Two weeks later I was summoned to a meeting in that very same restricted area. My task was to serve as secretary, recording the official minutes of that conference.
PACK A BAG AND YOUR CLERICAL TOOLS, MUDDLECOCK. YOU'RE LEAVING TOWN FOR A FEW DAYS.
On the way up into the hills I passed all manner of carriage, cart and mounted soldier coming and going.
And I was ordered to dress in only my finest clothes and robes of office. Apparently a very important meeting was in the offing.
BUT WHY INVOLVE ME? I'M NOT IMPORTANT AT ALL.

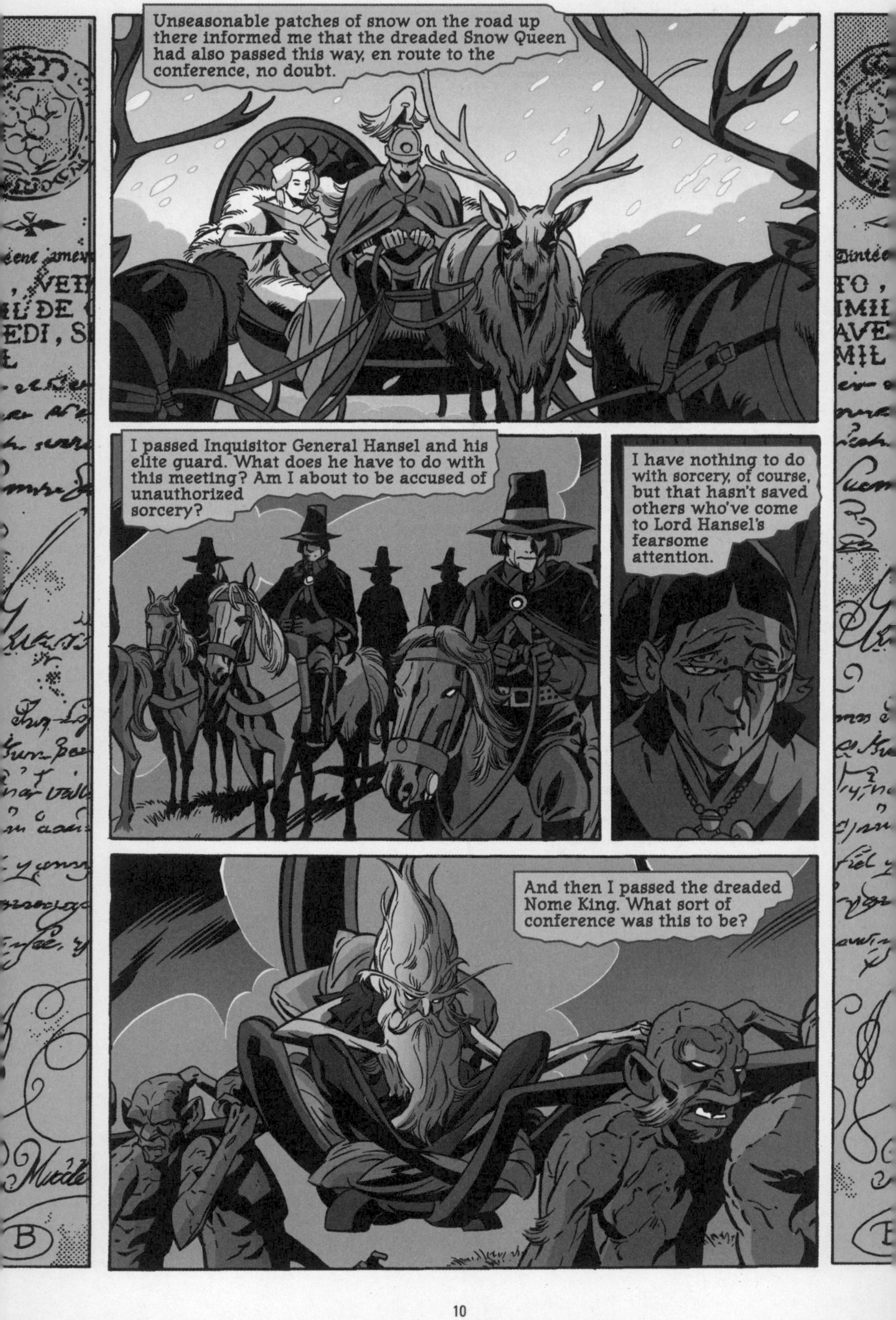
Unseasonable patches of snow on the road up there informed me that the dreaded Snow Queen had also passed this way, en route to the conference, no doubt.
I passed Inquisitor General Hansel and his elite guard. What does he have to do with this meeting? Am I about to be accused of unauthorized sorcery?
I have nothing to do with sorcery, of course, but that hasn't saved others who've come to Lord Hansel's fearsome attention.
And then I passed the dreaded Nome King. What sort of conference was this to be?

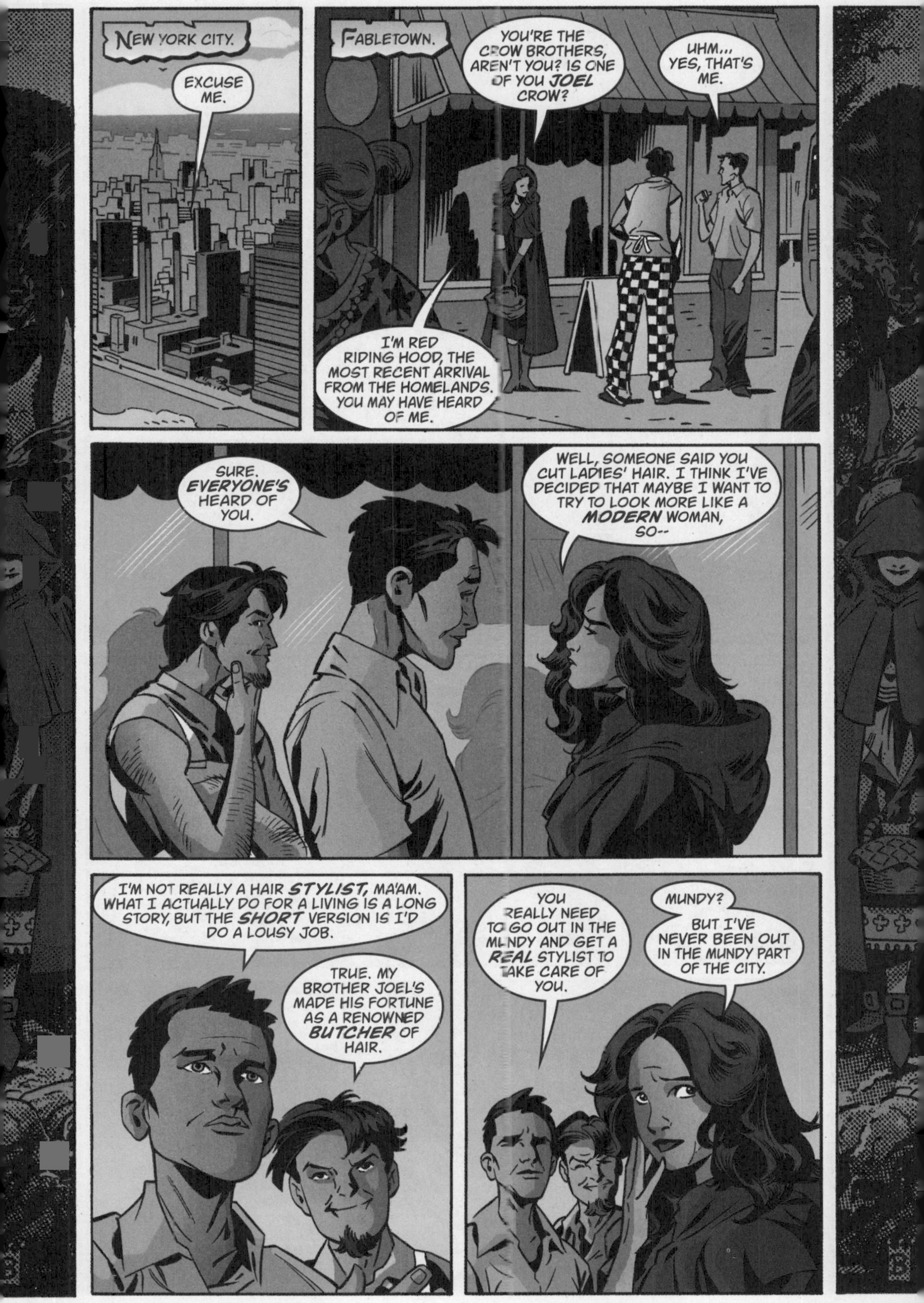
NEW YORK CITY.
EXCUSE ME.
FABLETOWN.
YOU'RE THE CROW BROTHERS, AREN'T YOU? IS ONE OF YOU JOEL CROW?
UHM... YES, THAT'S ME.
I'M RED RIDING HOOD, THE MOST RECENT ARRIVAL FROM THE HOMELANDS. YOU MAY HAVE HEARD OF ME.
SURE. EVERYONE'S HEARD OF YOU.
WELL, SOMEONE SAID YOU CUT LADIES' HAIR. I THINK I'VE DECIDED THAT MAYBE I WANT TO TRY TO LOOK MORE LIKE A MODERN WOMAN, SO--
I'M NOT REALLY A HAIR STYLIST, MA'AM. WHAT I ACTUALLY DO FOR A LIVING IS A LONG STORY, BUT THE SHORT VERSION IS I'D DO A LOUSY JOB.
TRUE. MY BROTHER JOEL'S MADE HIS FORTUNE AS A RENOWNED BUTCHER OF HAIR.
YOU REALLY NEED TO GO OUT IN THE MUNDY AND GET A REAL STYLIST TO TAKE CARE OF YOU.
MUNDY?
BUT I'VE NEVER BEEN OUT IN THE MUNDY PART OF THE CITY.

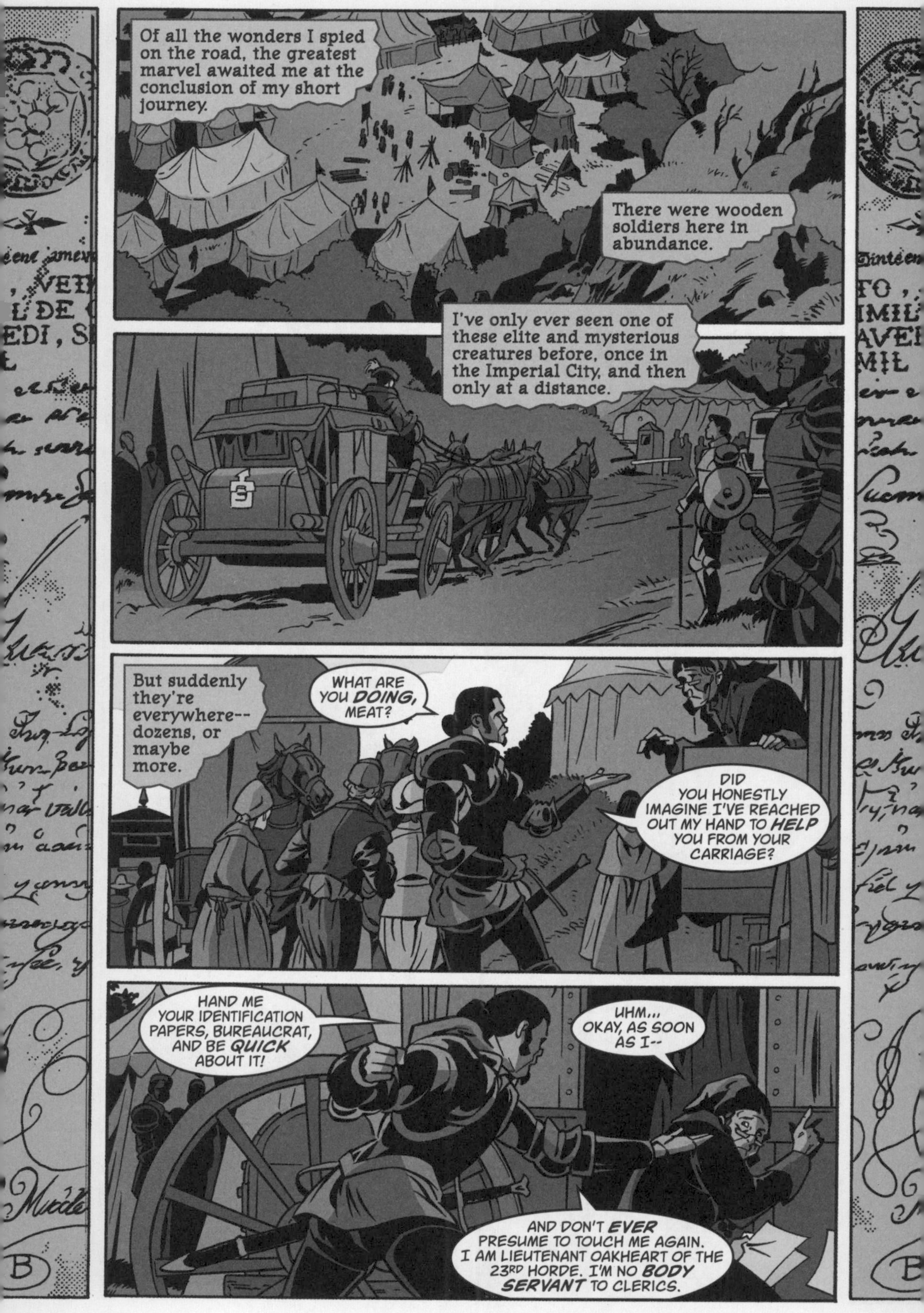

Of all the wonders I spied on the road, the greatest marvel awaited me at the conclusion of my short journey.
There were wooden soldiers here in abundance.
I've only ever seen one of these elite and mysterious creatures before, once in the Imperial City, and then only at a distance.
But suddenly they're everywhere--dozens, or maybe more.
WHAT ARE YOU DOING, MEAT?
DID YOU HONESTLY IMAGINE I'VE REACHED OUT MY HAND TO HELP YOU FROM YOUR CARRIAGE?
HAND ME YOUR IDENTIFICATION PAPERS, BUREAUCRAT, AND BE QUICK ABOUT IT!
UHM... OKAY, AS SOON AS I--
AND DON'T EVER PRESUME TO TOUCH ME AGAIN. I AM LIEUTENANT OAKHEART OF THE 23RD HORDE. I'M NO BODY SERVANT TO CLERICS.

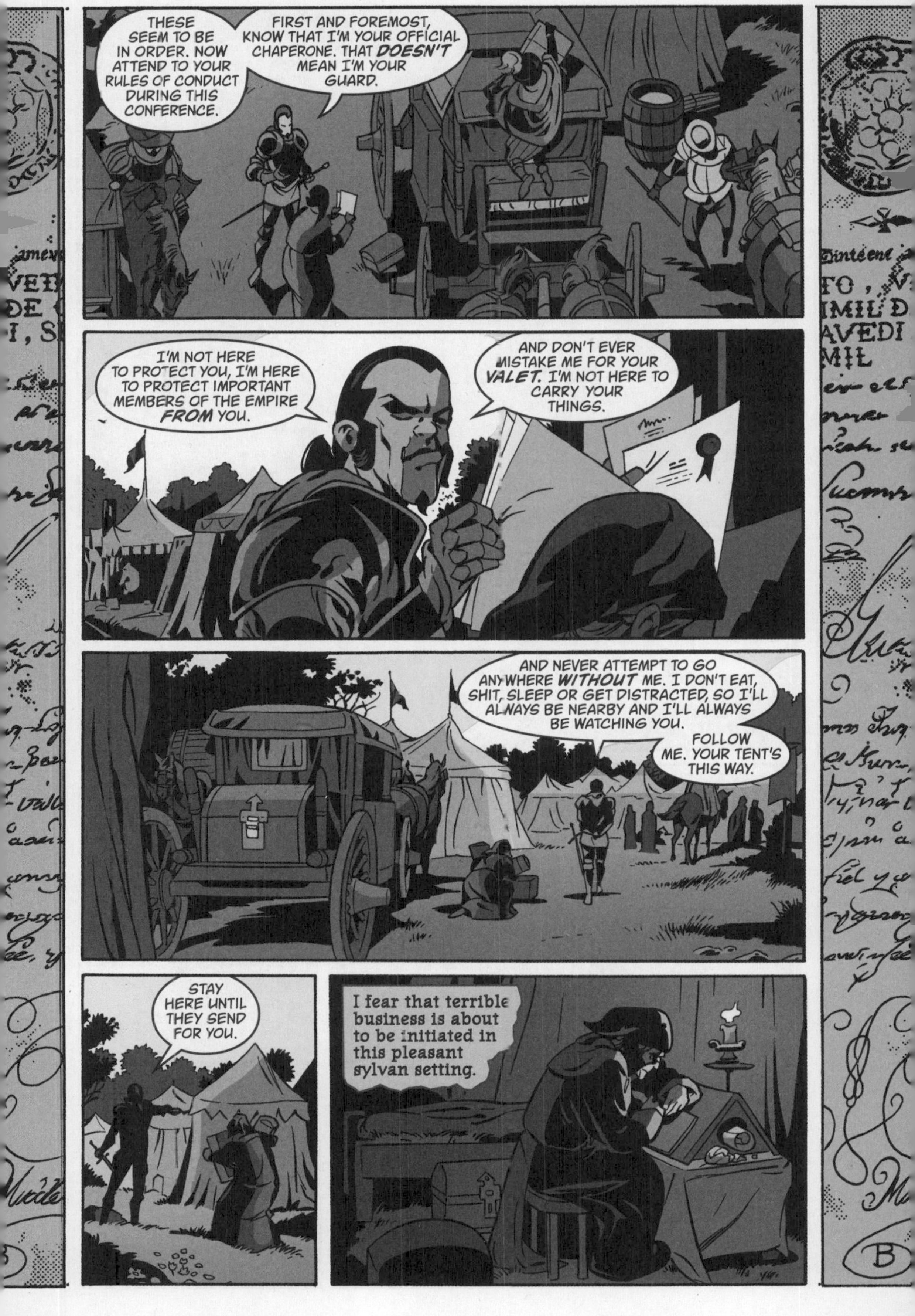
THESE SEEM TO BE IN ORDER. NOW ATTEND TO YOUR RULES OF CONDUCT DURING THIS CONFERENCE.
FIRST AND FOREMOST, KNOW THAT I'M YOUR OFFICIAL CHAPERONE. THAT DOESN'T MEAN I'M YOUR GUARD.
I'M NOT HERE TO PROTECT YOU, I'M HERE TO PROTECT IMPORTANT MEMBERS OF THE EMPIRE FROM YOU.
AND DON'T EVER MISTAKE ME FOR YOUR VALET. I'M NOT HERE TO CARRY YOUR THINGS.
AND NEVER ATTEMPT TO GO ANYWHERE WITHOUT ME. I DON'T EAT, SHIT, SLEEP OR GET DISTRACTED, SO I'LL ALWAYS BE NEARBY AND I'LL ALWAYS BE WATCHING YOU.
FOLLOW ME. YOUR TENT'S THIS WAY.
STAY HERE UNTIL THEY SEND FOR YOU.
I fear that terrible business is about to be initiated in this pleasant sylvan setting.

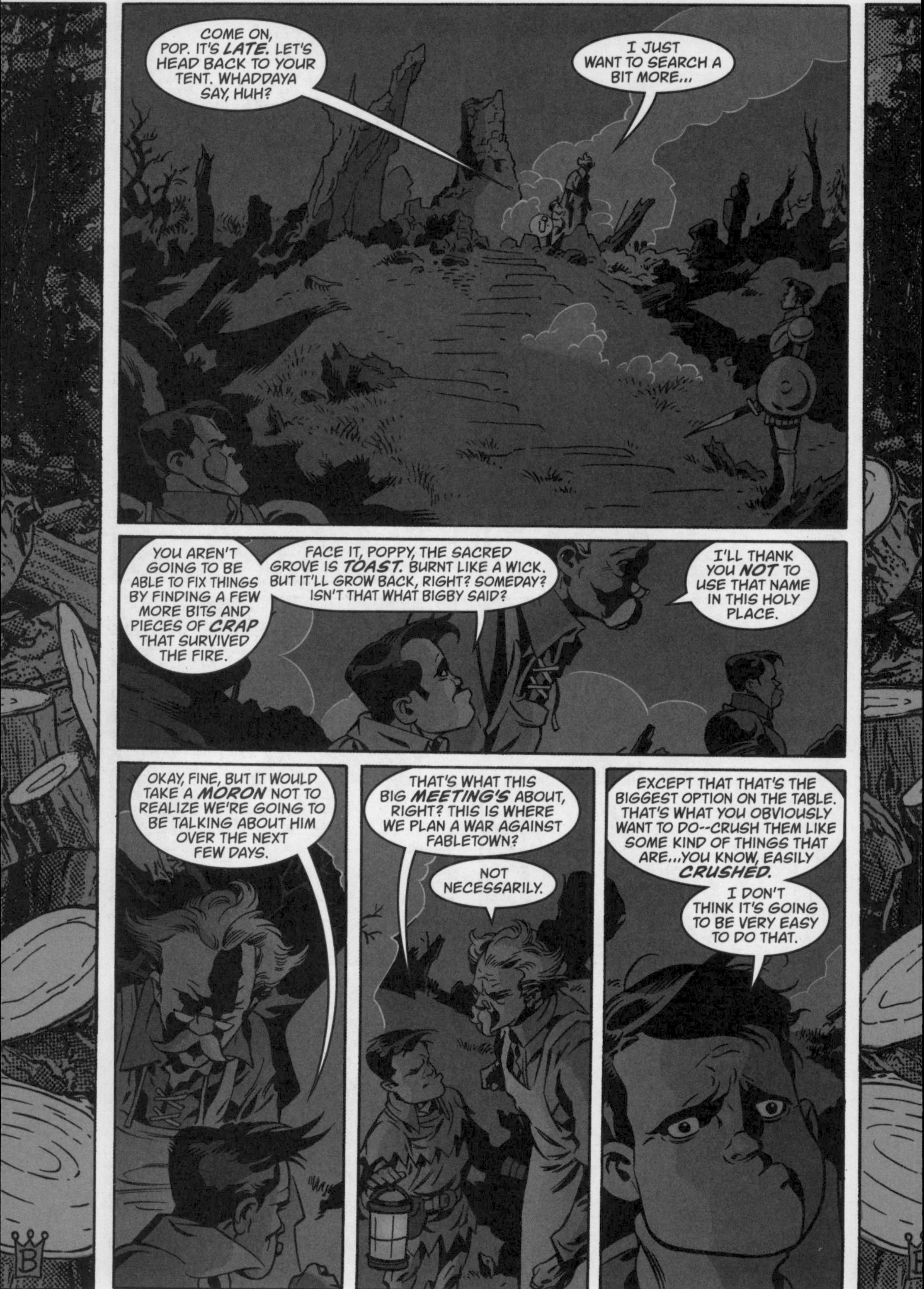
COME ON, POP. IT'S LATE. LET'S HEAD BACK TO YOUR TENT. WHADDAYA SAY, HUH?
I JUST WANT TO SEARCH A BIT MORE...
YOU AREN'T GOING TO BE ABLE TO FIX THINGS BY FINDING A FEW MORE BITS AND PIECES OF CRAP THAT SURVIVED THE FIRE.
FACE IT, POPPY, THE SACRED GROVE IS TOAST. BURNT LIKE A WICK. BUT IT'LL GROW BACK, RIGHT? SOMEDAY? ISN'T THAT WHAT BIGBY SAID?
I'LL THANK YOU NOT TO USE THAT NAME IN THIS HOLY PLACE.
OKAY, FINE, BUT IT WOULD TAKE A MORON NOT TO REALIZE WE'RE GOING TO BE TALKING ABOUT HIM OVER THE NEXT FEW DAYS.
THAT'S WHAT THIS BIG MEETING'S ABOUT, RIGHT? THIS IS WHERE WE PLAN A WAR AGAINST FABLETOWN?
NOT NECESSARILY.
EXCEPT THAT THAT'S THE BIGGEST OPTION ON THE TABLE. THAT'S WHAT YOU OBVIOUSLY WANT TO DO--CRUSH THEM LIKE SOME KIND OF THINGS THAT ARE...YOU KNOW, EASILY CRUSHED.
I DON'T THINK IT'S GOING TO BE VERY EASY TO DO THAT.

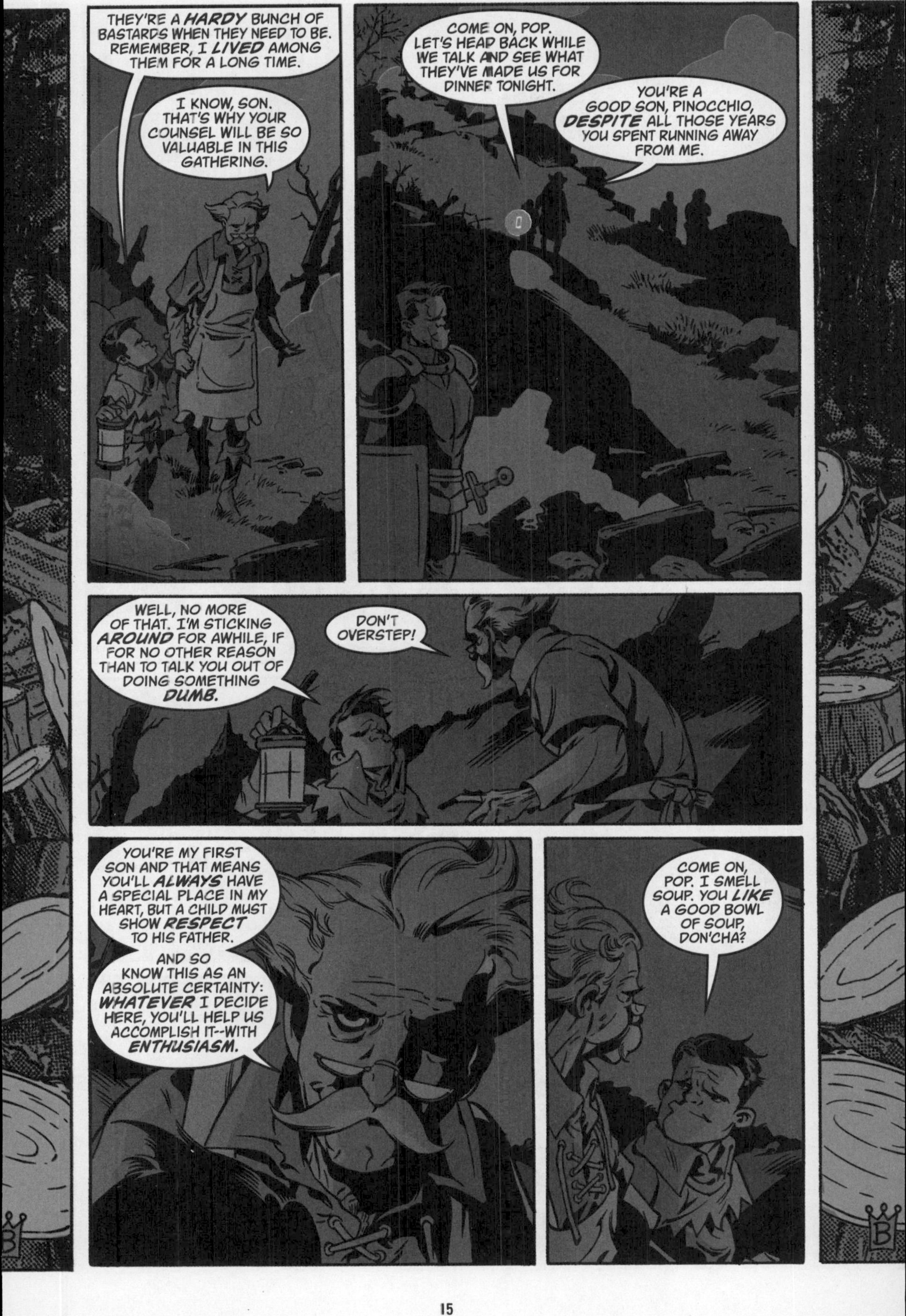
THEY'RE A HARDY BUNCH OF BASTARDS WHEN THEY NEED TO BE. REMEMBER, I LIVED AMONG THEM FOR A LONG TIME.
I KNOW, SON. THAT'S WHY YOUR COUNSEL WILL BE SO VALUABLE IN THIS GATHERING.
COME ON, POP. LET'S HEAD BACK WHILE WE TALK AND SEE WHAT THEY'VE MADE US FOR DINNER TONIGHT.
YOU'RE A GOOD SON, PINOCCHIO, DESPITE ALL THOSE YEARS YOU SPENT RUNNING AWAY FROM ME.
WELL, NO MORE OF THAT. I'M STICKING AROUND FOR AWHILE, IF FOR NO OTHER REASON THAN TO TALK YOU OUT OF DOING SOMETHING DUMB.
DON'T OVERSTEP!
YOU'RE MY FIRST SON AND THAT MEANS YOU'LL ALWAYS HAVE A SPECIAL PLACE IN MY HEART, BUT A CHILD MUST SHOW RESPECT TO HIS FATHER.
AND SO KNOW THIS AS AN ABSOLUTE CERTAINTY: WHATEVER I DECIDE HERE, YOU'LL HELP US ACCOMPLISH IT--WITH ENTHUSIASM.
COME ON, POP. I SMELL SOUP. YOU LIKE A GOOD BOWL OF SOUP, DON'CHA?

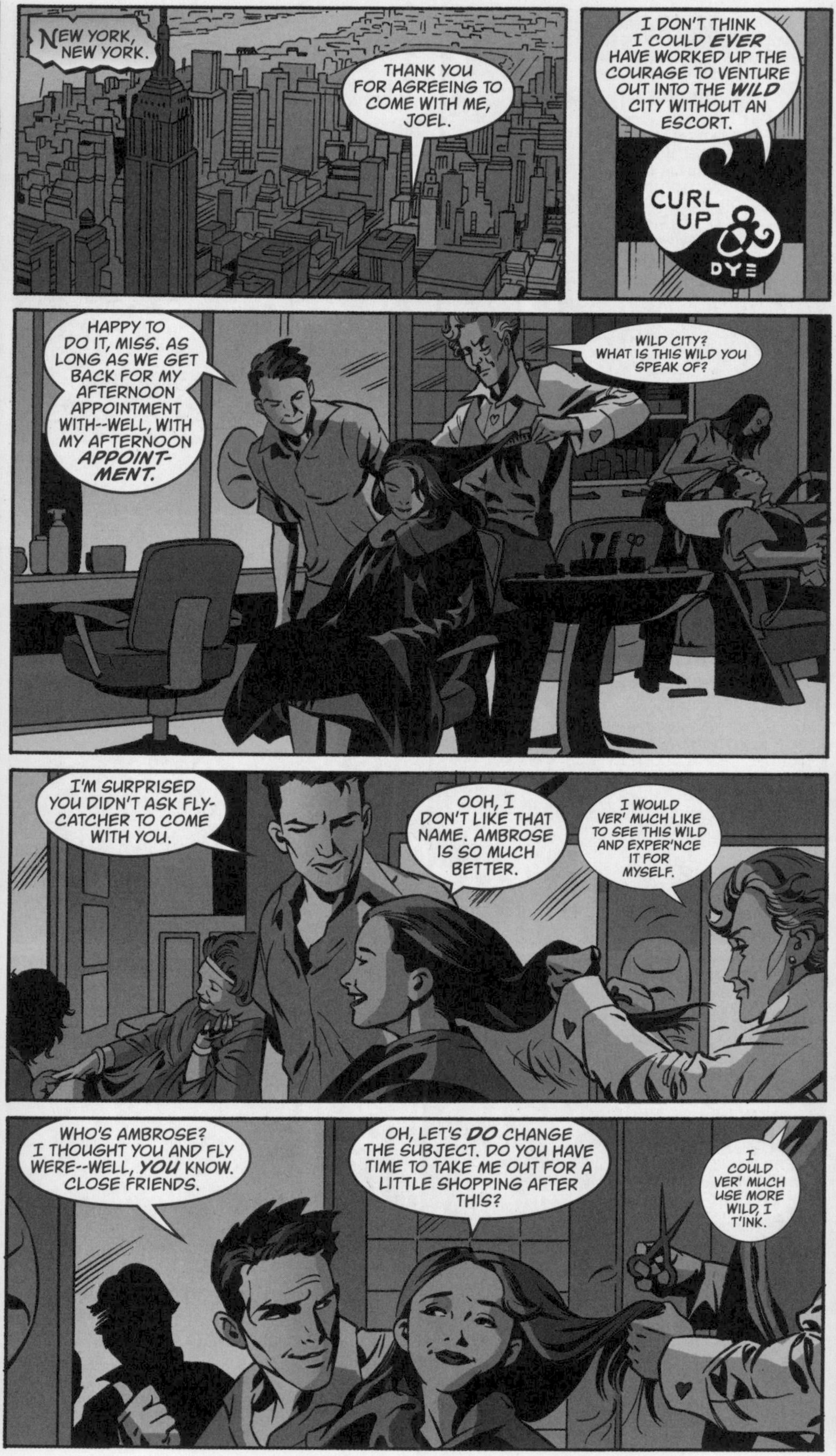
NEW YORK, NEW YORK.
THANK YOU FOR AGREEING TO COME WITH ME, JOEL.
I DON'T THINK I COULD EVER HAVE WORKED UP THE COURAGE TO VENTURE OUT INTO THE WILD CITY WITHOUT AN ESCORT.
CURL UP & DYE
HAPPY TO DO IT, MISS. AS LONG AS WE GET BACK FOR MY AFTERNOON APPOINTMENT WITH--WELL, WITH MY AFTERNOON APPOINTMENT.
WILD CITY? WHAT IS THIS WILD YOU SPEAK OF?
I'M SURPRISED YOU DIDN'T ASK FLY-CATCHER TO COME WITH YOU.
OOH, I DON'T LIKE THAT NAME. AMBROSE IS SO MUCH BETTER.
I WOULD VER' MUCH LIKE TO SEE THIS WILD AND EXPER'NCE IT FOR MYSELF.
WHO'S AMBROSE? I THOUGHT YOU AND FLY WERE--WELL, YOU KNOW. CLOSE FRIENDS.
OH, LET'S DO CHANGE THE SUBJECT. DO YOU HAVE TIME TO TAKE ME OUT FOR A LITTLE SHOPPING AFTER THIS?
I COULD VER' MUCH USE MORE WILD, I T'INK.

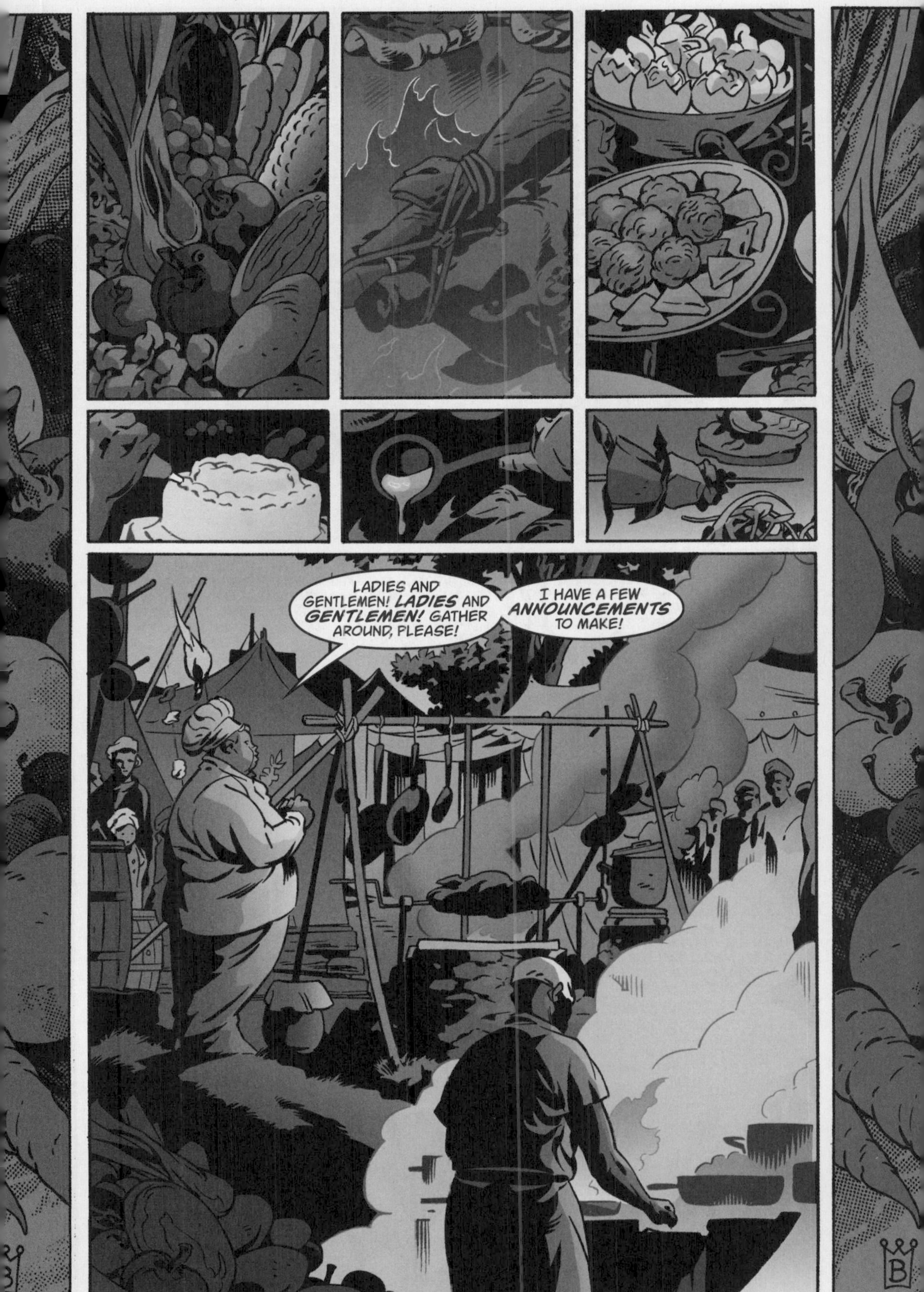
LADIES AND GENTLEMEN! LADIES AND GENTLEMEN! GATHER AROUND, PLEASE!
I HAVE A FEW ANNOUNCEMENTS TO MAKE!

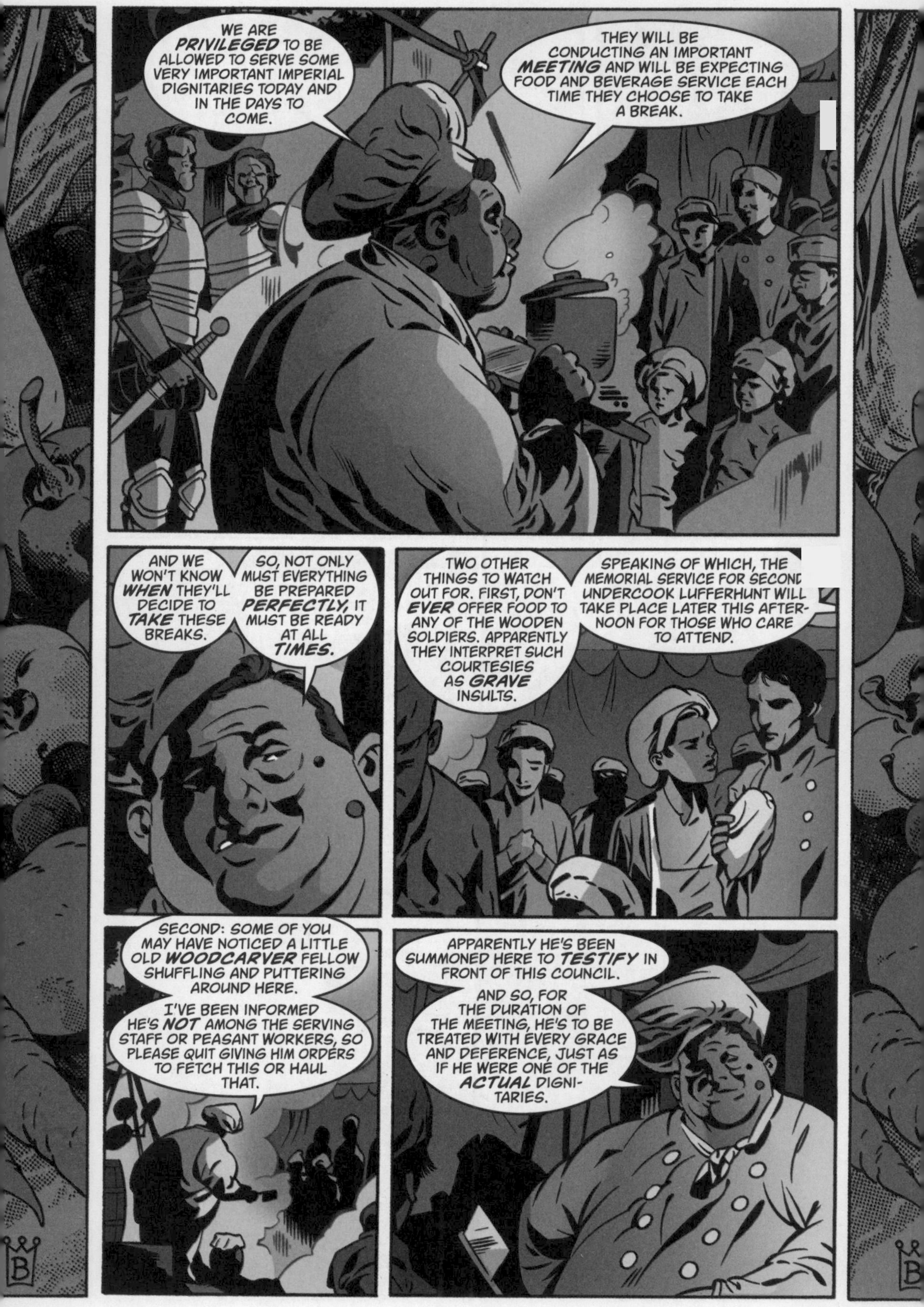
WE ARE PRIVILEGED TO BE ALLOWED TO SERVE SOME VERY IMPORTANT IMPERIAL DIGNITARIES TODAY AND IN THE DAYS TO COME.
THEY WILL BE CONDUCTING AN IMPORTANT MEETING AND WILL BE EXPECTING FOOD AND BEVERAGE SERVICE EACH TIME THEY CHOOSE TO TAKE A BREAK.
AND WE WON'T KNOW WHEN THEY'LL DECIDE TO TAKE THESE BREAKS.
SO, NOT ONLY MUST EVERYTHING BE PREPARED PERFECTLY, IT MUST BE READY AT ALL TIMES.
TWO OTHER THINGS TO WATCH OUT FOR. FIRST, DON'T EVER OFFER FOOD TO ANY OF THE WOODEN SOLDIERS. APPARENTLY THEY INTERPRET SUCH COURTESIES AS GRAVE INSULTS.
SPEAKING OF WHICH, THE MEMORIAL SERVICE FOR SECOND UNDERCOOK LUFFERHUNT WILL TAKE PLACE LATER THIS AFTERNOON FOR THOSE WHO CARE TO ATTEND.
SECOND: SOME OF YOU MAY HAVE NOTICED A LITTLE OLD WOODCARVER FELLOW SHUFFLING AND PUTTERING AROUND HERE.
I'VE BEEN INFORMED HE'S NOT AMONG THE SERVING STAFF OR PEASANT WORKERS, SO PLEASE QUIT GIVING HIM ORDERS TO FETCH THIS OR HAUL THAT.
APPARENTLY HE'S BEEN SUMMONED HERE TO TESTIFY IN FRONT OF THIS COUNCIL.
AND SO, FOR THE DURATION OF THE MEETING, HE'S TO BE TREATED WITH EVERY GRACE AND DEFERENCE, JUST AS IF HE WERE ONE OF THE ACTUAL DIGNITARIES.

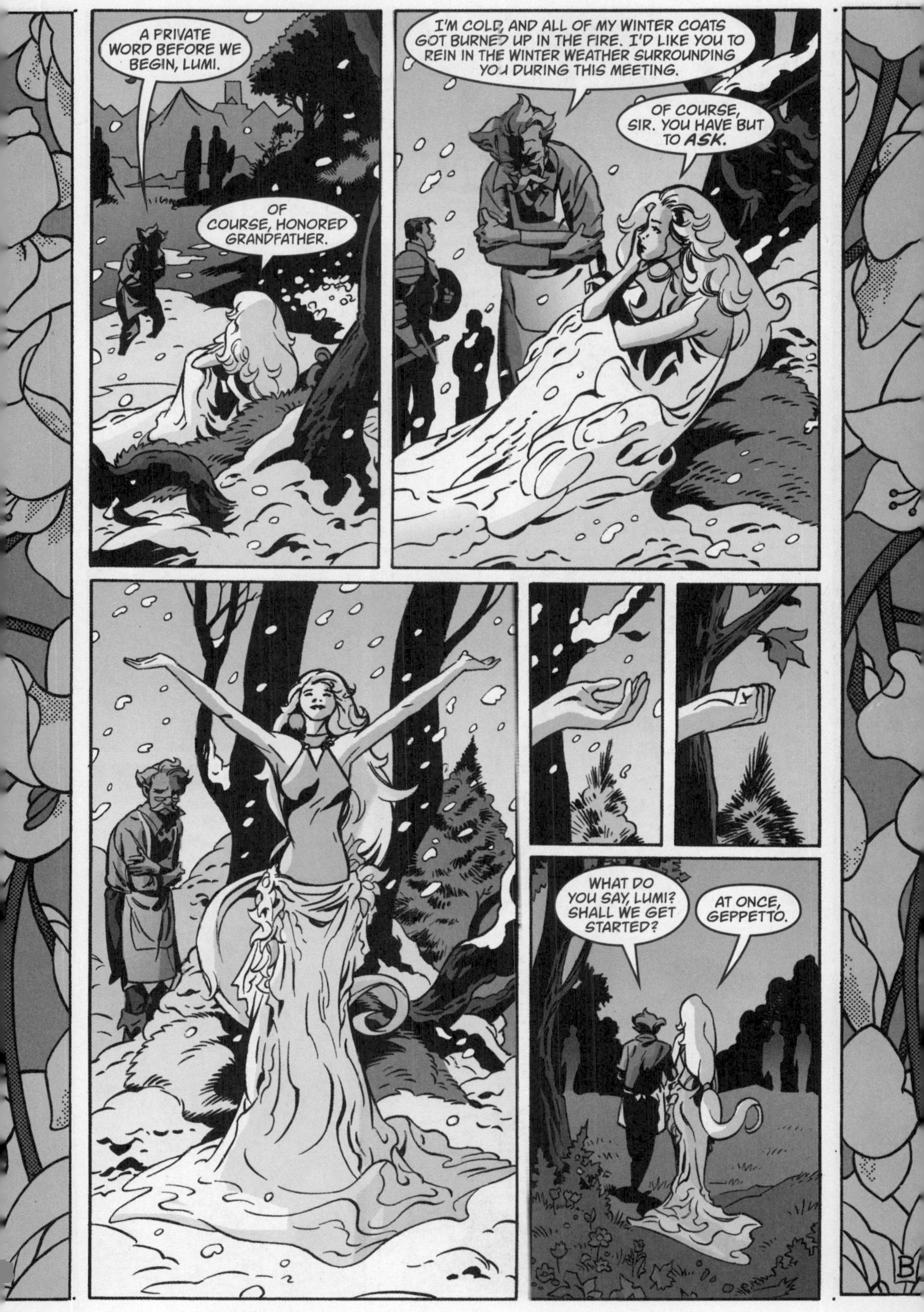

A PRIVATE WORD BEFORE WE BEGIN, LUMI.
OF COURSE, HONORED GRANDFATHER.
I'M COLD, AND ALL OF MY WINTER COATS GOT BURNED UP IN THE FIRE. I'D LIKE YOU TO REIN IN THE WINTER WEATHER SURROUNDING YOU DURING THIS MEETING.
OF COURSE, SIR. YOU HAVE BUT TO ASK.
WHAT DO YOU SAY, LUMI? SHALL WE GET STARTED?
AT ONCE, GEPPETTO.

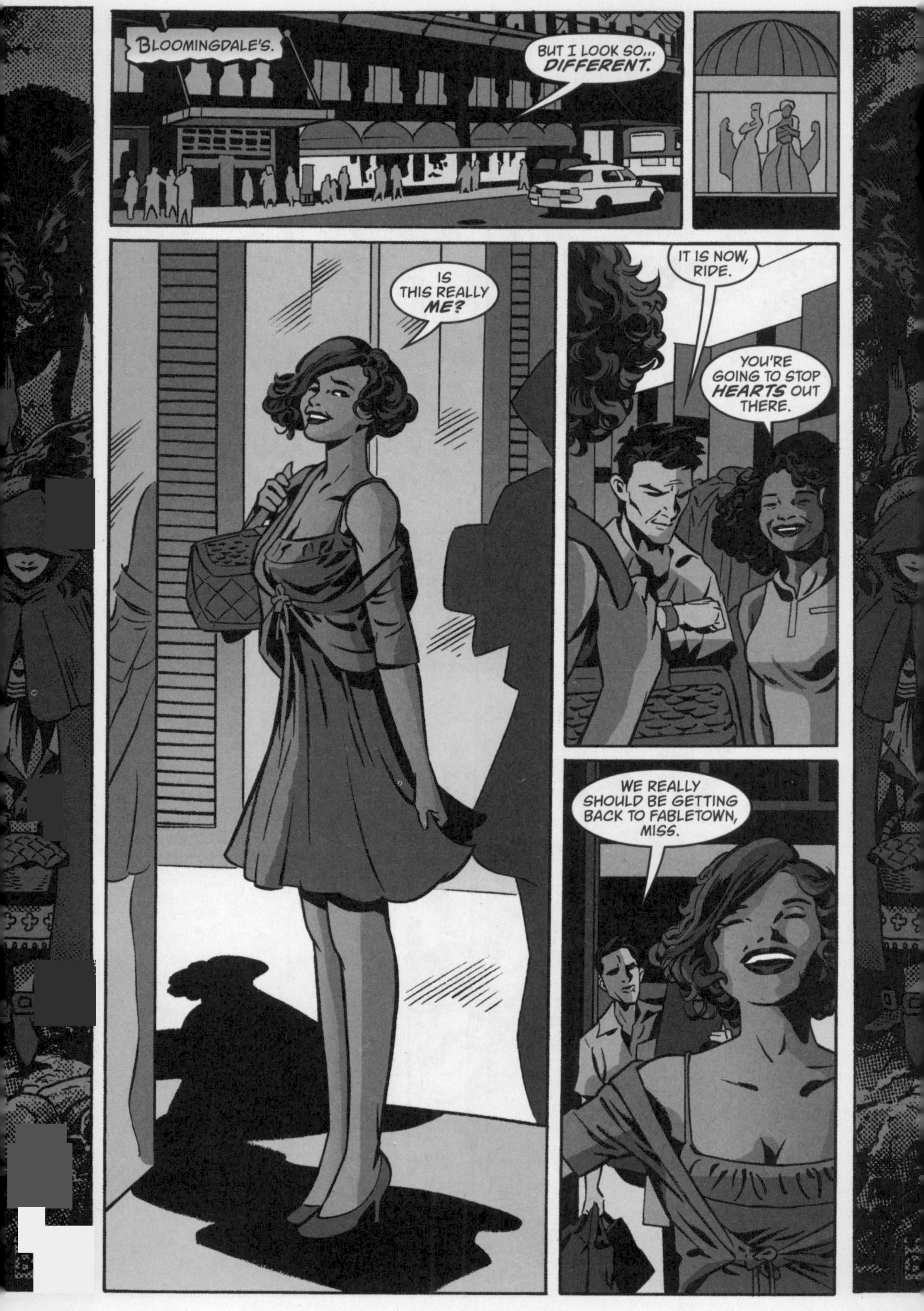
BLOOMINGDALE'S.
BUT I LOOK SO... DIFFERENT.
IS THIS REALLY ME?
IT IS NOW, RIDE.
YOU'RE GOING TO STOP HEARTS OUT THERE.
WE REALLY SHOULD BE GETTING BACK TO FABLETOWN, MISS.

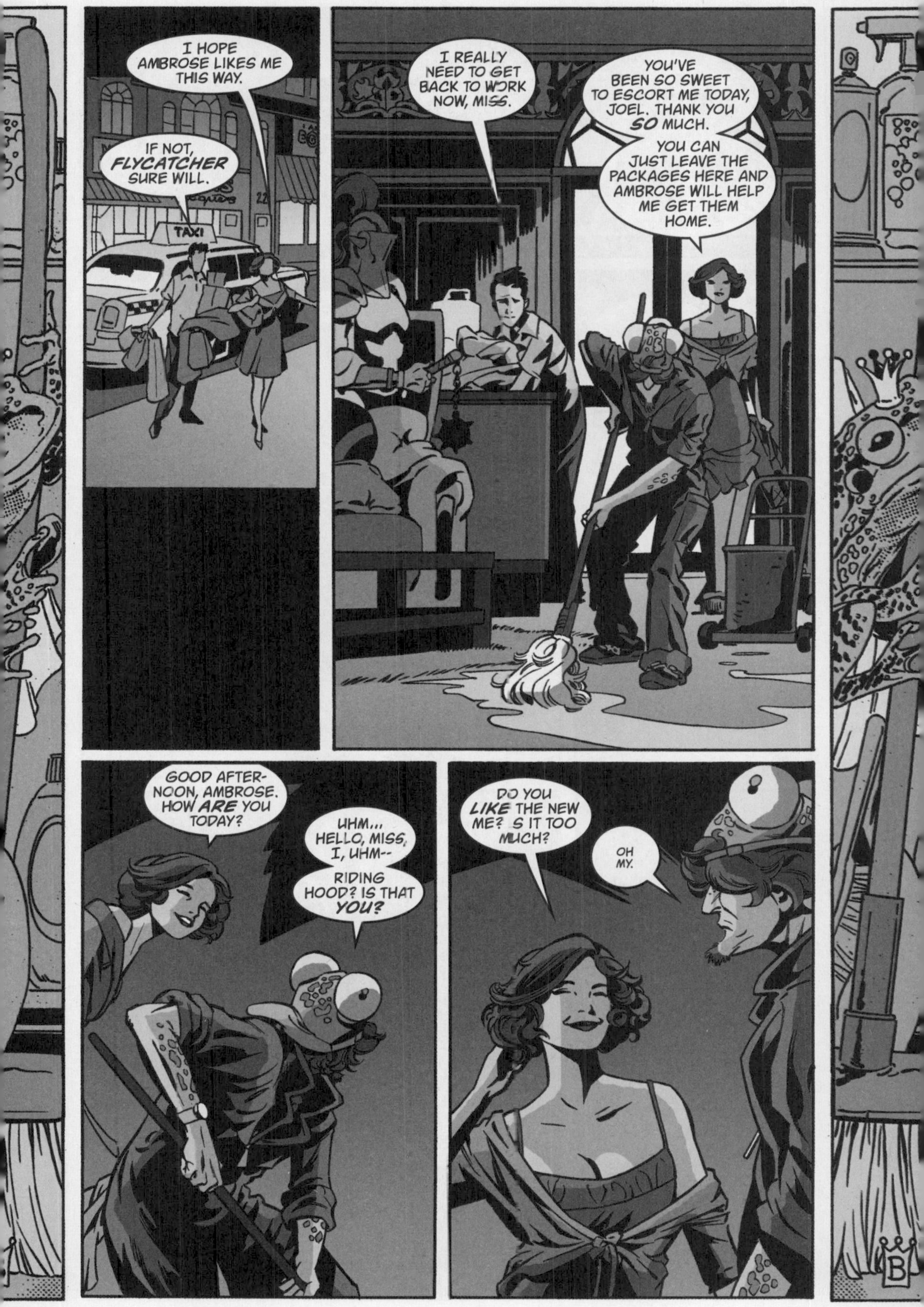

I HOPE AMBROSE LIKES ME THIS WAY.
IF NOT, FLYCATCHER SURE WILL.
TAXI
I REALLY NEED TO GET BACK TO WORK NOW, MISS.
YOU'VE BEEN SO SWEET TO ESCORT ME TODAY, JOEL. THANK YOU SO MUCH.
YOU CAN JUST LEAVE THE PACKAGES HERE AND AMBROSE WILL HELP ME GET THEM HOME.
GOOD AFTER-NOON, AMBROSE. HOW ARE YOU TODAY?
UHM... HELLO, MISS, I, UHM--
RIDING HOOD? IS THAT YOU?
DO YOU LIKE THE NEW ME? S IT TOO MUCH?
OH MY.

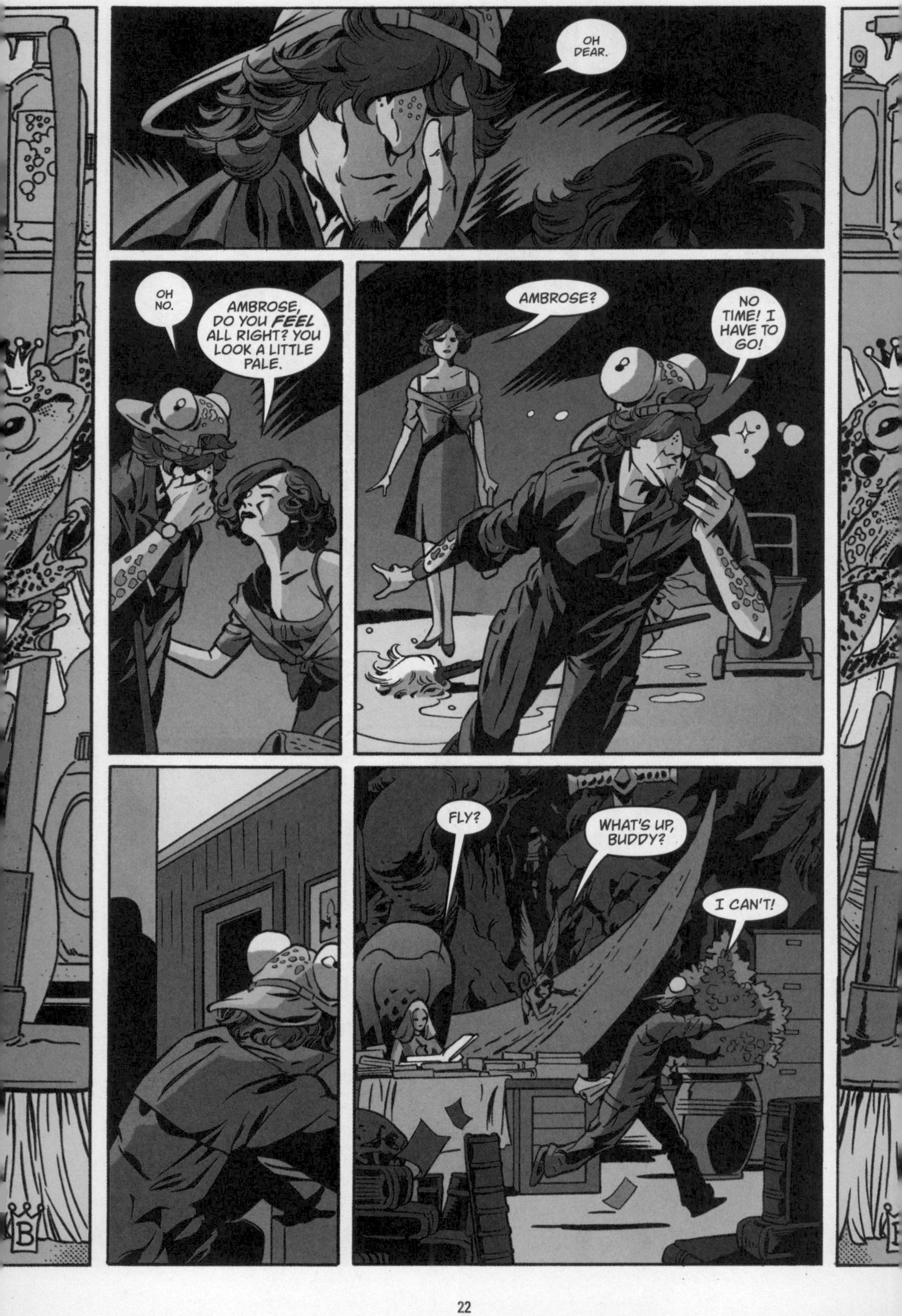
OH DEAR.
OH NO.
AMBROSE, DO YOU FEEL ALL RIGHT? YOU LOOK A LITTLE PALE.
AMBROSE?
NO TIME! I HAVE TO GO!
FLY?
WHAT'S UP, BUDDY?
I CAN'T!

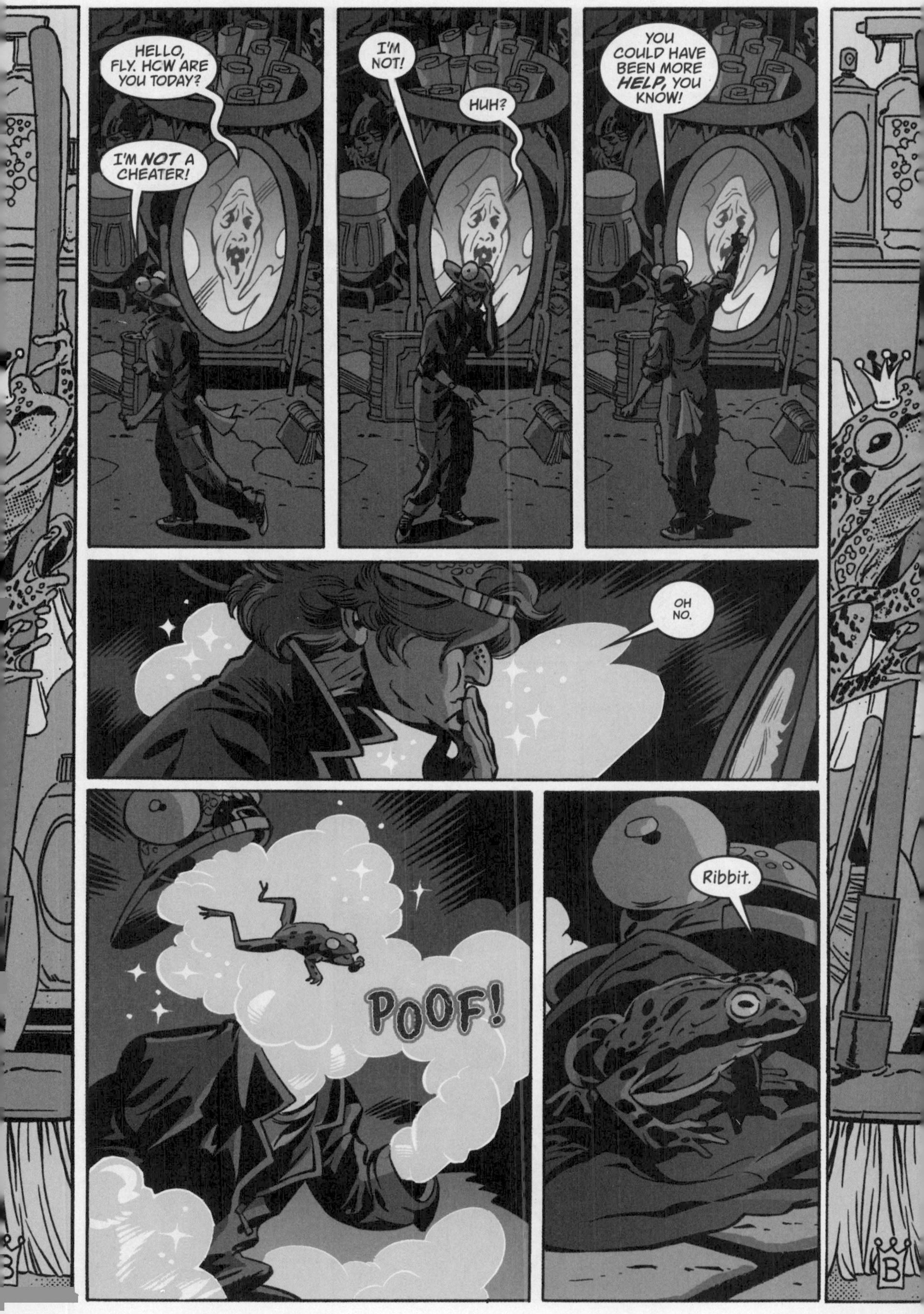
HELLO, FLY. HCW ARE YOU TODAY?
I'M NOT A CHEATER!
I'M NOT!
HUH?
YOU COULD HAVE BEEN MORE HELP, YOU KNOW!
OH NO.
POOF!
Ribbit.

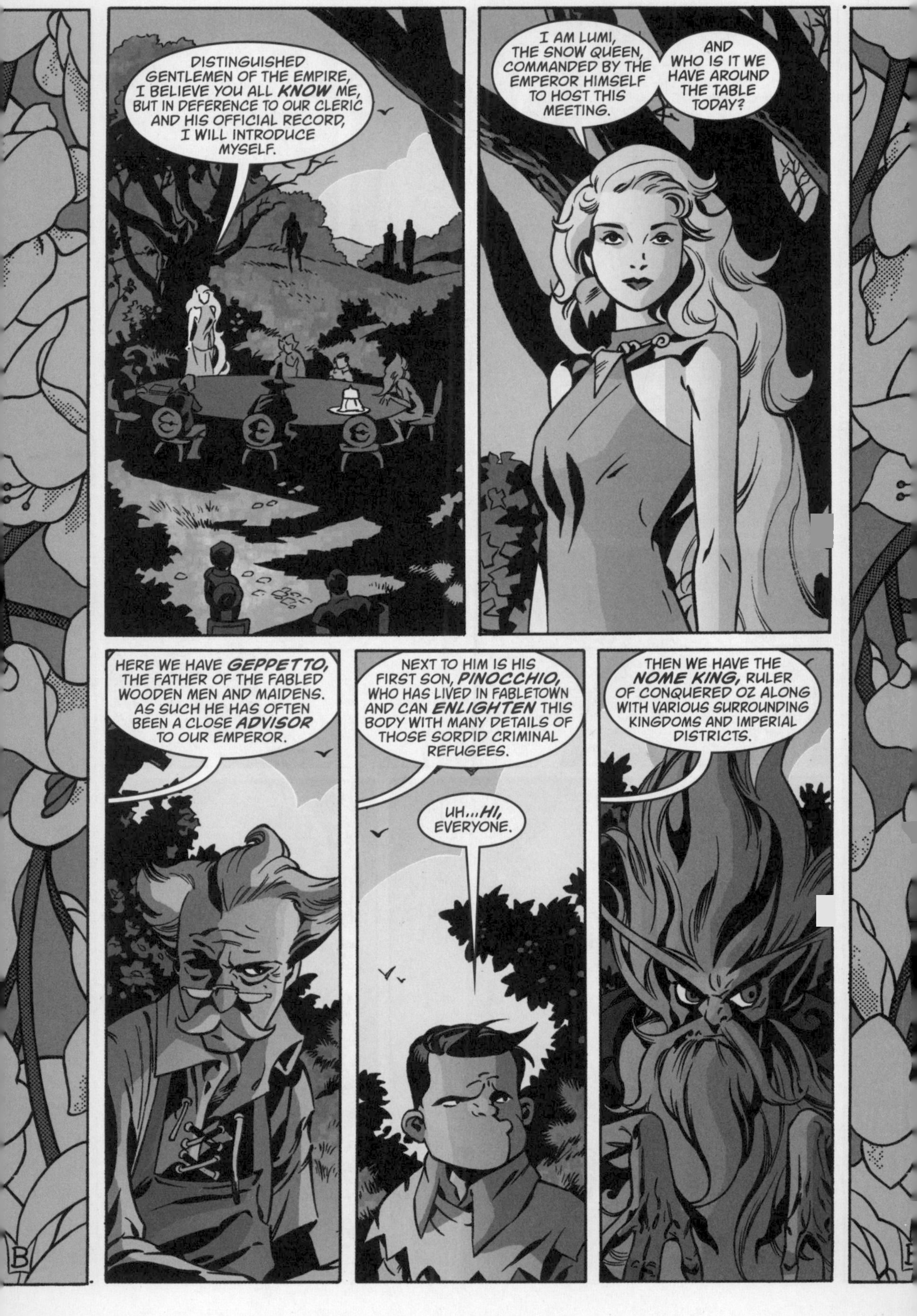
DISTINGUISHED GENTLEMEN OF THE EMPIRE, I BELIEVE YOU ALL KNOW ME, BUT IN DEFERENCE TO OUR CLERIC AND HIS OFFICIAL RECORD, I WILL INTRODUCE MYSELF.
I AM LUMI, THE SNOW QUEEN, COMMANDED BY THE EMPEROR HIMSELF TO HOST THIS MEETING.
AND WHO IS IT WE HAVE AROUND THE TABLE TODAY?
HERE WE HAVE GEPPETTO, THE FATHER OF THE FABLED WOODEN MEN AND MAIDENS. AS SUCH HE HAS OFTEN BEEN A CLOSE ADVISOR TO OUR EMPEROR.
NEXT TO HIM IS HIS FIRST SON, PINOCCHIO, WHO HAS LIVED IN FABLETOWN AND CAN ENLIGHTEN THIS BODY WITH MANY DETAILS OF THOSE SORDID CRIMINAL REFUGEES.
UH...HI, EVERYONE.
THEN WE HAVE THE NOME KING, RULER OF CONQUERED OZ ALONG WITH VARIOUS SURROUNDING KINGDOMS AND IMPERIAL DISTRICTS.

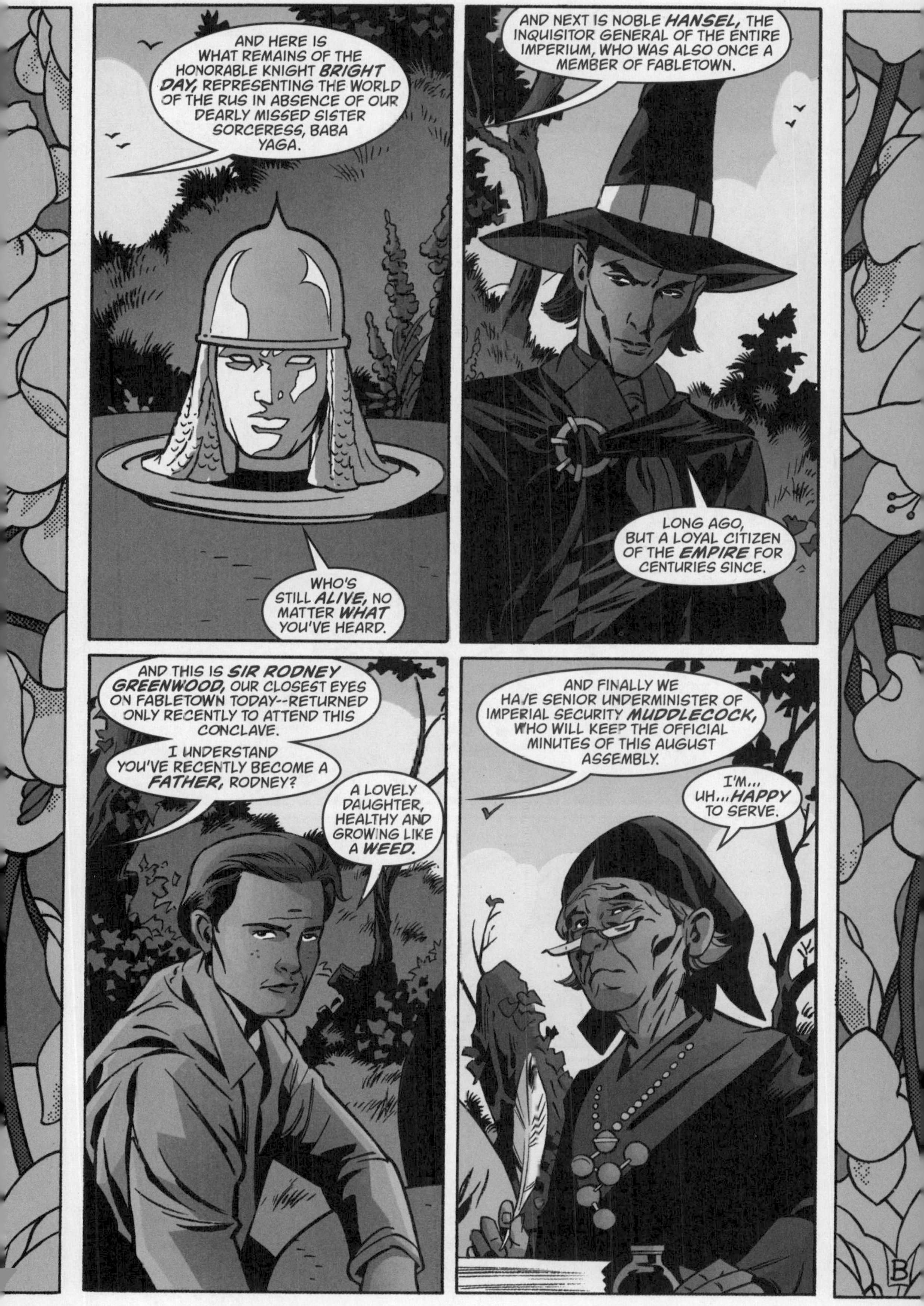
AND HERE IS WHAT REMAINS OF THE HONORABLE KNIGHT BRIGHT DAY, REPRESENTING THE WORLD OF THE RUS IN ABSENCE OF OUR DEARLY MISSED SISTER SORCERESS, BABA YAGA.
WHO'S STILL ALIVE, NO MATTER WHAT YOU'VE HEARD.
AND NEXT IS NOBLE HANSEL, THE INQUISITOR GENERAL OF THE ENTIRE IMPERIUM, WHO WAS ALSO ONCE A MEMBER OF FABLETOWN.
LONG AGO, BUT A LOYAL CITIZEN OF THE EMPIRE FOR CENTURIES SINCE.
AND THIS IS SIR RODNEY GREENWOOD, OUR CLOSEST EYES ON FABLETOWN TODAY--RETURNED ONLY RECENTLY TO ATTEND THIS CONCLAVE.
I UNDERSTAND YOU'VE RECENTLY BECOME A FATHER, RODNEY?
A LOVELY DAUGHTER, HEALTHY AND GROWING LIKE A WEED.
AND FINALLY WE HAVE SENIOR UNDERMINISTER OF IMPERIAL SECURITY MUDDLECOCK, WHO WILL KEEP THE OFFICIAL MINUTES OF THIS AUGUST ASSEMBLY.
I'M... UH...HAPPY TO SERVE.

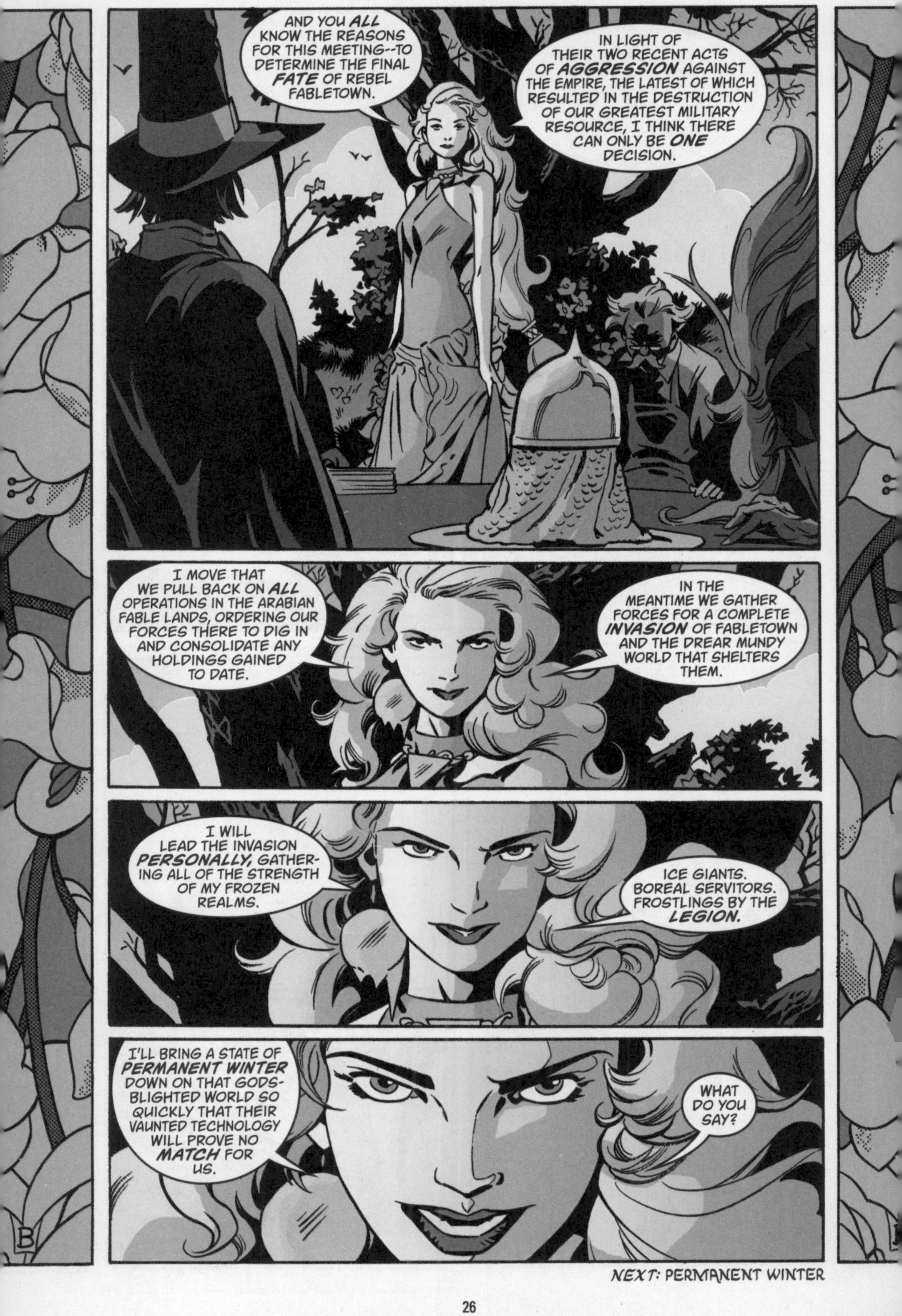
AND YOU ALL KNOW THE REASONS FOR THIS MEETING--TO DETERMINE THE FINAL FATE OF REBEL FABLETOWN.
IN LIGHT OF THEIR TWO RECENT ACTS OF AGGRESSION AGAINST THE EMPIRE, THE LATEST OF WHICH RESULTED IN THE DESTRUCTION OF OUR GREATEST MILITARY RESOURCE, I THINK THERE CAN ONLY BE ONE DECISION.
I MOVE THAT WE PULL BACK ON ALL OPERATIONS IN THE ARABIAN FABLE LANDS, ORDERING OUR FORCES THERE TO DIG IN AND CONSOLIDATE ANY HOLDINGS GAINED TO DATE.
IN THE MEANTIME WE GATHER FORCES FOR A COMPLETE INVASION OF FABLETOWN AND THE DREAR MUNDY WORLD THAT SHELTERS THEM.
I WILL LEAD THE INVASION PERSONALLY, GATHERING ALL OF THE STRENGTH OF MY FROZEN REALMS.
ICE GIANTS. BOREAL SERVITORS. FROSTLINGS BY THE LEGION.
I'LL BRING A STATE OF PERMANENT WINTER DOWN ON THAT GODS-BLIGHTED WORLD SO QUICKLY THAT THEIR VAUNTED TECHNOLOGY WILL PROVE NO MATCH FOR US.
WHAT DO YOU SAY?

NEXT: PERMANENT WINTER

HAIR

In which we present the first of four short-short Fables tales whose purpose is to introduce some of the other members of our (usually) happy community.

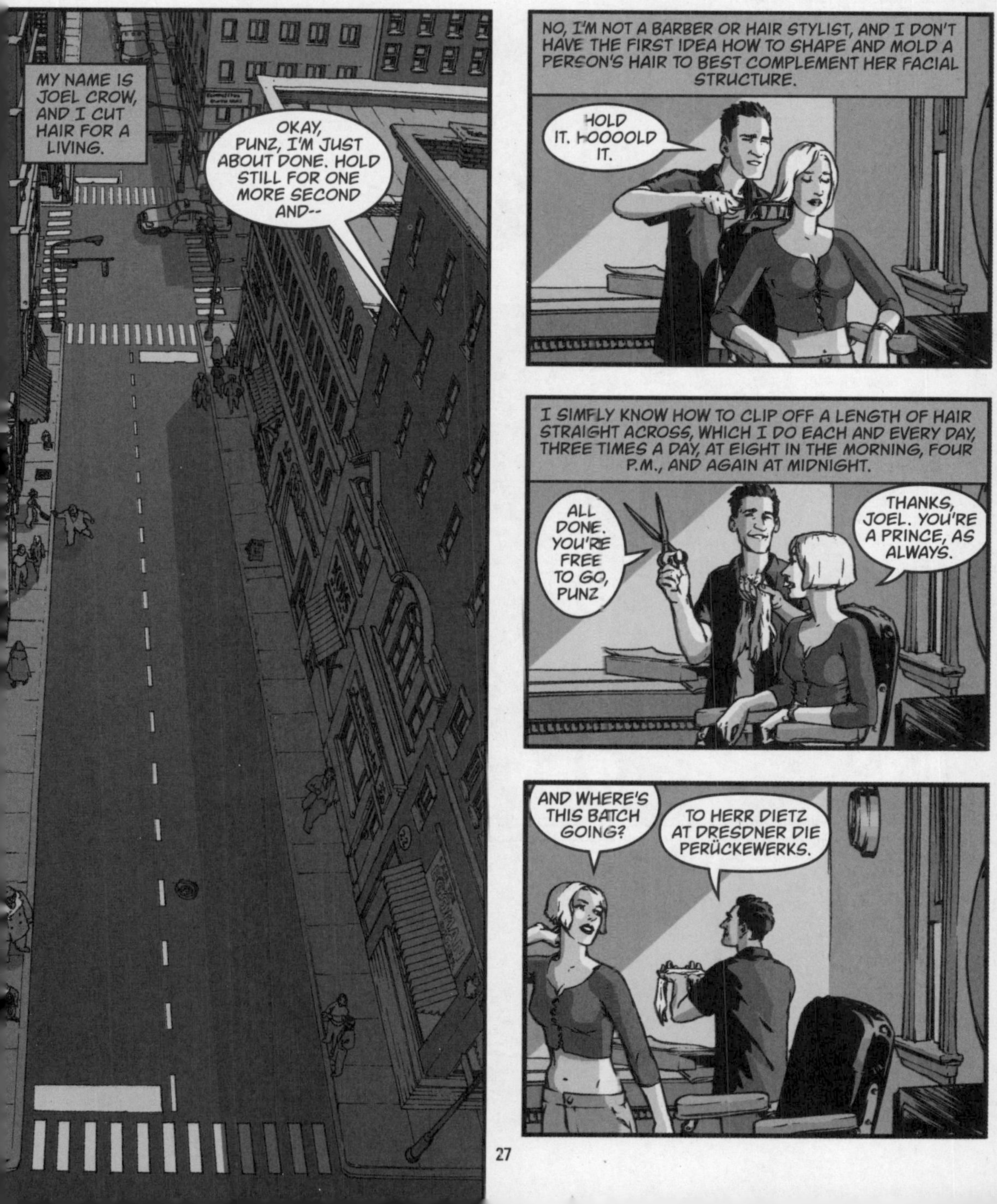

MY NAME IS JOEL CROW, AND I CUT HAIR FOR A LIVING.
OKAY, PUNZ, I'M JUST ABOUT DONE. HOLD STILL FOR ONE MORE SECOND AND--
NO, I'M NOT A BARBER OR HAIR STYLIST, AND I DON'T HAVE THE FIRST IDEA HOW TO SHAPE AND MOLD A PERSON'S HAIR TO BEST COMPLEMENT HER FACIAL STRUCTURE.
HOLD IT. HOOOOLD IT.
I SIMPLY KNOW HOW TO CLIP OFF A LENGTH OF HAIR STRAIGHT ACROSS, WHICH I DO EACH AND EVERY DAY, THREE TIMES A DAY, AT EIGHT IN THE MORNING, FOUR P.M., AND AGAIN AT MIDNIGHT.
ALL DONE. YOU'RE FREE TO GO, PUNZ
THANKS, JOEL. YOU'RE A PRINCE, AS ALWAYS.
AND WHERE'S THIS BATCH GOING?
TO HERR DIETZ AT DRESDNER DIE PERÜCKEWERKS.

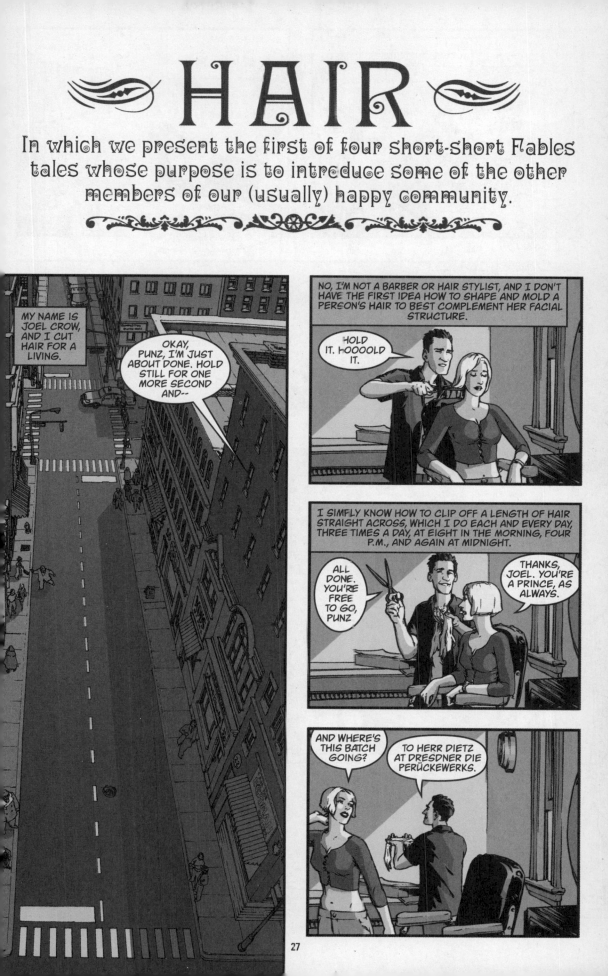

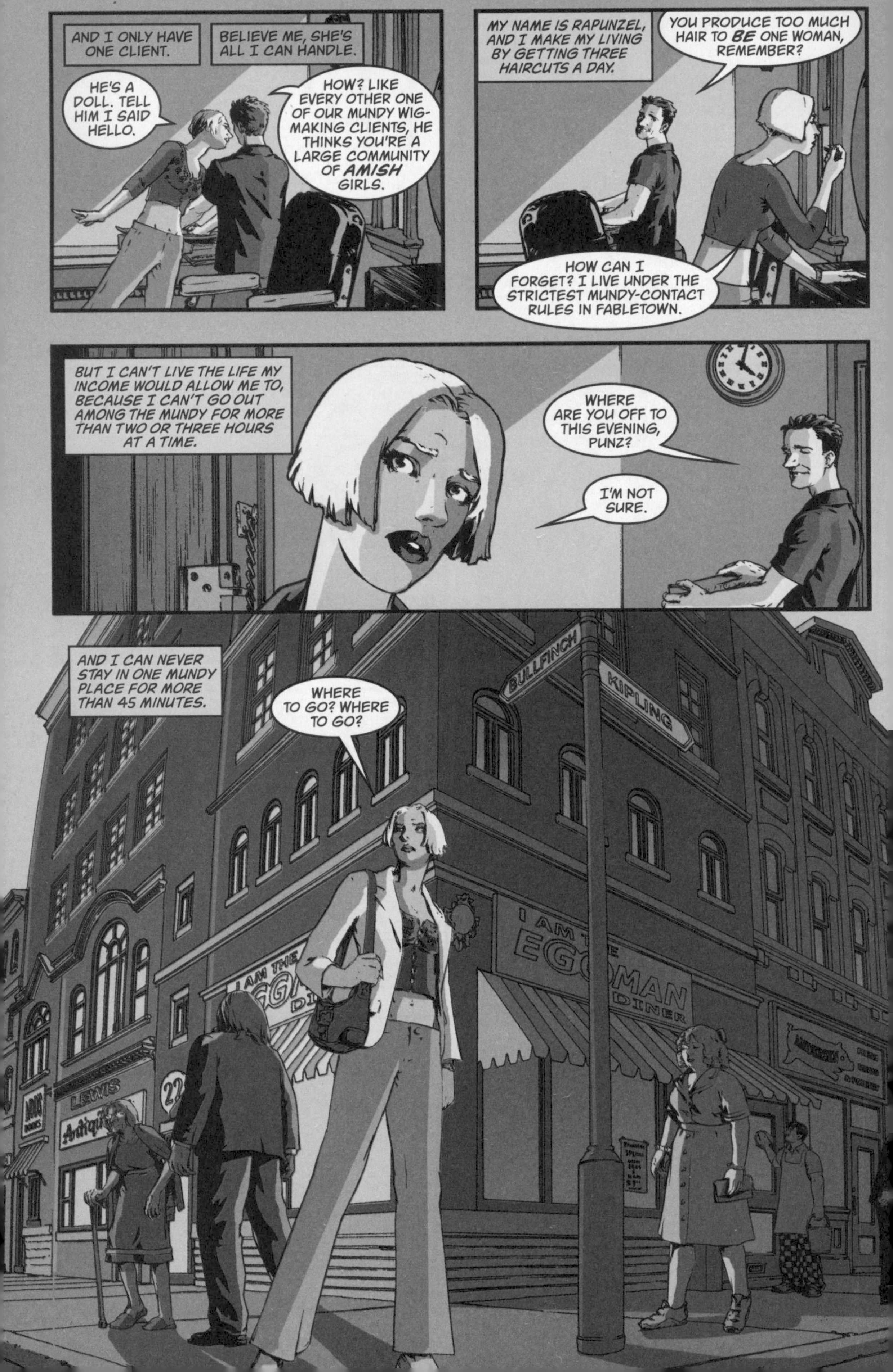

AND I ONLY HAVE ONE CLIENT.
BELIEVE ME, SHE'S ALL I CAN HANDLE.
HE'S A DOLL. TELL HIM I SAID HELLO.
HOW? LIKE EVERY OTHER ONE OF OUR MUNDY WIG-MAKING CLIENTS, HE THINKS YOU'RE A LARGE COMMUNITY OF AMISH GIRLS.
MY NAME IS RAPUNZEL, AND I MAKE MY LIVING BY GETTING THREE HAIRCUTS A DAY.
YOU PRODUCE TOO MUCH HAIR TO BE ONE WOMAN, REMEMBER?
HOW CAN I FORGET? I LIVE UNDER THE STRICTEST MUNDY-CONTACT RULES IN FABLETOWN.
BUT I CAN'T LIVE THE LIFE MY INCOME WOULD ALLOW ME TO, BECAUSE I CAN'T GO OUT AMONG THE MUNDY FOR MORE THAN TWO OR THREE HOURS AT A TIME.
WHERE ARE YOU OFF TO THIS EVENING, PUNZ?
I'M NOT SURE.
AND I CAN NEVER STAY IN ONE MUNDY PLACE FOR MORE THAN 45 MINUTES.
WHERE TO GO? WHERE TO GO?
BULLFINCH
KIPLING
I AM THE EGGMAN DINER
LEWIS

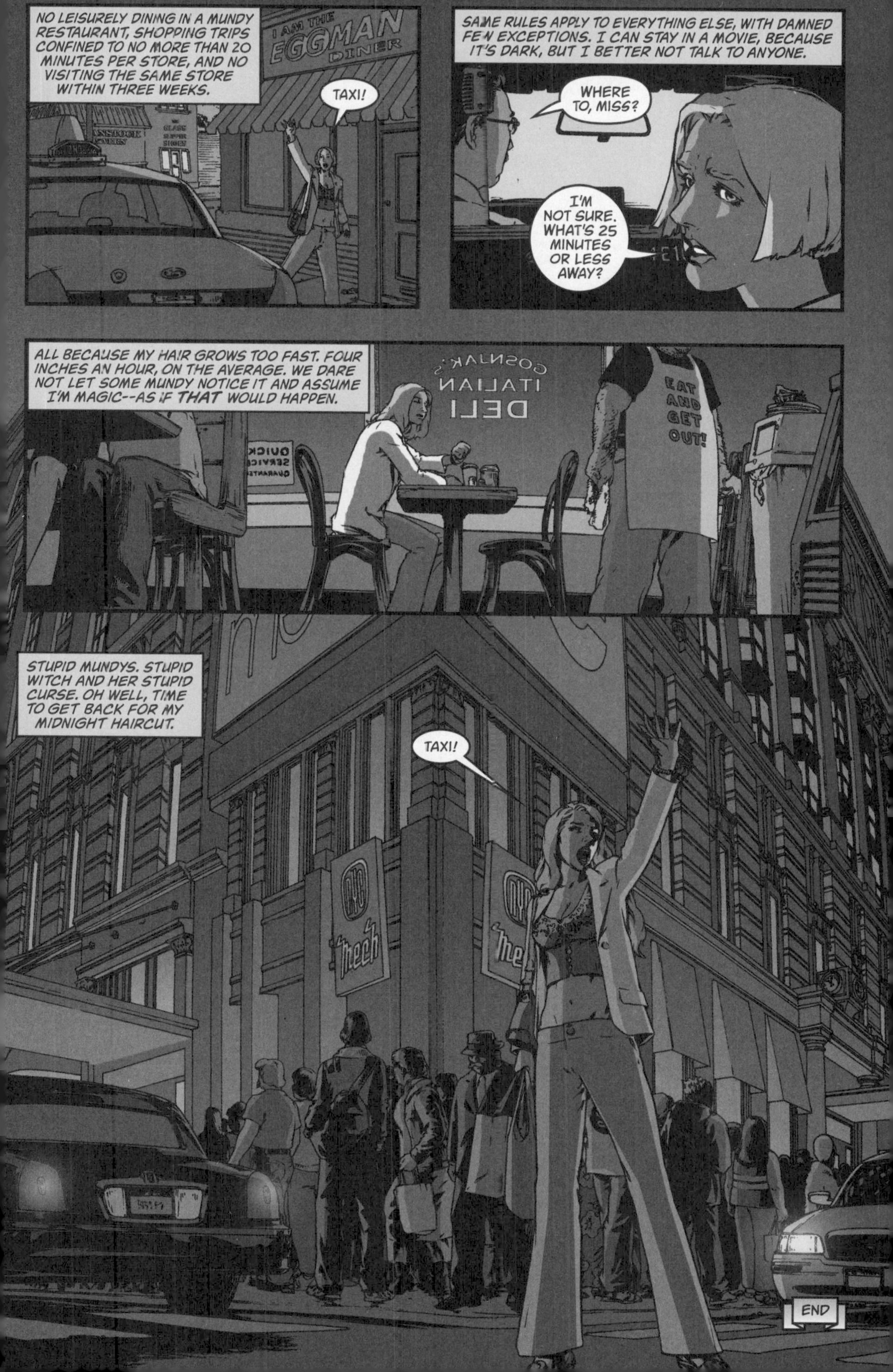
NO LEISURELY DINING IN A MUNDY RESTAURANT, SHOPPING TRIPS CONFINED TO NO MORE THAN 20 MINUTES PER STORE, AND NO VISITING THE SAME STORE WITHIN THREE WEEKS.
I AM THE EGGMAN DINER
TAXI!
SAME RULES APPLY TO EVERYTHING ELSE, WITH DAMNED FEW EXCEPTIONS. I CAN STAY IN A MOVIE, BECAUSE IT'S DARK, BUT I BETTER NOT TALK TO ANYONE.
WHERE TO, MISS?
I'M NOT SURE. WHAT'S 25 MINUTES OR LESS AWAY?
ALL BECAUSE MY HAIR GROWS TOO FAST. FOUR INCHES AN HOUR, ON THE AVERAGE. WE DARE NOT LET SOME MUNDY NOTICE IT AND ASSUME I'M MAGIC--AS IF *THAT* WOULD HAPPEN.
GOSNJAK'S ITALIAN DELI
EAT AND GET OUT!
STUPID MUNDYS. STUPID WITCH AND HER STUPID CURSE. OH WELL, TIME TO GET BACK FOR MY MIDNIGHT HAIRCUT.
TAXI!
END

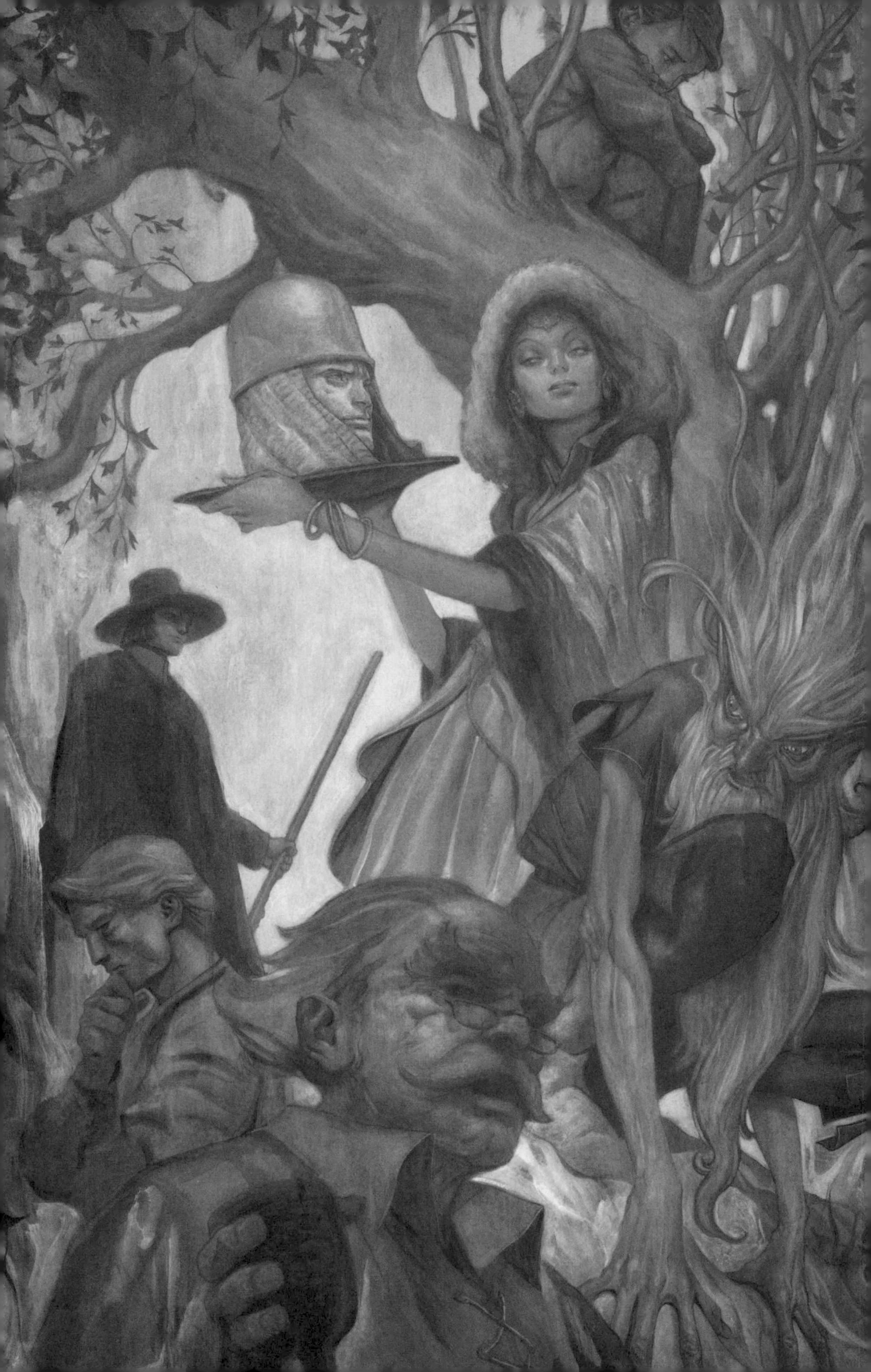

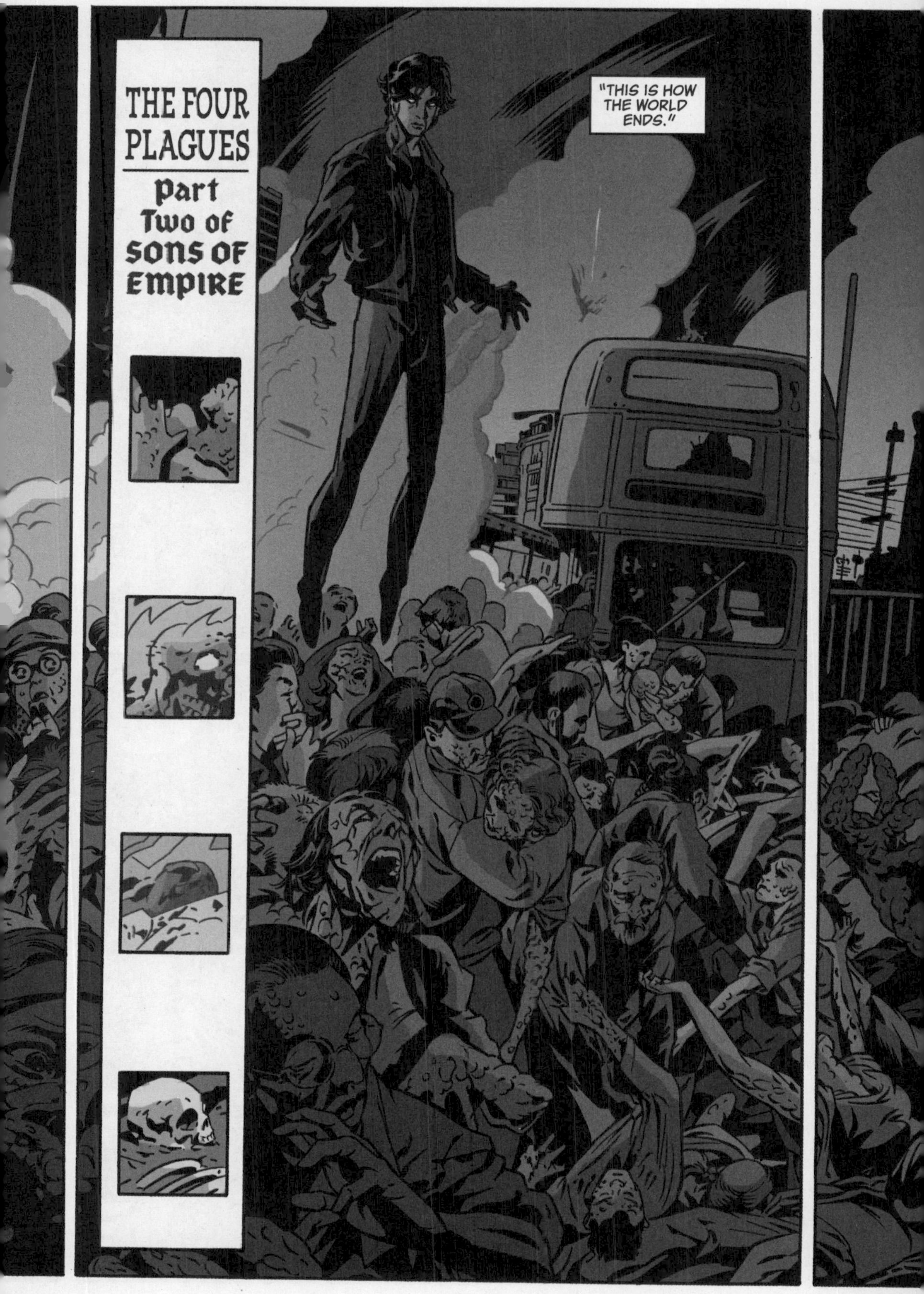
THE FOUR PLAGUES
Part Two of SONS OF EMPIRE
"THIS IS HOW THE WORLD ENDS."

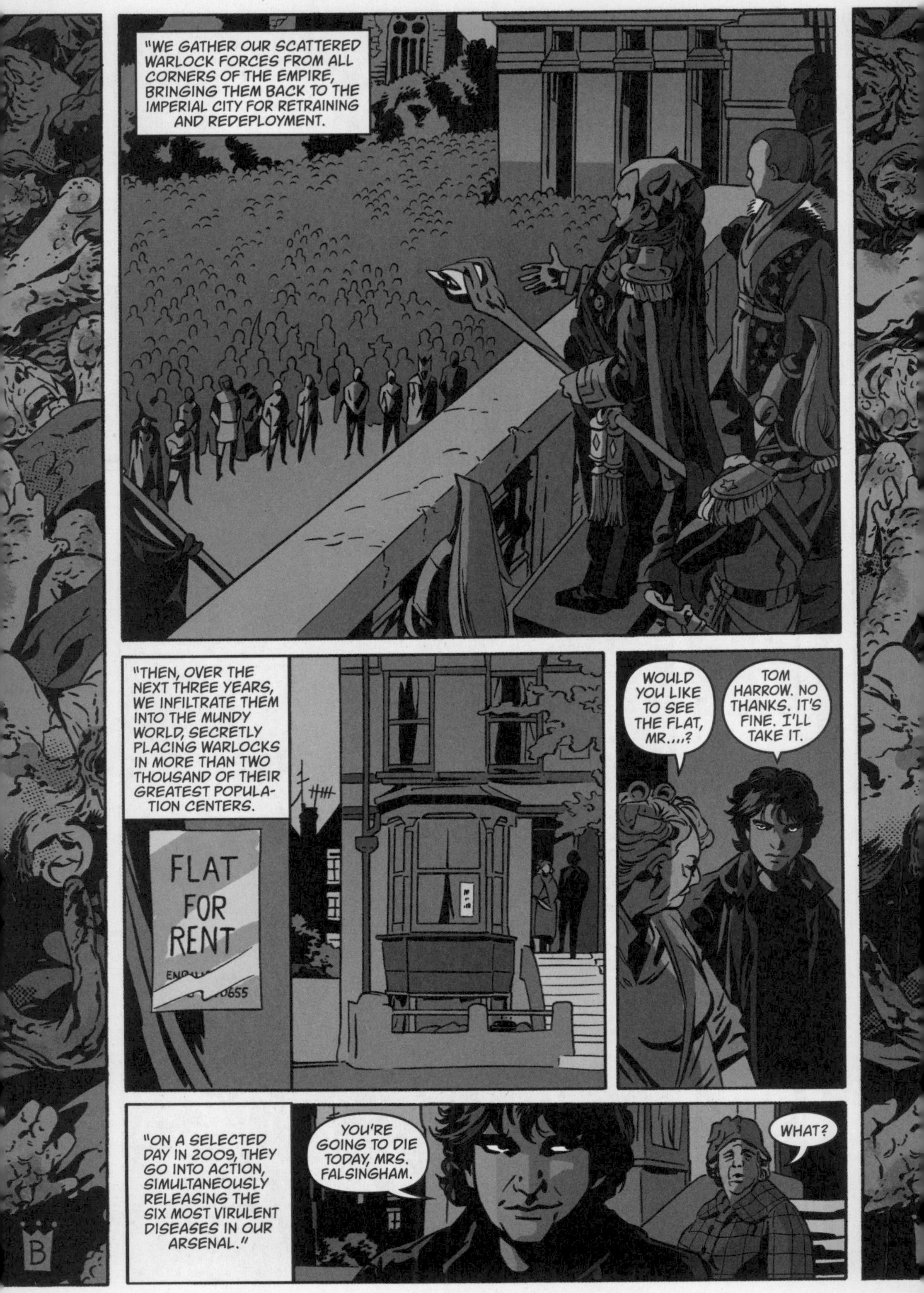
"WE GATHER OUR SCATTERED WARLOCK FORCES FROM ALL CORNERS OF THE EMPIRE, BRINGING THEM BACK TO THE IMPERIAL CITY FOR RETRAINING AND REDEPLOYMENT.
"THEN, OVER THE NEXT THREE YEARS, WE INFILTRATE THEM INTO THE MUNDY WORLD, SECRETLY PLACING WARLOCKS IN MORE THAN TWO THOUSAND OF THEIR GREATEST POPULATION CENTERS.
FLAT FOR RENT
WOULD YOU LIKE TO SEE THE FLAT, MR....?
TOM HARROW. NO THANKS. IT'S FINE. I'LL TAKE IT.
"ON A SELECTED DAY IN 2009, THEY GO INTO ACTION, SIMULTANEOUSLY RELEASING THE SIX MOST VIRULENT DISEASES IN OUR ARSENAL."
YOU'RE GOING TO DIE TODAY, MRS. FALSINGHAM.
WHAT?

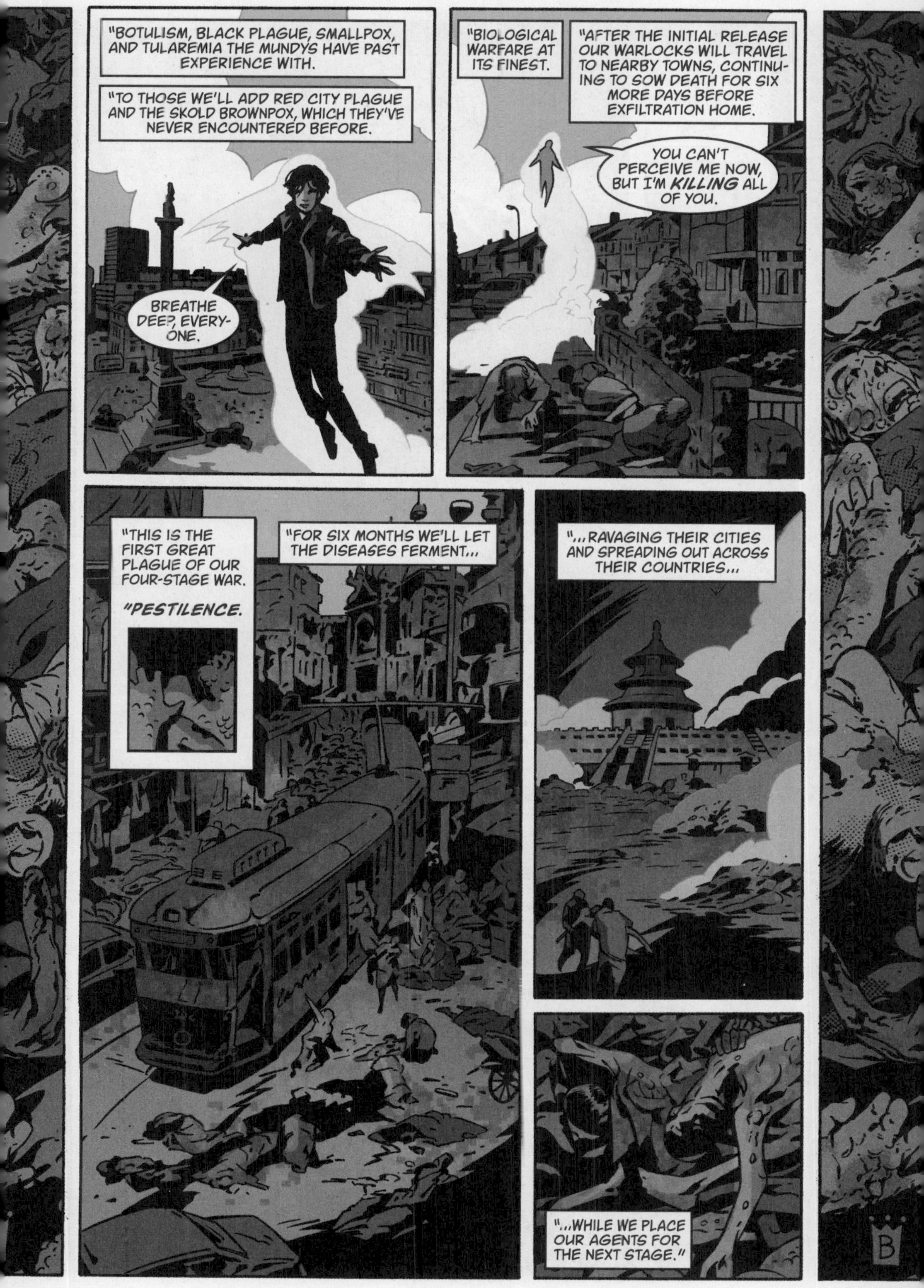
"BOTULISM, BLACK PLAGUE, SMALLPOX, AND TULAREMIA THE MUNDYS HAVE PAST EXPERIENCE WITH.
"TO THOSE WE'LL ADD RED CITY PLAGUE AND THE SKOLD BROWNPOX, WHICH THEY'VE NEVER ENCOUNTERED BEFORE.
BREATHE DEEP, EVERYONE.
"BIOLOGICAL WARFARE AT ITS FINEST.
"AFTER THE INITIAL RELEASE OUR WARLOCKS WILL TRAVEL TO NEARBY TOWNS, CONTINUING TO SOW DEATH FOR SIX MORE DAYS BEFORE EXFILTRATION HOME.
YOU CAN'T PERCEIVE ME NOW, BUT I'M KILLING ALL OF YOU.
"THIS IS THE FIRST GREAT PLAGUE OF OUR FOUR-STAGE WAR.
"PESTILENCE.
"FOR SIX MONTHS WE'LL LET THE DISEASES FERMENT...
"...RAVAGING THEIR CITIES AND SPREADING OUT ACROSS THEIR COUNTRIES...
"...WHILE WE PLACE OUR AGENTS FOR THE NEXT STAGE."

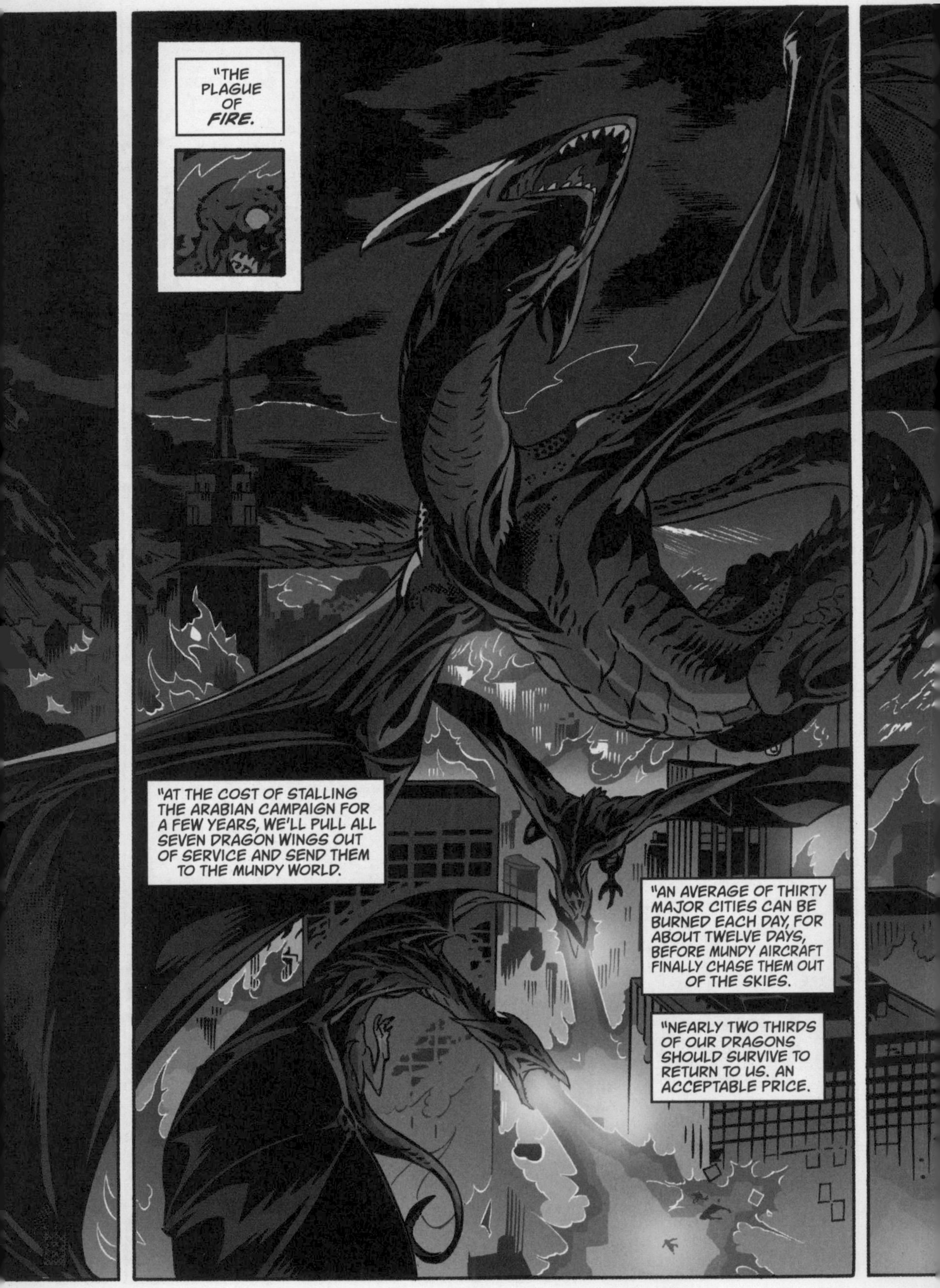
"THE PLAGUE OF FIRE.
"AT THE COST OF STALLING THE ARABIAN CAMPAIGN FOR A FEW YEARS, WE'LL PULL ALL SEVEN DRAGON WINGS OUT OF SERVICE AND SEND THEM TO THE MUNDY WORLD.
"AN AVERAGE OF THIRTY MAJOR CITIES CAN BE BURNED EACH DAY, FOR ABOUT TWELVE DAYS, BEFORE MUNDY AIRCRAFT FINALLY CHASE THEM OUT OF THE SKIES.
"NEARLY TWO THIRDS OF OUR DRAGONS SHOULD SURVIVE TO RETURN TO US. AN ACCEPTABLE PRICE.

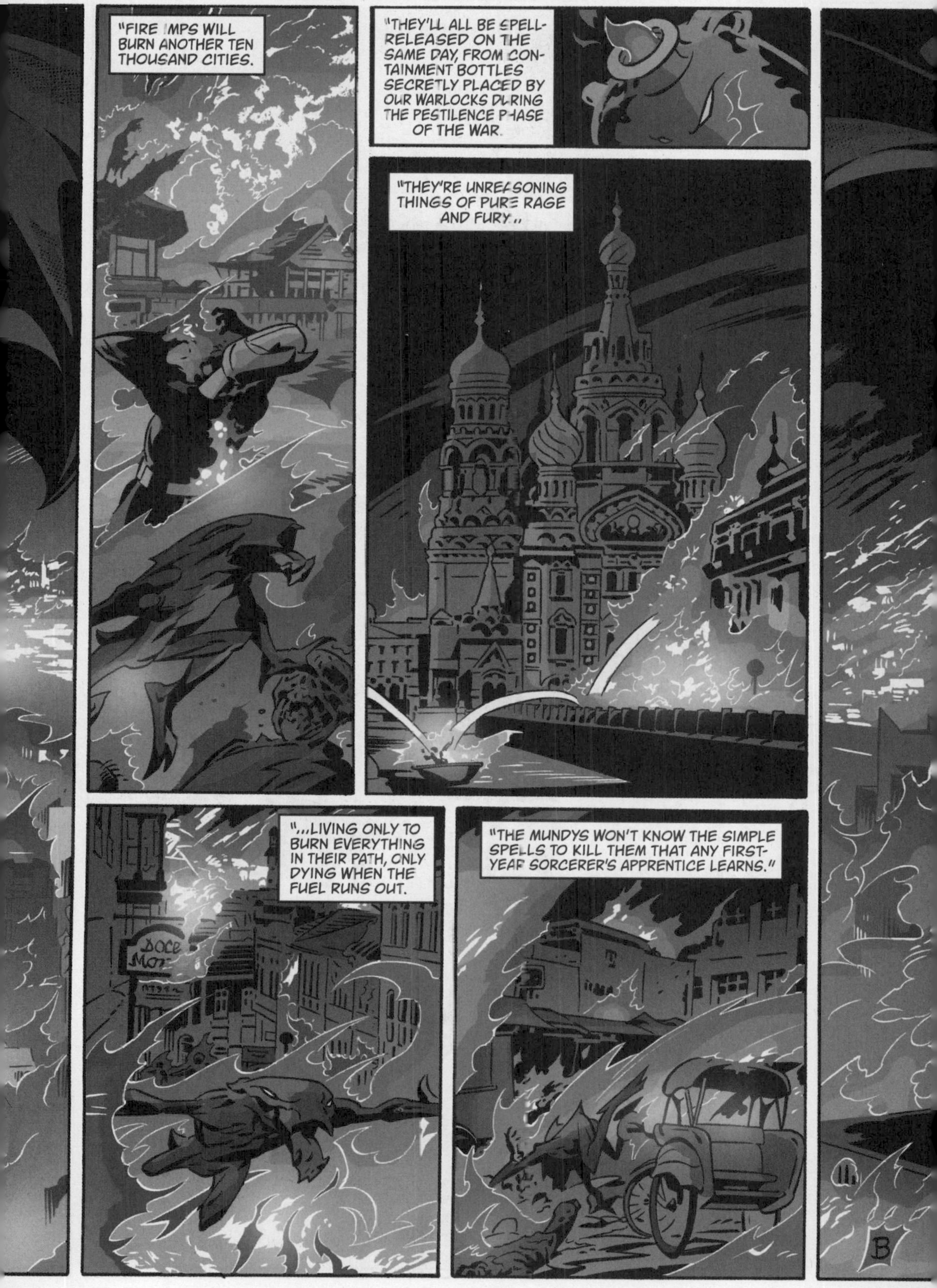
"FIRE IMPS WILL BURN ANOTHER TEN THOUSAND CITIES.
"THEY'LL ALL BE SPELL-RELEASED ON THE SAME DAY, FROM CONTAINMENT BOTTLES SECRETLY PLACED BY OUR WARLOCKS DURING THE PESTILENCE PHASE OF THE WAR.
"THEY'RE UNREASONING THINGS OF PURE RAGE AND FURY...
"...LIVING ONLY TO BURN EVERYTHING IN THEIR PATH, ONLY DYING WHEN THE FUEL RUNS OUT.
"THE MUNDYS WON'T KNOW THE SIMPLE SPELLS TO KILL THEM THAT ANY FIRST-YEAR SORCERER'S APPRENTICE LEARNS."

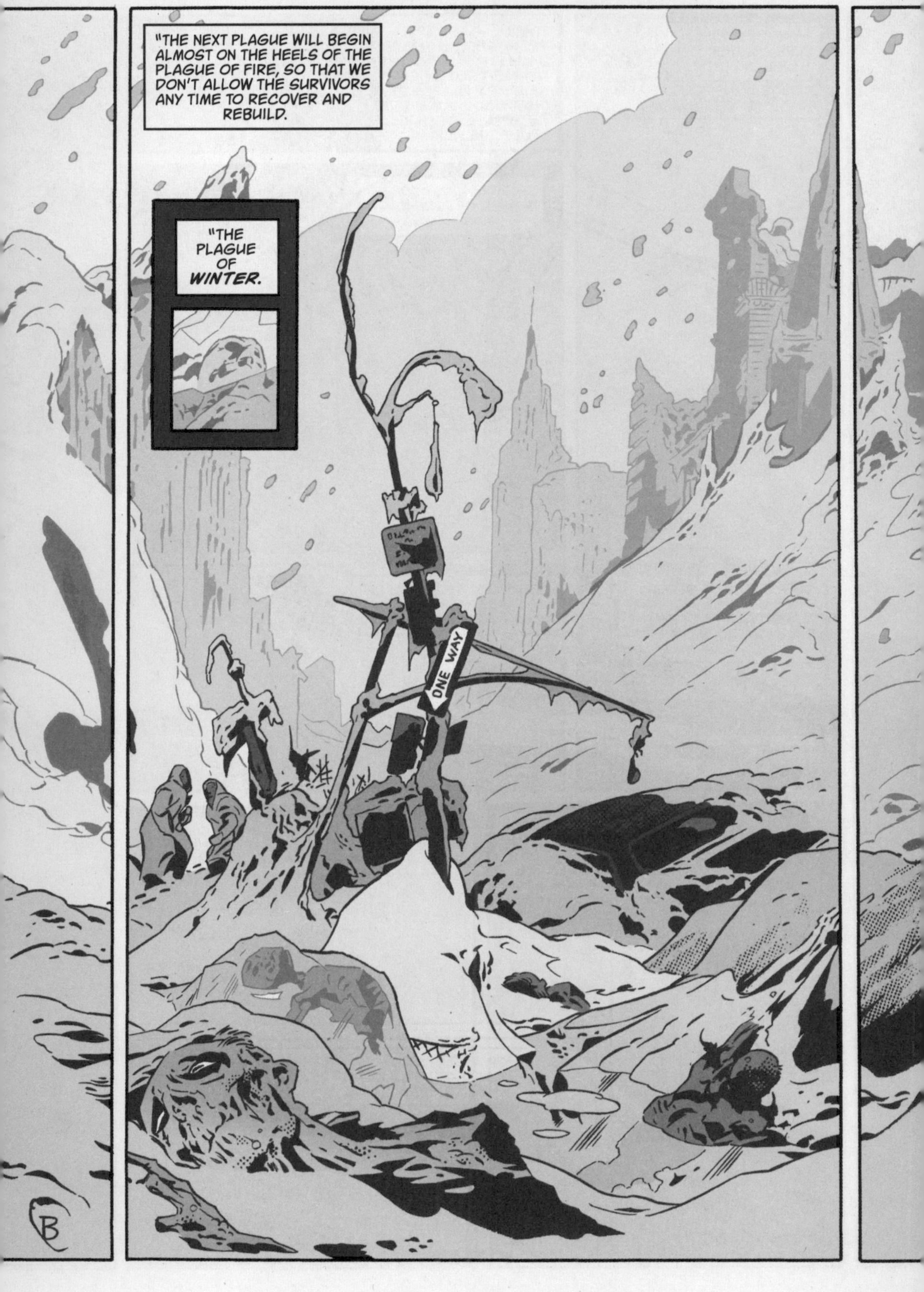
"THE NEXT PLAGUE WILL BEGIN ALMOST ON THE HEELS OF THE PLAGUE OF FIRE, SO THAT WE DON'T ALLOW THE SURVIVORS ANY TIME TO RECOVER AND REBUILD.
"THE PLAGUE OF *WINTER.*
ONE WAY

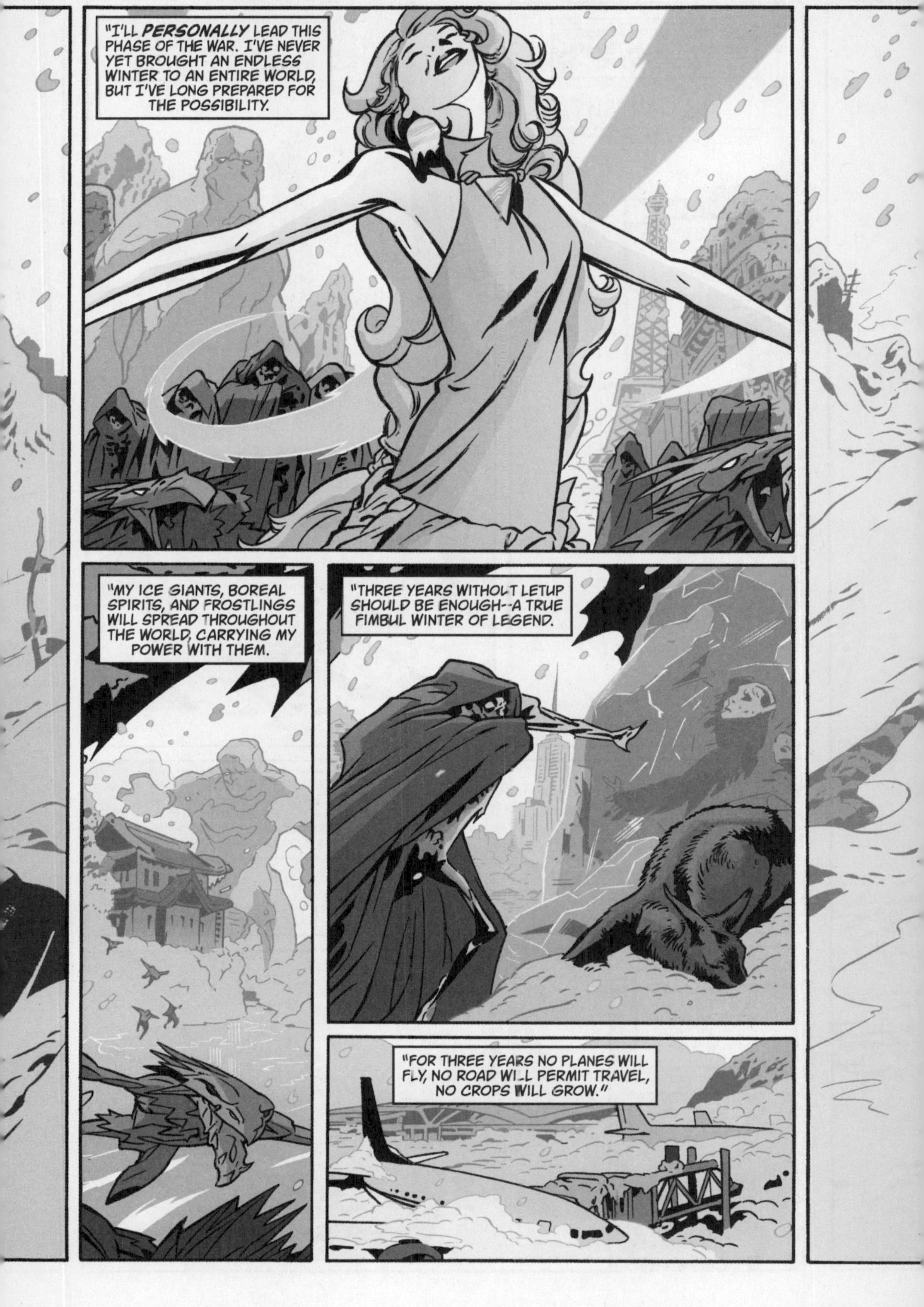
"I'LL PERSONALLY LEAD THIS PHASE OF THE WAR. I'VE NEVER YET BROUGHT AN ENDLESS WINTER TO AN ENTIRE WORLD, BUT I'VE LONG PREPARED FOR THE POSSIBILITY.
"MY ICE GIANTS, BOREAL SPIRITS, AND FROSTLINGS WILL SPREAD THROUGHOUT THE WORLD, CARRYING MY POWER WITH THEM.
"THREE YEARS WITHOUT LETUP SHOULD BE ENOUGH--A TRUE FIMBUL WINTER OF LEGEND.
"FOR THREE YEARS NO PLANES WILL FLY, NO ROAD WILL PERMIT TRAVEL, NO CROPS WILL GROW."

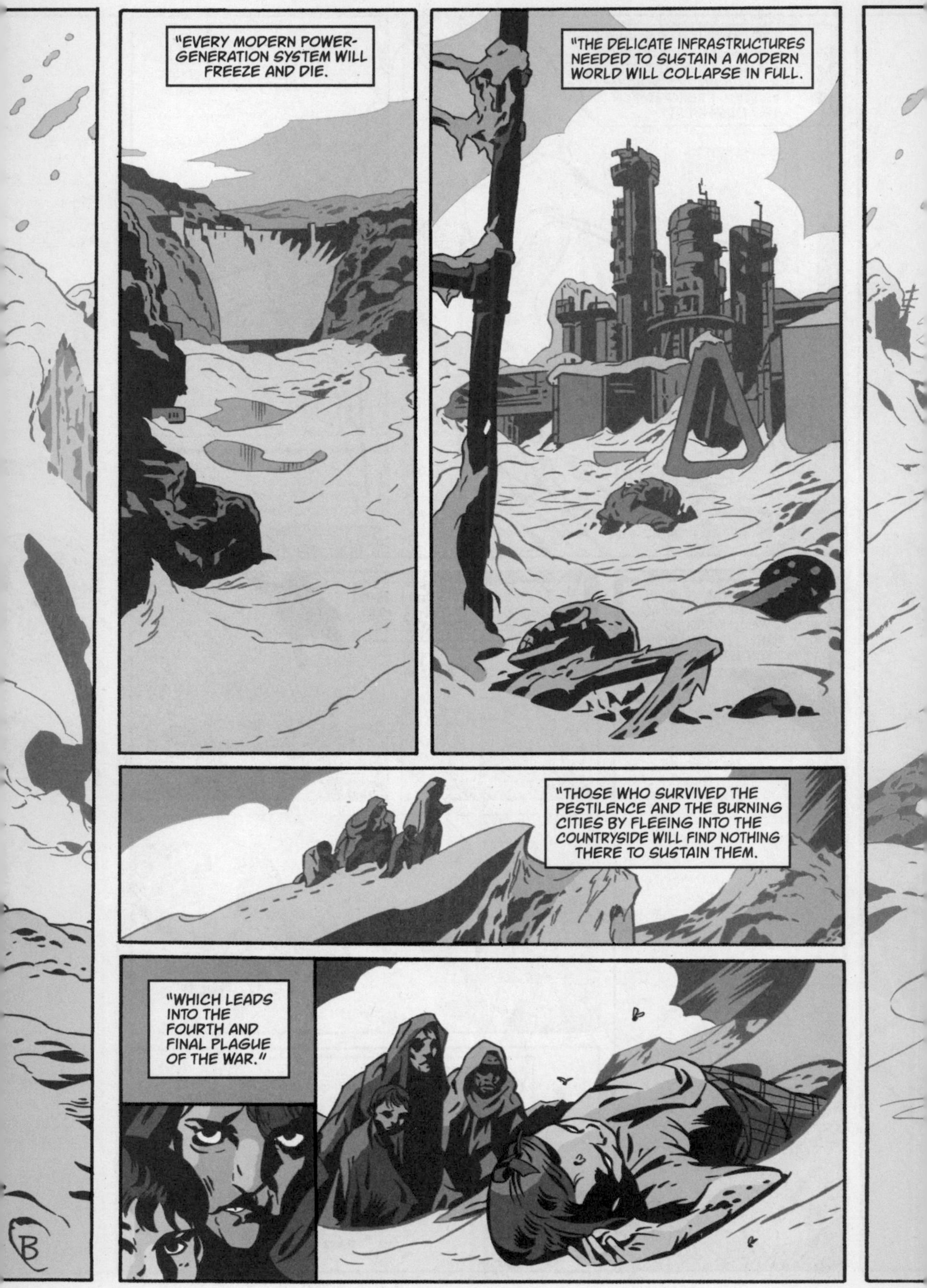
"EVERY MODERN POWER-GENERATION SYSTEM WILL FREEZE AND DIE.
"THE DELICATE INFRASTRUCTURES NEEDED TO SUSTAIN A MODERN WORLD WILL COLLAPSE IN FULL.
"THOSE WHO SURVIVED THE PESTILENCE AND THE BURNING CITIES BY FLEEING INTO THE COUNTRYSIDE WILL FIND NOTHING THERE TO SUSTAIN THEM.
"WHICH LEADS INTO THE FOURTH AND FINAL PLAGUE OF THE WAR."

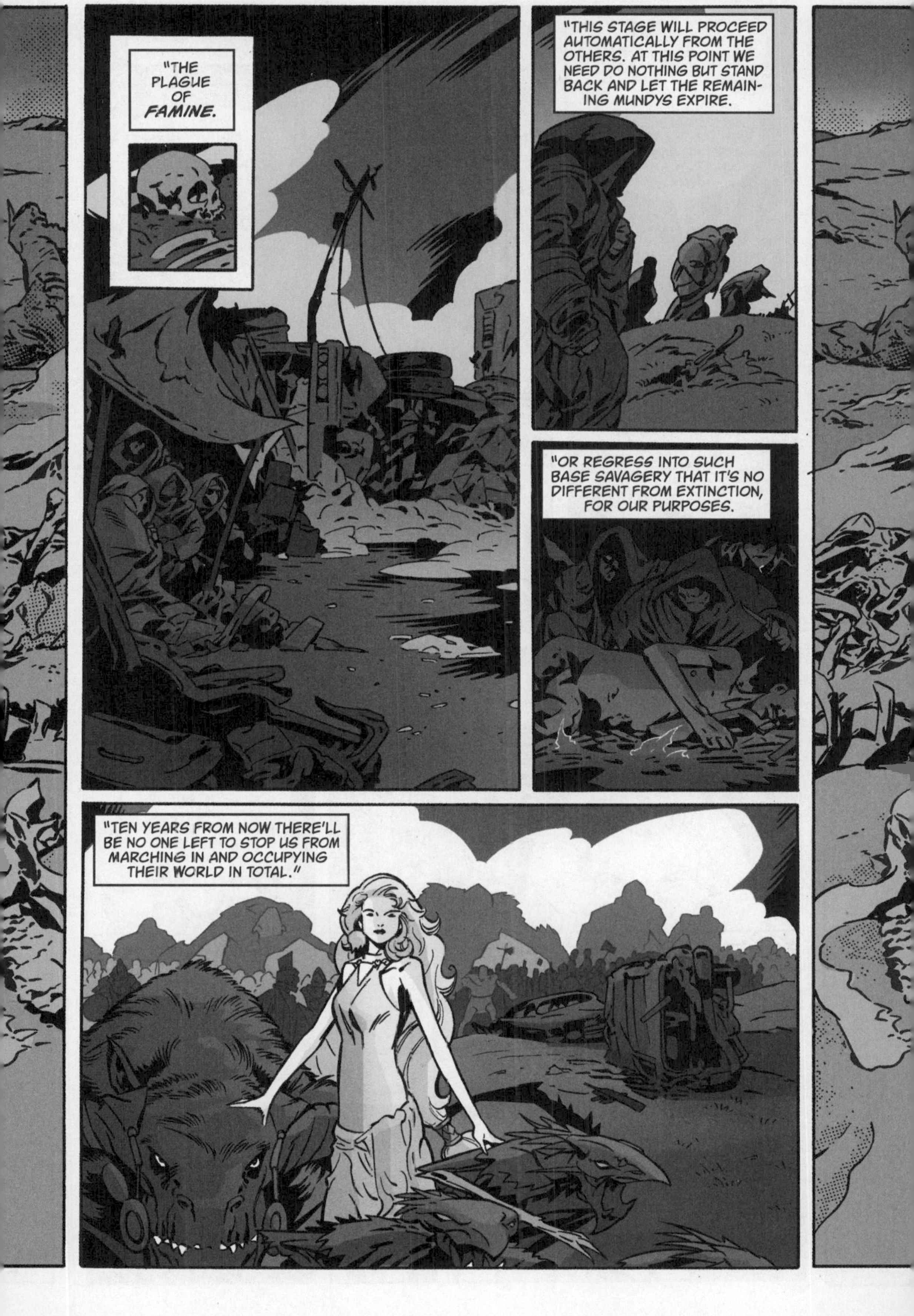
"THE PLAGUE OF FAMINE.
"THIS STAGE WILL PROCEED AUTOMATICALLY FROM THE OTHERS. AT THIS POINT WE NEED DO NOTHING BUT STAND BACK AND LET THE REMAINING MUNDYS EXPIRE.
"OR REGRESS INTO SUCH BASE SAVAGERY THAT IT'S NO DIFFERENT FROM EXTINCTION, FOR OUR PURPOSES.
"TEN YEARS FROM NOW THERE'LL BE NO ONE LEFT TO STOP US FROM MARCHING IN AND OCCUPYING THEIR WORLD IN TOTAL."

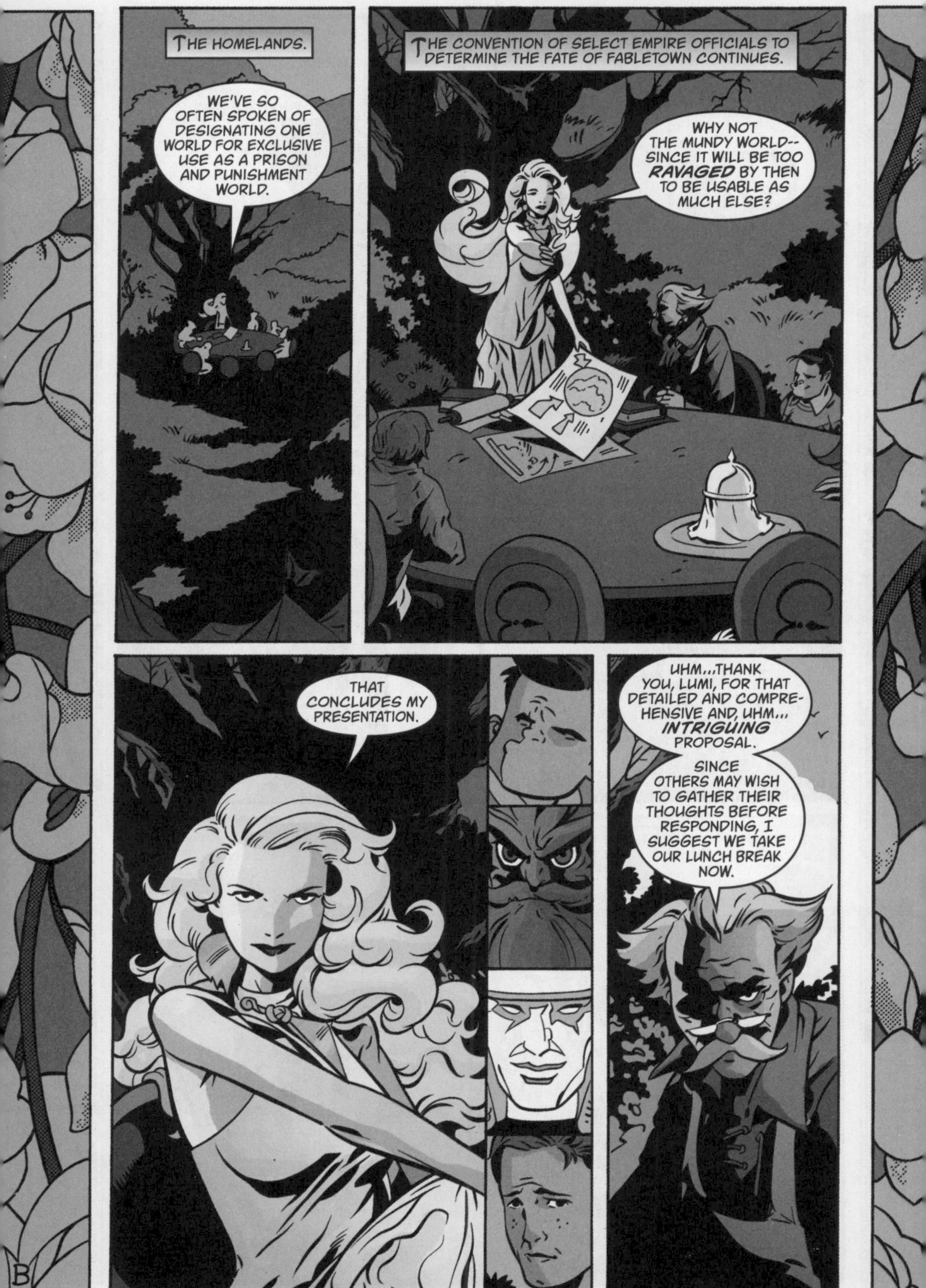
THE HOMELANDS.
WE'VE SO OFTEN SPOKEN OF DESIGNATING ONE WORLD FOR EXCLUSIVE USE AS A PRISON AND PUNISHMENT WORLD.
THE CONVENTION OF SELECT EMPIRE OFFICIALS TO DETERMINE THE FATE OF FABLETOWN CONTINUES.
WHY NOT THE MUNDY WORLD-- SINCE IT WILL BE TOO RAVAGED BY THEN TO BE USABLE AS MUCH ELSE?
THAT CONCLUDES MY PRESENTATION.
UHM...THANK YOU, LUMI, FOR THAT DETAILED AND COMPRE-HENSIVE AND, UHM... INTRIGUING PROPOSAL.
SINCE OTHERS MAY WISH TO GATHER THEIR THOUGHTS BEFORE RESPONDING, I SUGGEST WE TAKE OUR LUNCH BREAK NOW.

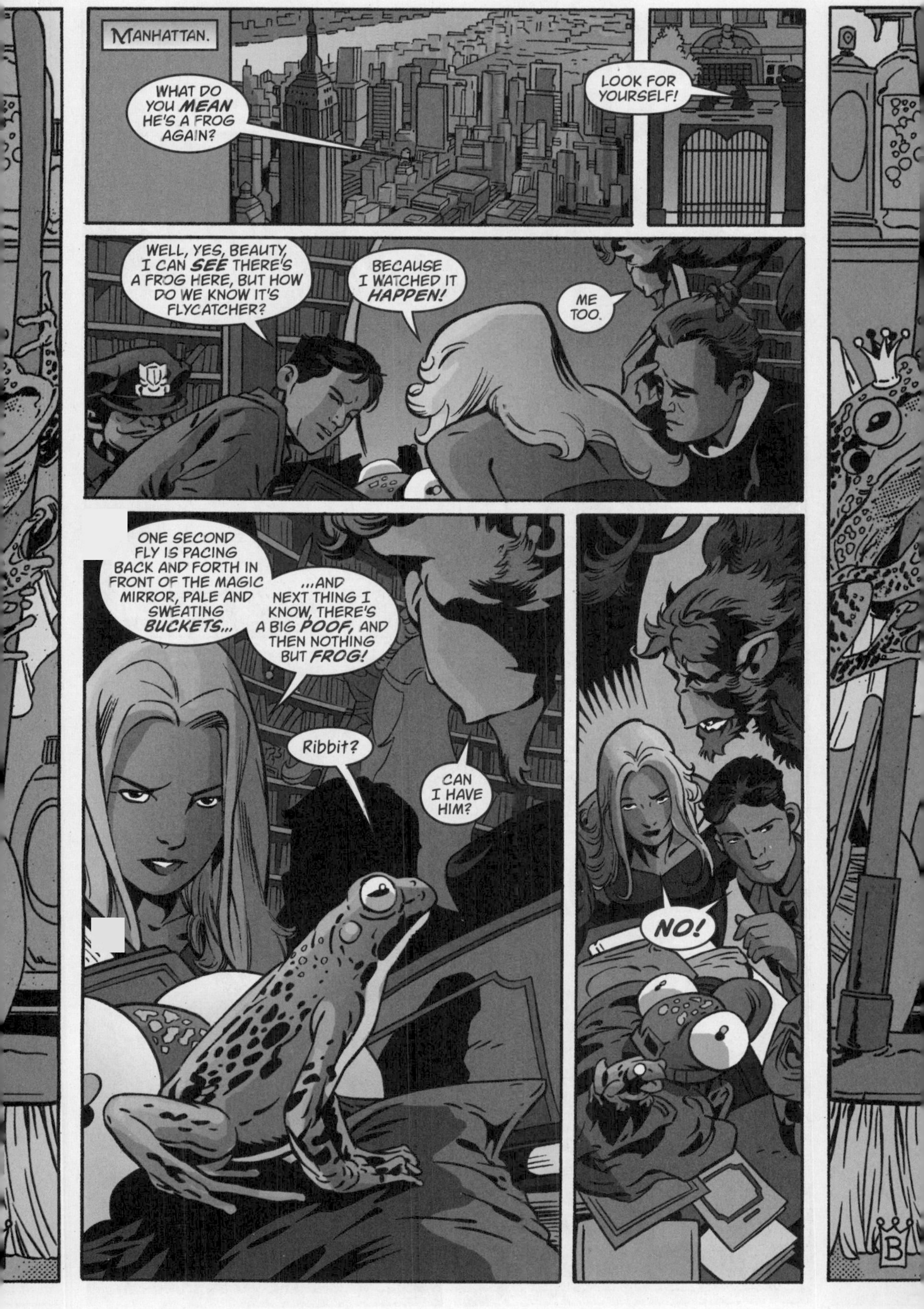
MANHATTAN.
WHAT DO YOU MEAN HE'S A FROG AGAIN?
LOOK FOR YOURSELF!
WELL, YES, BEAUTY, I CAN SEE THERE'S A FROG HERE, BUT HOW DO WE KNOW IT'S FLYCATCHER?
BECAUSE I WATCHED IT HAPPEN!
ME TOO.
ONE SECOND FLY IS PACING BACK AND FORTH IN FRONT OF THE MAGIC MIRROR, PALE AND SWEATING BUCKETS...
...AND NEXT THING I KNOW, THERE'S A BIG POOF, AND THEN NOTHING BUT FROG!
Ribbit?
CAN I HAVE HIM?
NO!

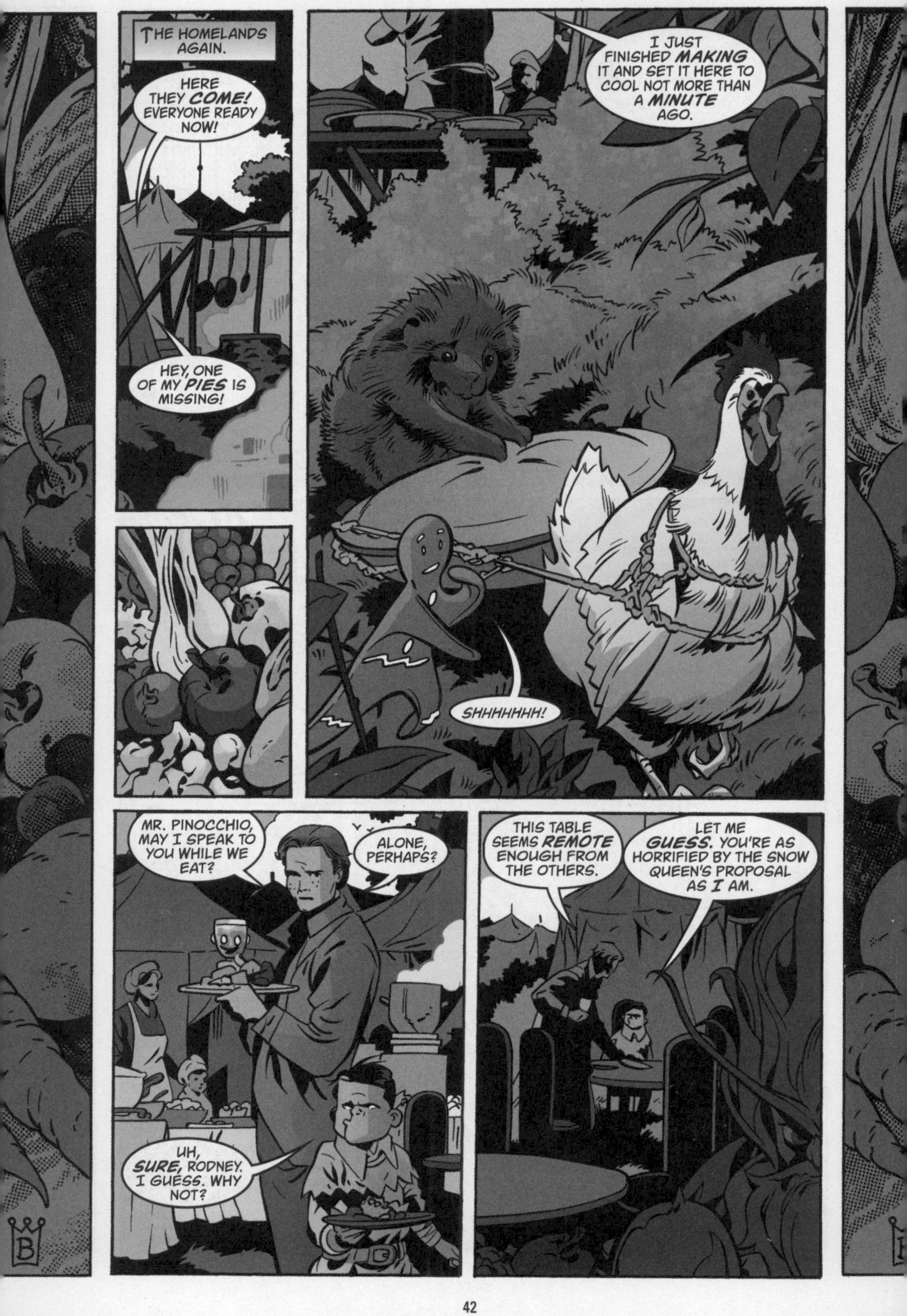
THE HOMELANDS AGAIN.
HERE THEY COME! EVERYONE READY NOW!
HEY, ONE OF MY PIES IS MISSING!
I JUST FINISHED MAKING IT AND SET IT HERE TO COOL NOT MORE THAN A MINUTE AGO.
SHHHHHHH!
MR. PINOCCHIO, MAY I SPEAK TO YOU WHILE WE EAT?
ALONE, PERHAPS?
UH, SURE, RODNEY. I GUESS. WHY NOT?
THIS TABLE SEEMS REMOTE ENOUGH FROM THE OTHERS.
LET ME GUESS. YOU'RE AS HORRIFIED BY THE SNOW QUEEN'S PROPOSAL AS I AM.

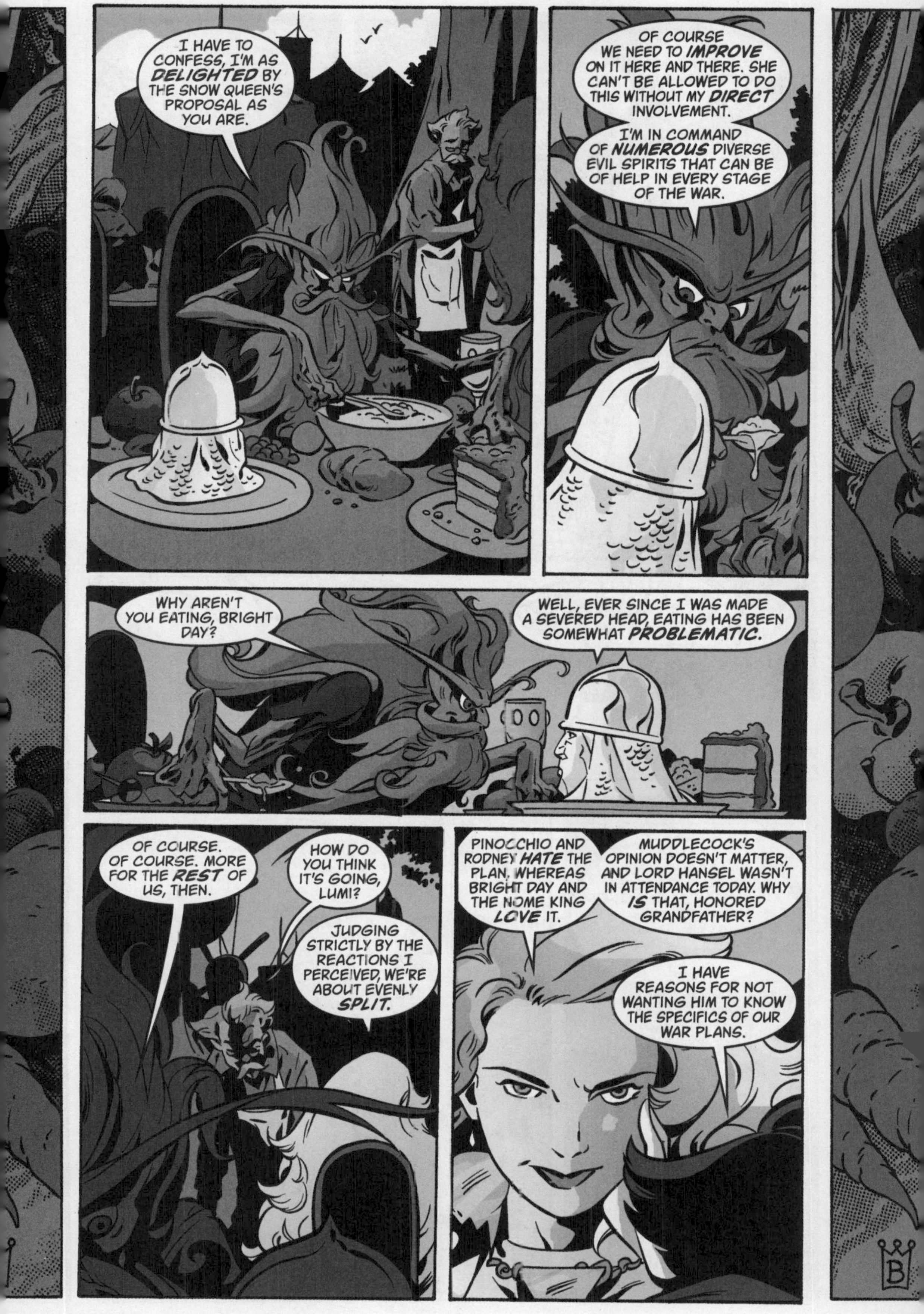
I HAVE TO CONFESS, I'M AS DELIGHTED BY THE SNOW QUEEN'S PROPOSAL AS YOU ARE.
OF COURSE WE NEED TO IMPROVE ON IT HERE AND THERE. SHE CAN'T BE ALLOWED TO DO THIS WITHOUT MY DIRECT INVOLVEMENT.
I'M IN COMMAND OF NUMEROUS DIVERSE EVIL SPIRITS THAT CAN BE OF HELP IN EVERY STAGE OF THE WAR.
WHY AREN'T YOU EATING, BRIGHT DAY?
WELL, EVER SINCE I WAS MADE A SEVERED HEAD, EATING HAS BEEN SOMEWHAT PROBLEMATIC.
OF COURSE. OF COURSE. MORE FOR THE REST OF US, THEN.
HOW DO YOU THINK IT'S GOING, LUMI?
JUDGING STRICTLY BY THE REACTIONS I PERCEIVED, WE'RE ABOUT EVENLY SPLIT.
PINOCCHIO AND RODNEY HATE THE PLAN, WHEREAS BRIGHT DAY AND THE NOME KING LOVE IT.
MUDDLECOCK'S OPINION DOESN'T MATTER, AND LORD HANSEL WASN'T IN ATTENDANCE TODAY. WHY IS THAT, HONORED GRANDFATHER?
I HAVE REASONS FOR NOT WANTING HIM TO KNOW THE SPECIFICS OF OUR WAR PLANS.

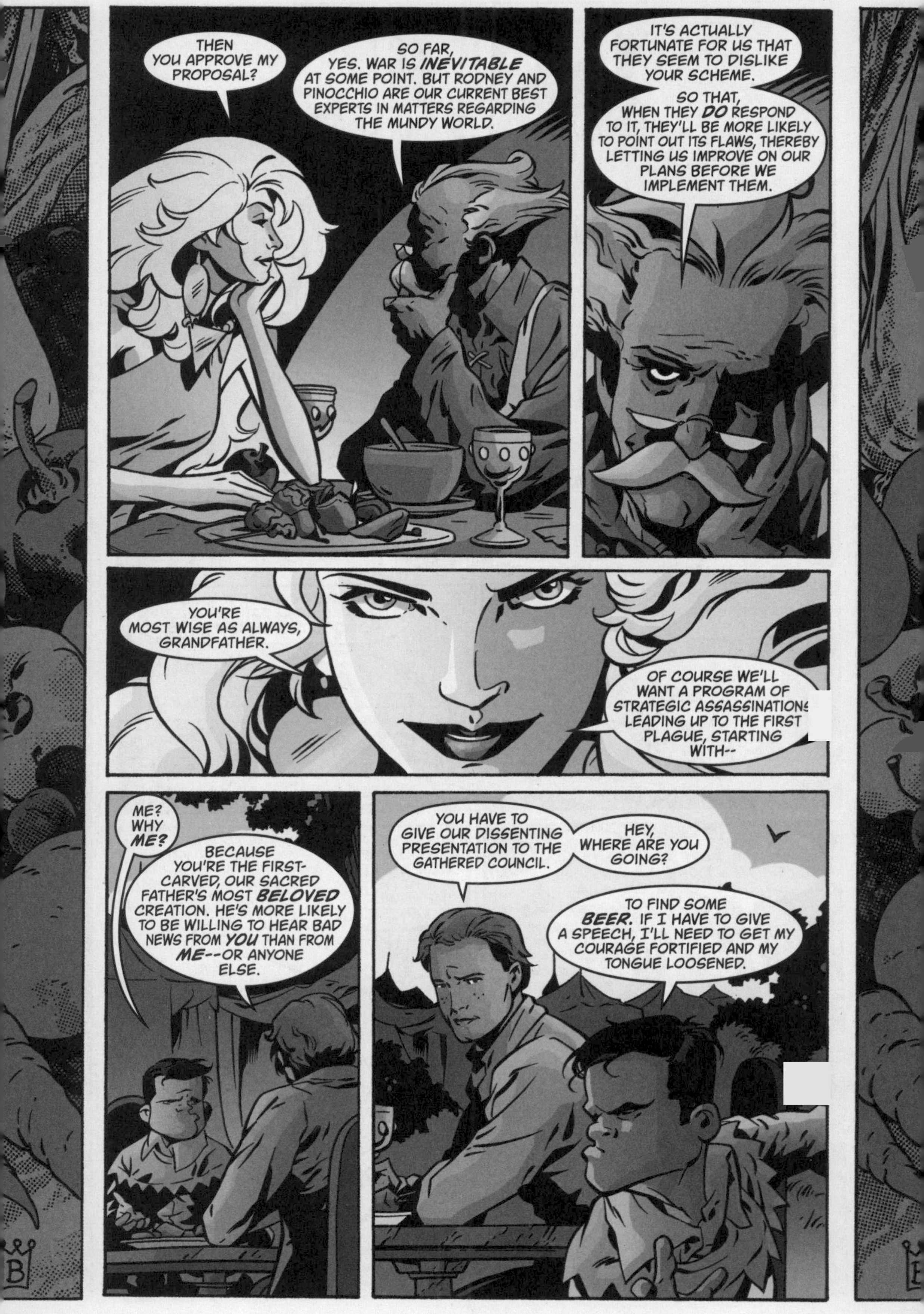
THEN YOU APPROVE MY PROPOSAL?
SO FAR, YES. WAR IS INEVITABLE AT SOME POINT. BUT RODNEY AND PINOCCHIO ARE OUR CURRENT BEST EXPERTS IN MATTERS REGARDING THE MUNDY WORLD.
IT'S ACTUALLY FORTUNATE FOR US THAT THEY SEEM TO DISLIKE YOUR SCHEME.
SO THAT, WHEN THEY DO RESPOND TO IT, THEY'LL BE MORE LIKELY TO POINT OUT ITS FLAWS, THEREBY LETTING US IMPROVE ON OUR PLANS BEFORE WE IMPLEMENT THEM.
YOU'RE MOST WISE AS ALWAYS, GRANDFATHER.
OF COURSE WE'LL WANT A PROGRAM OF STRATEGIC ASSASSINATIONS LEADING UP TO THE FIRST PLAGUE, STARTING WITH--
ME? WHY ME?
BECAUSE YOU'RE THE FIRST-CARVED, OUR SACRED FATHER'S MOST BELOVED CREATION. HE'S MORE LIKELY TO BE WILLING TO HEAR BAD NEWS FROM YOU THAN FROM ME--OR ANYONE ELSE.
YOU HAVE TO GIVE OUR DISSENTING PRESENTATION TO THE GATHERED COUNCIL.
HEY, WHERE ARE YOU GOING?
TO FIND SOME BEER. IF I HAVE TO GIVE A SPEECH, I'LL NEED TO GET MY COURAGE FORTIFIED AND MY TONGUE LOOSENED.

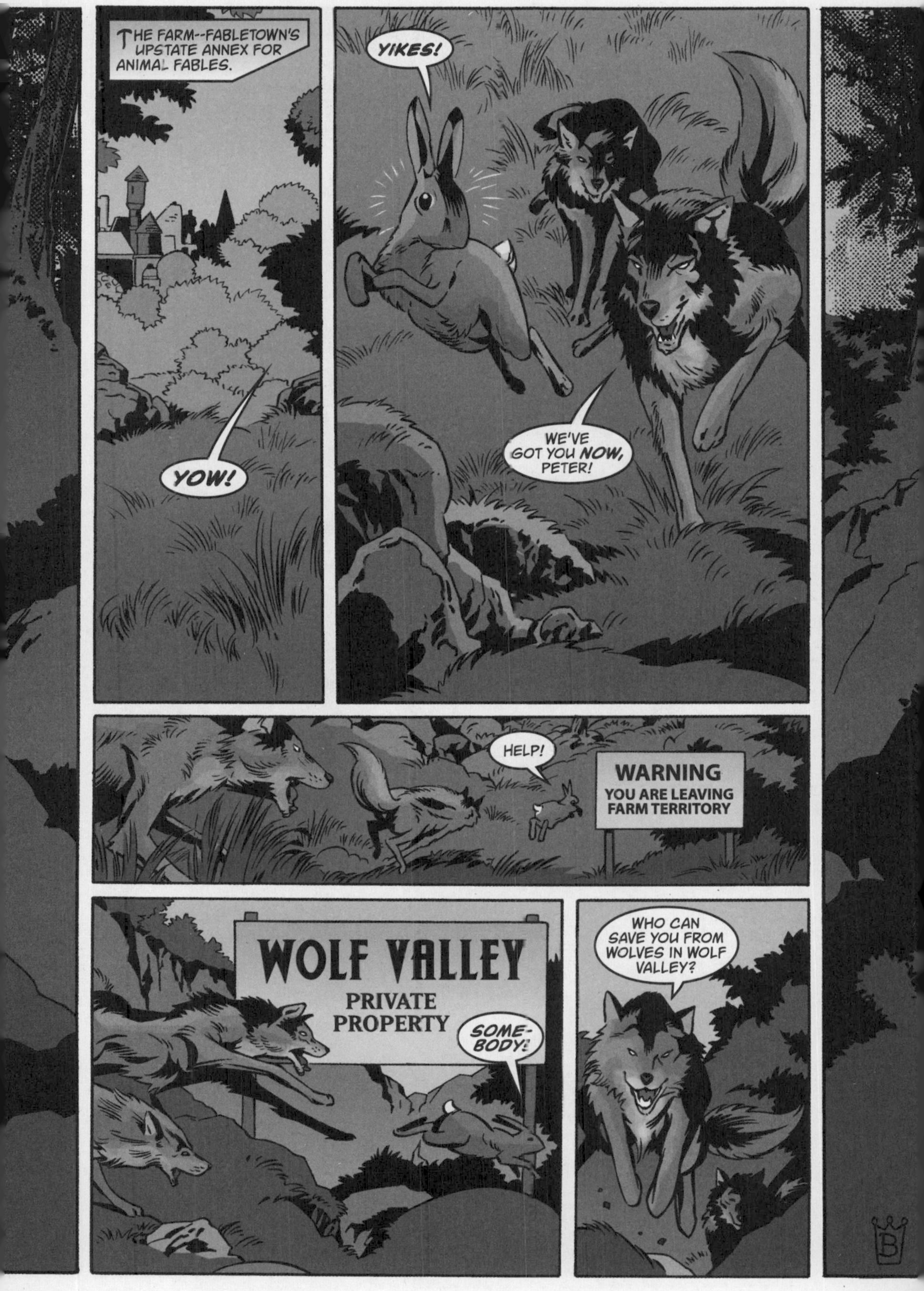
THE FARM--FABLETOWN'S UPSTATE ANNEX FOR ANIMAL FABLES.
YOW!
YIKES!
WE'VE GOT YOU NOW, PETER!
HELP!
WARNING
YOU ARE LEAVING FARM TERRITORY
WOLF VALLEY
PRIVATE PROPERTY
SOME-BODY!
WHO CAN SAVE YOU FROM WOLVES IN WOLF VALLEY?

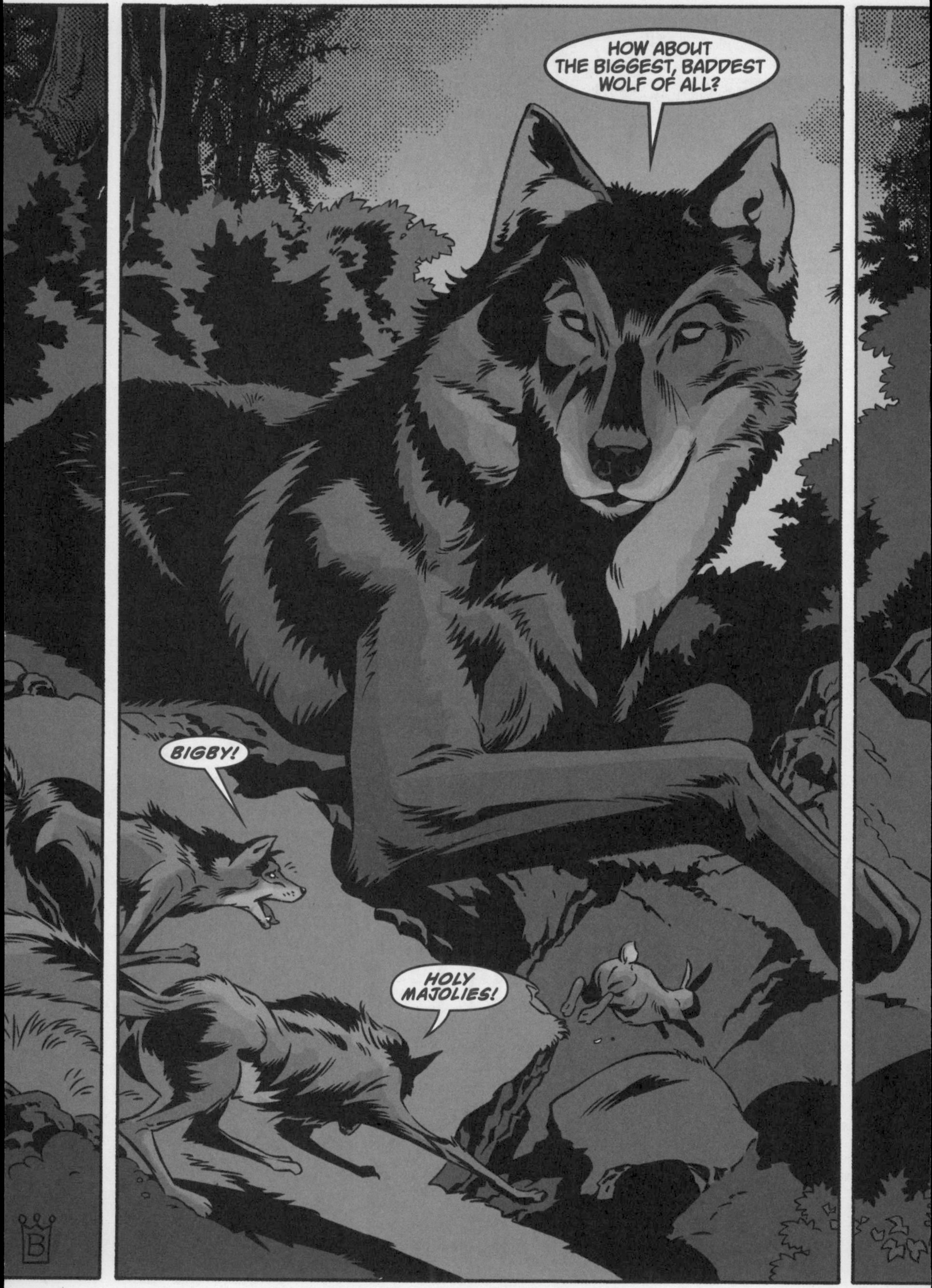
HOW ABOUT THE BIGGEST, BADDEST WOLF OF ALL?
BIGBY!
HOLY MAJOLIES!

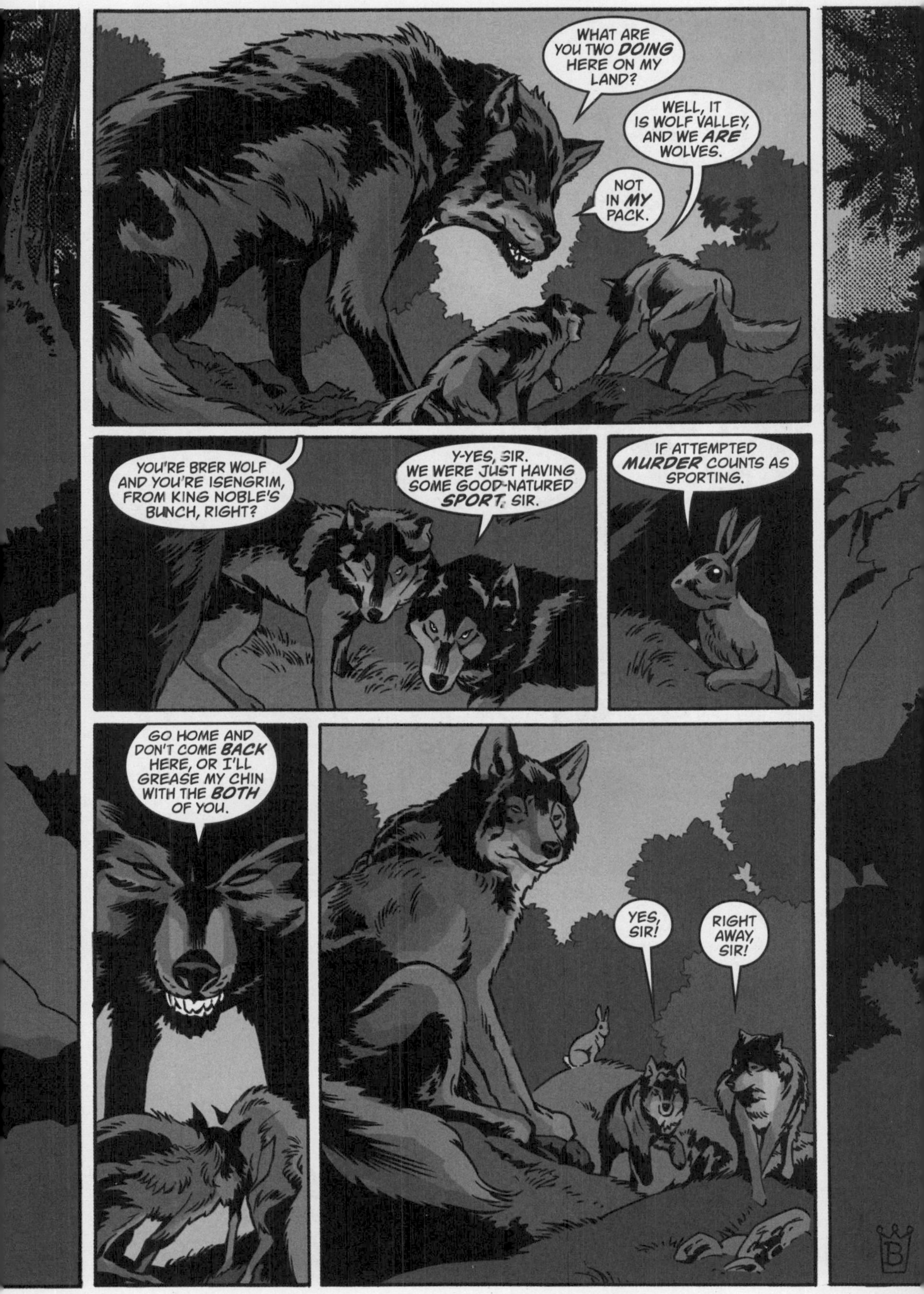
WHAT ARE YOU TWO DOING HERE ON MY LAND?
WELL, IT IS WOLF VALLEY, AND WE ARE WOLVES.
NOT IN MY PACK.
YOU'RE BRER WOLF AND YOU'RE ISENGRIM, FROM KING NOBLE'S BUNCH, RIGHT?
Y-YES, SIR. WE WERE JUST HAVING SOME GOOD-NATURED SPORT, SIR.
IF ATTEMPTED MURDER COUNTS AS SPORTING.
GO HOME AND DON'T COME BACK HERE, OR I'LL GREASE MY CHIN WITH THE BOTH OF YOU.
YES, SIR!
RIGHT AWAY, SIR!

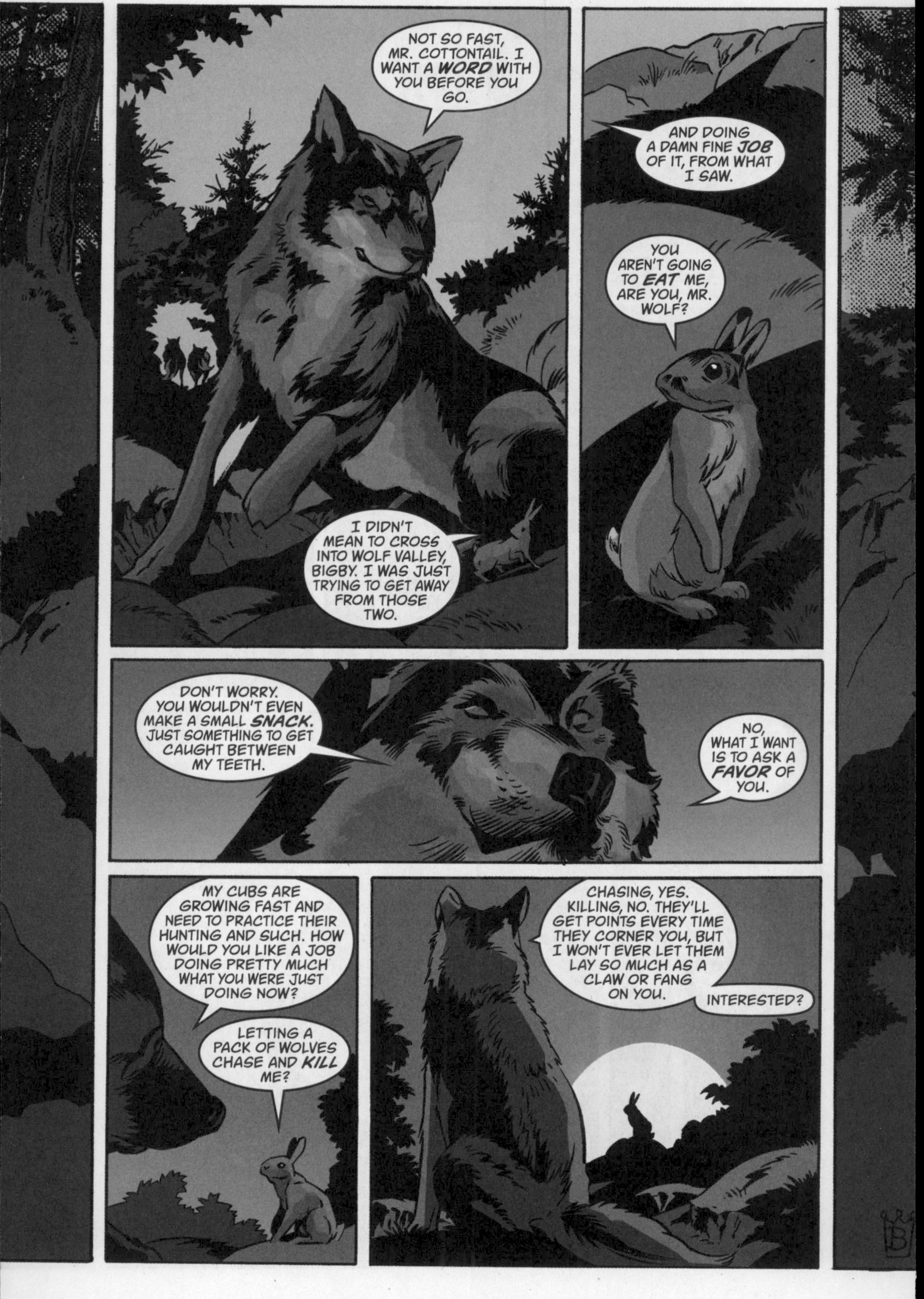
NOT SO FAST, MR. COTTONTAIL. I WANT A WORD WITH YOU BEFORE YOU GO.
I DIDN'T MEAN TO CROSS INTO WOLF VALLEY, BIGBY. I WAS JUST TRYING TO GET AWAY FROM THOSE TWO.
AND DOING A DAMN FINE JOB OF IT, FROM WHAT I SAW.
YOU AREN'T GOING TO EAT ME, ARE YOU, MR. WOLF?
DON'T WORRY. YOU WOULDN'T EVEN MAKE A SMALL SNACK. JUST SOMETHING TO GET CAUGHT BETWEEN MY TEETH.
NO, WHAT I WANT IS TO ASK A FAVOR OF YOU.
MY CUBS ARE GROWING FAST AND NEED TO PRACTICE THEIR HUNTING AND SUCH. HOW WOULD YOU LIKE A JOB DOING PRETTY MUCH WHAT YOU WERE JUST DOING NOW?
LETTING A PACK OF WOLVES CHASE AND KILL ME?
CHASING, YES. KILLING, NO. THEY'LL GET POINTS EVERY TIME THEY CORNER YOU, BUT I WON'T EVER LET THEM LAY SO MUCH AS A CLAW OR FANG ON YOU.
INTERESTED?

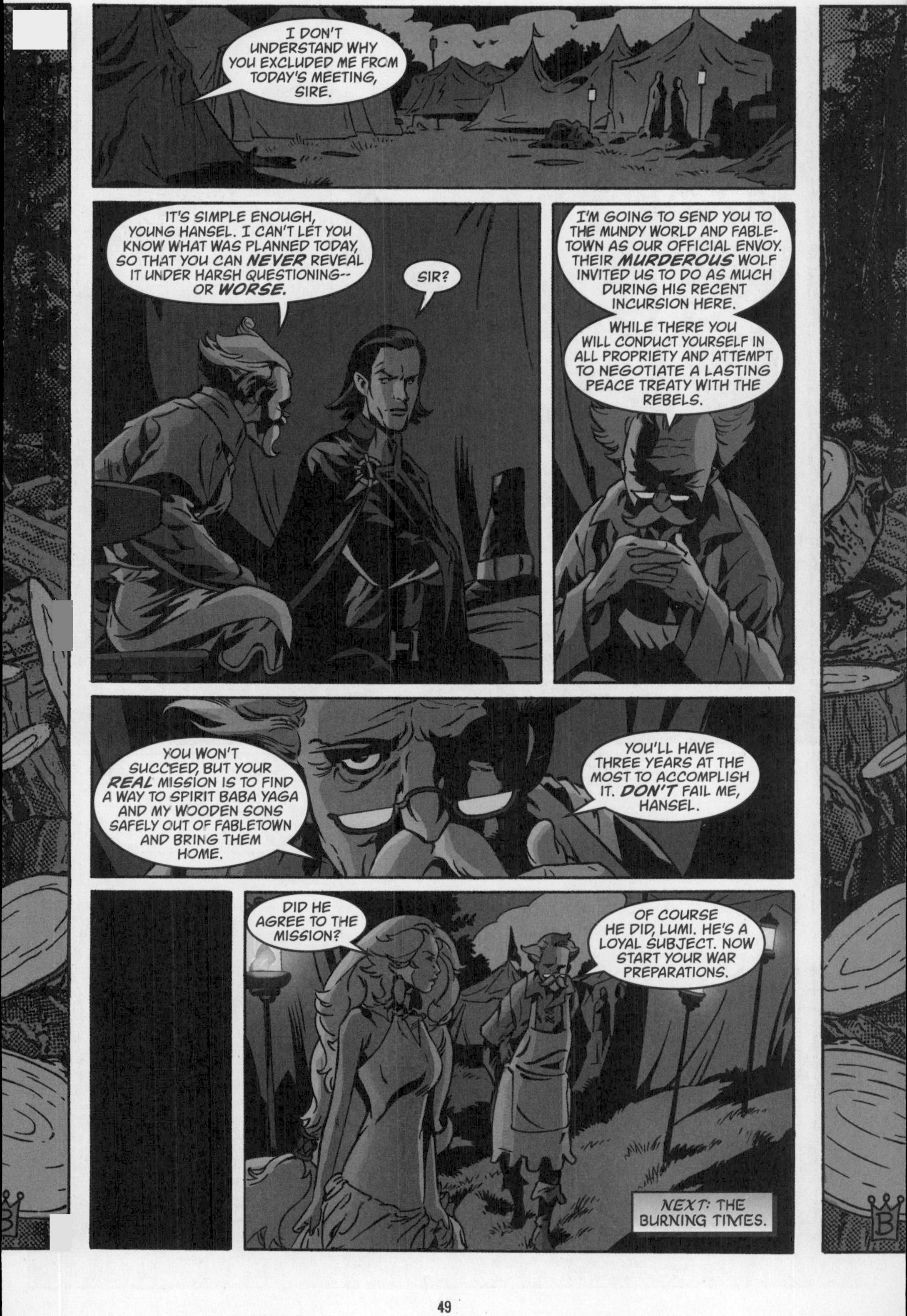
I DON'T UNDERSTAND WHY YOU EXCLUDED ME FROM TODAY'S MEETING, SIRE.
IT'S SIMPLE ENOUGH, YOUNG HANSEL. I CAN'T LET YOU KNOW WHAT WAS PLANNED TODAY, SO THAT YOU CAN NEVER REVEAL IT UNDER HARSH QUESTIONING-- OR WORSE.
SIR?
I'M GOING TO SEND YOU TO THE MUNDY WORLD AND FABLE-TOWN AS OUR OFFICIAL ENVOY. THEIR MURDEROUS WOLF INVITED US TO DO AS MUCH DURING HIS RECENT INCURSION HERE.
WHILE THERE YOU WILL CONDUCT YOURSELF IN ALL PROPRIETY AND ATTEMPT TO NEGOTIATE A LASTING PEACE TREATY WITH THE REBELS.
YOU WON'T SUCCEED, BUT YOUR REAL MISSION IS TO FIND A WAY TO SPIRIT BABA YAGA AND MY WOODEN SONS SAFELY OUT OF FABLETOWN AND BRING THEM HOME.
YOU'LL HAVE THREE YEARS AT THE MOST TO ACCOMPLISH IT. DON'T FAIL ME, HANSEL.
DID HE AGREE TO THE MISSION?
OF COURSE HE DID, LUMI. HE'S A LOYAL SUBJECT. NOW START YOUR WAR PREPARATIONS.
NEXT: THE BURNING TIMES.

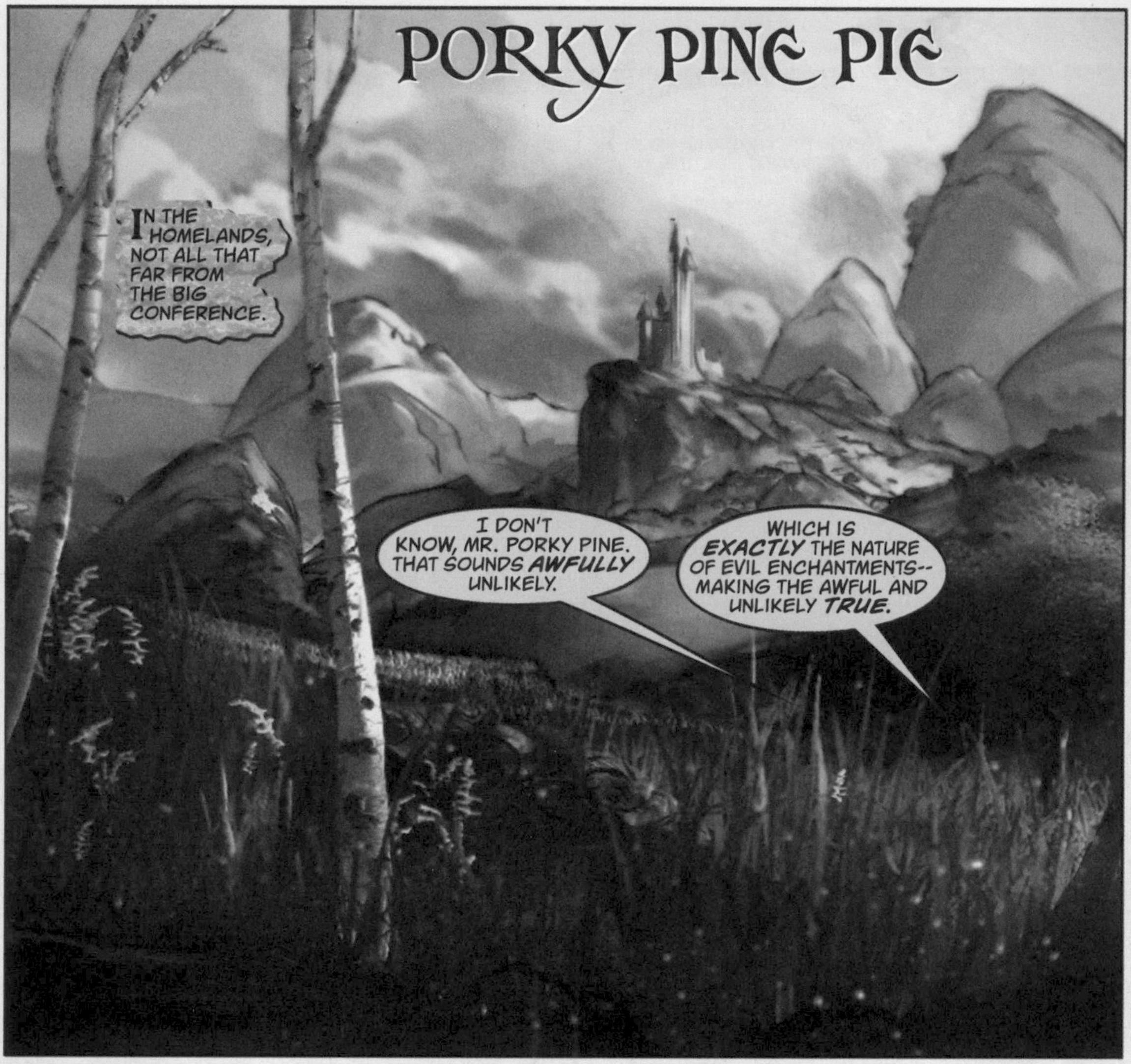
PORKY PINE PIE
IN THE HOMELANDS, NOT ALL THAT FAR FROM THE BIG CONFERENCE.
I DON'T KNOW, MR. PORKY PINE. THAT SOUNDS AWFULLY UNLIKELY.
WHICH IS EXACTLY THE NATURE OF EVIL ENCHANTMENTS-- MAKING THE AWFUL AND UNLIKELY TRUE.

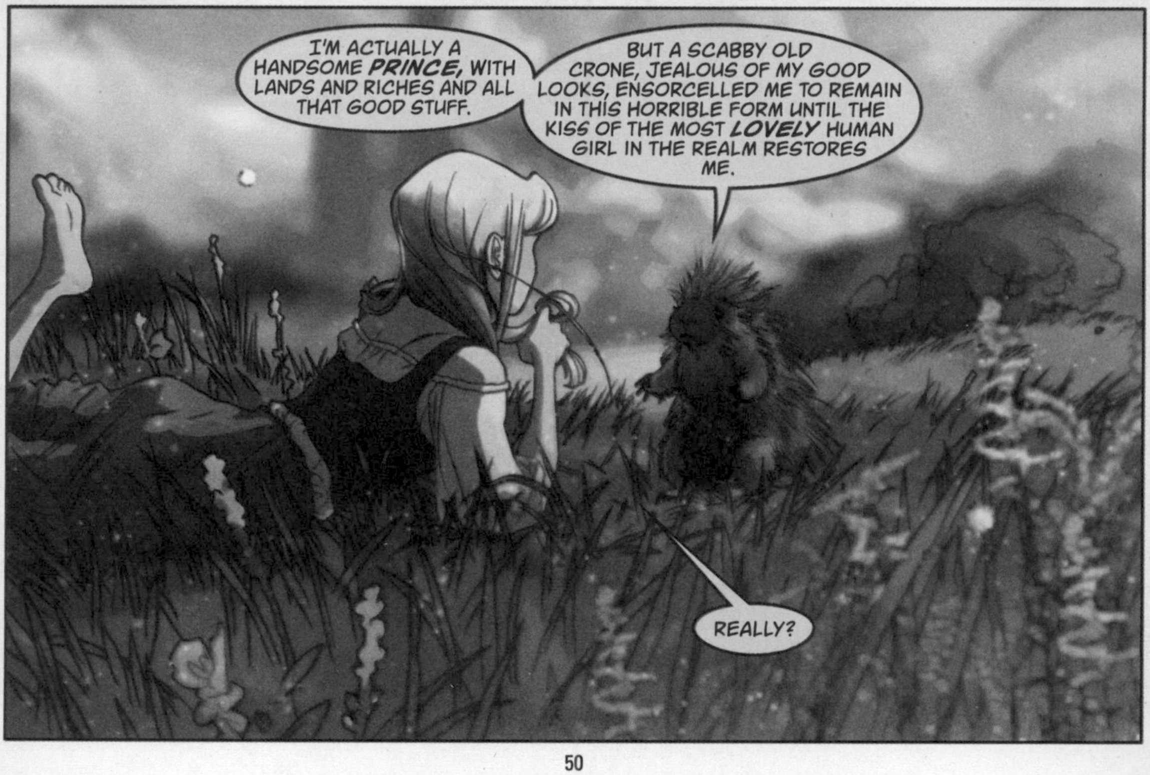
I'M ACTUALLY A HANDSOME PRINCE, WITH LANDS AND RICHES AND ALL THAT GOOD STUFF.
BUT A SCABBY OLD CRONE, JEALOUS OF MY GOOD LOOKS, ENSORCELLED ME TO REMAIN IN THIS HORRIBLE FORM UNTIL THE KISS OF THE MOST LOVELY HUMAN GIRL IN THE REALM RESTORES ME.
REALLY?

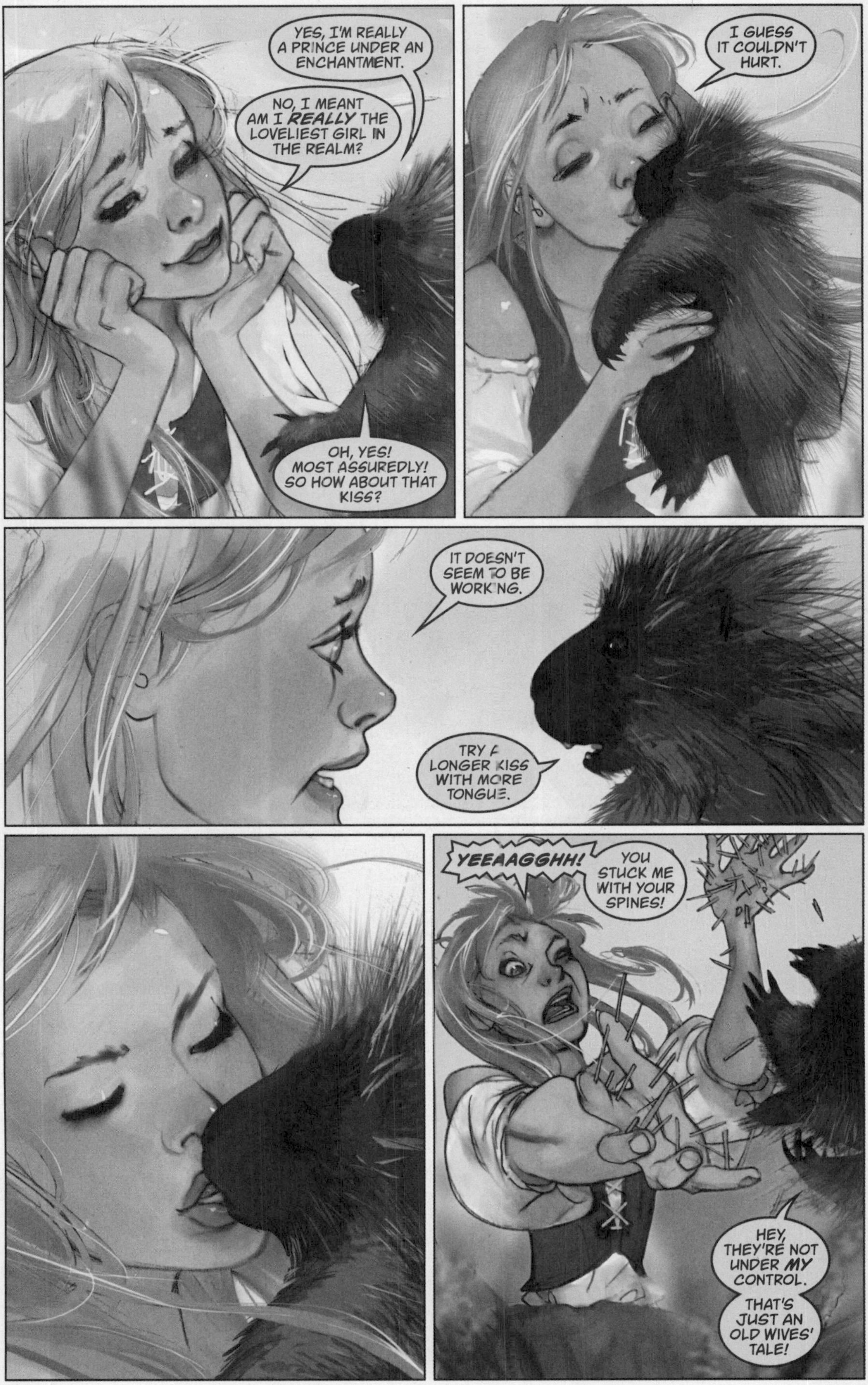
YES, I'M REALLY A PRINCE UNDER AN ENCHANTMENT.
NO, I MEANT AM I REALLY THE LOVELIEST GIRL IN THE REALM?
OH, YES! MOST ASSUREDLY! SO HOW ABOUT THAT KISS?
I GUESS IT COULDN'T HURT.
IT DOESN'T SEEM TO BE WORKING.
TRY A LONGER KISS WITH MORE TONGUE.
YEEAAGGHH!
YOU STUCK ME WITH YOUR SPINES!
HEY, THEY'RE NOT UNDER MY CONTROL.
THAT'S JUST AN OLD WIVES' TALE!

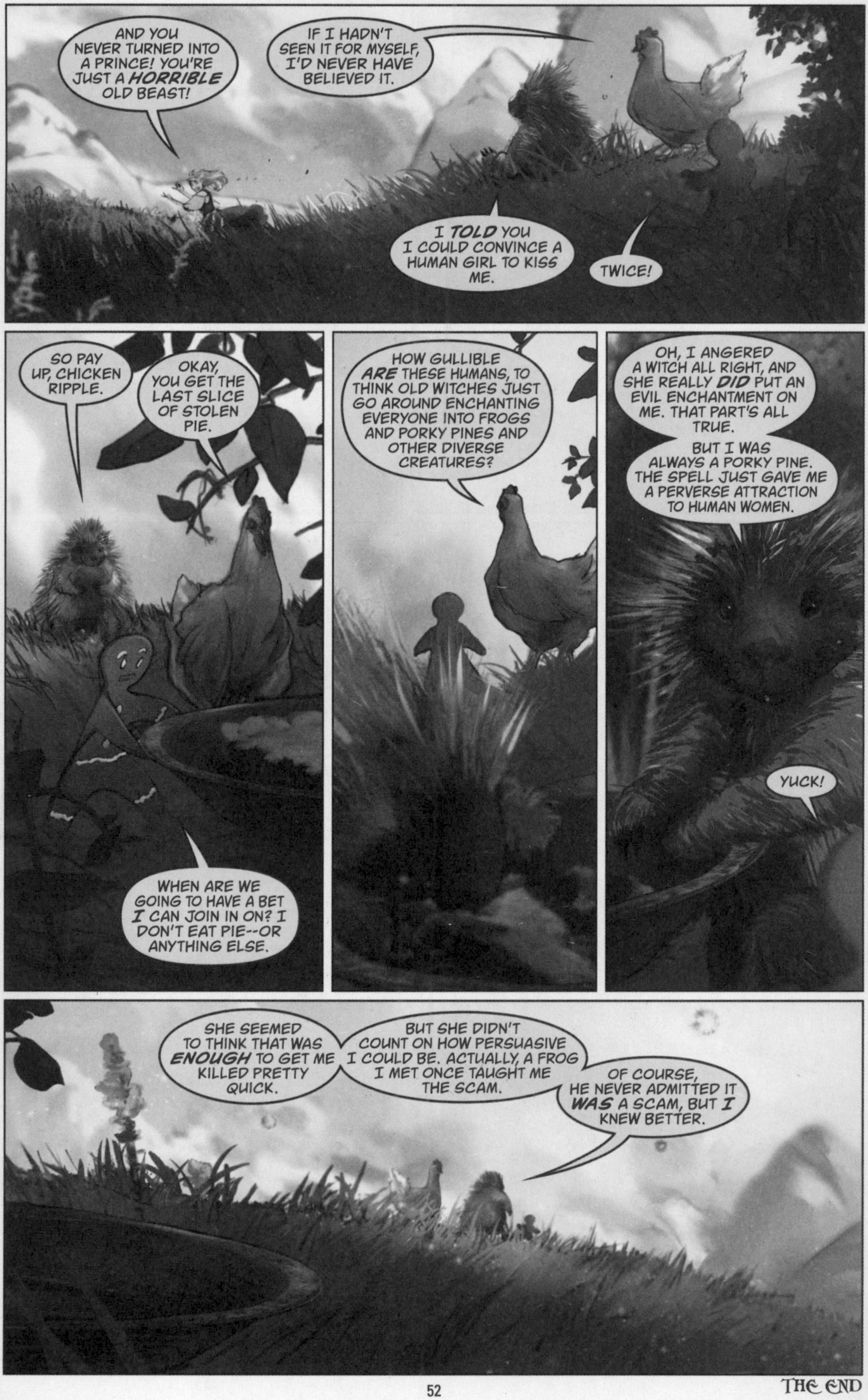
AND YOU NEVER TURNED INTO A PRINCE! YOU'RE JUST A HORRIBLE OLD BEAST!
IF I HADN'T SEEN IT FOR MYSELF, I'D NEVER HAVE BELIEVED IT.
I TOLD YOU I COULD CONVINCE A HUMAN GIRL TO KISS ME.
TWICE!
SO PAY UP, CHICKEN RIPPLE.
OKAY, YOU GET THE LAST SLICE OF STOLEN PIE.
WHEN ARE WE GOING TO HAVE A BET I CAN JOIN IN ON? I DON'T EAT PIE--OR ANYTHING ELSE.
HOW GULLIBLE ARE THESE HUMANS, TO THINK OLD WITCHES JUST GO AROUND ENCHANTING EVERYONE INTO FROGS AND PORKY PINES AND OTHER DIVERSE CREATURES?
OH, I ANGERED A WITCH ALL RIGHT, AND SHE REALLY DID PUT AN EVIL ENCHANTMENT ON ME. THAT PART'S ALL TRUE.
BUT I WAS ALWAYS A PORKY PINE. THE SPELL JUST GAVE ME A PERVERSE ATTRACTION TO HUMAN WOMEN.
YUCK!
SHE SEEMED TO THINK THAT WAS ENOUGH TO GET ME KILLED PRETTY QUICK.
BUT SHE DIDN'T COUNT ON HOW PERSUASIVE I COULD BE. ACTUALLY, A FROG I MET ONCE TAUGHT ME THE SCAM.
OF COURSE, HE NEVER ADMITTED IT WAS A SCAM, BUT I KNEW BETTER.

THE END

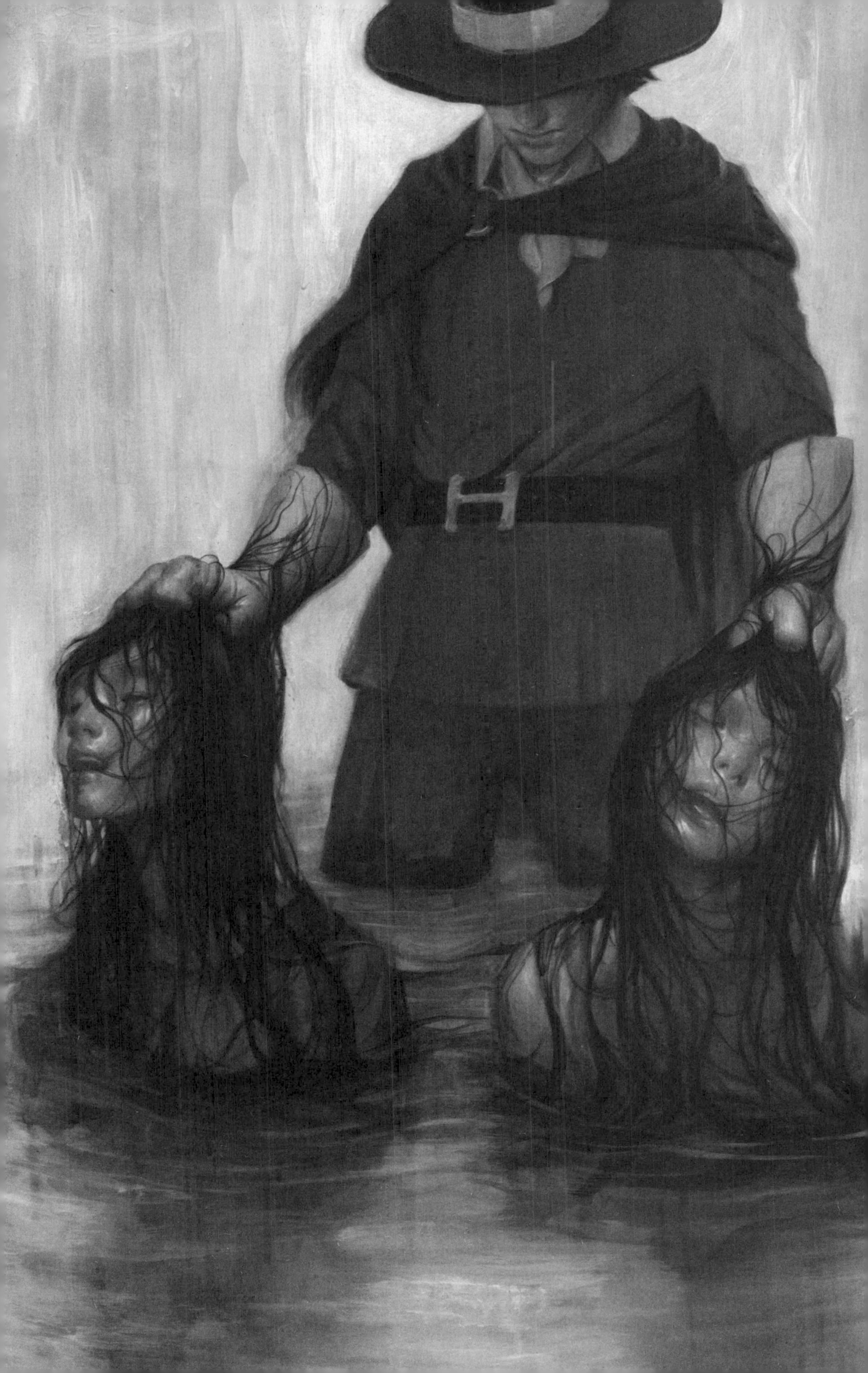

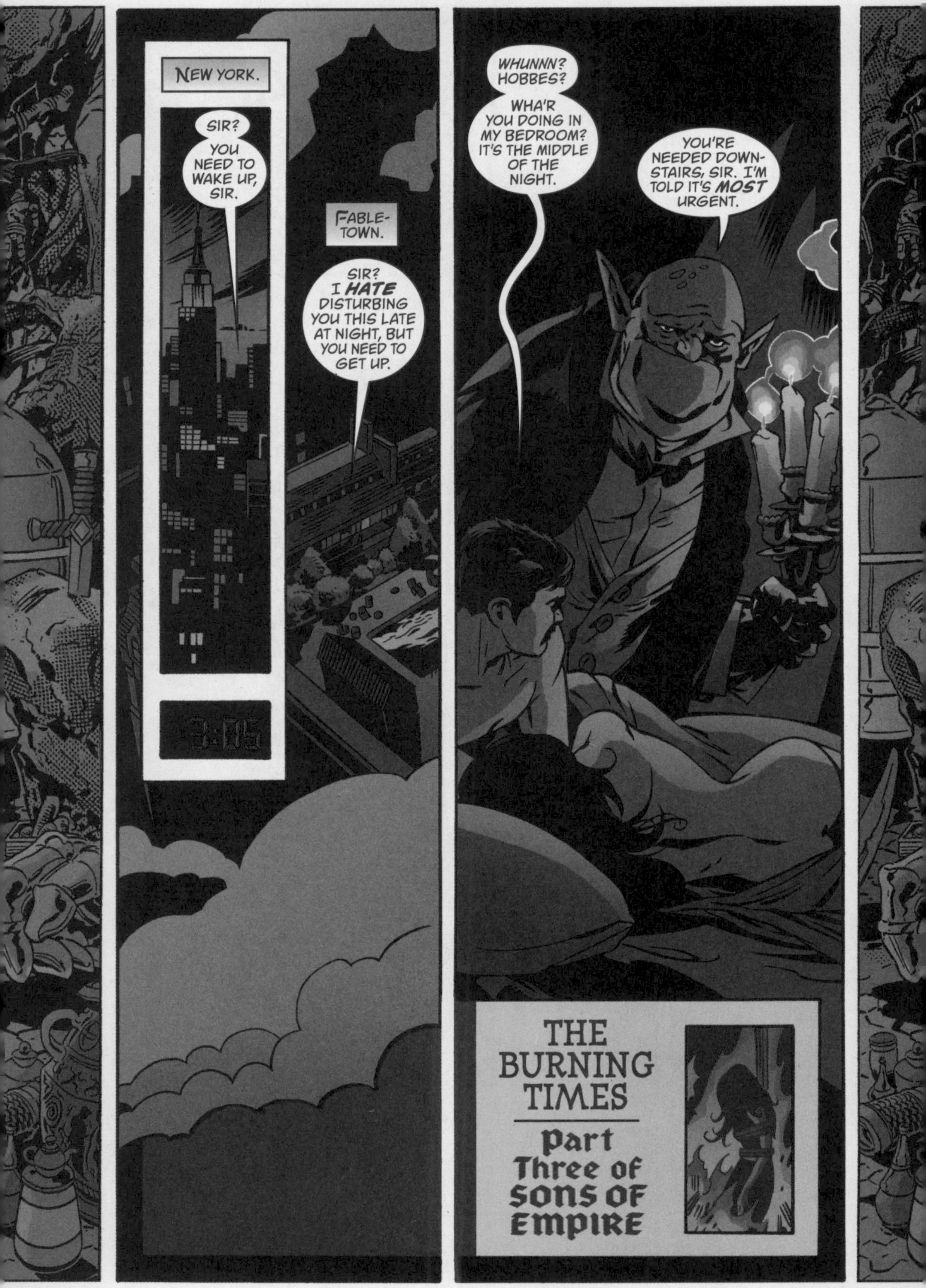

NEW YORK.
SIR?
YOU NEED TO WAKE UP, SIR.
3:05
FABLE-TOWN.
SIR? I HATE DISTURBING YOU THIS LATE AT NIGHT, BUT YOU NEED TO GET UP.
WHUNNN? HOBBES?
WHA'R YOU DOING IN MY BEDROOM? IT'S THE MIDDLE OF THE NIGHT.
YOU'RE NEEDED DOWN-STAIRS, SIR. I'M TOLD IT'S MOST URGENT.
THE BURNING TIMES
Part Three of SONS OF EMPIRE

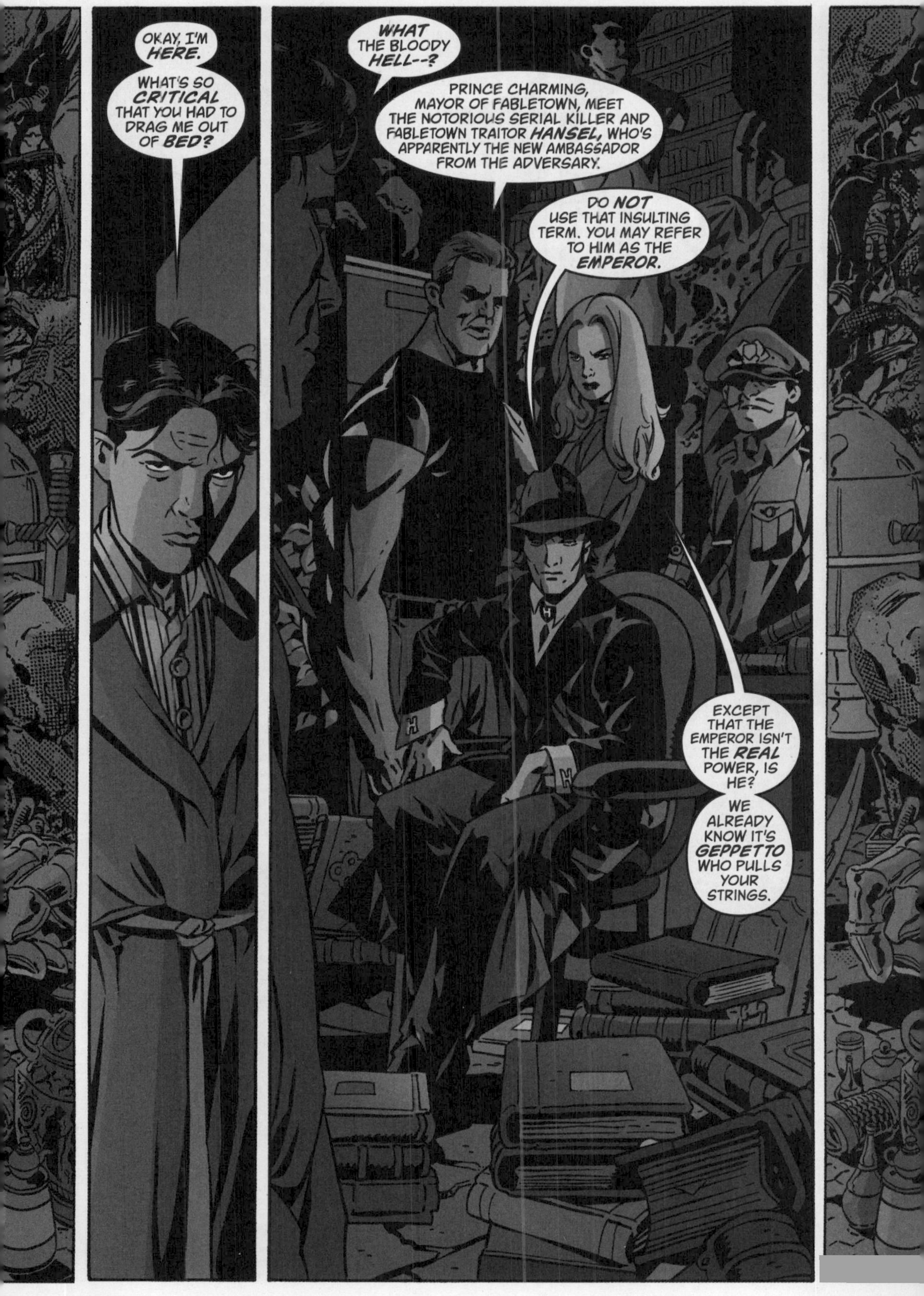
OKAY, I'M HERE.
WHAT'S SO CRITICAL THAT YOU HAD TO DRAG ME OUT OF BED?
WHAT THE BLOODY HELL--?
PRINCE CHARMING, MAYOR OF FABLETOWN, MEET THE NOTORIOUS SERIAL KILLER AND FABLETOWN TRAITOR HANSEL, WHO'S APPARENTLY THE NEW AMBASSADOR FROM THE ADVERSARY.
DO NOT USE THAT INSULTING TERM. YOU MAY REFER TO HIM AS THE EMPEROR.
EXCEPT THAT THE EMPEROR ISN'T THE REAL POWER, IS HE?
WE ALREADY KNOW IT'S GEPPETTO WHO PULLS YOUR STRINGS.

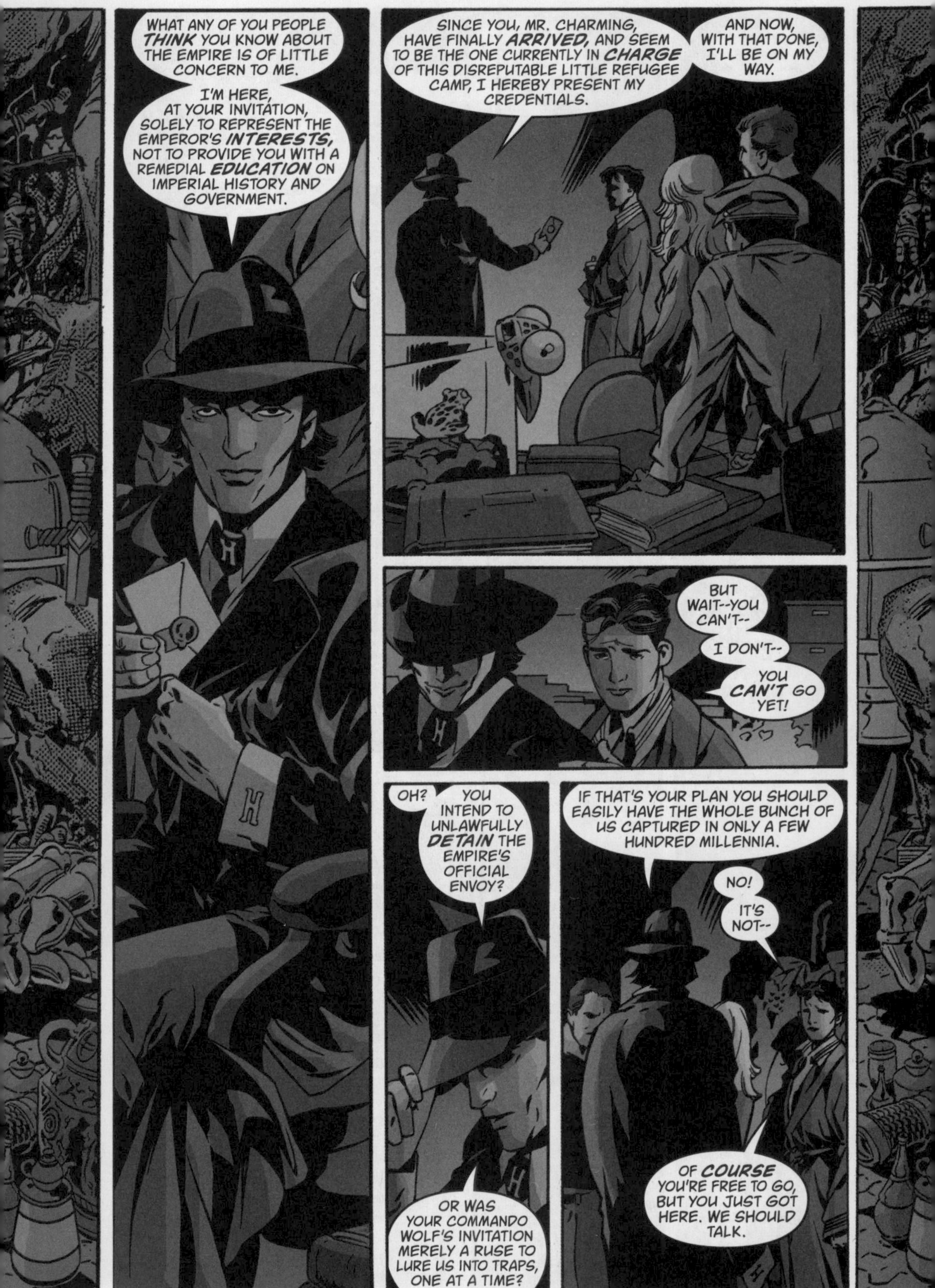
WHAT ANY OF YOU PEOPLE THINK YOU KNOW ABOUT THE EMPIRE IS OF LITTLE CONCERN TO ME.
I'M HERE, AT YOUR INVITATION, SOLELY TO REPRESENT THE EMPEROR'S INTERESTS, NOT TO PROVIDE YOU WITH A REMEDIAL EDUCATION ON IMPERIAL HISTORY AND GOVERNMENT.
SINCE YOU, MR. CHARMING, HAVE FINALLY ARRIVED, AND SEEM TO BE THE ONE CURRENTLY IN CHARGE OF THIS DISREPUTABLE LITTLE REFUGEE CAMP, I HEREBY PRESENT MY CREDENTIALS.
AND NOW, WITH THAT DONE, I'LL BE ON MY WAY.
BUT WAIT--YOU CAN'T--
I DON'T--
YOU CAN'T GO YET!
OH?
YOU INTEND TO UNLAWFULLY DETAIN THE EMPIRE'S OFFICIAL ENVOY?
OR WAS YOUR COMMANDO WOLF'S INVITATION MERELY A RUSE TO LURE US INTO TRAPS, ONE AT A TIME?
IF THAT'S YOUR PLAN YOU SHOULD EASILY HAVE THE WHOLE BUNCH OF US CAPTURED IN ONLY A FEW HUNDRED MILLENNIA.
NO!
IT'S NOT--
OF COURSE YOU'RE FREE TO GO, BUT YOU JUST GOT HERE. WE SHOULD TALK.

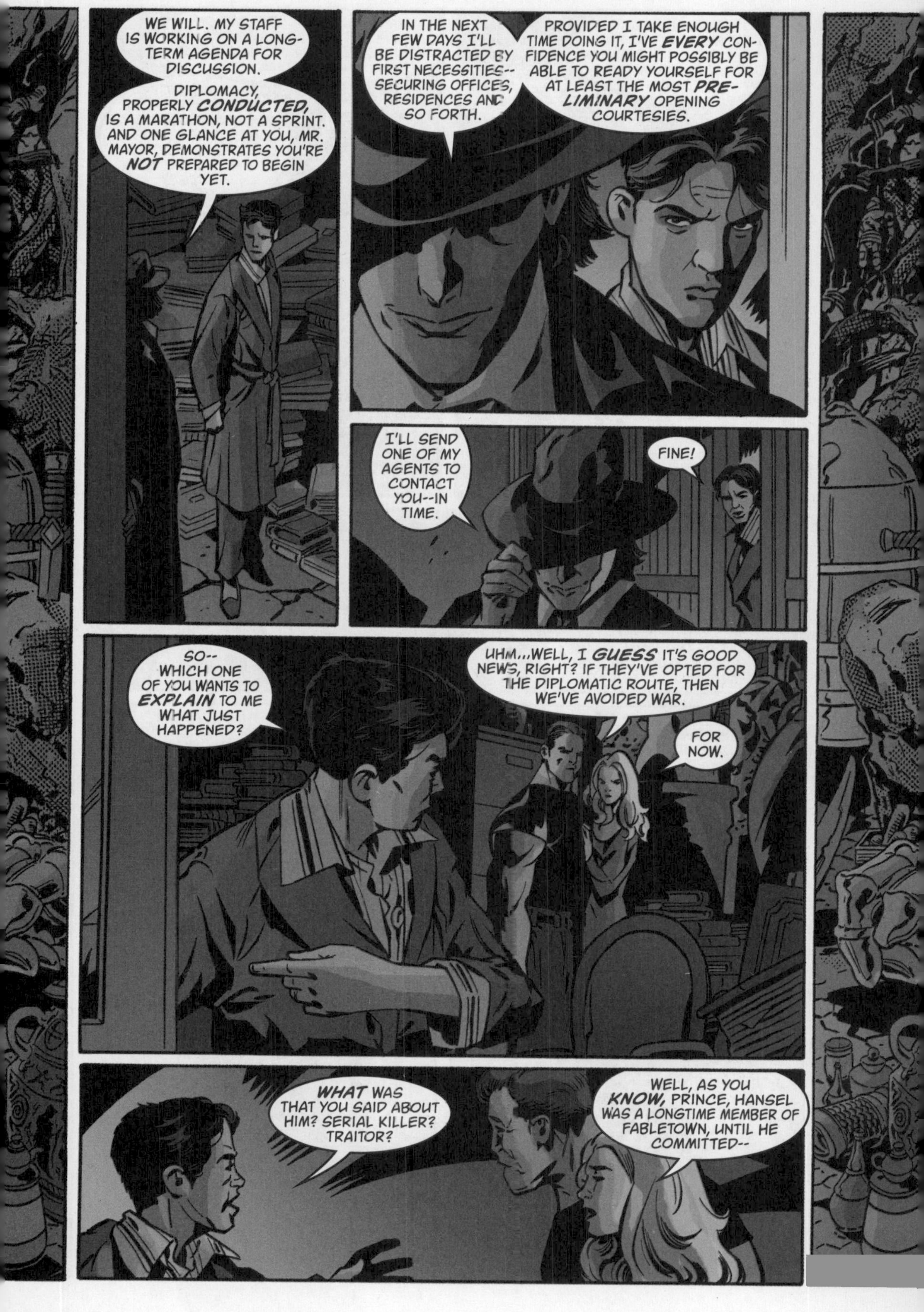
WE WILL. MY STAFF IS WORKING ON A LONG-TERM AGENDA FOR DISCUSSION.
DIPLOMACY, PROPERLY CONDUCTED, IS A MARATHON, NOT A SPRINT. AND ONE GLANCE AT YOU, MR. MAYOR, DEMONSTRATES YOU'RE NOT PREPARED TO BEGIN YET.
IN THE NEXT FEW DAYS I'LL BE DISTRACTED BY FIRST NECESSITIES--SECURING OFFICES, RESIDENCES AND SO FORTH.
PROVIDED I TAKE ENOUGH TIME DOING IT, I'VE EVERY CONFIDENCE YOU MIGHT POSSIBLY BE ABLE TO READY YOURSELF FOR AT LEAST THE MOST PRELIMINARY OPENING COURTESIES.
I'LL SEND ONE OF MY AGENTS TO CONTACT YOU--IN TIME.
FINE!
SO--WHICH ONE OF YOU WANTS TO EXPLAIN TO ME WHAT JUST HAPPENED?
UHM...WELL, I GUESS IT'S GOOD NEWS, RIGHT? IF THEY'VE OPTED FOR THE DIPLOMATIC ROUTE, THEN WE'VE AVOIDED WAR.
FOR NOW.
WHAT WAS THAT YOU SAID ABOUT HIM? SERIAL KILLER? TRAITOR?
WELL, AS YOU KNOW, PRINCE, HANSEL WAS A LONGTIME MEMBER OF FABLETOWN, UNTIL HE COMMITTED--

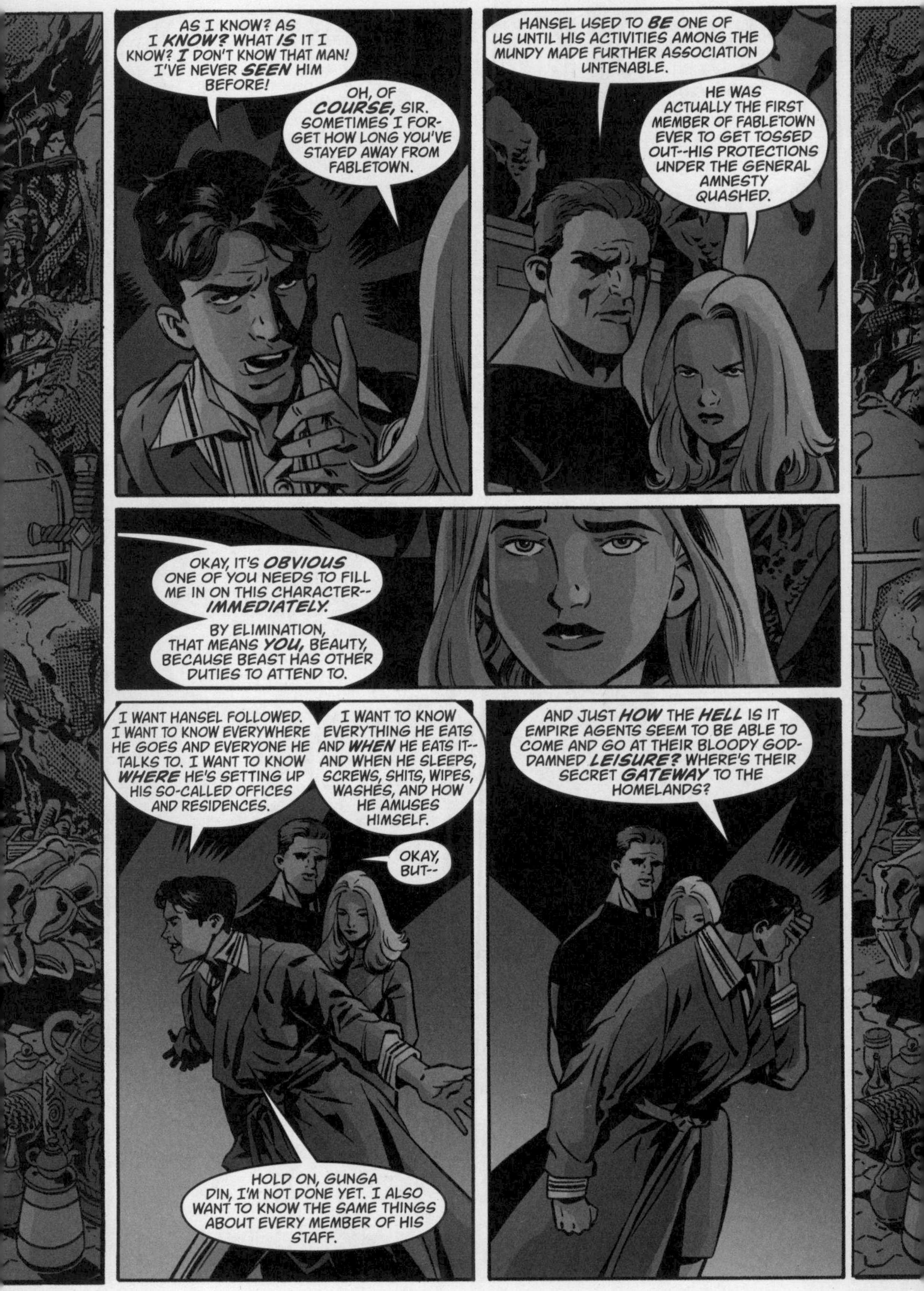
AS I KNOW? AS I KNOW? WHAT IS IT I KNOW? I DON'T KNOW THAT MAN! I'VE NEVER SEEN HIM BEFORE!
OH, OF COURSE, SIR. SOMETIMES I FORGET HOW LONG YOU'VE STAYED AWAY FROM FABLETOWN.
HANSEL USED TO BE ONE OF US UNTIL HIS ACTIVITIES AMONG THE MUNDY MADE FURTHER ASSOCIATION UNTENABLE.
HE WAS ACTUALLY THE FIRST MEMBER OF FABLETOWN EVER TO GET TOSSED OUT--HIS PROTECTIONS UNDER THE GENERAL AMNESTY QUASHED.
OKAY, IT'S OBVIOUS ONE OF YOU NEEDS TO FILL ME IN ON THIS CHARACTER--IMMEDIATELY.
BY ELIMINATION, THAT MEANS YOU, BEAUTY, BECAUSE BEAST HAS OTHER DUTIES TO ATTEND TO.
I WANT HANSEL FOLLOWED. I WANT TO KNOW EVERYWHERE HE GOES AND EVERYONE HE TALKS TO. I WANT TO KNOW WHERE HE'S SETTING UP HIS SO-CALLED OFFICES AND RESIDENCES.
I WANT TO KNOW EVERYTHING HE EATS AND WHEN HE EATS IT--AND WHEN HE SLEEPS, SCREWS, SHITS, WIPES, WASHES, AND HOW HE AMUSES HIMSELF.
OKAY, BUT--
HOLD ON, GUNGA DIN, I'M NOT DONE YET. I ALSO WANT TO KNOW THE SAME THINGS ABOUT EVERY MEMBER OF HIS STAFF.
AND JUST HOW THE HELL IS IT EMPIRE AGENTS SEEM TO BE ABLE TO COME AND GO AT THEIR BLOODY GOD-DAMNED LEISURE? WHERE'S THEIR SECRET GATEWAY TO THE HOMELANDS?

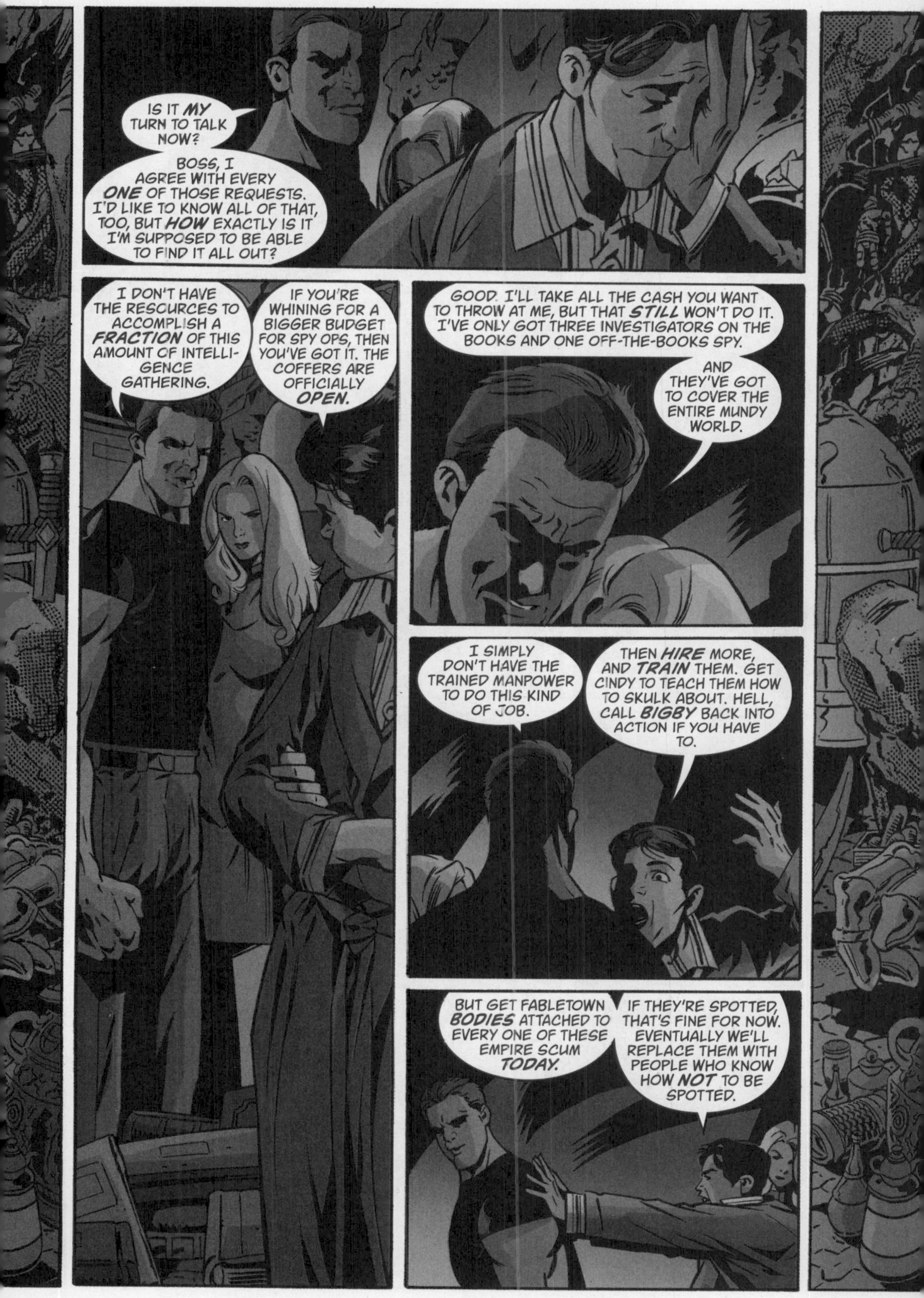
IS IT MY TURN TO TALK NOW?
BOSS, I AGREE WITH EVERY ONE OF THOSE REQUESTS. I'D LIKE TO KNOW ALL OF THAT, TOO, BUT HOW EXACTLY IS IT I'M SUPPOSED TO BE ABLE TO FIND IT ALL OUT?
I DON'T HAVE THE RESOURCES TO ACCOMPLISH A FRACTION OF THIS AMOUNT OF INTELLIGENCE GATHERING.
IF YOU'RE WHINING FOR A BIGGER BUDGET FOR SPY OPS, THEN YOU'VE GOT IT. THE COFFERS ARE OFFICIALLY OPEN.
GOOD. I'LL TAKE ALL THE CASH YOU WANT TO THROW AT ME, BUT THAT STILL WON'T DO IT. I'VE ONLY GOT THREE INVESTIGATORS ON THE BOOKS AND ONE OFF-THE-BOOKS SPY.
AND THEY'VE GOT TO COVER THE ENTIRE MUNDY WORLD.
I SIMPLY DON'T HAVE THE TRAINED MANPOWER TO DO THIS KIND OF JOB.
THEN HIRE MORE, AND TRAIN THEM. GET CINDY TO TEACH THEM HOW TO SKULK ABOUT. HELL, CALL BIGBY BACK INTO ACTION IF YOU HAVE TO.
BUT GET FABLETOWN BODIES ATTACHED TO EVERY ONE OF THESE EMPIRE SCUM TODAY.
IF THEY'RE SPOTTED, THAT'S FINE FOR NOW. EVENTUALLY WE'LL REPLACE THEM WITH PEOPLE WHO KNOW HOW NOT TO BE SPOTTED.

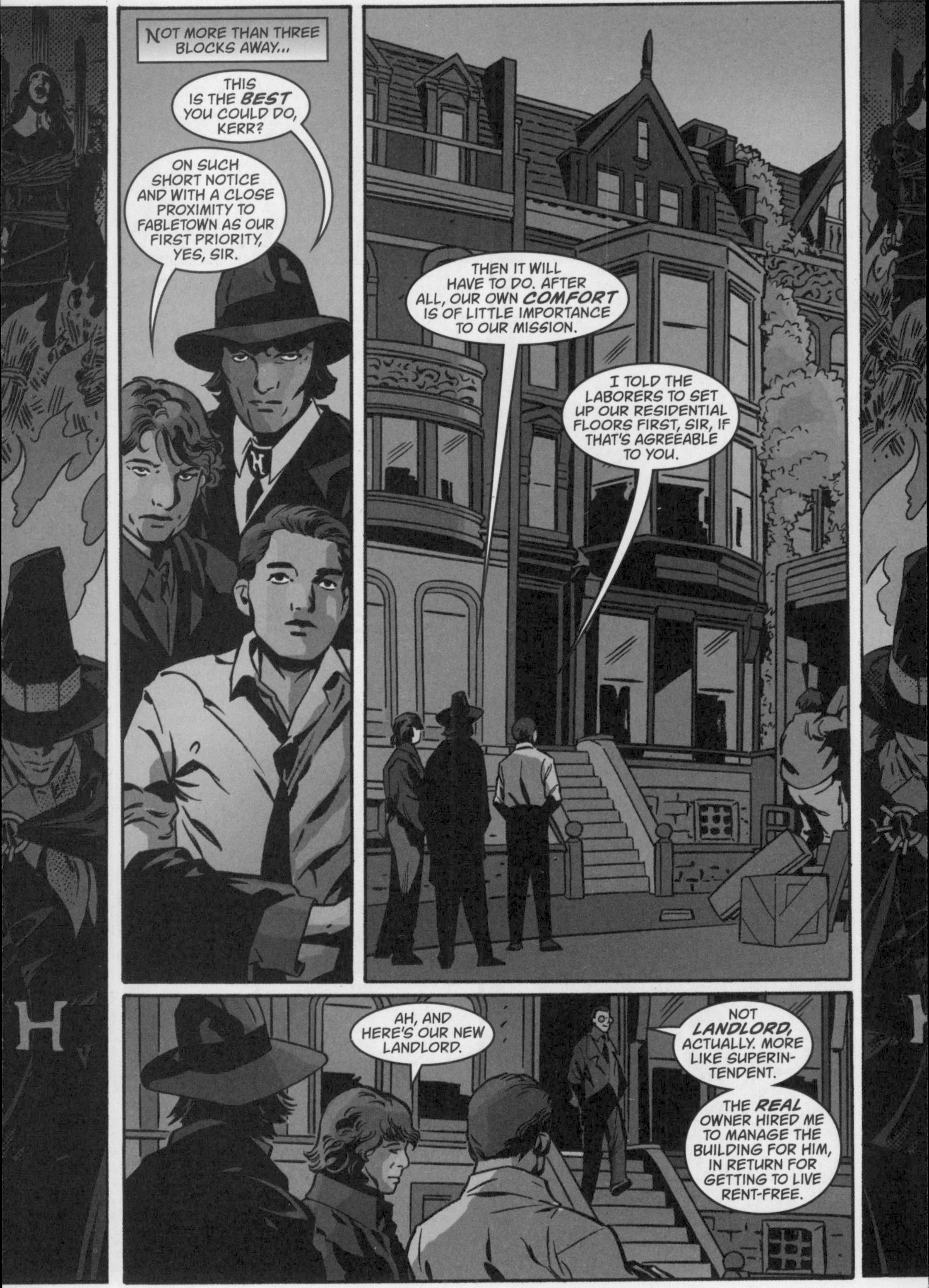
NOT MORE THAN THREE BLOCKS AWAY...
THIS IS THE BEST YOU COULD DO, KERR?
ON SUCH SHORT NOTICE AND WITH A CLOSE PROXIMITY TO FABLETOWN AS OUR FIRST PRIORITY, YES, SIR.
THEN IT WILL HAVE TO DO. AFTER ALL, OUR OWN COMFORT IS OF LITTLE IMPORTANCE TO OUR MISSION.
I TOLD THE LABORERS TO SET UP OUR RESIDENTIAL FLOORS FIRST, SIR, IF THAT'S AGREEABLE TO YOU.
AH, AND HERE'S OUR NEW LANDLORD.
NOT LANDLORD, ACTUALLY. MORE LIKE SUPERIN-TENDENT.
THE REAL OWNER HIRED ME TO MANAGE THE BUILDING FOR HIM, IN RETURN FOR GETTING TO LIVE RENT-FREE.

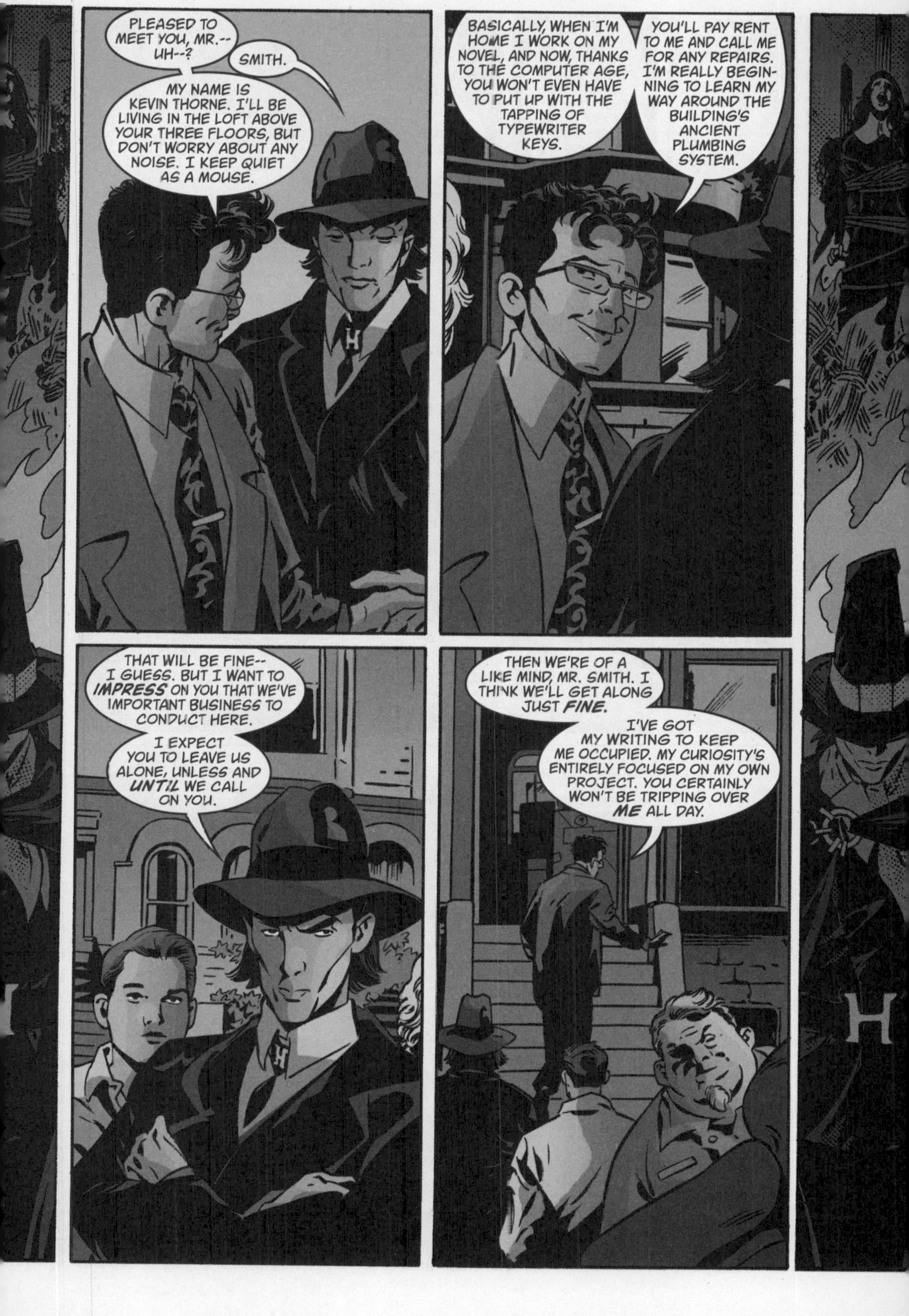
PLEASED TO MEET YOU, MR.-- UH--?
SMITH.
MY NAME IS KEVIN THORNE. I'LL BE LIVING IN THE LOFT ABOVE YOUR THREE FLOORS, BUT DON'T WORRY ABOUT ANY NOISE. I KEEP QUIET AS A MOUSE.
BASICALLY, WHEN I'M HOME I WORK ON MY NOVEL, AND NOW, THANKS TO THE COMPUTER AGE, YOU WON'T EVEN HAVE TO PUT UP WITH THE TAPPING OF TYPEWRITER KEYS.
YOU'LL PAY RENT TO ME AND CALL ME FOR ANY REPAIRS. I'M REALLY BEGINNING TO LEARN MY WAY AROUND THE BUILDING'S ANCIENT PLUMBING SYSTEM.
THAT WILL BE FINE-- I GUESS. BUT I WANT TO *IMPRESS* ON YOU THAT WE'VE IMPORTANT BUSINESS TO CONDUCT HERE.
I EXPECT YOU TO LEAVE US ALONE, UNLESS AND *UNTIL* WE CALL ON YOU.
THEN WE'RE OF A LIKE MIND, MR. SMITH. I THINK WE'LL GET ALONG JUST *FINE.*
I'VE GOT MY WRITING TO KEEP ME OCCUPIED. MY CURIOSITY'S ENTIRELY FOCUSED ON MY OWN PROJECT. YOU CERTAINLY WON'T BE TRIPPING OVER *ME* ALL DAY.

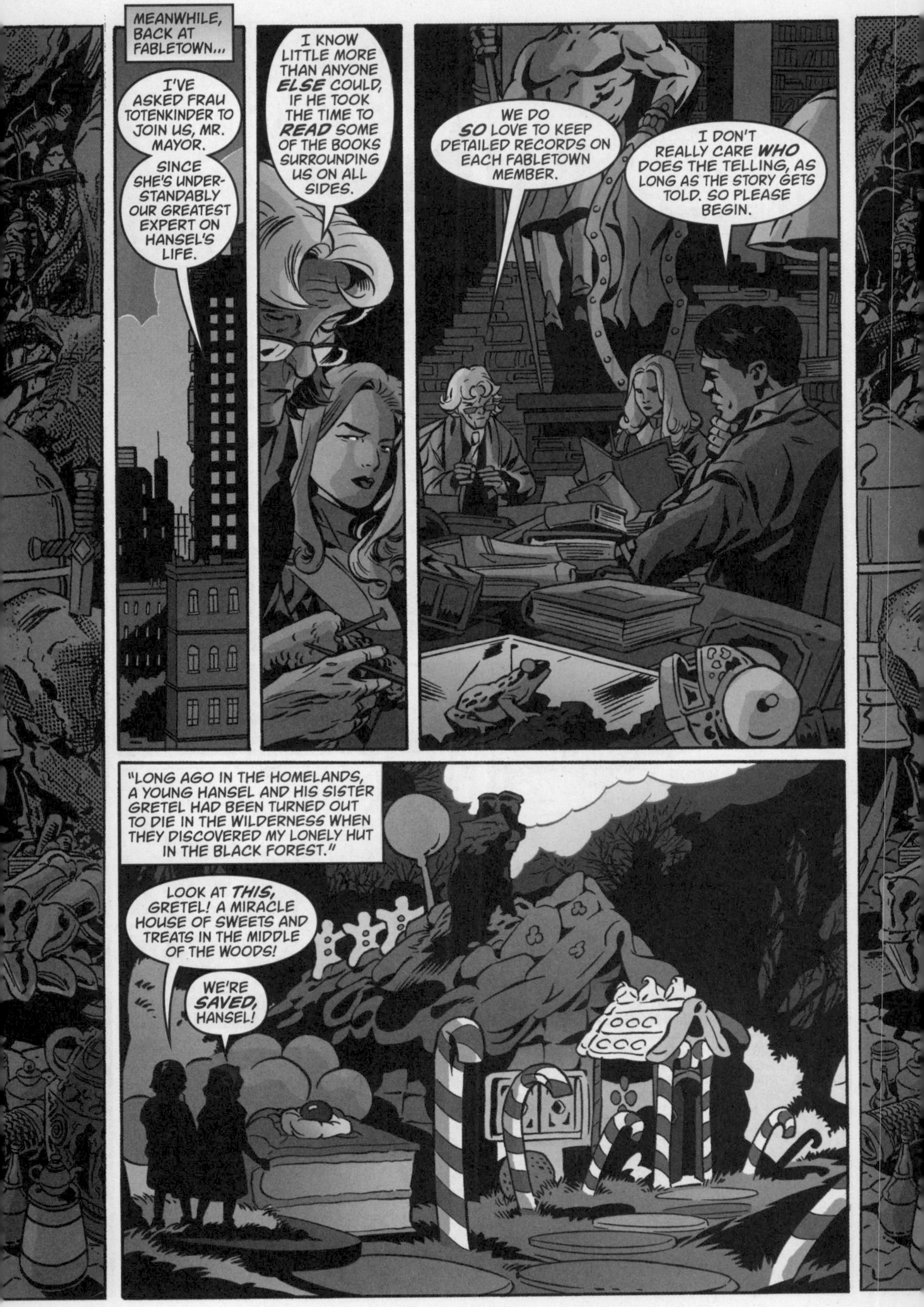
MEANWHILE, BACK AT FABLETOWN...
I'VE ASKED FRAU TOTENKINDER TO JOIN US, MR. MAYOR.
SINCE SHE'S UNDER-STANDABLY OUR GREATEST EXPERT ON HANSEL'S LIFE.
I KNOW LITTLE MORE THAN ANYONE ELSE COULD, IF HE TOOK THE TIME TO READ SOME OF THE BOOKS SURROUNDING US ON ALL SIDES.
WE DO SO LOVE TO KEEP DETAILED RECORDS ON EACH FABLETOWN MEMBER.
I DON'T REALLY CARE WHO DOES THE TELLING, AS LONG AS THE STORY GETS TOLD. SO PLEASE BEGIN.
"LONG AGO IN THE HOMELANDS, A YOUNG HANSEL AND HIS SISTER GRETEL HAD BEEN TURNED OUT TO DIE IN THE WILDERNESS WHEN THEY DISCOVERED MY LONELY HUT IN THE BLACK FOREST."
LOOK AT THIS, GRETEL! A MIRACLE HOUSE OF SWEETS AND TREATS IN THE MIDDLE OF THE WOODS!
WE'RE SAVED, HANSEL!

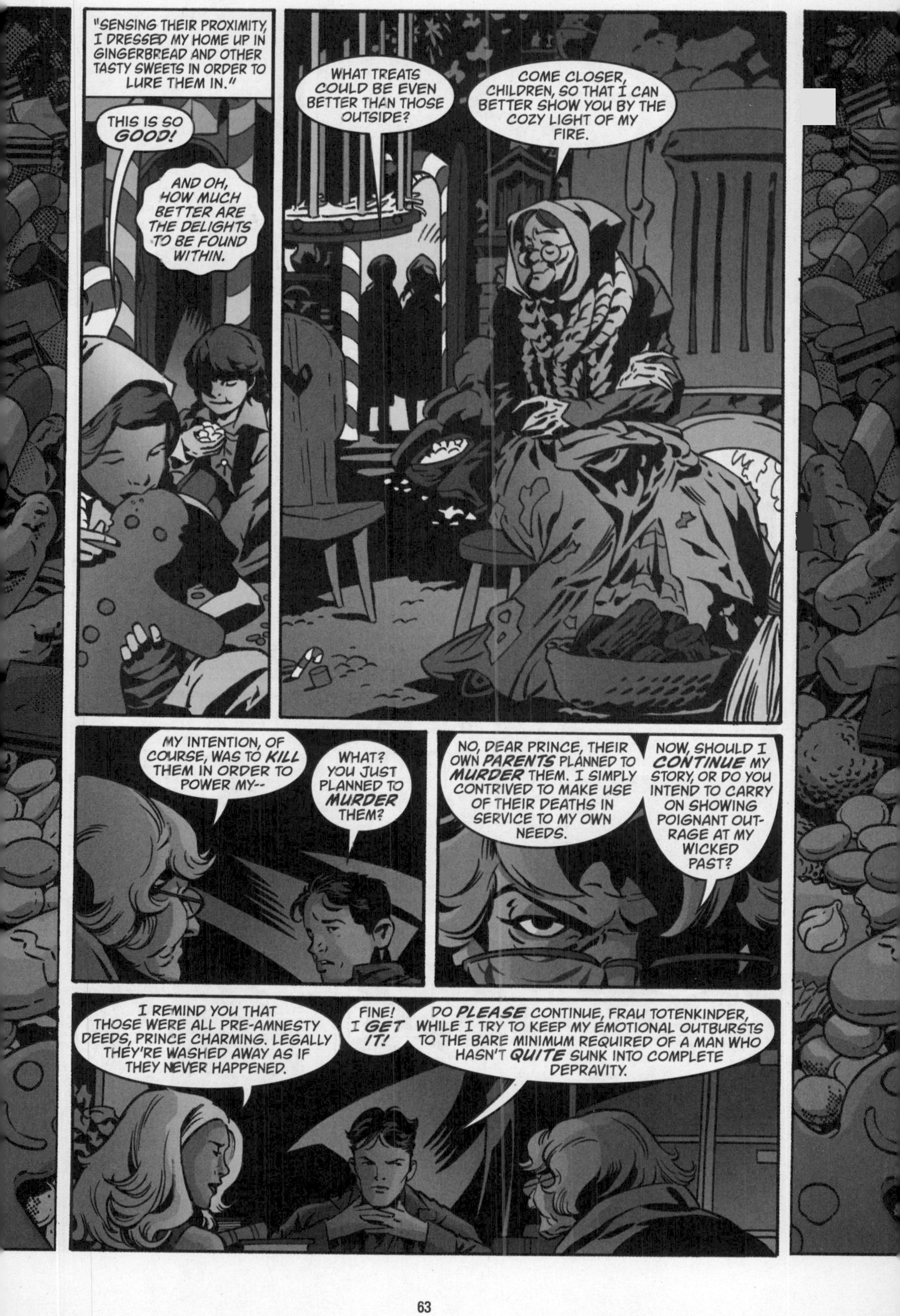
"SENSING THEIR PROXIMITY, I DRESSED MY HOME UP IN GINGERBREAD AND OTHER TASTY SWEETS IN ORDER TO LURE THEM IN."
THIS IS SO GOOD!
AND OH, HOW MUCH BETTER ARE THE DELIGHTS TO BE FOUND WITHIN.
WHAT TREATS COULD BE EVEN BETTER THAN THOSE OUTSIDE?
COME CLOSER, CHILDREN, SO THAT I CAN BETTER SHOW YOU BY THE COZY LIGHT OF MY FIRE.
MY INTENTION, OF COURSE, WAS TO KILL THEM IN ORDER TO POWER MY--
WHAT? YOU JUST PLANNED TO MURDER THEM?
NO, DEAR PRINCE, THEIR OWN PARENTS PLANNED TO MURDER THEM. I SIMPLY CONTRIVED TO MAKE USE OF THEIR DEATHS IN SERVICE TO MY OWN NEEDS.
NOW, SHOULD I CONTINUE MY STORY, OR DO YOU INTEND TO CARRY ON SHOWING POIGNANT OUTRAGE AT MY WICKED PAST?
I REMIND YOU THAT THOSE WERE ALL PRE-AMNESTY DEEDS, PRINCE CHARMING. LEGALLY THEY'RE WASHED AWAY AS IF THEY NEVER HAPPENED.
FINE! I GET IT!
DO PLEASE CONTINUE, FRAU TOTENKINDER, WHILE I TRY TO KEEP MY EMOTIONAL OUTBURSTS TO THE BARE MINIMUM REQUIRED OF A MAN WHO HASN'T QUITE SUNK INTO COMPLETE DEPRAVITY.

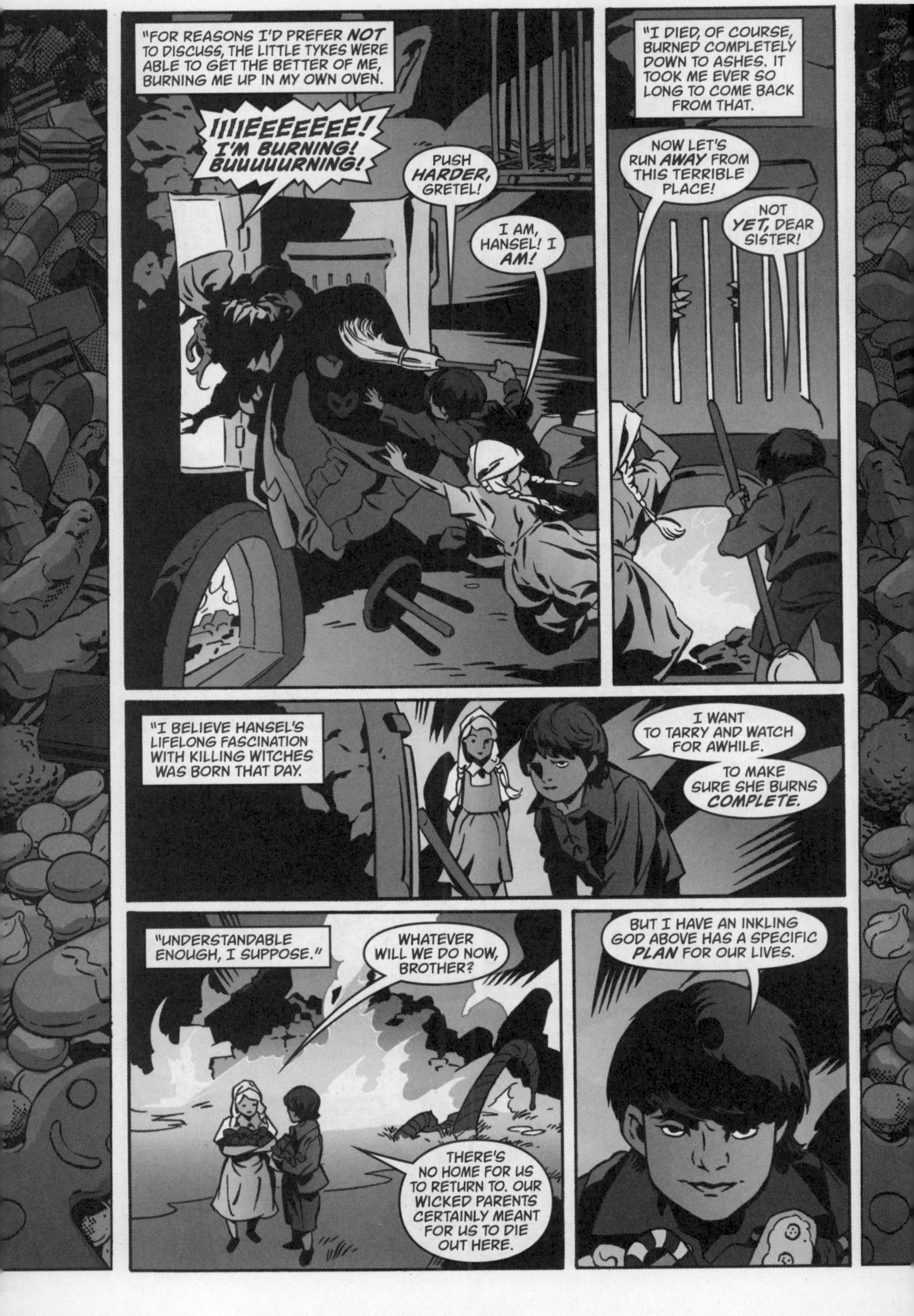
"FOR REASONS I'D PREFER NOT TO DISCUSS, THE LITTLE TYKES WERE ABLE TO GET THE BETTER OF ME, BURNING ME UP IN MY OWN OVEN.
IIIIEEEEEEE! I'M BURNING! BUUUUURNING!
PUSH HARDER, GRETEL!
I AM, HANSEL! I AM!
"I DIED, OF COURSE, BURNED COMPLETELY DOWN TO ASHES. IT TOOK ME EVER SO LONG TO COME BACK FROM THAT.
NOW LET'S RUN AWAY FROM THIS TERRIBLE PLACE!
NOT YET, DEAR SISTER!
"I BELIEVE HANSEL'S LIFELONG FASCINATION WITH KILLING WITCHES WAS BORN THAT DAY.
I WANT TO TARRY AND WATCH FOR AWHILE.
TO MAKE SURE SHE BURNS COMPLETE.
"UNDERSTANDABLE ENOUGH, I SUPPOSE."
WHATEVER WILL WE DO NOW, BROTHER?
THERE'S NO HOME FOR US TO RETURN TO. OUR WICKED PARENTS CERTAINLY MEANT FOR US TO DIE OUT HERE.
BUT I HAVE AN INKLING GOD ABOVE HAS A SPECIFIC PLAN FOR OUR LIVES.

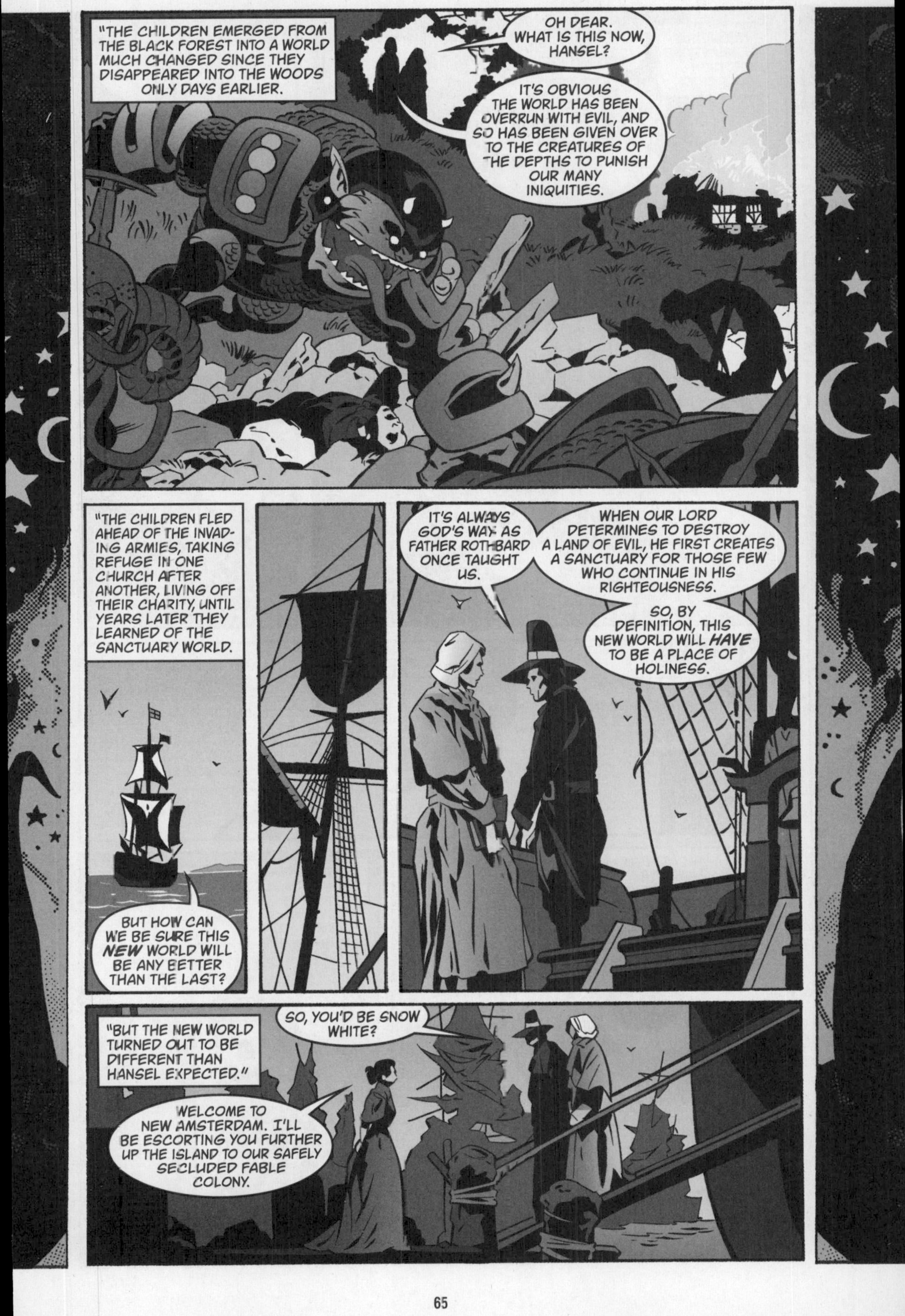
"THE CHILDREN EMERGED FROM THE BLACK FOREST INTO A WORLD MUCH CHANGED SINCE THEY DISAPPEARED INTO THE WOODS ONLY DAYS EARLIER.
OH DEAR. WHAT IS THIS NOW, HANSEL?
IT'S OBVIOUS THE WORLD HAS BEEN OVERRUN WITH EVIL, AND SO HAS BEEN GIVEN OVER TO THE CREATURES OF THE DEPTHS TO PUNISH OUR MANY INIQUITIES.
"THE CHILDREN FLED AHEAD OF THE INVADING ARMIES, TAKING REFUGE IN ONE CHURCH AFTER ANOTHER, LIVING OFF THEIR CHARITY, UNTIL YEARS LATER THEY LEARNED OF THE SANCTUARY WORLD.
BUT HOW CAN WE BE SURE THIS NEW WORLD WILL BE ANY BETTER THAN THE LAST?
IT'S ALWAYS GOD'S WAY AS FATHER ROTHBARD ONCE TAUGHT US.
WHEN OUR LORD DETERMINES TO DESTROY A LAND OF EVIL, HE FIRST CREATES A SANCTUARY FOR THOSE FEW WHO CONTINUE IN HIS RIGHTEOUSNESS.
SO, BY DEFINITION, THIS NEW WORLD WILL HAVE TO BE A PLACE OF HOLINESS.
"BUT THE NEW WORLD TURNED OUT TO BE DIFFERENT THAN HANSEL EXPECTED."
SO, YOU'D BE SNOW WHITE?
WELCOME TO NEW AMSTERDAM. I'LL BE ESCORTING YOU FURTHER UP THE ISLAND TO OUR SAFELY SECLUDED FABLE COLONY.

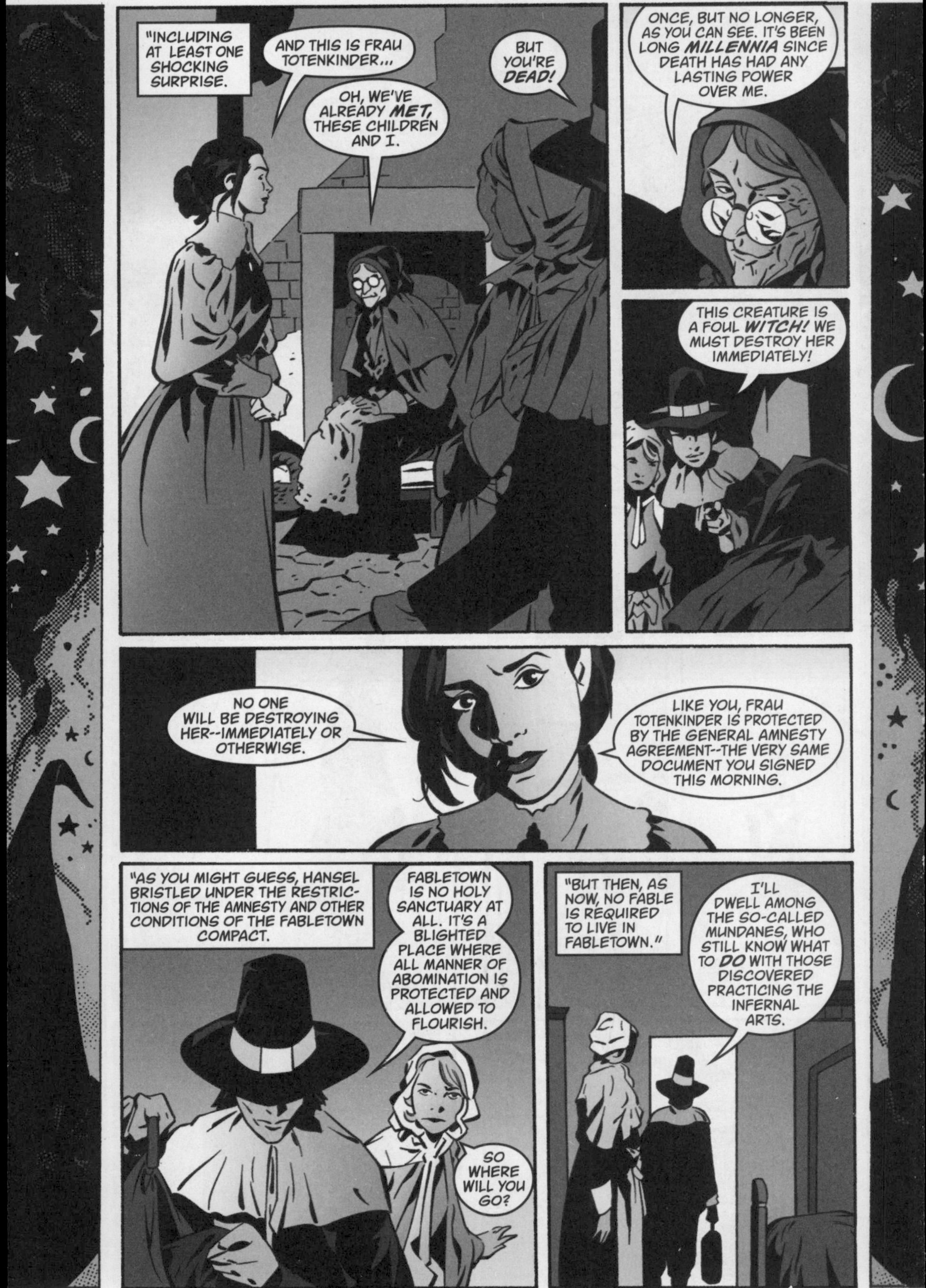
"INCLUDING AT LEAST ONE SHOCKING SURPRISE.
AND THIS IS FRAU TOTENKINDER...
OH, WE'VE ALREADY MET, THESE CHILDREN AND I.
BUT YOU'RE DEAD!
ONCE, BUT NO LONGER, AS YOU CAN SEE. IT'S BEEN LONG MILLENNIA SINCE DEATH HAS HAD ANY LASTING POWER OVER ME.
THIS CREATURE IS A FOUL WITCH! WE MUST DESTROY HER IMMEDIATELY!
NO ONE WILL BE DESTROYING HER--IMMEDIATELY OR OTHERWISE.
LIKE YOU, FRAU TOTENKINDER IS PROTECTED BY THE GENERAL AMNESTY AGREEMENT--THE VERY SAME DOCUMENT YOU SIGNED THIS MORNING.
"AS YOU MIGHT GUESS, HANSEL BRISTLED UNDER THE RESTRICTIONS OF THE AMNESTY AND OTHER CONDITIONS OF THE FABLETOWN COMPACT.
FABLETOWN IS NO HOLY SANCTUARY AT ALL. IT'S A BLIGHTED PLACE WHERE ALL MANNER OF ABOMINATION IS PROTECTED AND ALLOWED TO FLOURISH.
SO WHERE WILL YOU GO?
"BUT THEN, AS NOW, NO FABLE IS REQUIRED TO LIVE IN FABLETOWN."
I'LL DWELL AMONG THE SO-CALLED MUNDANES, WHO STILL KNOW WHAT TO DO WITH THOSE DISCOVERED PRACTICING THE INFERNAL ARTS.

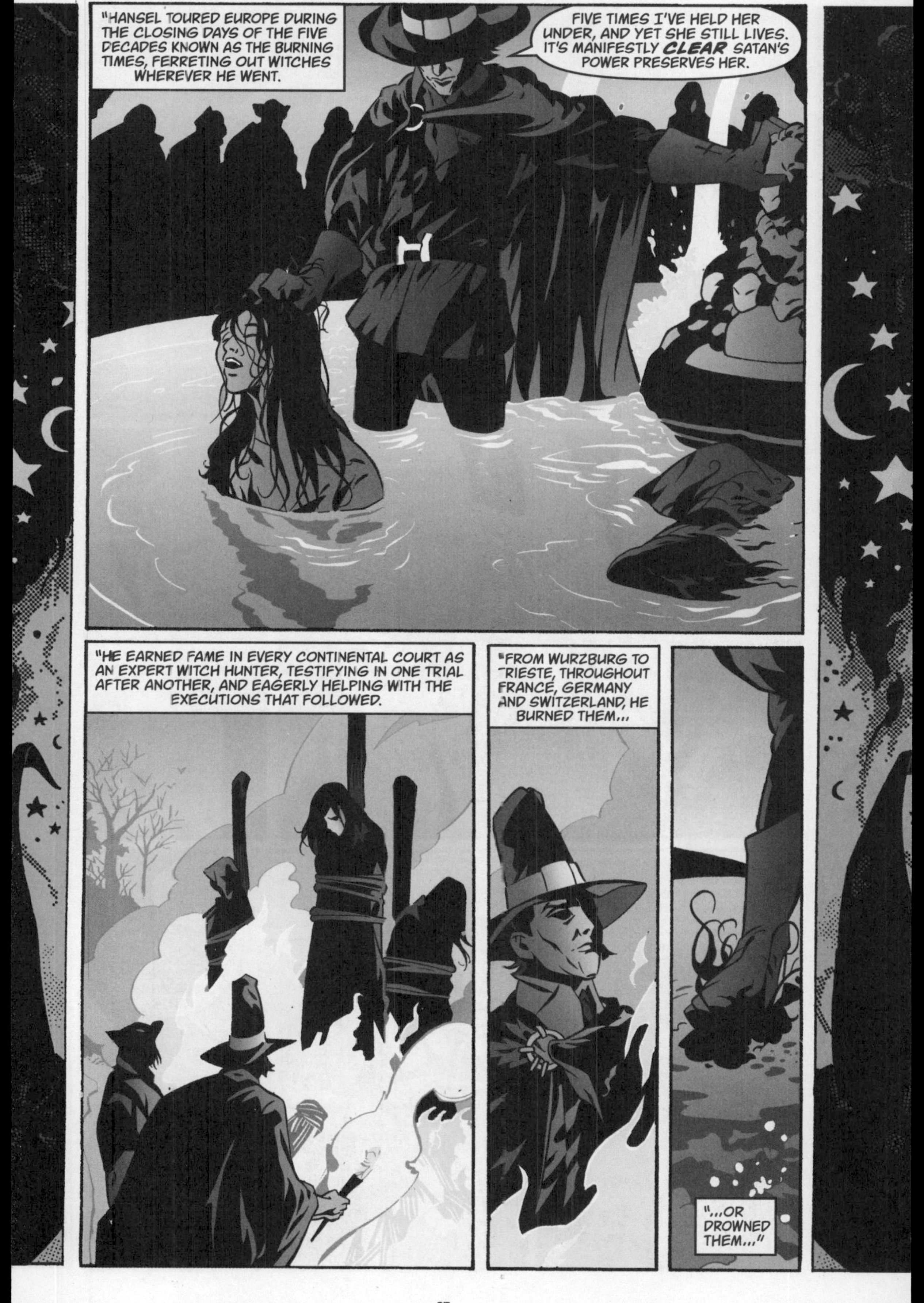
"HANSEL TOURED EUROPE DURING THE CLOSING DAYS OF THE FIVE DECADES KNOWN AS THE BURNING TIMES, FERRETING OUT WITCHES WHEREVER HE WENT.
FIVE TIMES I'VE HELD HER UNDER, AND YET SHE STILL LIVES. IT'S MANIFESTLY CLEAR SATAN'S POWER PRESERVES HER.
"HE EARNED FAME IN EVERY CONTINENTAL COURT AS AN EXPERT WITCH HUNTER, TESTIFYING IN ONE TRIAL AFTER ANOTHER, AND EAGERLY HELPING WITH THE EXECUTIONS THAT FOLLOWED.
"FROM WURZBURG TO TRIESTE, THROUGHOUT FRANCE, GERMANY AND SWITZERLAND, HE BURNED THEM...
"...OR DROWNED THEM..."

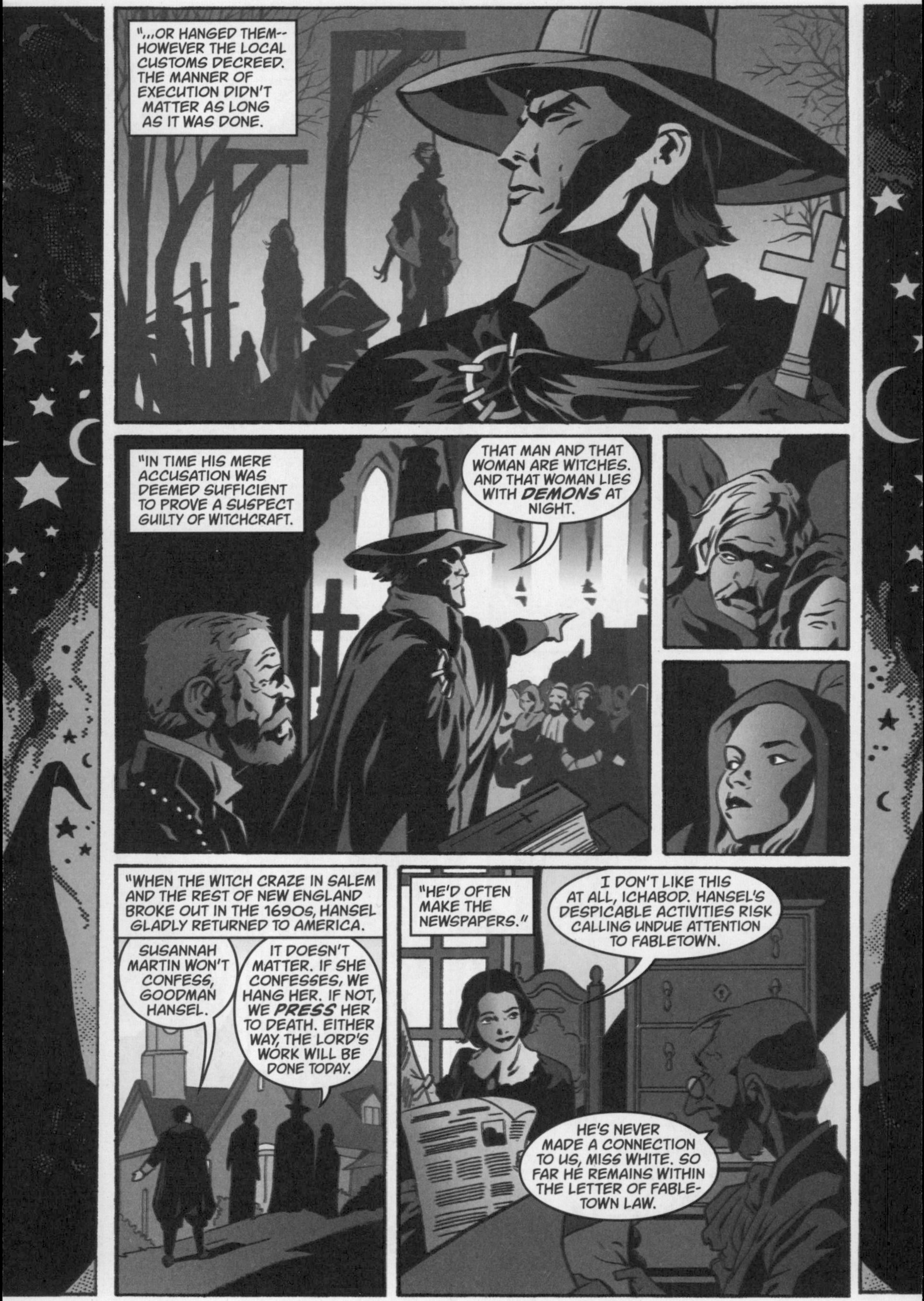
"...OR HANGED THEM--HOWEVER THE LOCAL CUSTOMS DECREED. THE MANNER OF EXECUTION DIDN'T MATTER AS LONG AS IT WAS DONE.
"IN TIME HIS MERE ACCUSATION WAS DEEMED SUFFICIENT TO PROVE A SUSPECT GUILTY OF WITCHCRAFT.
THAT MAN AND THAT WOMAN ARE WITCHES. AND THAT WOMAN LIES WITH DEMONS AT NIGHT.
"WHEN THE WITCH CRAZE IN SALEM AND THE REST OF NEW ENGLAND BROKE OUT IN THE 1690s, HANSEL GLADLY RETURNED TO AMERICA.
SUSANNAH MARTIN WON'T CONFESS, GOODMAN HANSEL.
IT DOESN'T MATTER. IF SHE CONFESSES, WE HANG HER. IF NOT, WE PRESS HER TO DEATH. EITHER WAY, THE LORD'S WORK WILL BE DONE TODAY.
"HE'D OFTEN MAKE THE NEWSPAPERS."
I DON'T LIKE THIS AT ALL, ICHABOD. HANSEL'S DESPICABLE ACTIVITIES RISK CALLING UNDUE ATTENTION TO FABLETOWN.
HE'S NEVER MADE A CONNECTION TO US, MISS WHITE. SO FAR HE REMAINS WITHIN THE LETTER OF FABLE-TOWN LAW.

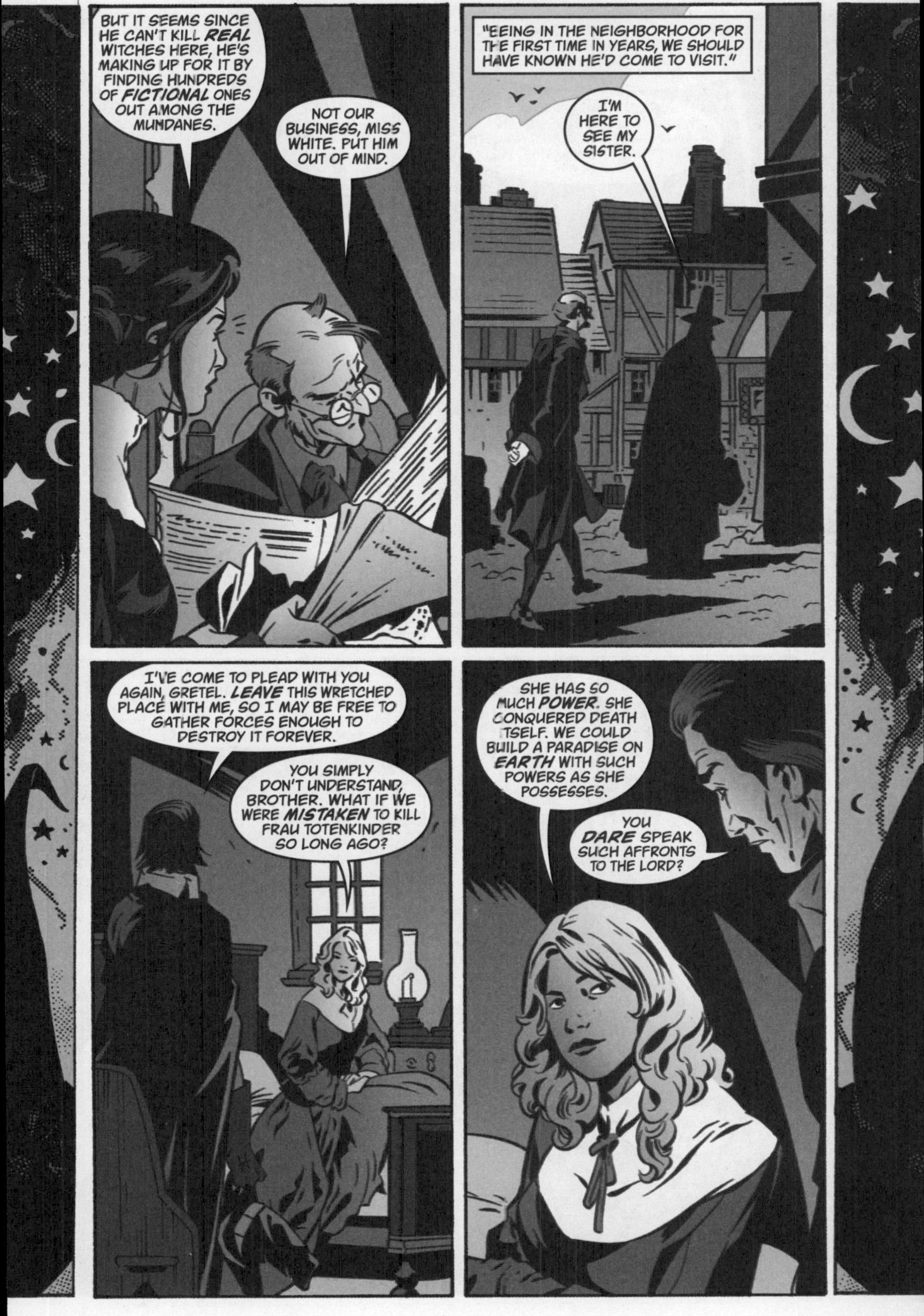
BUT IT SEEMS SINCE HE CAN'T KILL REAL WITCHES HERE, HE'S MAKING UP FOR IT BY FINDING HUNDREDS OF FICTIONAL ONES OUT AMONG THE MUNDANES.
NOT OUR BUSINESS, MISS WHITE. PUT HIM OUT OF MIND.
"BEING IN THE NEIGHBORHOOD FOR THE FIRST TIME IN YEARS, WE SHOULD HAVE KNOWN HE'D COME TO VISIT."
I'M HERE TO SEE MY SISTER.
I'VE COME TO PLEAD WITH YOU AGAIN, GRETEL. LEAVE THIS WRETCHED PLACE WITH ME, SO I MAY BE FREE TO GATHER FORCES ENOUGH TO DESTROY IT FOREVER.
YOU SIMPLY DON'T UNDERSTAND, BROTHER. WHAT IF WE WERE MISTAKEN TO KILL FRAU TOTENKINDER SO LONG AGO?
SHE HAS SO MUCH POWER. SHE CONQUERED DEATH ITSELF. WE COULD BUILD A PARADISE ON EARTH WITH SUCH POWERS AS SHE POSSESSES.
YOU DARE SPEAK SUCH AFFRONTS TO THE LORD?

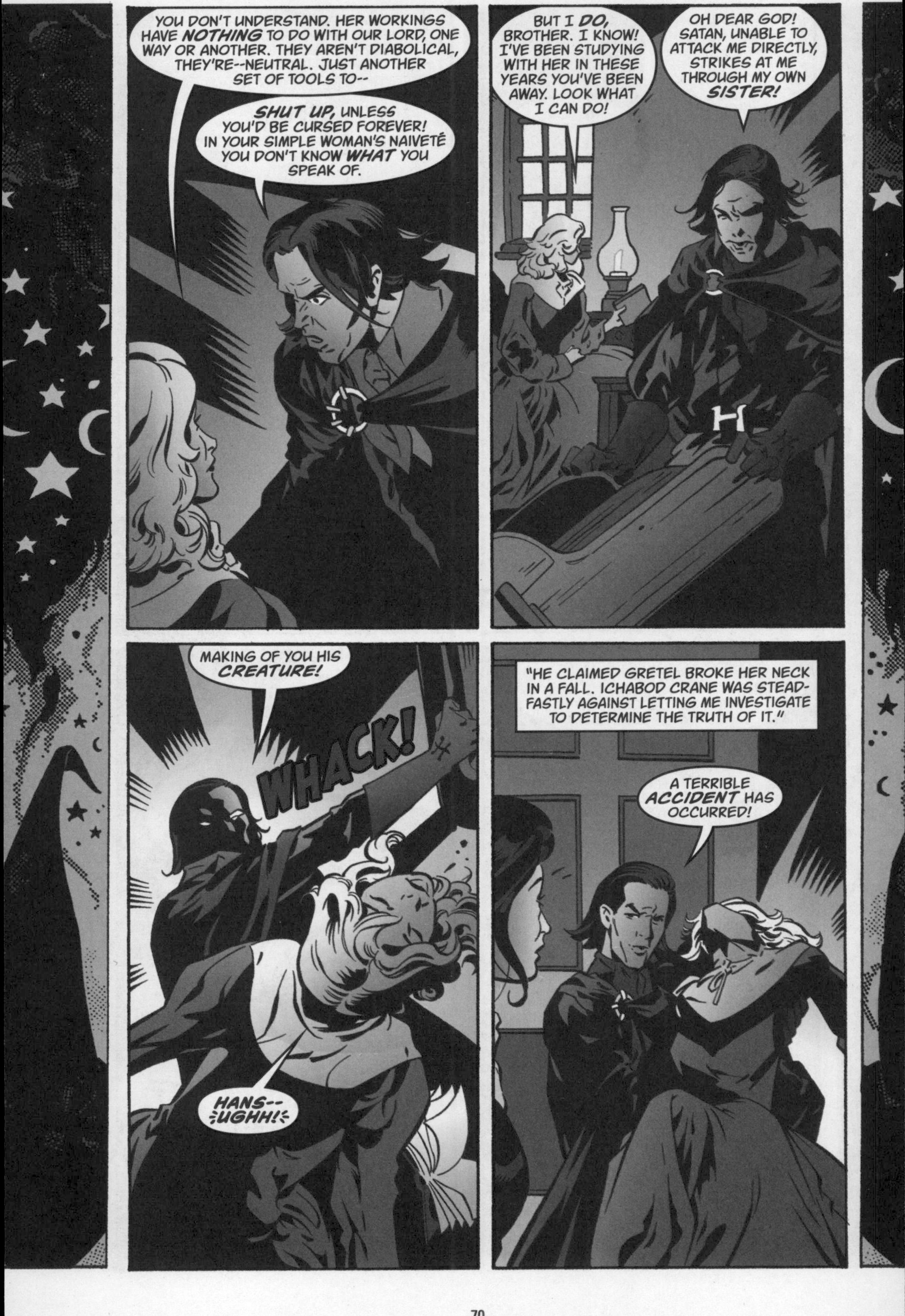
YOU DON'T UNDERSTAND. HER WORKINGS HAVE NOTHING TO DO WITH OUR LORD, ONE WAY OR ANOTHER. THEY AREN'T DIABOLICAL, THEY'RE--NEUTRAL. JUST ANOTHER SET OF TOOLS TO--
SHUT UP, UNLESS YOU'D BE CURSED FOREVER! IN YOUR SIMPLE WOMAN'S NAIVETÉ YOU DON'T KNOW WHAT YOU SPEAK OF.
BUT I DO, BROTHER. I KNOW! I'VE BEEN STUDYING WITH HER IN THESE YEARS YOU'VE BEEN AWAY. LOOK WHAT I CAN DO!
OH DEAR GOD! SATAN, UNABLE TO ATTACK ME DIRECTLY, STRIKES AT ME THROUGH MY OWN SISTER!
MAKING OF YOU HIS CREATURE!
WHACK!
HANS-- UGHH!
"HE CLAIMED GRETEL BROKE HER NECK IN A FALL. ICHABOD CRANE WAS STEADFASTLY AGAINST LETTING ME INVESTIGATE TO DETERMINE THE TRUTH OF IT."
A TERRIBLE ACCIDENT HAS OCCURRED!

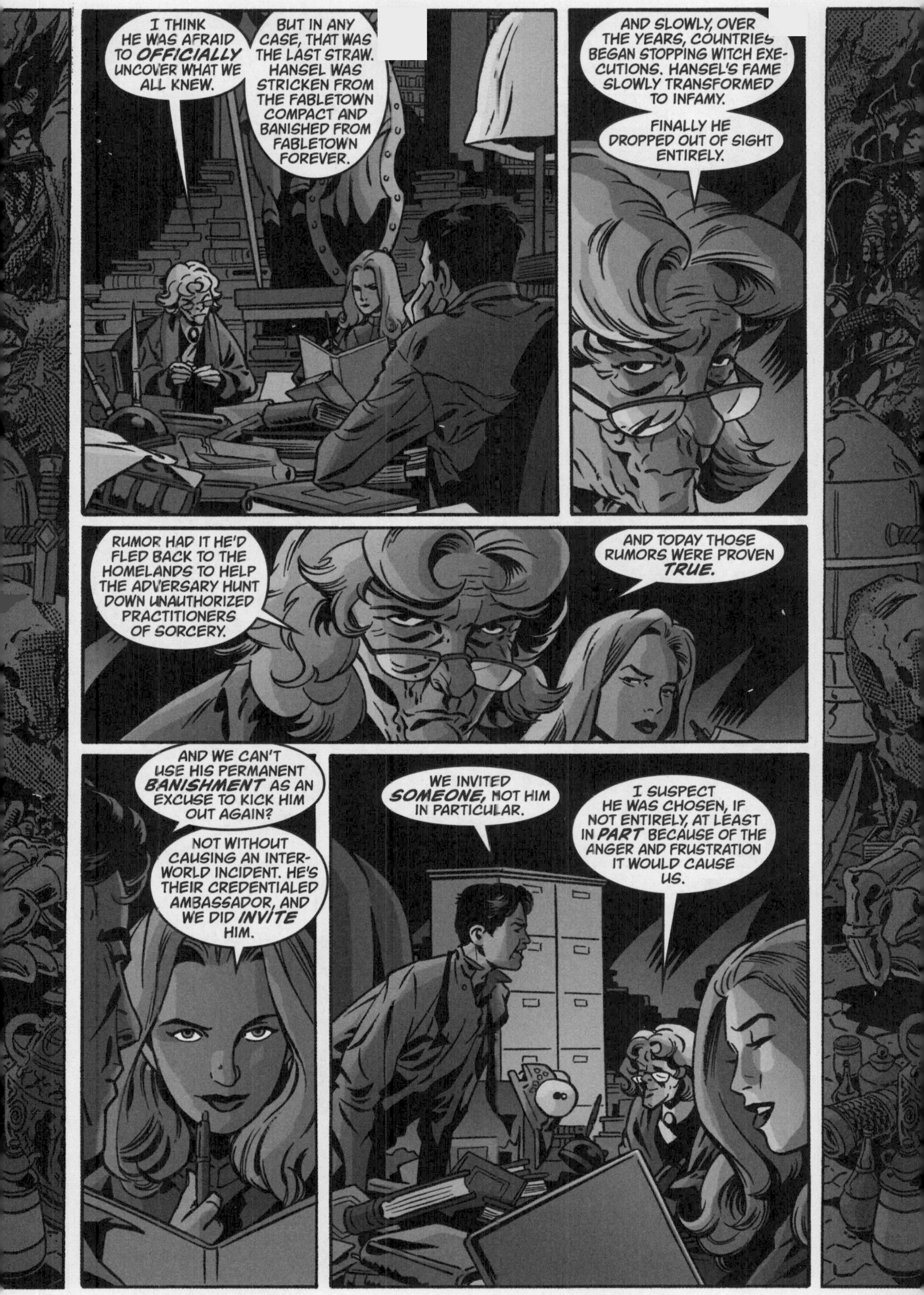
I THINK HE WAS AFRAID TO OFFICIALLY UNCOVER WHAT WE ALL KNEW.
BUT IN ANY CASE, THAT WAS THE LAST STRAW. HANSEL WAS STRICKEN FROM THE FABLETOWN COMPACT AND BANISHED FROM FABLETOWN FOREVER.
AND SLOWLY, OVER THE YEARS, COUNTRIES BEGAN STOPPING WITCH EXECUTIONS. HANSEL'S FAME SLOWLY TRANSFORMED TO INFAMY.
FINALLY HE DROPPED OUT OF SIGHT ENTIRELY.
RUMOR HAD IT HE'D FLED BACK TO THE HOMELANDS TO HELP THE ADVERSARY HUNT DOWN UNAUTHORIZED PRACTITIONERS OF SORCERY.
AND TODAY THOSE RUMORS WERE PROVEN TRUE.
AND WE CAN'T USE HIS PERMANENT BANISHMENT AS AN EXCUSE TO KICK HIM OUT AGAIN?
NOT WITHOUT CAUSING AN INTER-WORLD INCIDENT. HE'S THEIR CREDENTIALED AMBASSADOR, AND WE DID INVITE HIM.
WE INVITED SOMEONE, NOT HIM IN PARTICULAR.
I SUSPECT HE WAS CHOSEN, IF NOT ENTIRELY, AT LEAST IN PART BECAUSE OF THE ANGER AND FRUSTRATION IT WOULD CAUSE US.

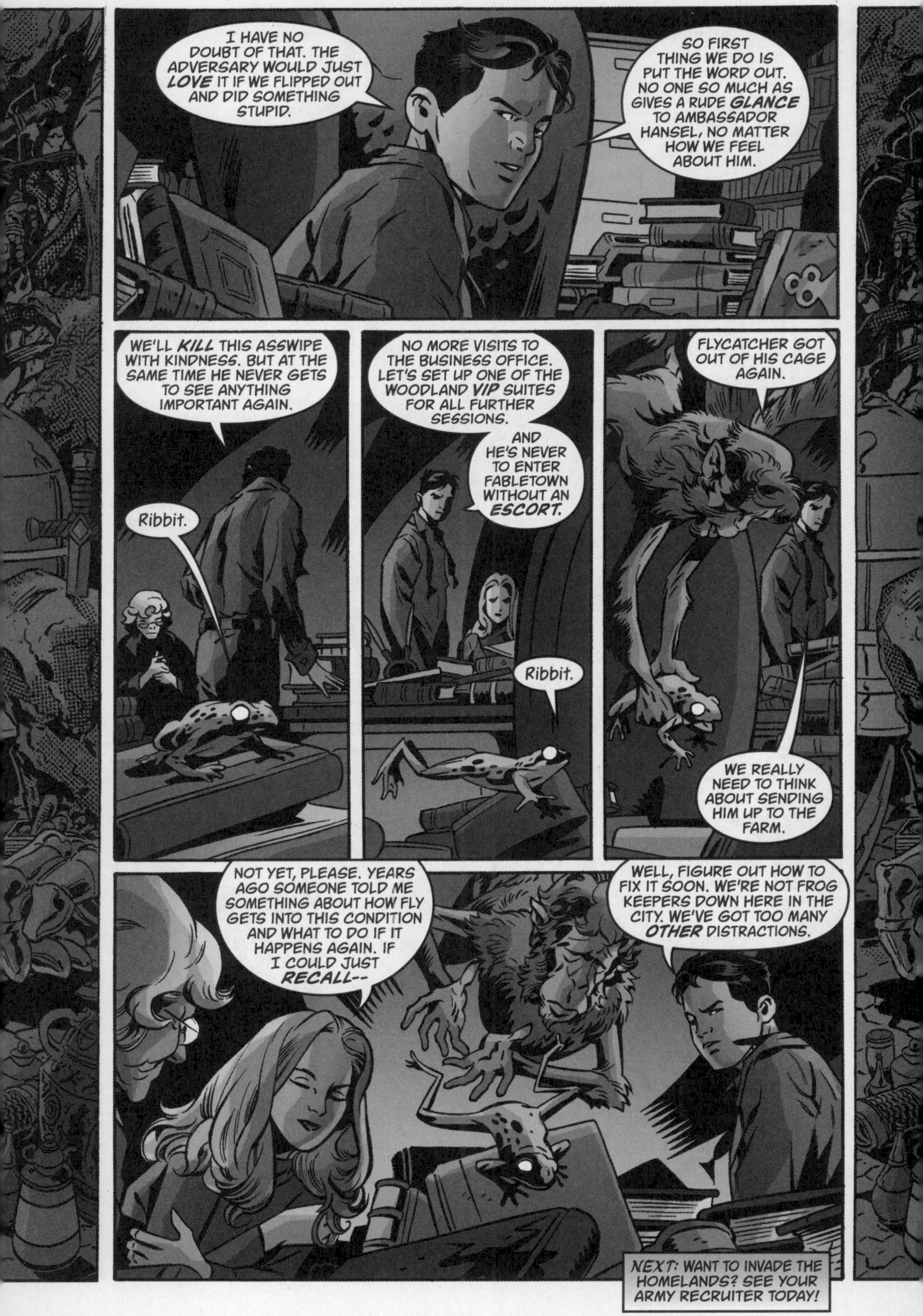
I HAVE NO DOUBT OF THAT. THE ADVERSARY WOULD JUST LOVE IT IF WE FLIPPED OUT AND DID SOMETHING STUPID.
SO FIRST THING WE DO IS PUT THE WORD OUT. NO ONE SO MUCH AS GIVES A RUDE GLANCE TO AMBASSADOR HANSEL, NO MATTER HOW WE FEEL ABOUT HIM.
WE'LL KILL THIS ASSWIPE WITH KINDNESS. BUT AT THE SAME TIME HE NEVER GETS TO SEE ANYTHING IMPORTANT AGAIN.
Ribbit.
NO MORE VISITS TO THE BUSINESS OFFICE. LET'S SET UP ONE OF THE WOODLAND VIP SUITES FOR ALL FURTHER SESSIONS.
AND HE'S NEVER TO ENTER FABLETOWN WITHOUT AN ESCORT.
Ribbit.
FLYCATCHER GOT OUT OF HIS CAGE AGAIN.
WE REALLY NEED TO THINK ABOUT SENDING HIM UP TO THE FARM.
NOT YET, PLEASE. YEARS AGO SOMEONE TOLD ME SOMETHING ABOUT HOW FLY GETS INTO THIS CONDITION AND WHAT TO DO IF IT HAPPENS AGAIN. IF I COULD JUST RECALL--
WELL, FIGURE OUT HOW TO FIX IT SOON. WE'RE NOT FROG KEEPERS DOWN HERE IN THE CITY. WE'VE GOT TOO MANY OTHER DISTRACTIONS.
NEXT: WANT TO INVADE THE HOMELANDS? SEE YOUR ARMY RECRUITER TODAY!

A Thorn in Their Side?

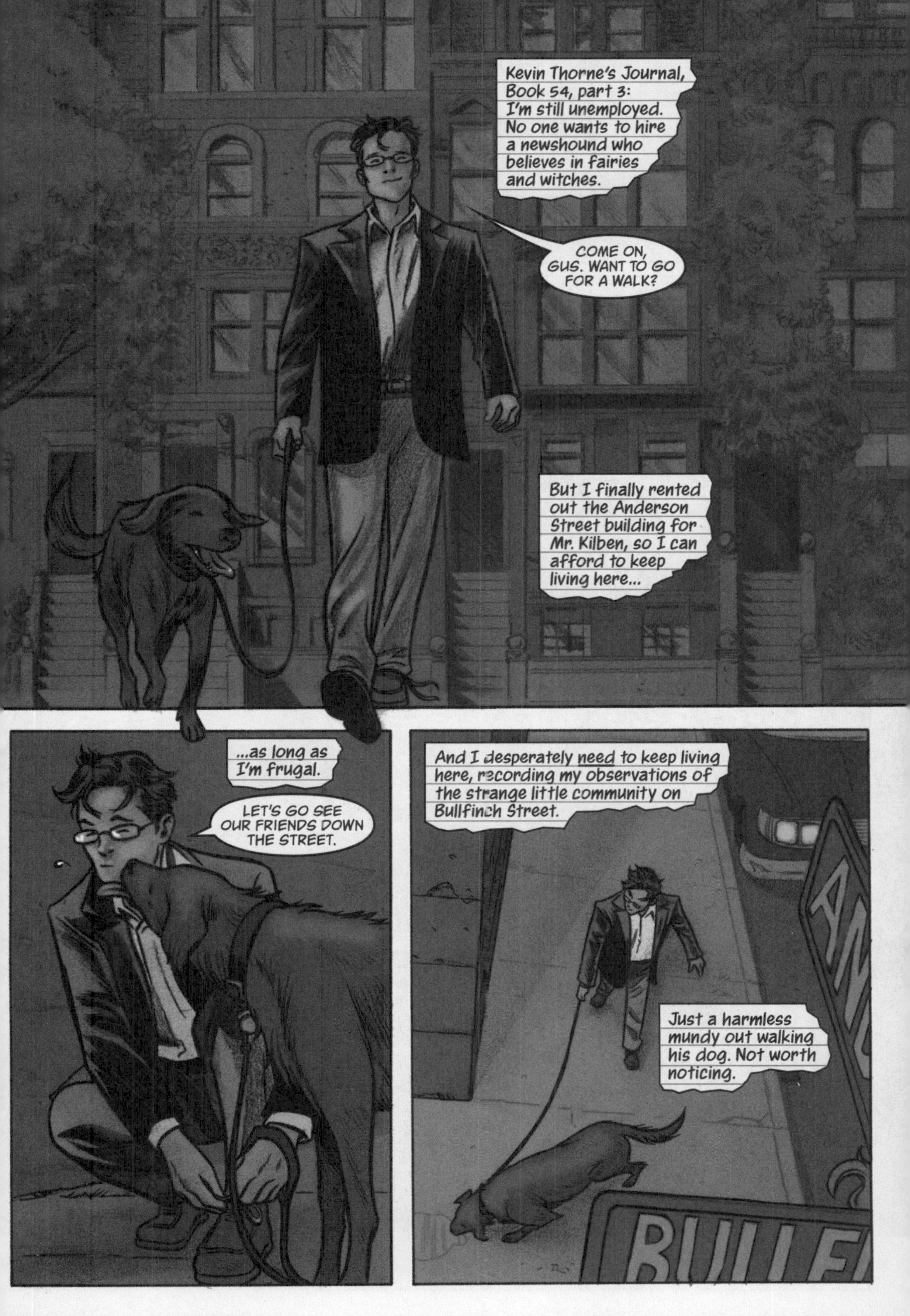
Kevin Thorne's Journal, Book 54, part 3: I'm still unemployed. No one wants to hire a newshound who believes in fairies and witches.
COME ON, GUS. WANT TO GO FOR A WALK?
But I finally rented out the Anderson Street building for Mr. Kilben, so I can afford to keep living here...
...as long as I'm frugal.
LET'S GO SEE OUR FRIENDS DOWN THE STREET.
And I desperately need to keep living here, recording my observations of the strange little community on Bullfinch Street.
Just a harmless mundy out walking his dog. Not worth noticing.

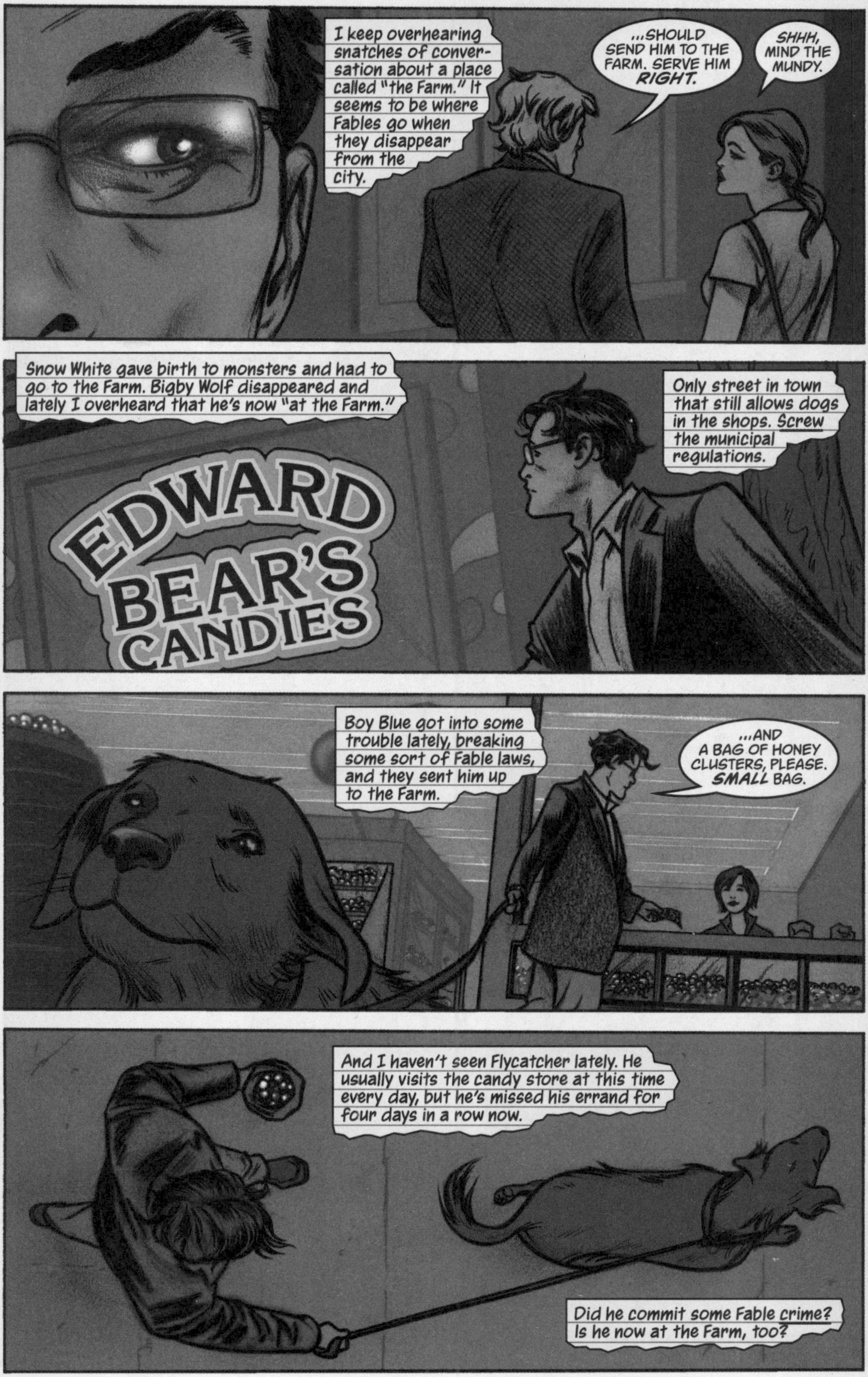
I keep overhearing snatches of conversation about a place called "the Farm." It seems to be where Fables go when they disappear from the city.
...SHOULD SEND HIM TO THE FARM. SERVE HIM RIGHT.
SHHH, MIND THE MUNDY.
Snow White gave birth to monsters and had to go to the Farm. Bigby Wolf disappeared and lately I overheard that he's now "at the Farm."
EDWARD BEAR'S CANDIES
Only street in town that still allows dogs in the shops. Screw the municipal regulations.
Boy Blue got into some trouble lately, breaking some sort of Fable laws, and they sent him up to the Farm.
...AND A BAG OF HONEY CLUSTERS, PLEASE. SMALL BAG.
And I haven't seen Flycatcher lately. He usually visits the candy store at this time every day, but he's missed his errand for four days in a row now.
Did he commit some Fable crime? Is he now at the Farm, too?

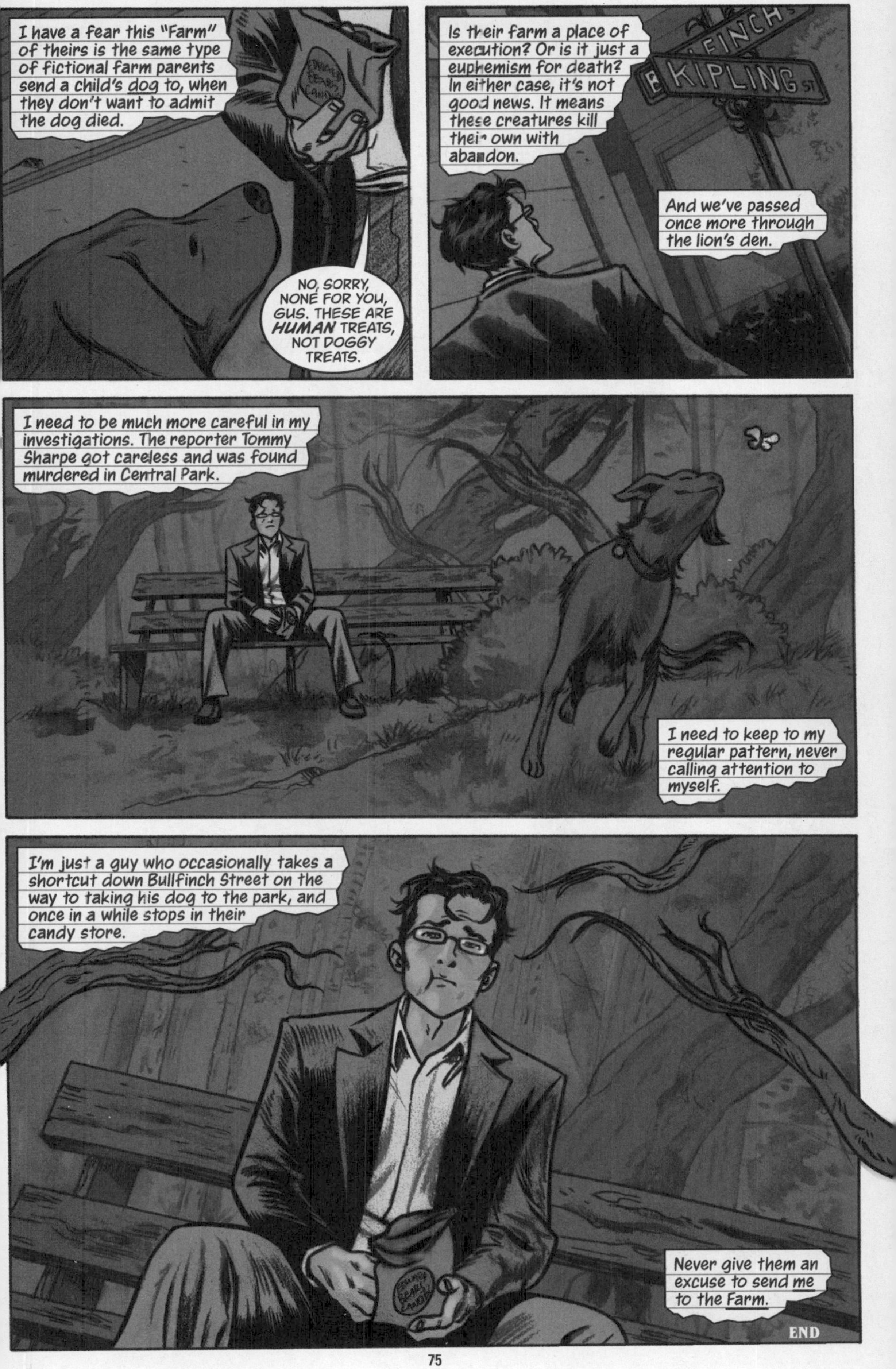
I have a fear this "Farm" of theirs is the same type of fictional farm parents send a child's dog to, when they don't want to admit the dog died.
NO, SORRY, NONE FOR YOU, GUS. THESE ARE HUMAN TREATS, NOT DOGGY TREATS.
Is their farm a place of execution? Or is it just a euphemism for death? In either case, it's not good news. It means these creatures kill their own with abandon.
FINCH
KIPLING ST
And we've passed once more through the lion's den.
I need to be much more careful in my investigations. The reporter Tommy Sharpe got careless and was found murdered in Central Park.
I need to keep to my regular pattern, never calling attention to myself.
I'm just a guy who occasionally takes a shortcut down Bullfinch Street on the way to taking his dog to the park, and once in a while stops in their candy store.
Never give them an excuse to send me to the Farm.
END

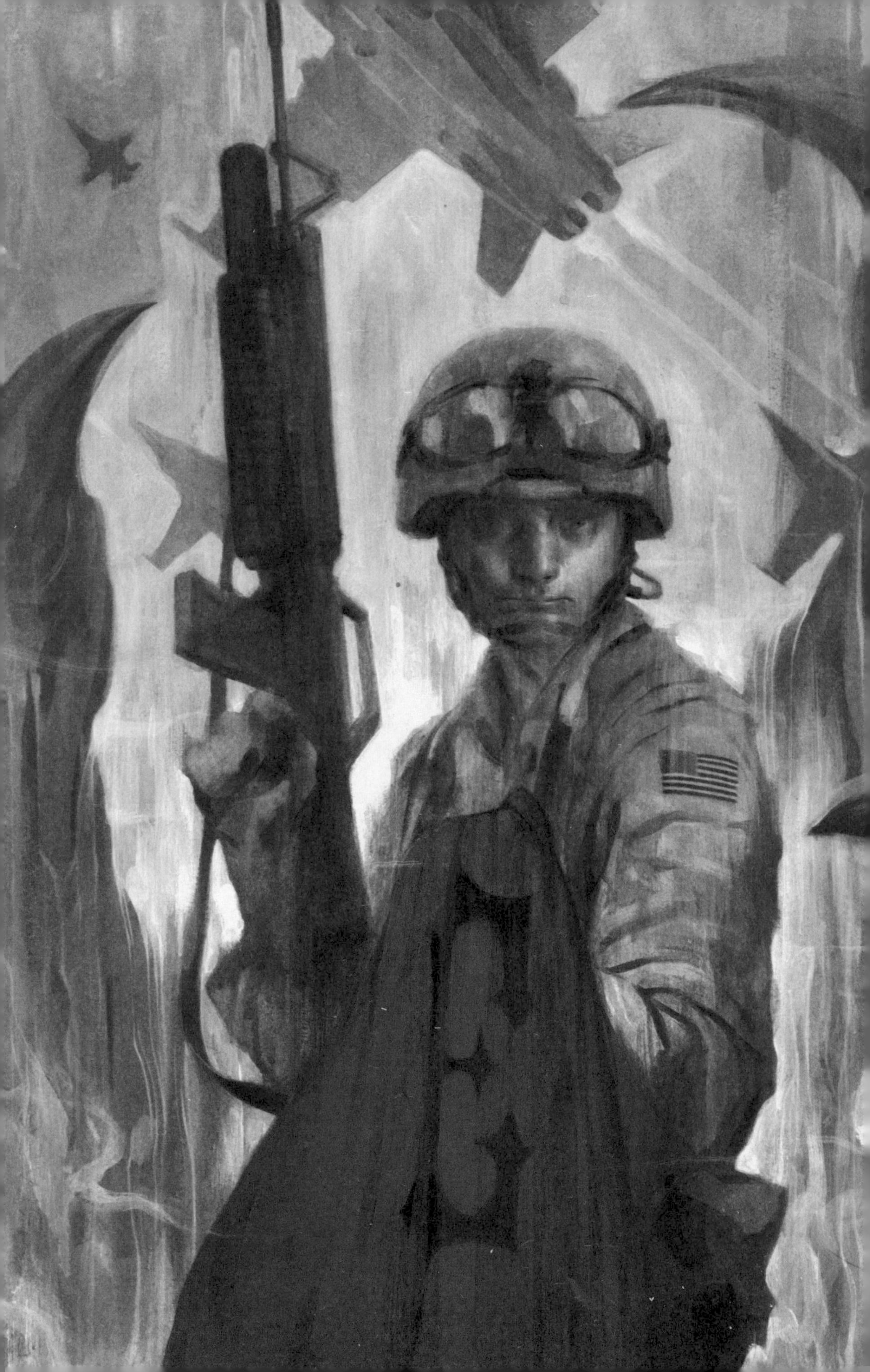

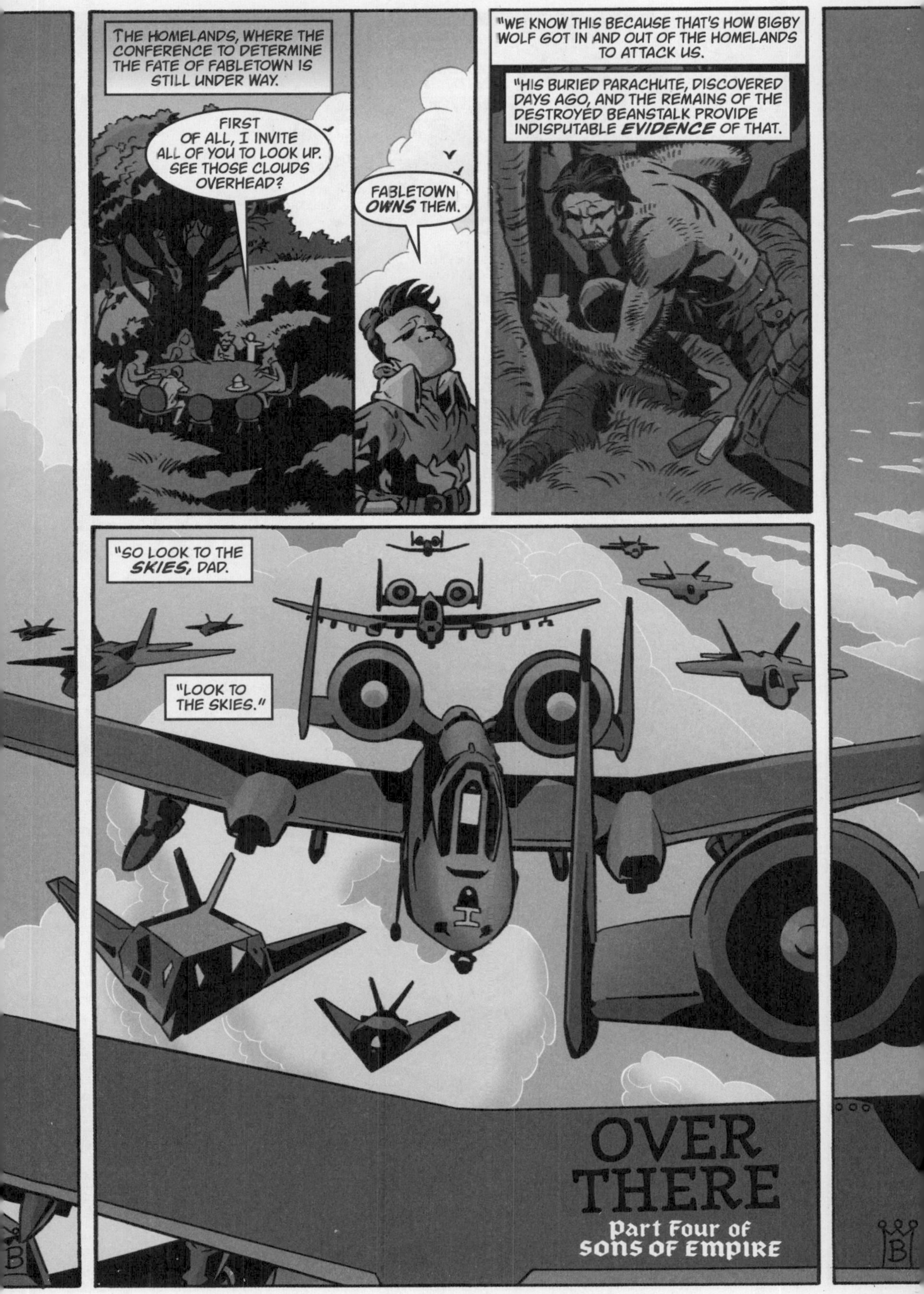
THE HOMELANDS, WHERE THE CONFERENCE TO DETERMINE THE FATE OF FABLETOWN IS STILL UNDER WAY.
FIRST OF ALL, I INVITE ALL OF YOU TO LOOK UP. SEE THOSE CLOUDS OVERHEAD?
FABLETOWN OWNS THEM.
"WE KNOW THIS BECAUSE THAT'S HOW BIGBY WOLF GOT IN AND OUT OF THE HOMELANDS TO ATTACK US.
"HIS BURIED PARACHUTE, DISCOVERED DAYS AGO, AND THE REMAINS OF THE DESTROYED BEANSTALK PROVIDE INDISPUTABLE EVIDENCE OF THAT.
"SO LOOK TO THE SKIES, DAD.
"LOOK TO THE SKIES."
OVER THERE
Part Four of SONS OF EMPIRE

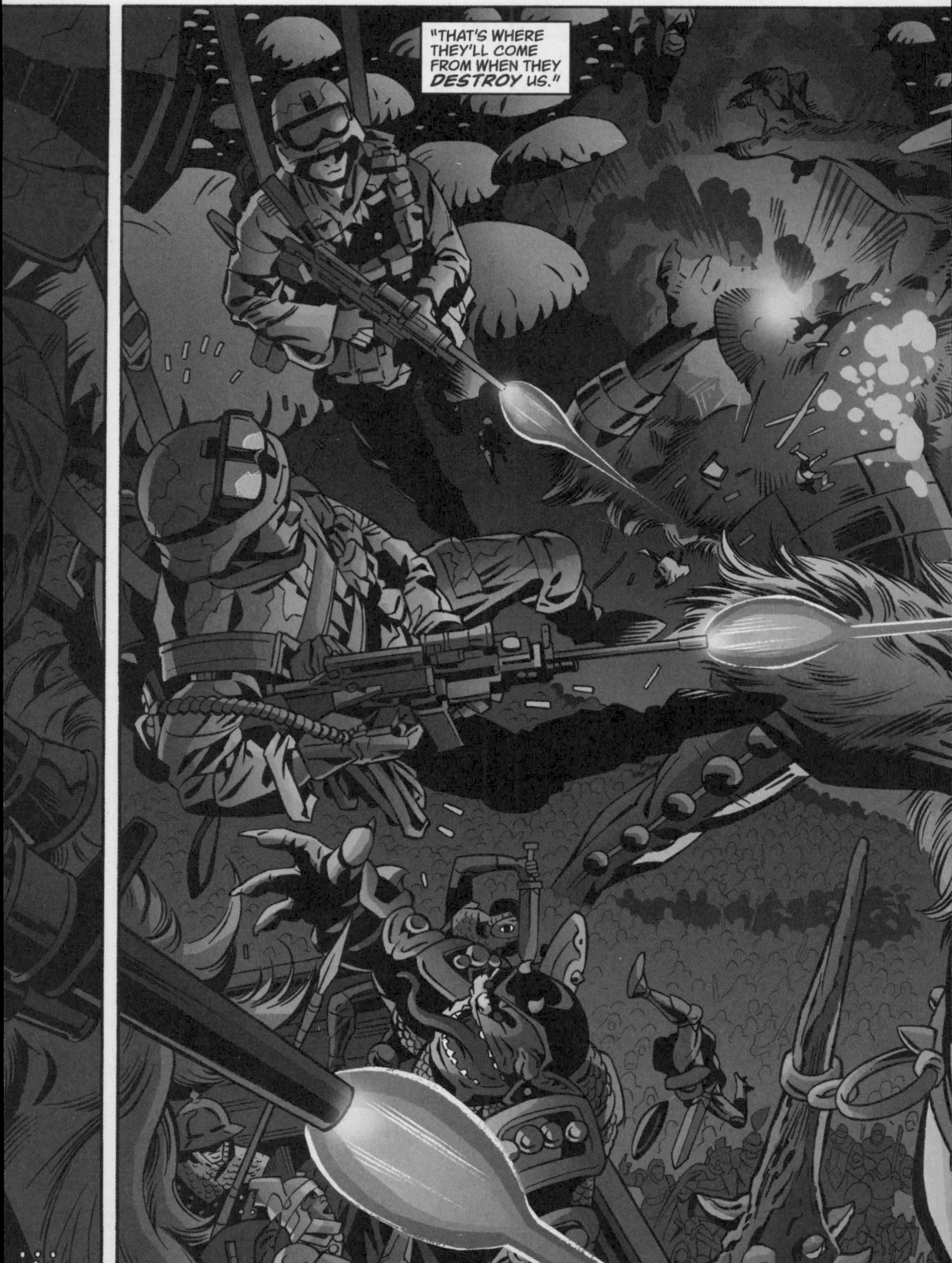
"THAT'S WHERE THEY'LL COME FROM WHEN THEY DESTROY US."

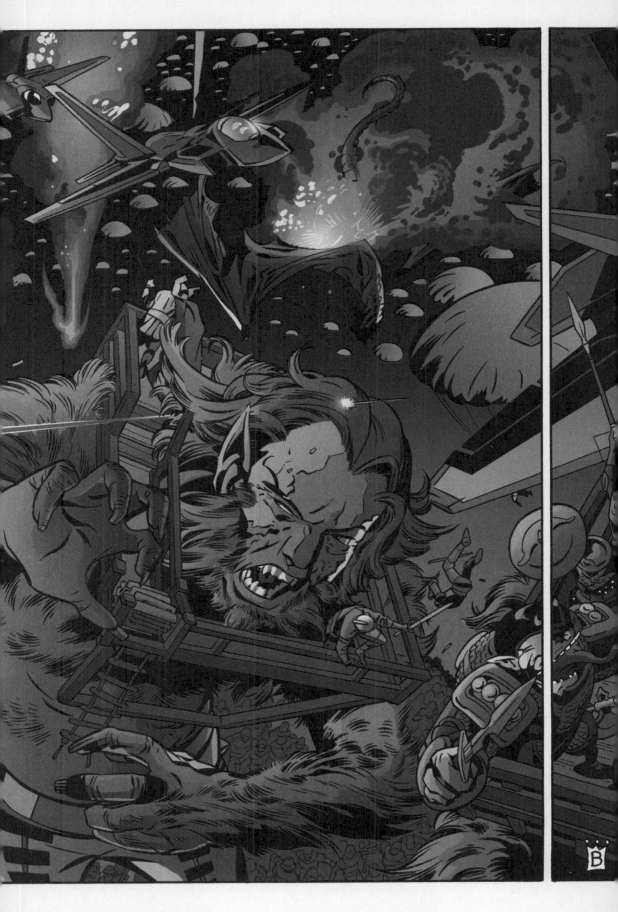

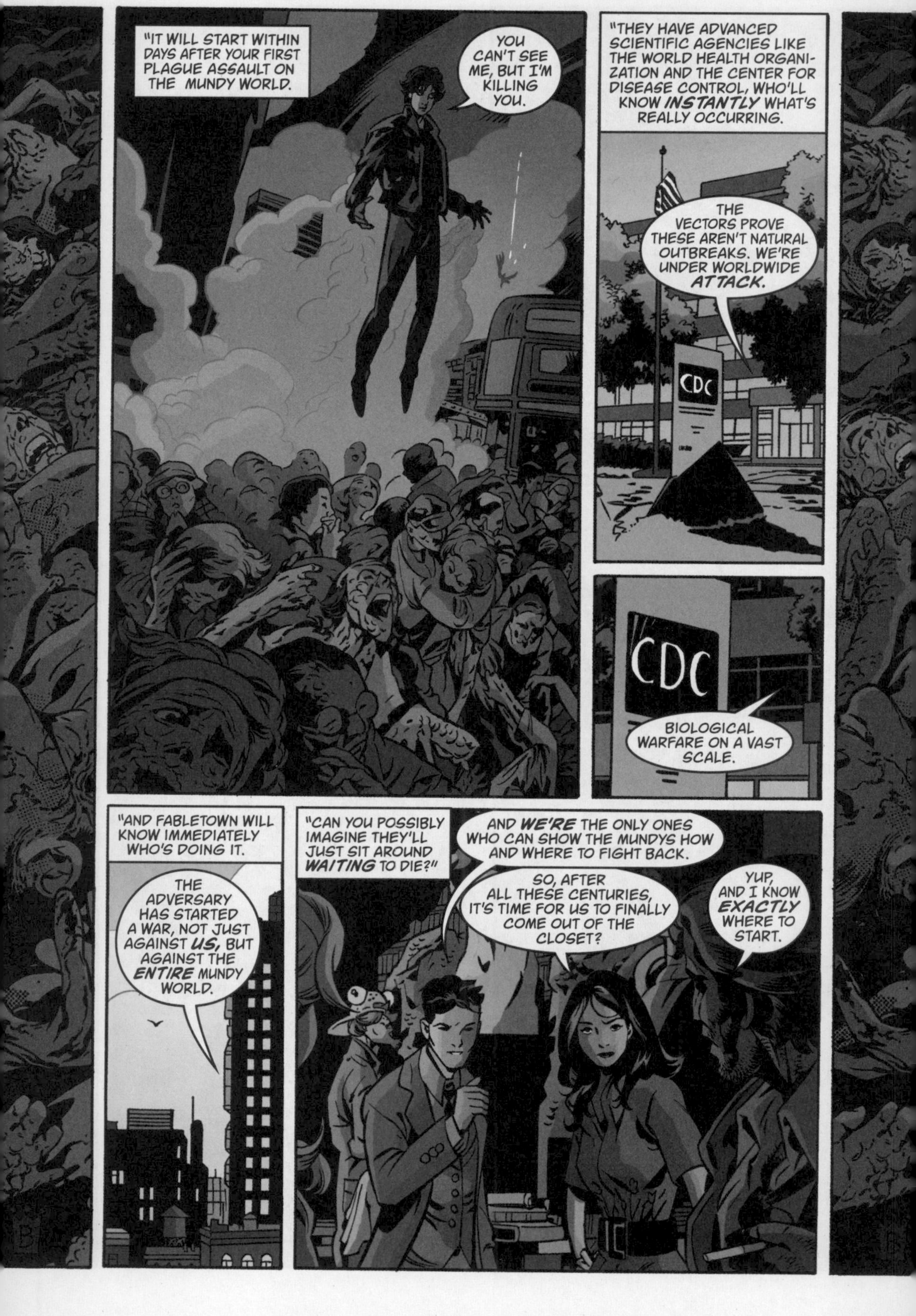
"IT WILL START WITHIN DAYS AFTER YOUR FIRST PLAGUE ASSAULT ON THE MUNDY WORLD.
YOU CAN'T SEE ME, BUT I'M KILLING YOU.
"THEY HAVE ADVANCED SCIENTIFIC AGENCIES LIKE THE WORLD HEALTH ORGANIZATION AND THE CENTER FOR DISEASE CONTROL, WHO'LL KNOW INSTANTLY WHAT'S REALLY OCCURRING.
THE VECTORS PROVE THESE AREN'T NATURAL OUTBREAKS. WE'RE UNDER WORLDWIDE ATTACK.
CDC
CDC
BIOLOGICAL WARFARE ON A VAST SCALE.
"AND FABLETOWN WILL KNOW IMMEDIATELY WHO'S DOING IT.
THE ADVERSARY HAS STARTED A WAR, NOT JUST AGAINST US, BUT AGAINST THE ENTIRE MUNDY WORLD.
"CAN YOU POSSIBLY IMAGINE THEY'LL JUST SIT AROUND WAITING TO DIE?"
AND WE'RE THE ONLY ONES WHO CAN SHOW THE MUNDYS HOW AND WHERE TO FIGHT BACK.
SO, AFTER ALL THESE CENTURIES, IT'S TIME FOR US TO FINALLY COME OUT OF THE CLOSET?
YUP, AND I KNOW EXACTLY WHERE TO START.

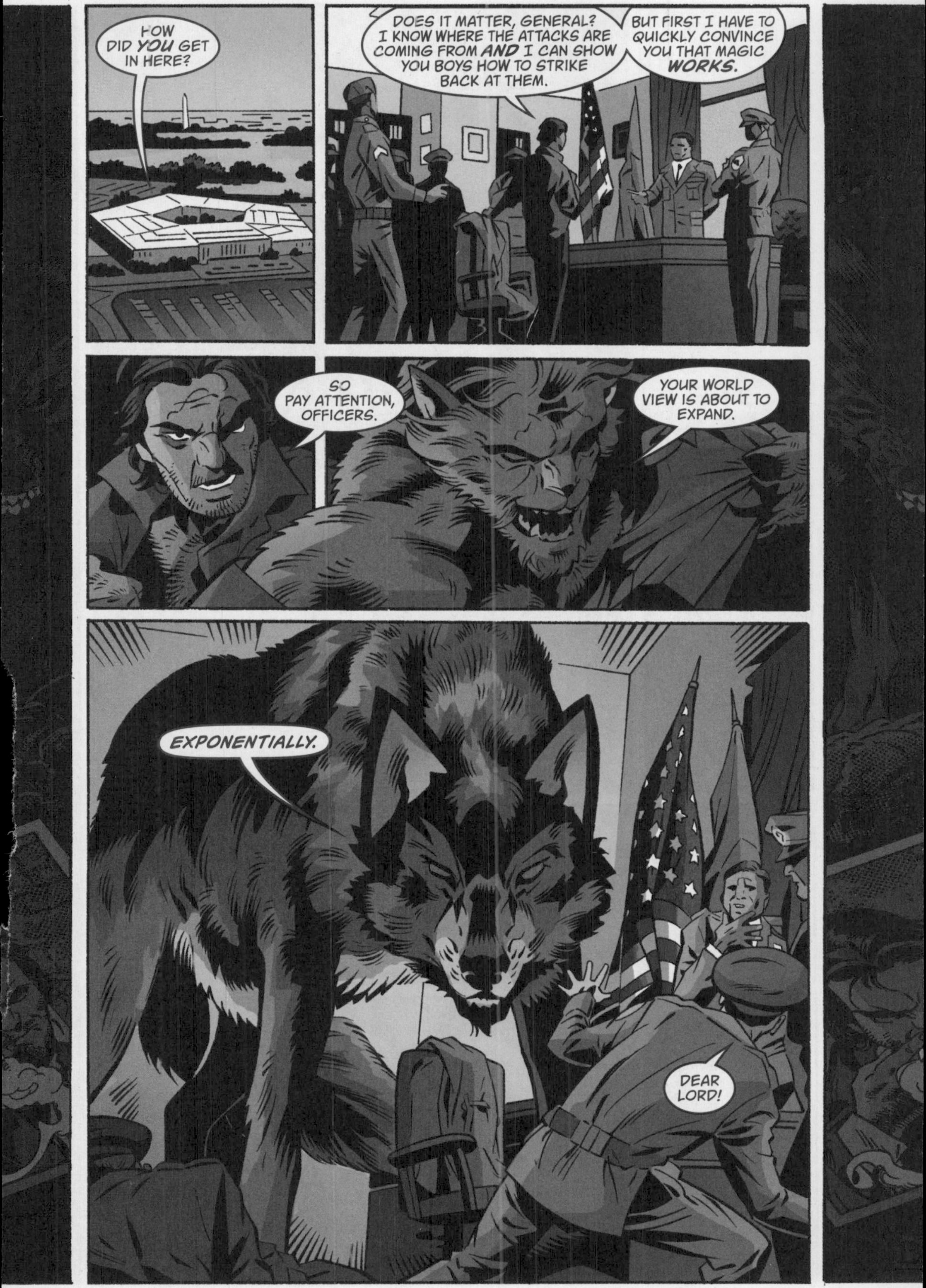
HOW DID YOU GET IN HERE?
DOES IT MATTER, GENERAL? I KNOW WHERE THE ATTACKS ARE COMING FROM AND I CAN SHOW YOU BOYS HOW TO STRIKE BACK AT THEM.
BUT FIRST I HAVE TO QUICKLY CONVINCE YOU THAT MAGIC WORKS.
SO PAY ATTENTION, OFFICERS.
YOUR WORLD VIEW IS ABOUT TO EXPAND.
EXPONENTIALLY.
DEAR LORD!

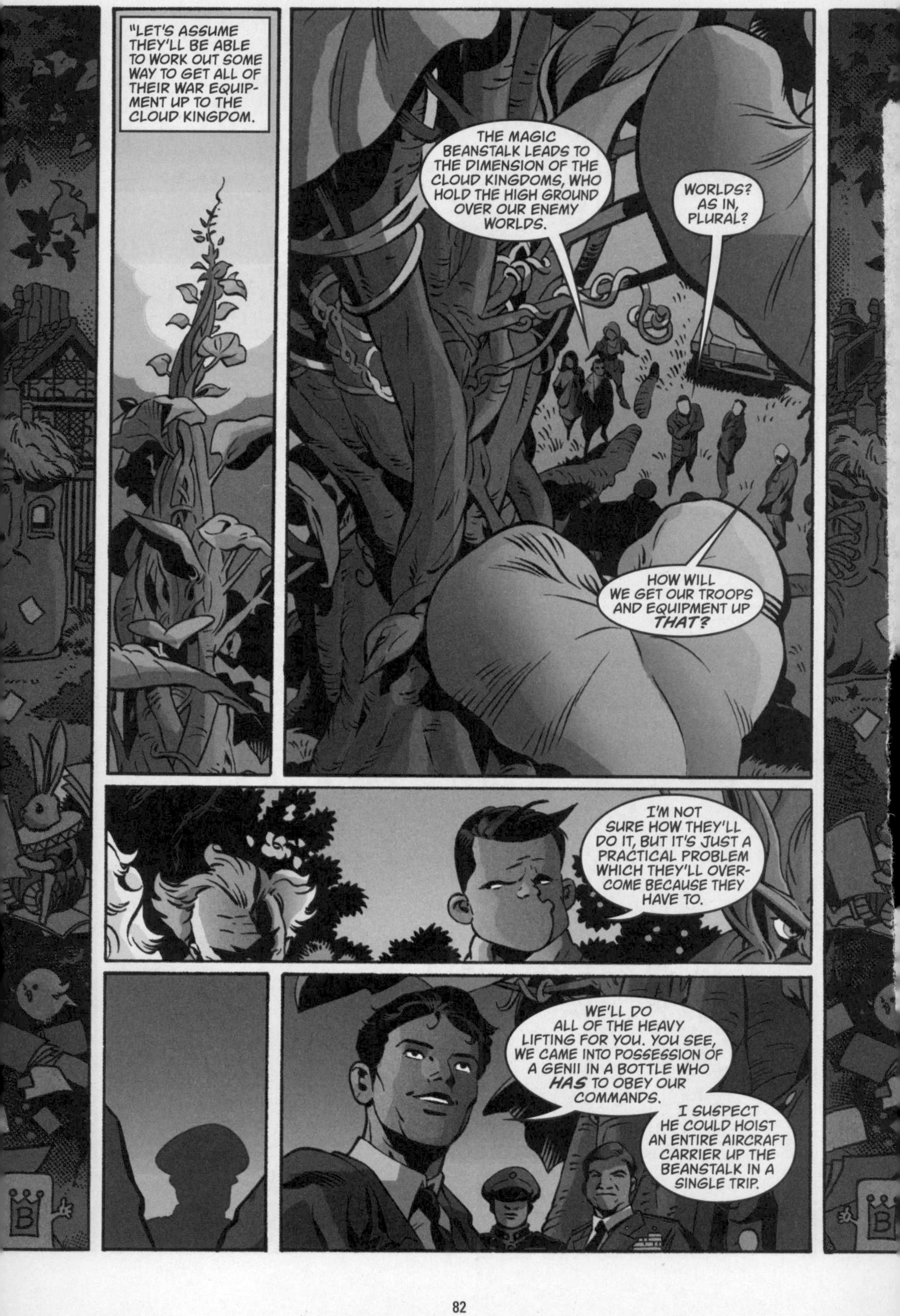
"LET'S ASSUME THEY'LL BE ABLE TO WORK OUT SOME WAY TO GET ALL OF THEIR WAR EQUIPMENT UP TO THE CLOUD KINGDOM.
THE MAGIC BEANSTALK LEADS TO THE DIMENSION OF THE CLOUD KINGDOMS, WHO HOLD THE HIGH GROUND OVER OUR ENEMY WORLDS.
WORLDS? AS IN, PLURAL?
HOW WILL WE GET OUR TROOPS AND EQUIPMENT UP THAT?
I'M NOT SURE HOW THEY'LL DO IT, BUT IT'S JUST A PRACTICAL PROBLEM WHICH THEY'LL OVERCOME BECAUSE THEY HAVE TO.
WE'LL DO ALL OF THE HEAVY LIFTING FOR YOU. YOU SEE, WE CAME INTO POSSESSION OF A GENII IN A BOTTLE WHO HAS TO OBEY OUR COMMANDS.
I SUSPECT HE COULD HOIST AN ENTIRE AIRCRAFT CARRIER UP THE BEANSTALK IN A SINGLE TRIP.

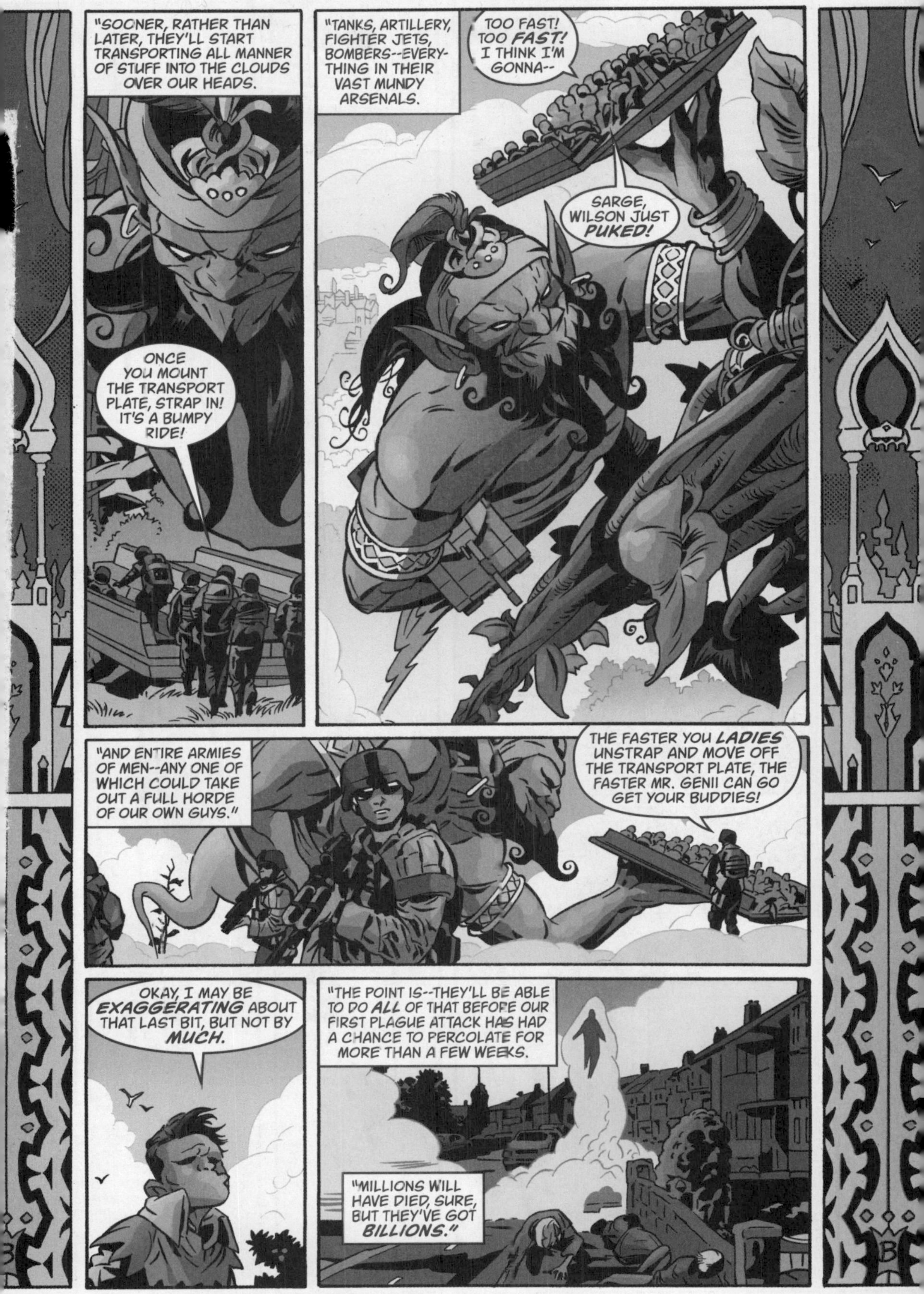
"SOONER, RATHER THAN LATER, THEY'LL START TRANSPORTING ALL MANNER OF STUFF INTO THE CLOUDS OVER OUR HEADS.
ONCE YOU MOUNT THE TRANSPORT PLATE, STRAP IN! IT'S A BUMPY RIDE!
"TANKS, ARTILLERY, FIGHTER JETS, BOMBERS--EVERYTHING IN THEIR VAST MUNDY ARSENALS.
TOO FAST! TOO FAST! I THINK I'M GONNA--
SARGE, WILSON JUST PUKED!
"AND ENTIRE ARMIES OF MEN--ANY ONE OF WHICH COULD TAKE OUT A FULL HORDE OF OUR OWN GUYS."
THE FASTER YOU LADIES UNSTRAP AND MOVE OFF THE TRANSPORT PLATE, THE FASTER MR. GENII CAN GO GET YOUR BUDDIES!
OKAY, I MAY BE EXAGGERATING ABOUT THAT LAST BIT, BUT NOT BY MUCH.
"THE POINT IS--THEY'LL BE ABLE TO DO ALL OF THAT BEFORE OUR FIRST PLAGUE ATTACK HAS HAD A CHANCE TO PERCOLATE FOR MORE THAN A FEW WEEKS.
"MILLIONS WILL HAVE DIED, SURE, BUT THEY'VE GOT BILLIONS."

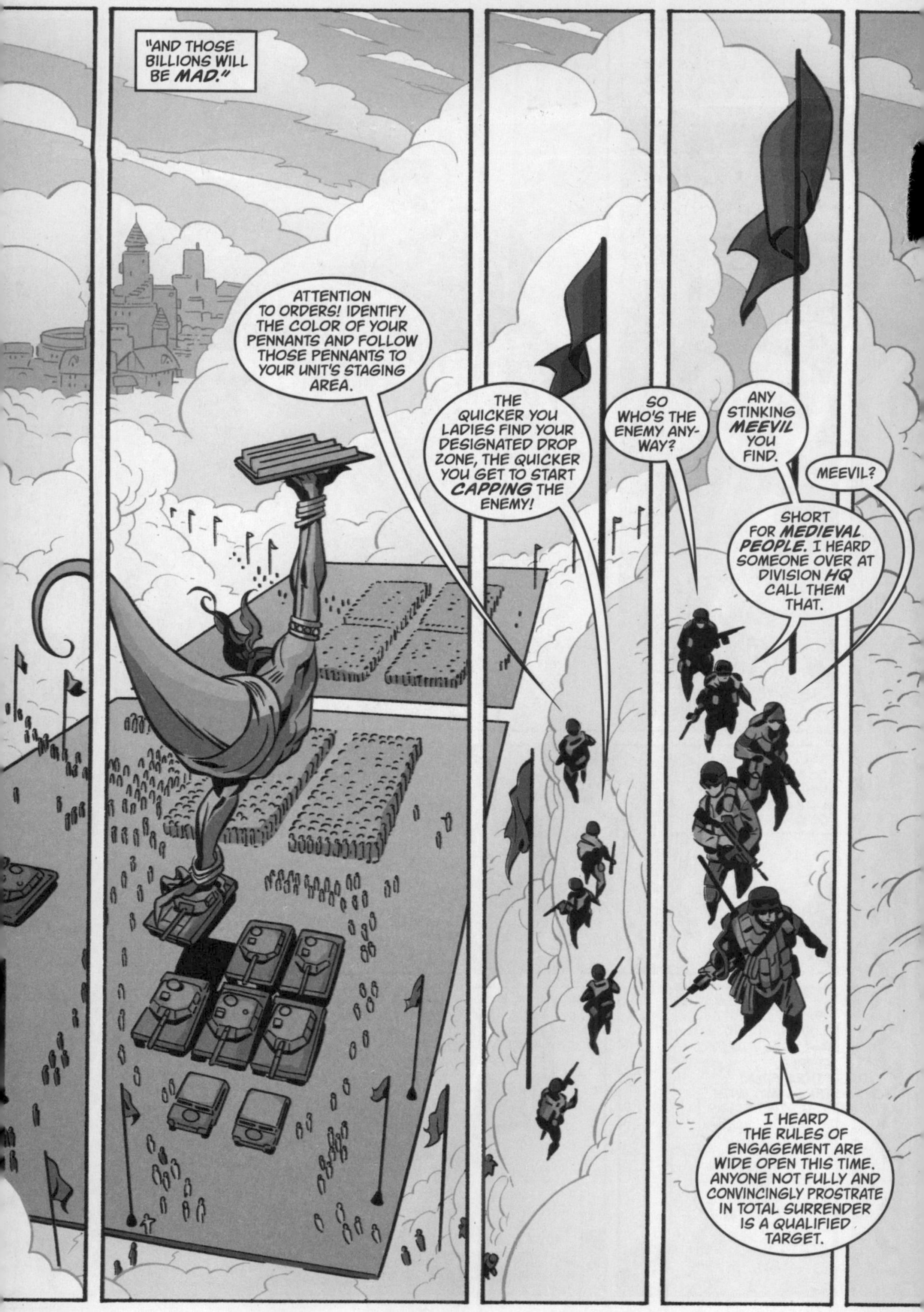
"AND THOSE BILLIONS WILL BE MAD."
ATTENTION TO ORDERS! IDENTIFY THE COLOR OF YOUR PENNANTS AND FOLLOW THOSE PENNANTS TO YOUR UNIT'S STAGING AREA.
THE QUICKER YOU LADIES FIND YOUR DESIGNATED DROP ZONE, THE QUICKER YOU GET TO START CAPPING THE ENEMY!
SO WHO'S THE ENEMY ANY-WAY?
ANY STINKING MEEVIL YOU FIND.
MEEVIL?
SHORT FOR MEDIEVAL PEOPLE. I HEARD SOMEONE OVER AT DIVISION HQ CALL THEM THAT.
I HEARD THE RULES OF ENGAGEMENT ARE WIDE OPEN THIS TIME. ANYONE NOT FULLY AND CONVINCINGLY PROSTRATE IN TOTAL SURRENDER IS A QUALIFIED TARGET.

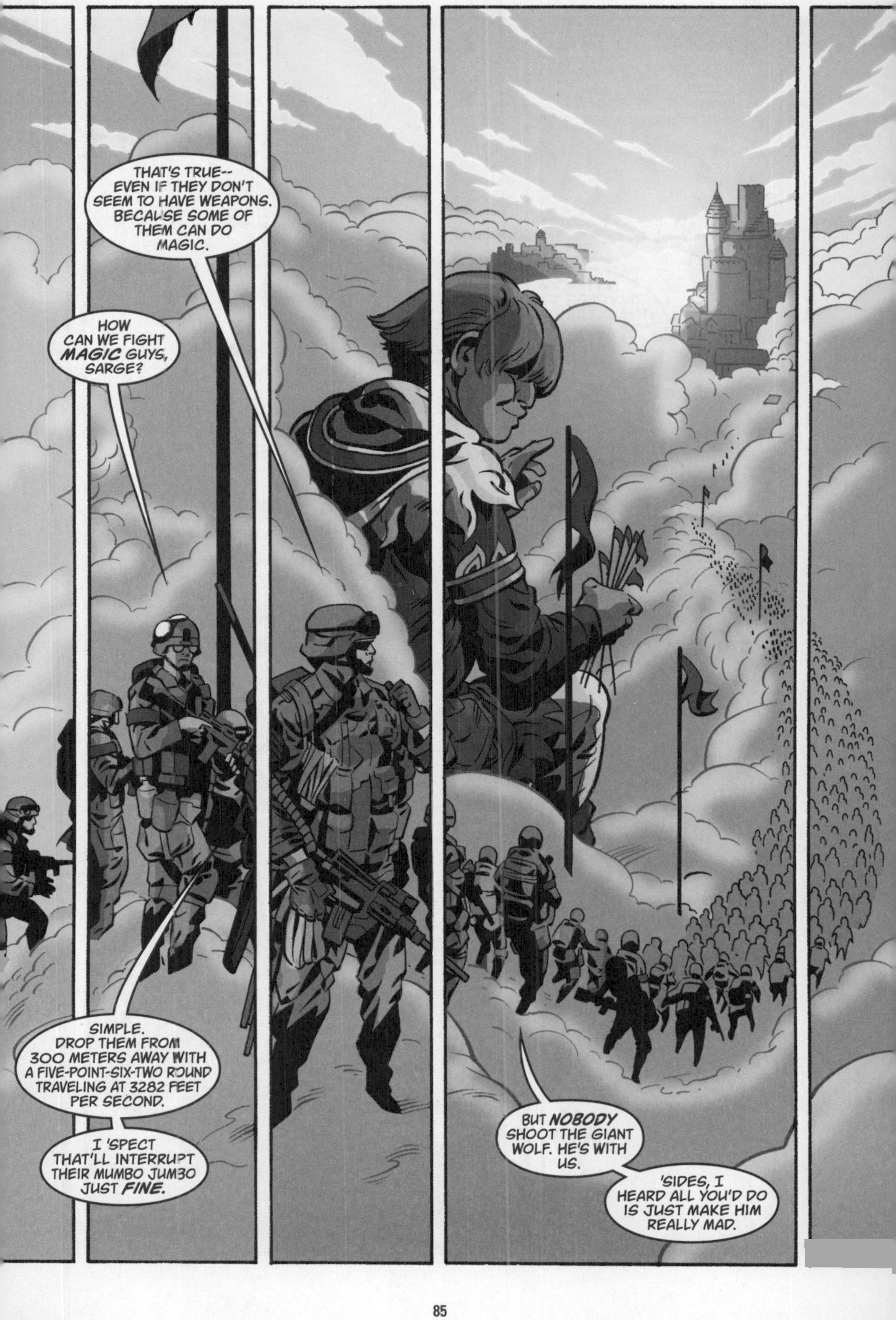
HOW CAN WE FIGHT MAGIC GUYS, SARGE?
THAT'S TRUE-- EVEN IF THEY DON'T SEEM TO HAVE WEAPONS. BECAUSE SOME OF THEM CAN DO MAGIC.
SIMPLE. DROP THEM FROM 300 METERS AWAY WITH A FIVE-POINT-SIX-TWO ROUND TRAVELING AT 3282 FEET PER SECOND.
I 'SPECT THAT'LL INTERRUPT THEIR MUMBO JUMBO JUST FINE.
BUT NOBODY SHOOT THE GIANT WOLF. HE'S WITH US.
'SIDES, I HEARD ALL YOU'D DO IS JUST MAKE HIM REALLY MAD.

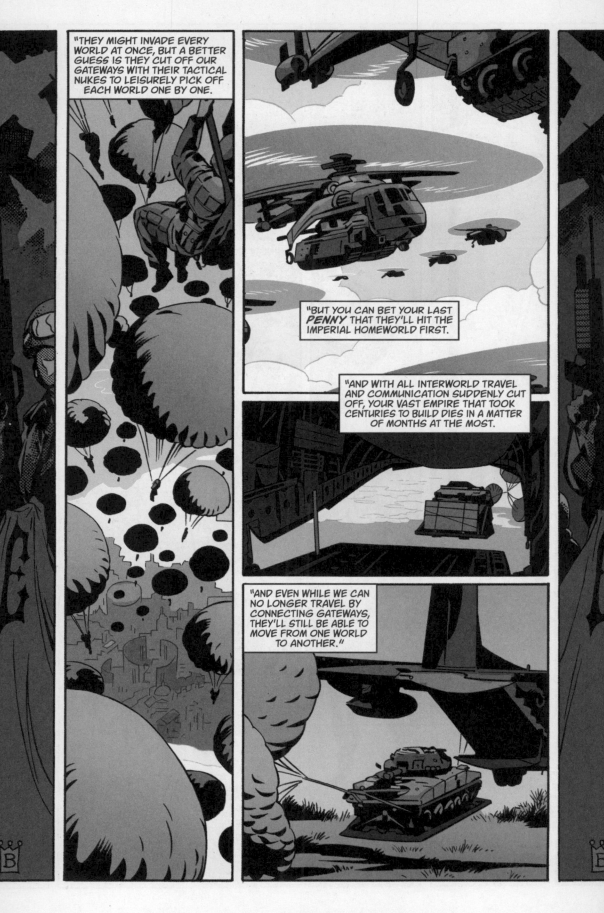

"THEY MIGHT INVADE EVERY WORLD AT ONCE, BUT A BETTER GUESS IS THEY CUT OFF OUR GATEWAYS WITH THEIR TACTICAL NUKES TO LEISURELY PICK OFF EACH WORLD ONE BY ONE.

"BUT YOU CAN BET YOUR LAST *PENNY* THAT THEY'LL HIT THE IMPERIAL HOMEWORLD FIRST.

"AND WITH ALL INTERWORLD TRAVEL AND COMMUNICATION SUDDENLY CUT OFF, YOUR VAST EMPIRE THAT TOOK CENTURIES TO BUILD DIES IN A MATTER OF MONTHS AT THE MOST.

"AND EVEN WHILE WE CAN NO LONGER TRAVEL BY CONNECTING GATEWAYS, THEY'LL STILL BE ABLE TO MOVE FROM ONE WORLD TO ANOTHER."

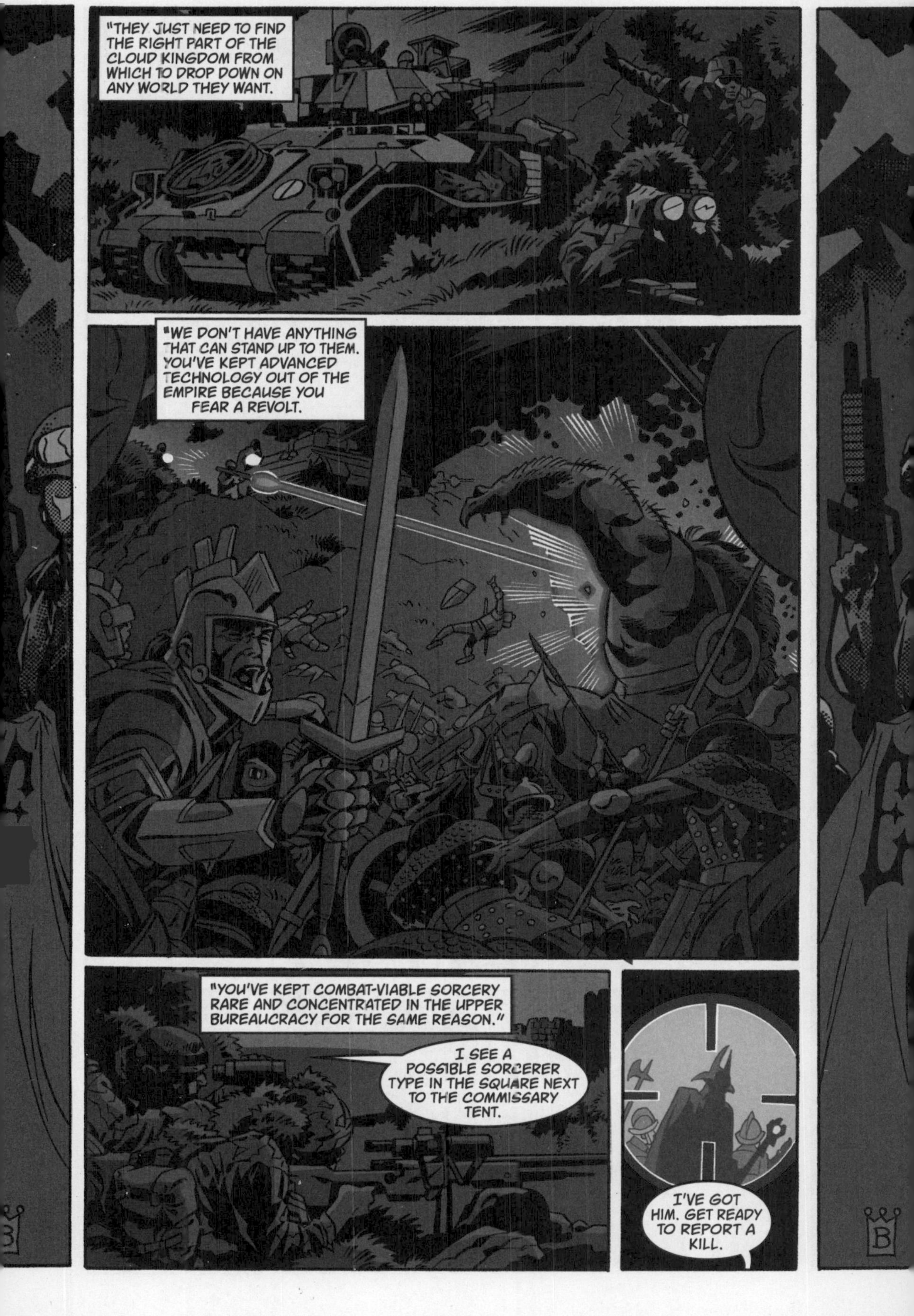
"THEY JUST NEED TO FIND THE RIGHT PART OF THE CLOUD KINGDOM FROM WHICH TO DROP DOWN ON ANY WORLD THEY WANT.
"WE DON'T HAVE ANYTHING THAT CAN STAND UP TO THEM. YOU'VE KEPT ADVANCED TECHNOLOGY OUT OF THE EMPIRE BECAUSE YOU FEAR A REVOLT.
"YOU'VE KEPT COMBAT-VIABLE SORCERY RARE AND CONCENTRATED IN THE UPPER BUREAUCRACY FOR THE SAME REASON."
I SEE A POSSIBLE SORCERER TYPE IN THE SQUARE NEXT TO THE COMMISSARY TENT.
I'VE GOT HIM. GET READY TO REPORT A KILL.

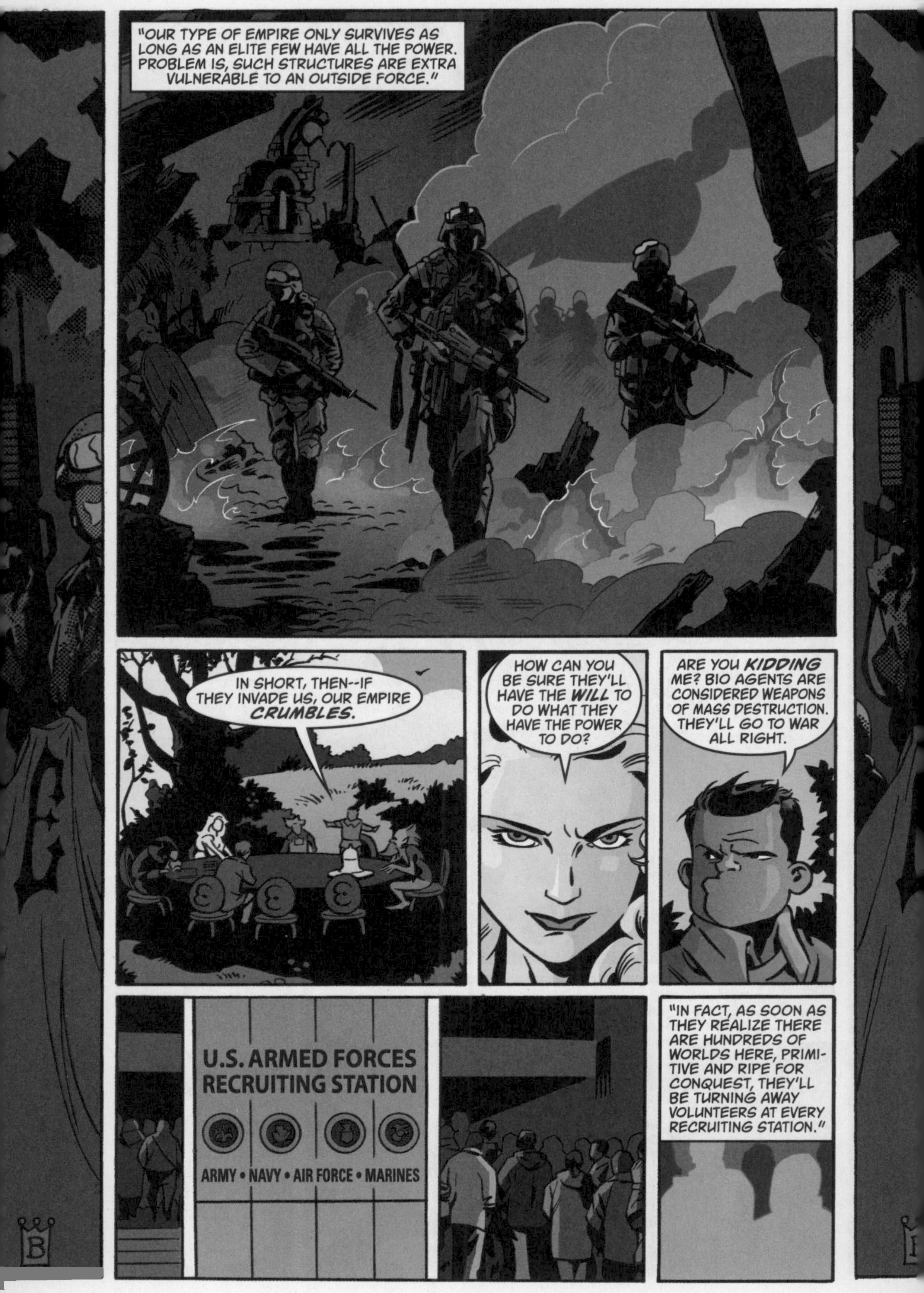
"OUR TYPE OF EMPIRE ONLY SURVIVES AS LONG AS AN ELITE FEW HAVE ALL THE POWER. PROBLEM IS, SUCH STRUCTURES ARE EXTRA VULNERABLE TO AN OUTSIDE FORCE."
IN SHORT, THEN--IF THEY INVADE US, OUR EMPIRE *CRUMBLES.*
HOW CAN YOU BE SURE THEY'LL HAVE THE *WILL* TO DO WHAT THEY HAVE THE POWER TO DO?
ARE YOU *KIDDING* ME? BIO AGENTS ARE CONSIDERED WEAPONS OF MASS DESTRUCTION. THEY'LL GO TO WAR ALL RIGHT.
U.S. ARMED FORCES RECRUITING STATION
ARMY • NAVY • AIR FORCE • MARINES
"IN FACT, AS SOON AS THEY REALIZE THERE ARE HUNDREDS OF WORLDS HERE, PRIMITIVE AND RIPE FOR CONQUEST, THEY'LL BE TURNING AWAY VOLUNTEERS AT EVERY RECRUITING STATION."

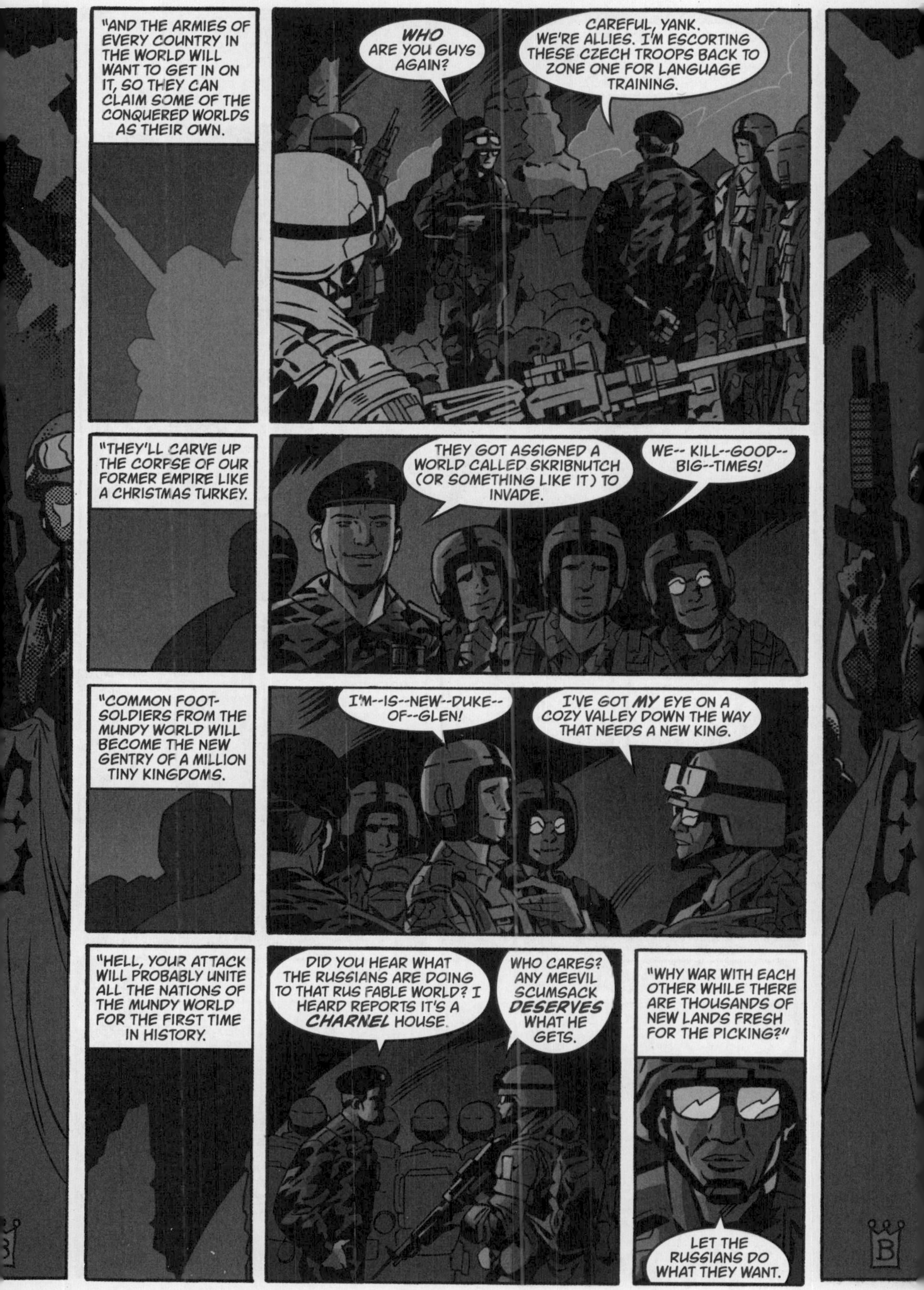
"AND THE ARMIES OF EVERY COUNTRY IN THE WORLD WILL WANT TO GET IN ON IT, SO THEY CAN CLAIM SOME OF THE CONQUERED WORLDS AS THEIR OWN.
WHO ARE YOU GUYS AGAIN?
CAREFUL, YANK. WE'RE ALLIES. I'M ESCORTING THESE CZECH TROOPS BACK TO ZONE ONE FOR LANGUAGE TRAINING.
"THEY'LL CARVE UP THE CORPSE OF OUR FORMER EMPIRE LIKE A CHRISTMAS TURKEY.
THEY GOT ASSIGNED A WORLD CALLED SKRIBNUTCH (OR SOMETHING LIKE IT) TO INVADE.
WE-- KILL--GOOD-- BIG--TIMES!
"COMMON FOOT-SOLDIERS FROM THE MUNDY WORLD WILL BECOME THE NEW GENTRY OF A MILLION TINY KINGDOMS.
I'M--IS--NEW--DUKE-- OF--GLEN!
I'VE GOT MY EYE ON A COZY VALLEY DOWN THE WAY THAT NEEDS A NEW KING.
"HELL, YOUR ATTACK WILL PROBABLY UNITE ALL THE NATIONS OF THE MUNDY WORLD FOR THE FIRST TIME IN HISTORY.
DID YOU HEAR WHAT THE RUSSIANS ARE DOING TO THAT RUS FABLE WORLD? I HEARD REPORTS IT'S A CHARNEL HOUSE.
WHO CARES? ANY MEEVIL SCUMSACK DESERVES WHAT HE GETS.
"WHY WAR WITH EACH OTHER WHILE THERE ARE THOUSANDS OF NEW LANDS FRESH FOR THE PICKING?"
LET THE RUSSIANS DO WHAT THEY WANT.

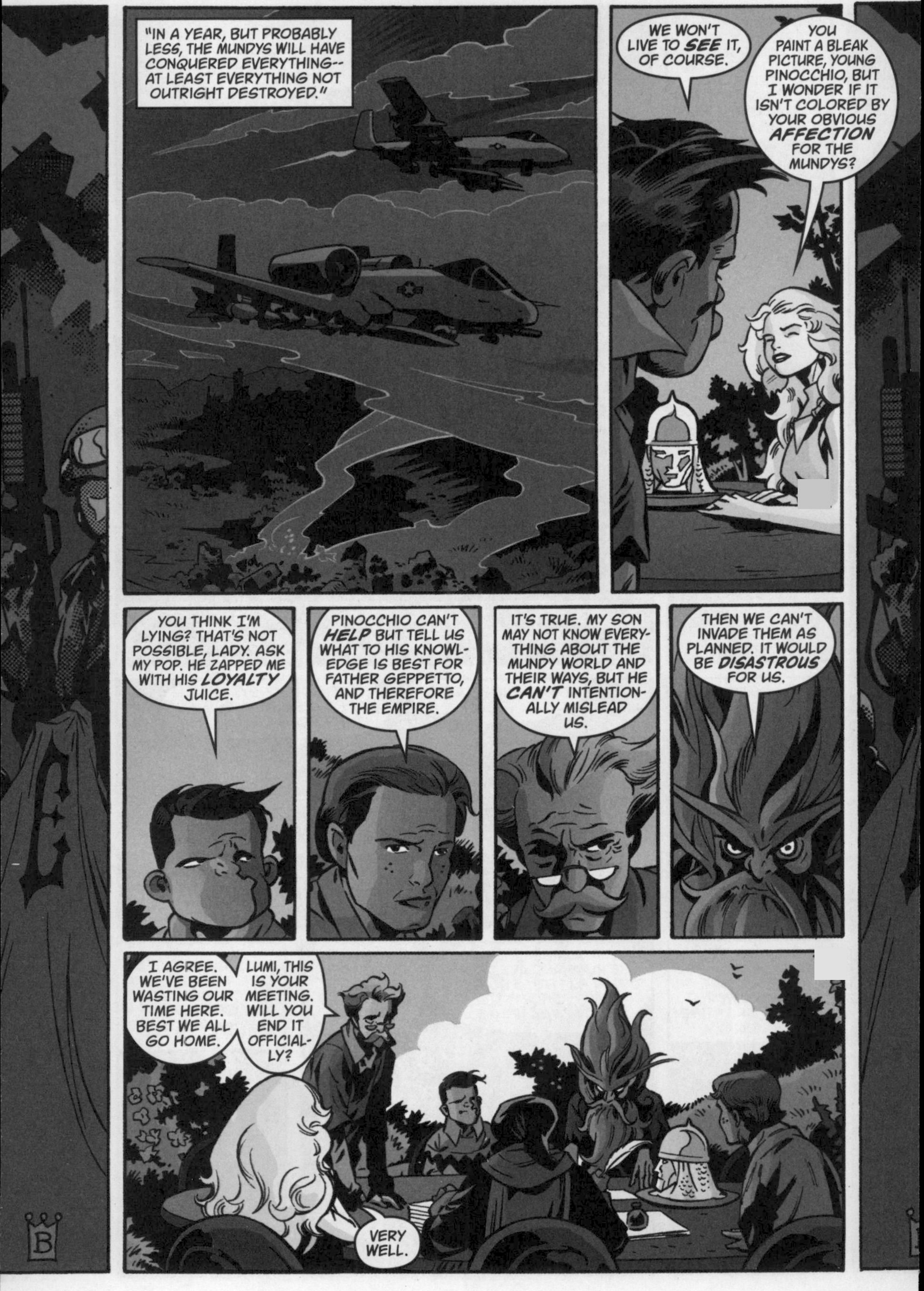

"IN A YEAR, BUT PROBABLY LESS, THE MUNDYS WILL HAVE CONQUERED EVERYTHING--AT LEAST EVERYTHING NOT OUTRIGHT DESTROYED."
WE WON'T LIVE TO SEE IT, OF COURSE.
YOU PAINT A BLEAK PICTURE, YOUNG PINOCCHIO, BUT I WONDER IF IT ISN'T COLORED BY YOUR OBVIOUS AFFECTION FOR THE MUNDYS?
YOU THINK I'M LYING? THAT'S NOT POSSIBLE, LADY. ASK MY POP. HE ZAPPED ME WITH HIS LOYALTY JUICE.
PINOCCHIO CAN'T HELP BUT TELL US WHAT TO HIS KNOWLEDGE IS BEST FOR FATHER GEPPETTO, AND THEREFORE THE EMPIRE.
IT'S TRUE. MY SON MAY NOT KNOW EVERYTHING ABOUT THE MUNDY WORLD AND THEIR WAYS, BUT HE CAN'T INTENTIONALLY MISLEAD US.
THEN WE CAN'T INVADE THEM AS PLANNED. IT WOULD BE DISASTROUS FOR US.
I AGREE. WE'VE BEEN WASTING OUR TIME HERE. BEST WE ALL GO HOME.
LUMI, THIS IS YOUR MEETING. WILL YOU END IT OFFICIALLY?
VERY WELL.

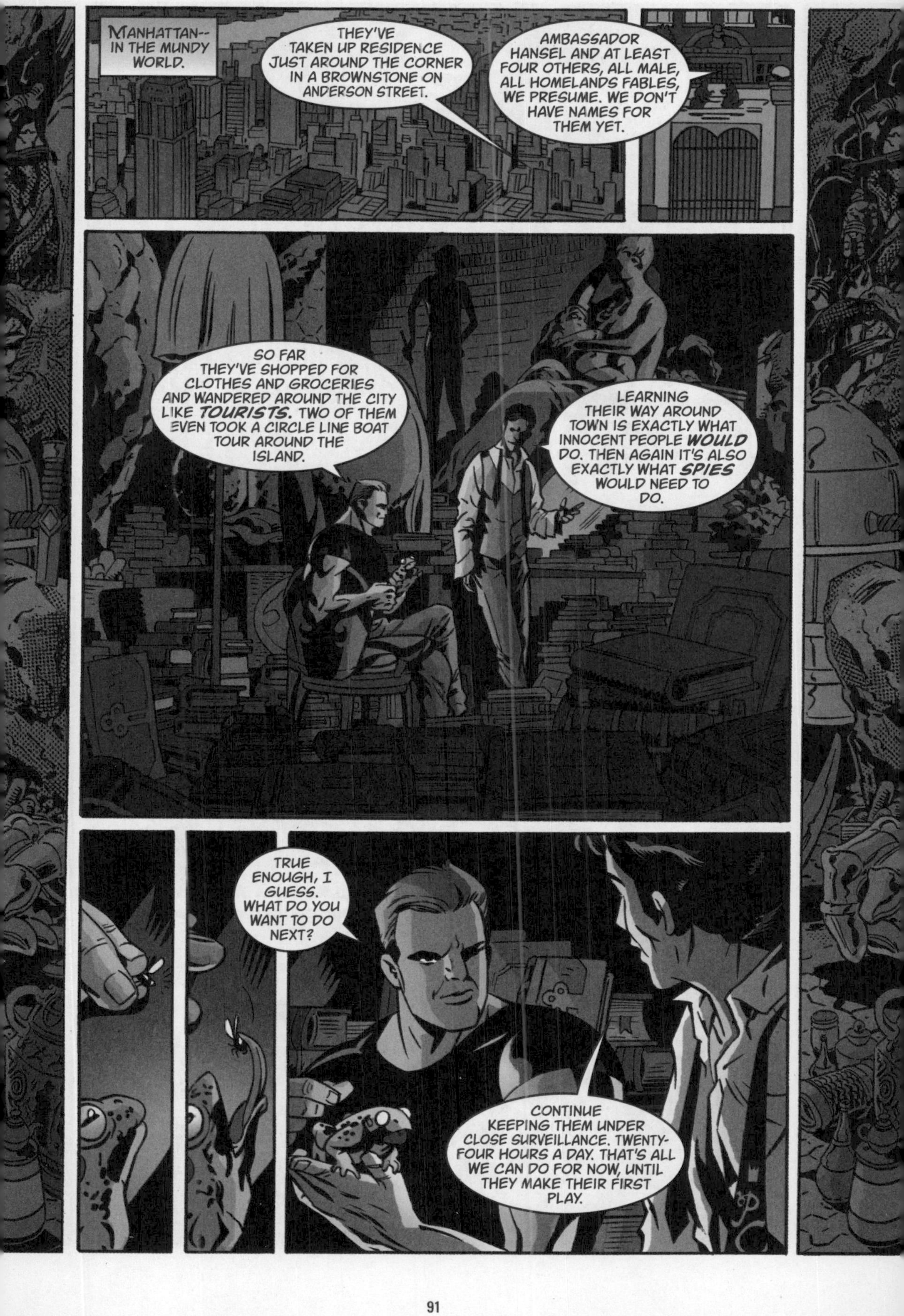
MANHATTAN-- IN THE MUNDY WORLD.
THEY'VE TAKEN UP RESIDENCE JUST AROUND THE CORNER IN A BROWNSTONE ON ANDERSON STREET.
AMBASSADOR HANSEL AND AT LEAST FOUR OTHERS, ALL MALE, ALL HOMELANDS FABLES, WE PRESUME. WE DON'T HAVE NAMES FOR THEM YET.
SO FAR THEY'VE SHOPPED FOR CLOTHES AND GROCERIES AND WANDERED AROUND THE CITY LIKE TOURISTS. TWO OF THEM EVEN TOOK A CIRCLE LINE BOAT TOUR AROUND THE ISLAND.
LEARNING THEIR WAY AROUND TOWN IS EXACTLY WHAT INNOCENT PEOPLE WOULD DO. THEN AGAIN IT'S ALSO EXACTLY WHAT SPIES WOULD NEED TO DO.
TRUE ENOUGH, I GUESS. WHAT DO YOU WANT TO DO NEXT?
CONTINUE KEEPING THEM UNDER CLOSE SURVEILLANCE. TWENTY-FOUR HOURS A DAY. THAT'S ALL WE CAN DO FOR NOW, UNTIL THEY MAKE THEIR FIRST PLAY.

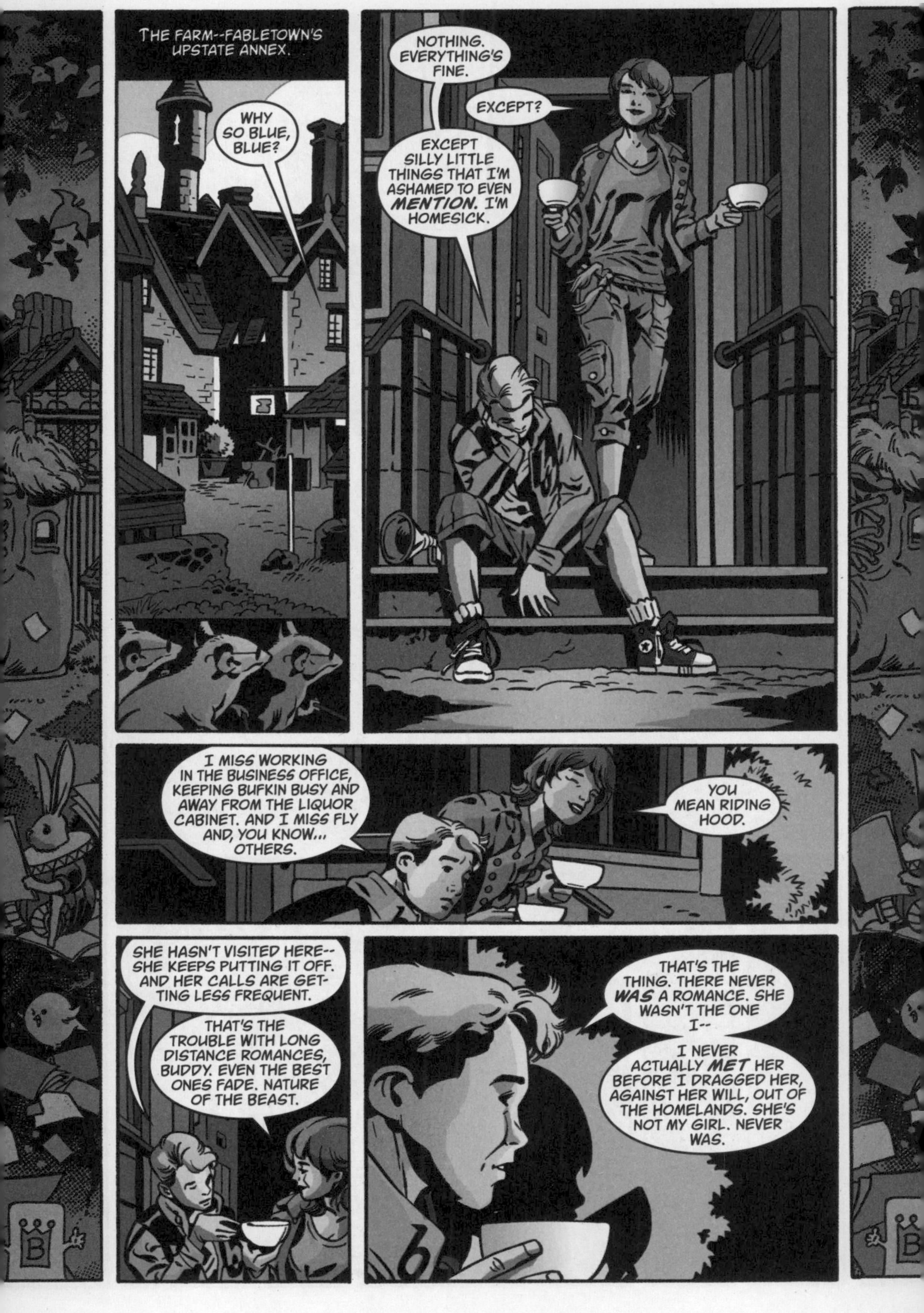
THE FARM--FABLETOWN'S UPSTATE ANNEX.
WHY SO BLUE, BLUE?
NOTHING. EVERYTHING'S FINE.
EXCEPT?
EXCEPT SILLY LITTLE THINGS THAT I'M ASHAMED TO EVEN MENTION. I'M HOMESICK.
I MISS WORKING IN THE BUSINESS OFFICE, KEEPING BUFKIN BUSY AND AWAY FROM THE LIQUOR CABINET. AND I MISS FLY AND, YOU KNOW... OTHERS.
YOU MEAN RIDING HOOD.
SHE HASN'T VISITED HERE-- SHE KEEPS PUTTING IT OFF. AND HER CALLS ARE GETTING LESS FREQUENT.
THAT'S THE TROUBLE WITH LONG DISTANCE ROMANCES, BUDDY. EVEN THE BEST ONES FADE. NATURE OF THE BEAST.
THAT'S THE THING. THERE NEVER WAS A ROMANCE. SHE WASN'T THE ONE I--
I NEVER ACTUALLY MET HER BEFORE I DRAGGED HER, AGAINST HER WILL, OUT OF THE HOMELANDS. SHE'S NOT MY GIRL. NEVER WAS.

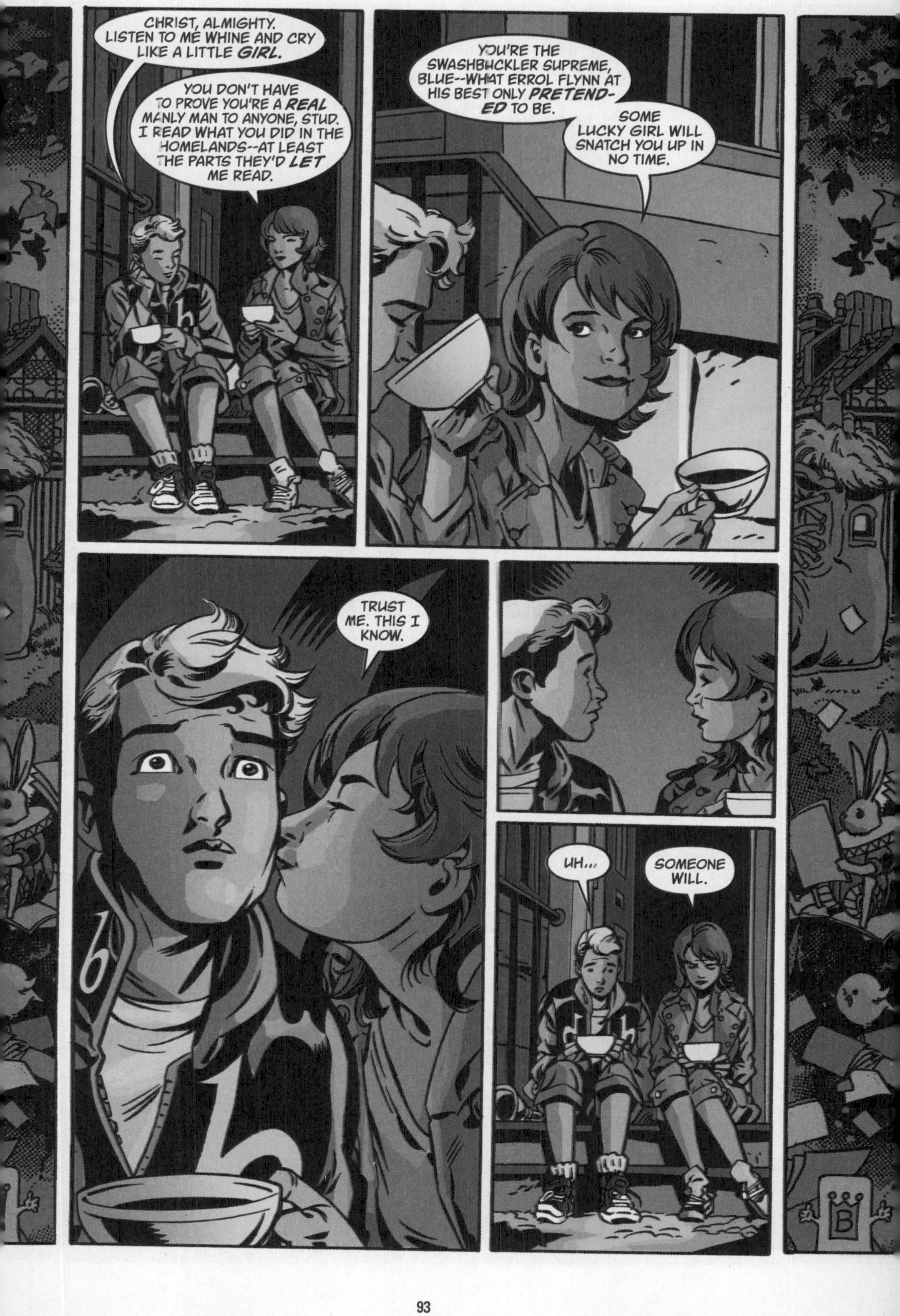
CHRIST, ALMIGHTY. LISTEN TO ME WHINE AND CRY LIKE A LITTLE GIRL.
YOU DON'T HAVE TO PROVE YOU'RE A REAL MANLY MAN TO ANYONE, STUD. I READ WHAT YOU DID IN THE HOMELANDS--AT LEAST THE PARTS THEY'D LET ME READ.
YOU'RE THE SWASHBUCKLER SUPREME, BLUE--WHAT ERROL FLYNN AT HIS BEST ONLY PRETEND-ED TO BE.
SOME LUCKY GIRL WILL SNATCH YOU UP IN NO TIME.
TRUST ME. THIS I KNOW.
UH...
SOMEONE WILL.

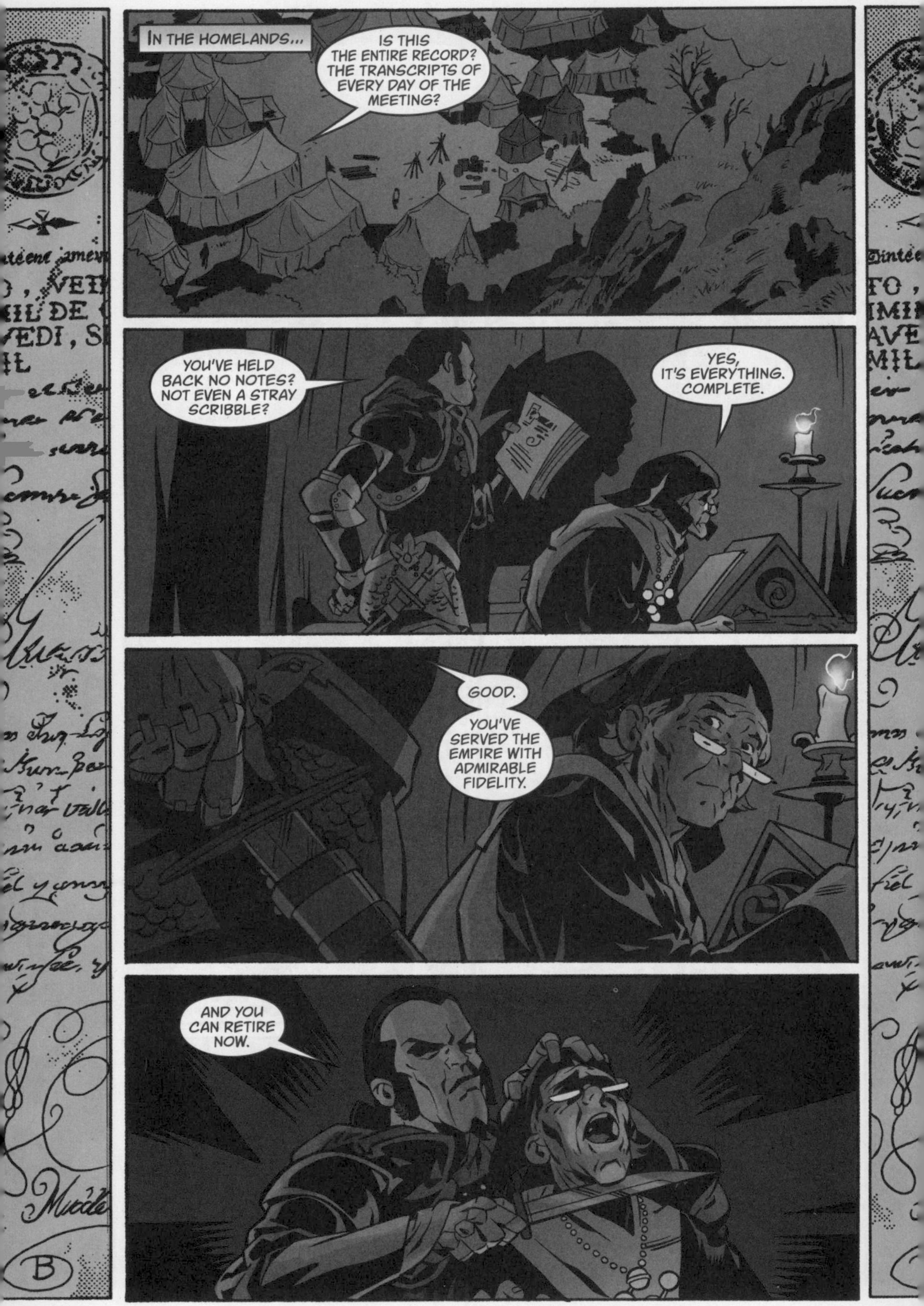
IN THE HOMELANDS...
IS THIS THE ENTIRE RECORD? THE TRANSCRIPTS OF EVERY DAY OF THE MEETING?
YOU'VE HELD BACK NO NOTES? NOT EVEN A STRAY SCRIBBLE?
YES, IT'S EVERYTHING. COMPLETE.
GOOD.
YOU'VE SERVED THE EMPIRE WITH ADMIRABLE FIDELITY.
AND YOU CAN RETIRE NOW.

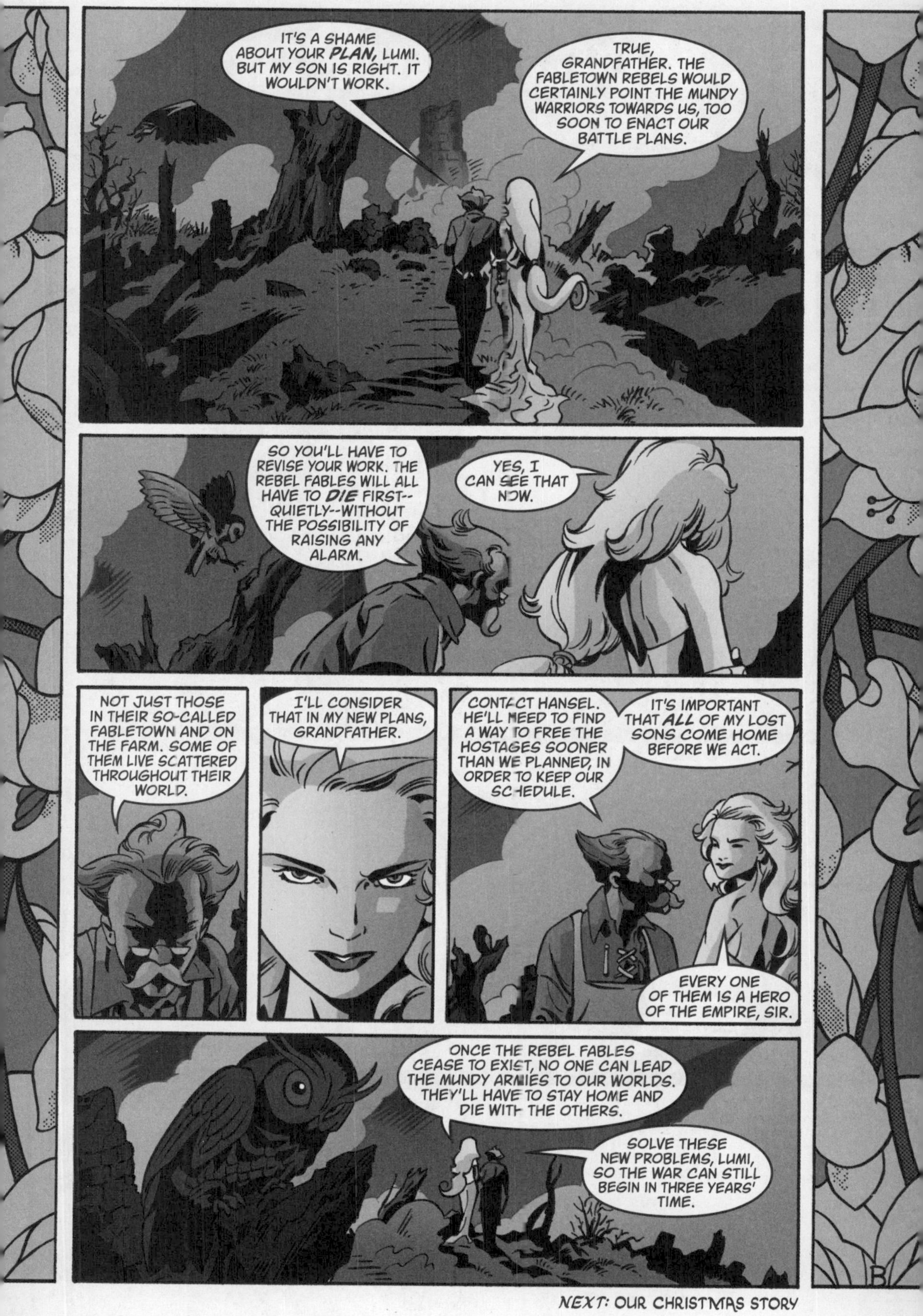

IT'S A SHAME ABOUT YOUR PLAN, LUMI. BUT MY SON IS RIGHT. IT WOULDN'T WORK.
TRUE, GRANDFATHER. THE FABLETOWN REBELS WOULD CERTAINLY POINT THE MUNDY WARRIORS TOWARDS US, TOO SOON TO ENACT OUR BATTLE PLANS.
SO YOU'LL HAVE TO REVISE YOUR WORK. THE REBEL FABLES WILL ALL HAVE TO DIE FIRST--QUIETLY--WITHOUT THE POSSIBILITY OF RAISING ANY ALARM.
YES, I CAN SEE THAT NOW.
NOT JUST THOSE IN THEIR SO-CALLED FABLETOWN AND ON THE FARM. SOME OF THEM LIVE SCATTERED THROUGHOUT THEIR WORLD.
I'LL CONSIDER THAT IN MY NEW PLANS, GRANDFATHER.
CONTACT HANSEL. HE'LL NEED TO FIND A WAY TO FREE THE HOSTAGES SOONER THAN WE PLANNED, IN ORDER TO KEEP OUR SCHEDULE.
IT'S IMPORTANT THAT ALL OF MY LOST SONS COME HOME BEFORE WE ACT.
EVERY ONE OF THEM IS A HERO OF THE EMPIRE, SIR.
ONCE THE REBEL FABLES CEASE TO EXIST, NO ONE CAN LEAD THE MUNDY ARMIES TO OUR WORLDS. THEY'LL HAVE TO STAY HOME AND DIE WITH THE OTHERS.
SOLVE THESE NEW PROBLEMS, LUMI, SO THE WAR CAN STILL BEGIN IN THREE YEARS' TIME.

NEXT: OUR CHRISTMAS STORY

The Road to Paradise

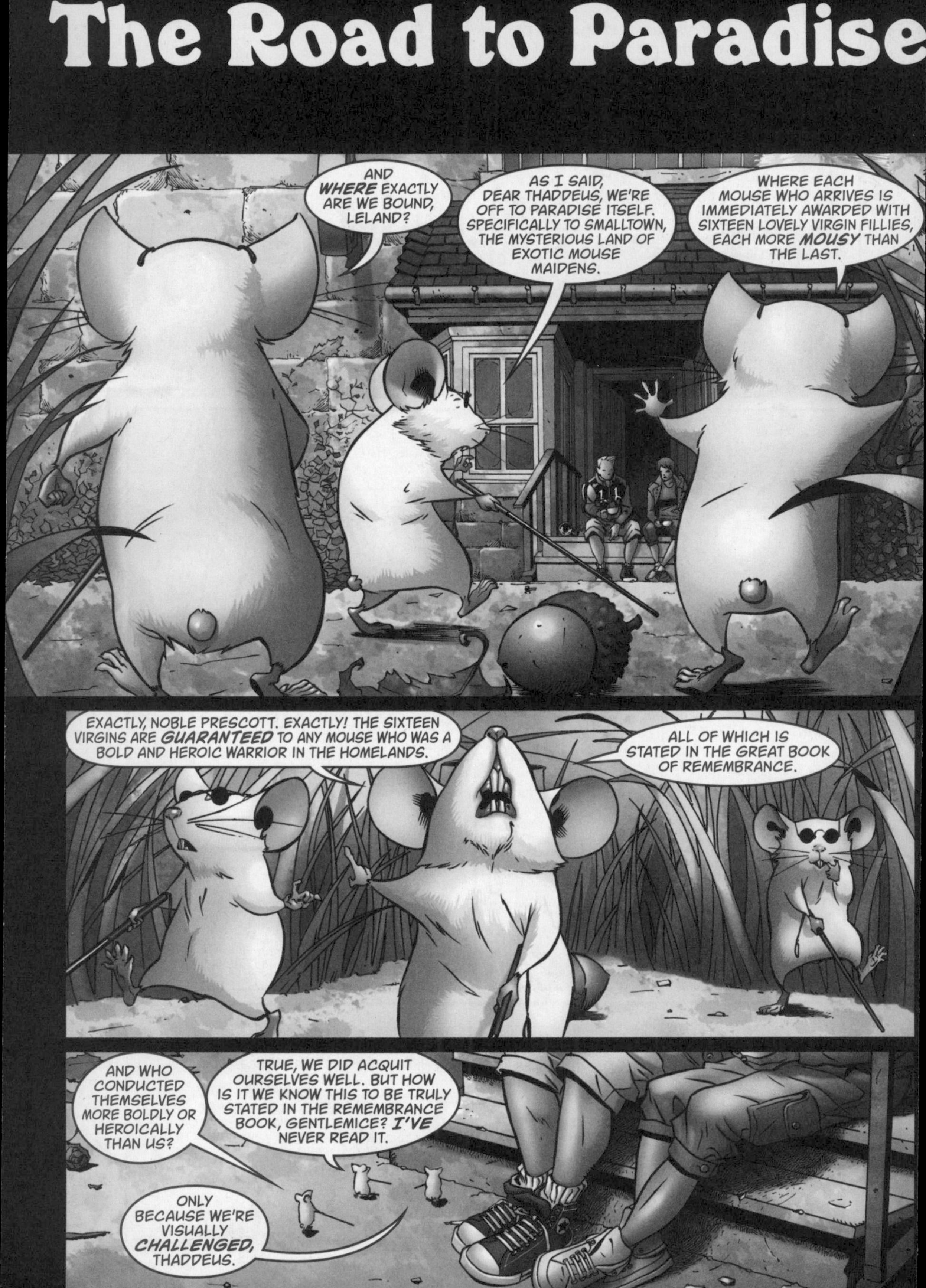

AND WHERE EXACTLY ARE WE BOUND, LELAND?
AS I SAID, DEAR THADDEUS, WE'RE OFF TO PARADISE ITSELF. SPECIFICALLY TO SMALLTOWN, THE MYSTERIOUS LAND OF EXOTIC MOUSE MAIDENS.
WHERE EACH MOUSE WHO ARRIVES IS IMMEDIATELY AWARDED WITH SIXTEEN LOVELY VIRGIN FILLIES, EACH MORE MOUSY THAN THE LAST.
EXACTLY, NOBLE PRESCOTT. EXACTLY! THE SIXTEEN VIRGINS ARE GUARANTEED TO ANY MOUSE WHO WAS A BOLD AND HEROIC WARRIOR IN THE HOMELANDS.
ALL OF WHICH IS STATED IN THE GREAT BOOK OF REMEMBRANCE.
AND WHO CONDUCTED THEMSELVES MORE BOLDLY OR HEROICALLY THAN US?
TRUE, WE DID ACQUIT OURSELVES WELL. BUT HOW IS IT WE KNOW THIS TO BE TRULY STATED IN THE REMEMBRANCE BOOK, GENTLEMICE? I'VE NEVER READ IT.
ONLY BECAUSE WE'RE VISUALLY CHALLENGED, THADDEUS.

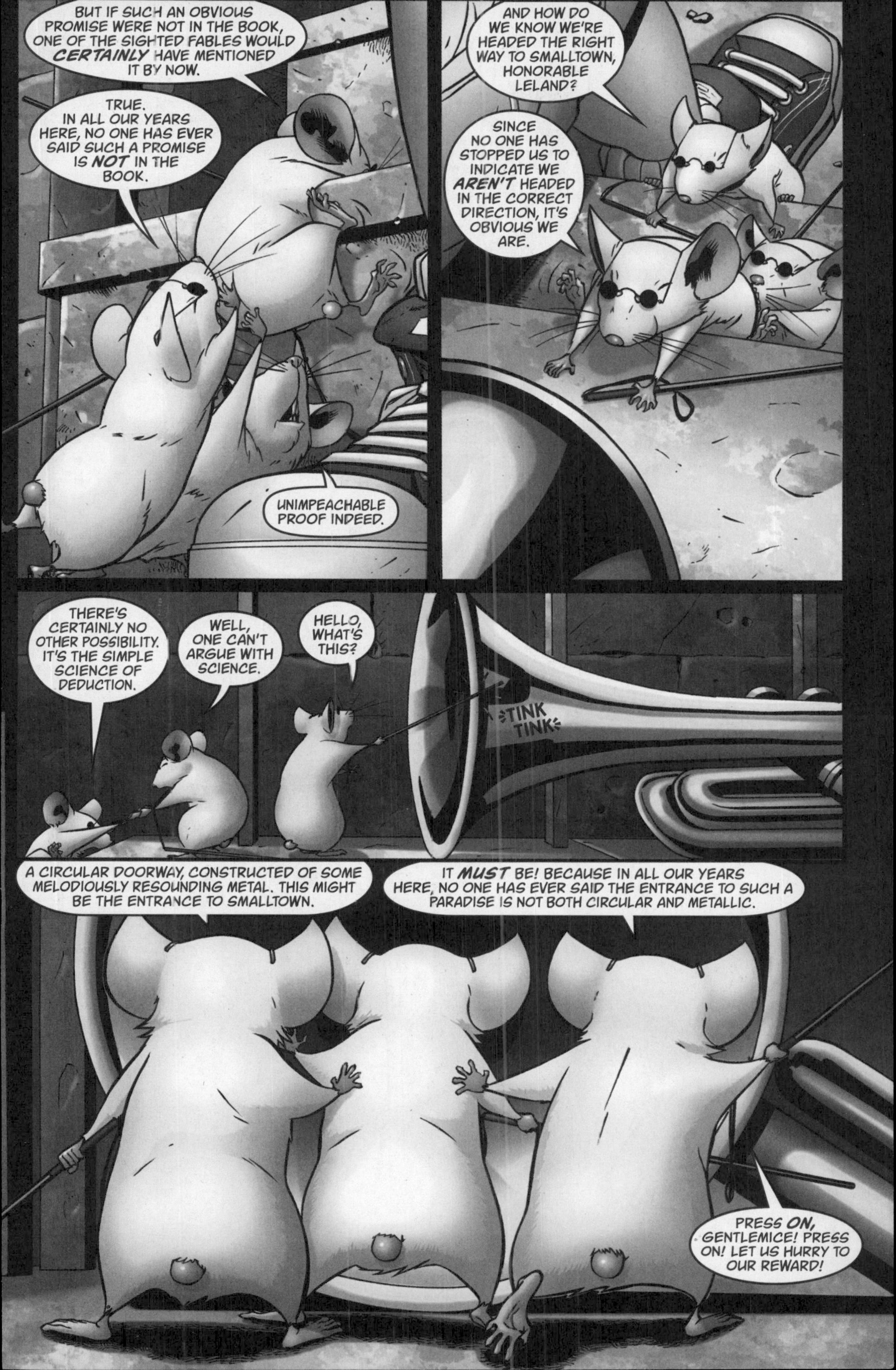

BUT IF SUCH AN OBVIOUS PROMISE WERE NOT IN THE BOOK, ONE OF THE SIGHTED FABLES WOULD CERTAINLY HAVE MENTIONED IT BY NOW.
TRUE. IN ALL OUR YEARS HERE, NO ONE HAS EVER SAID SUCH A PROMISE IS NOT IN THE BOOK.
UNIMPEACHABLE PROOF INDEED.
AND HOW DO WE KNOW WE'RE HEADED THE RIGHT WAY TO SMALLTOWN, HONORABLE LELAND?
SINCE NO ONE HAS STOPPED US TO INDICATE WE AREN'T HEADED IN THE CORRECT DIRECTION, IT'S OBVIOUS WE ARE.
THERE'S CERTAINLY NO OTHER POSSIBILITY. IT'S THE SIMPLE SCIENCE OF DEDUCTION.
WELL, ONE CAN'T ARGUE WITH SCIENCE.
HELLO, WHAT'S THIS?
TINK TINK
A CIRCULAR DOORWAY, CONSTRUCTED OF SOME MELODIOUSLY RESOUNDING METAL. THIS MIGHT BE THE ENTRANCE TO SMALLTOWN.
IT MUST BE! BECAUSE IN ALL OUR YEARS HERE, NO ONE HAS EVER SAID THE ENTRANCE TO SUCH A PARADISE IS NOT BOTH CIRCULAR AND METALLIC.
PRESS ON, GENTLEMICE! PRESS ON! LET US HURRY TO OUR REWARD!

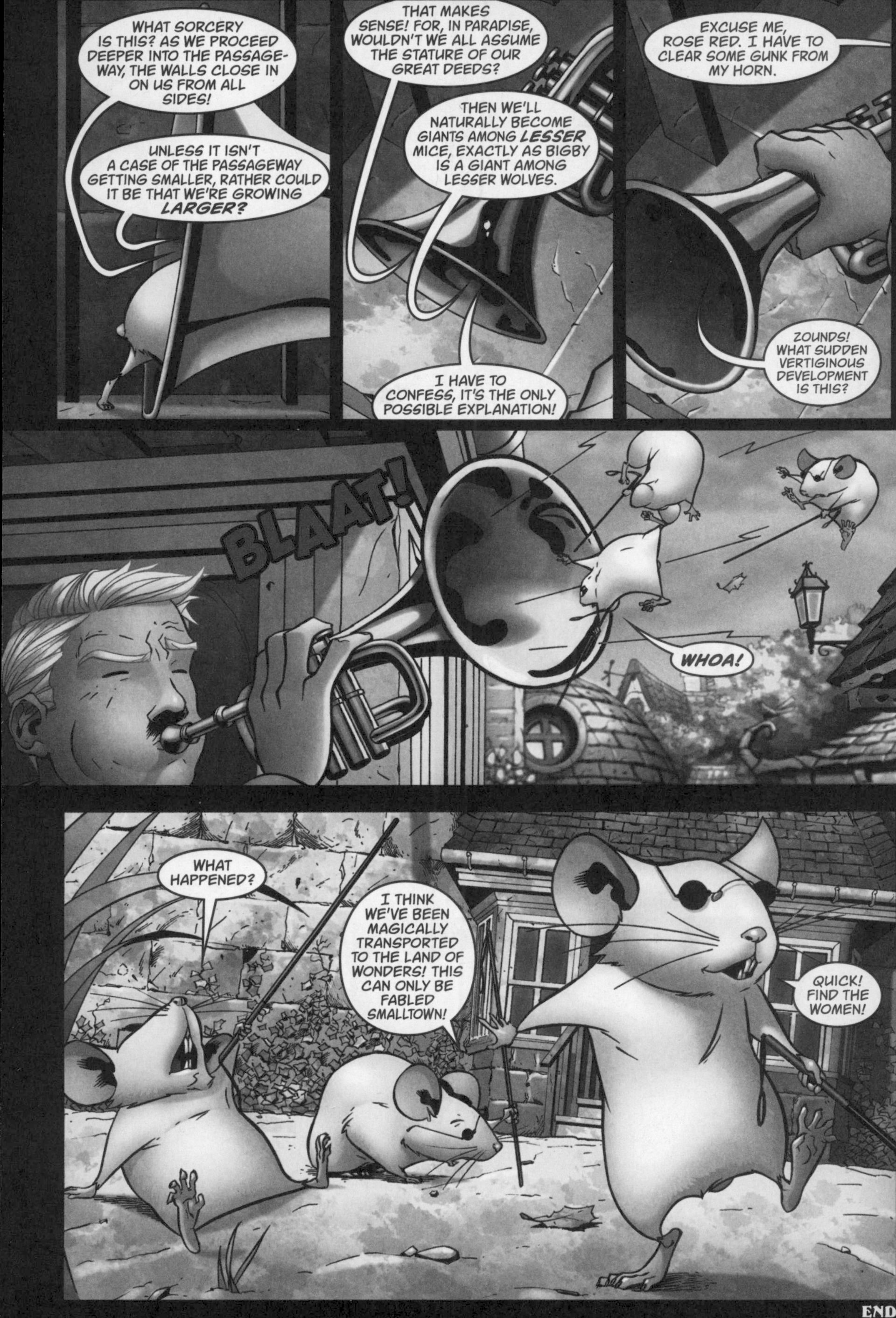
WHAT SORCERY IS THIS? AS WE PROCEED DEEPER INTO THE PASSAGEWAY, THE WALLS CLOSE IN ON US FROM ALL SIDES!
UNLESS IT ISN'T A CASE OF THE PASSAGEWAY GETTING SMALLER, RATHER COULD IT BE THAT WE'RE GROWING LARGER?
THAT MAKES SENSE! FOR, IN PARADISE, WOULDN'T WE ALL ASSUME THE STATURE OF OUR GREAT DEEDS?
THEN WE'LL NATURALLY BECOME GIANTS AMONG LESSER MICE, EXACTLY AS BIGBY IS A GIANT AMONG LESSER WOLVES.
I HAVE TO CONFESS, IT'S THE ONLY POSSIBLE EXPLANATION!
EXCUSE ME, ROSE RED. I HAVE TO CLEAR SOME GUNK FROM MY HORN.
ZOUNDS! WHAT SUDDEN VERTIGINOUS DEVELOPMENT IS THIS?
BLAAT!
WHOA!
WHAT HAPPENED?
I THINK WE'VE BEEN MAGICALLY TRANSPORTED TO THE LAND OF WONDERS! THIS CAN ONLY BE FABLED SMALLTOWN!
QUICK! FIND THE WOMEN!
END

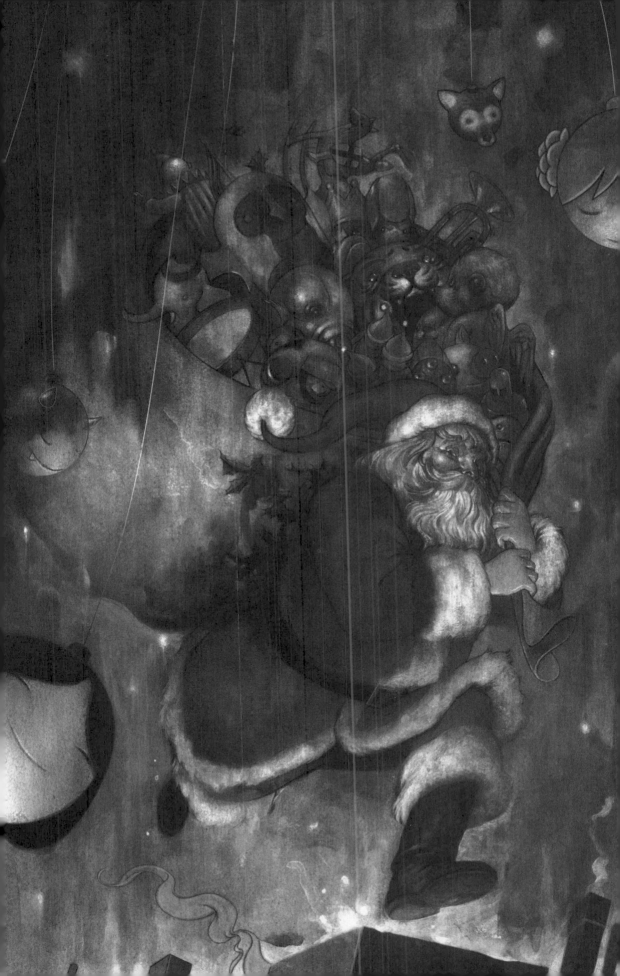

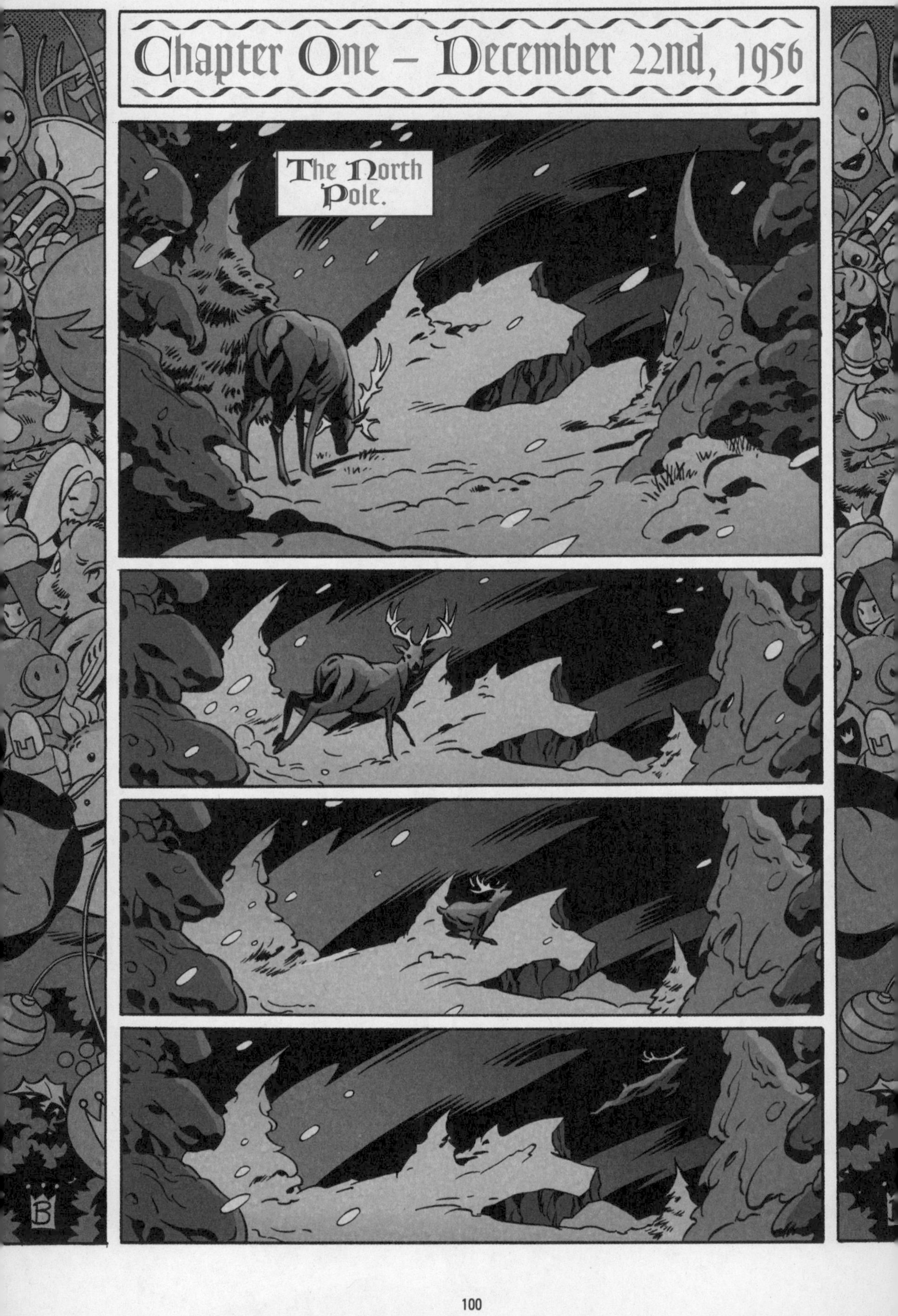
Chapter One – December 22nd, 1956
The North Pole.

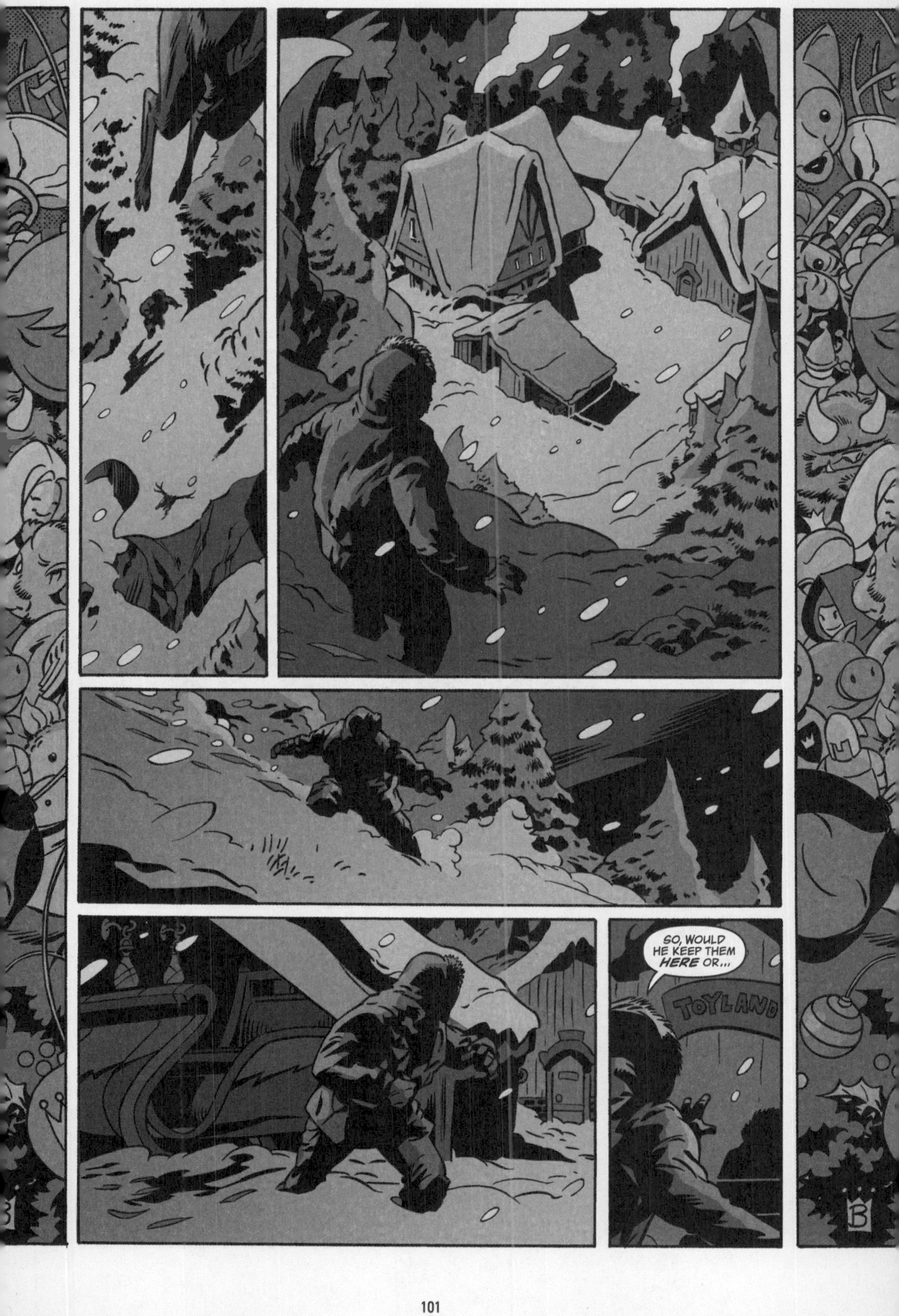
SO, WOULD HE KEEP THEM *HERE* OR...
TOYLAND

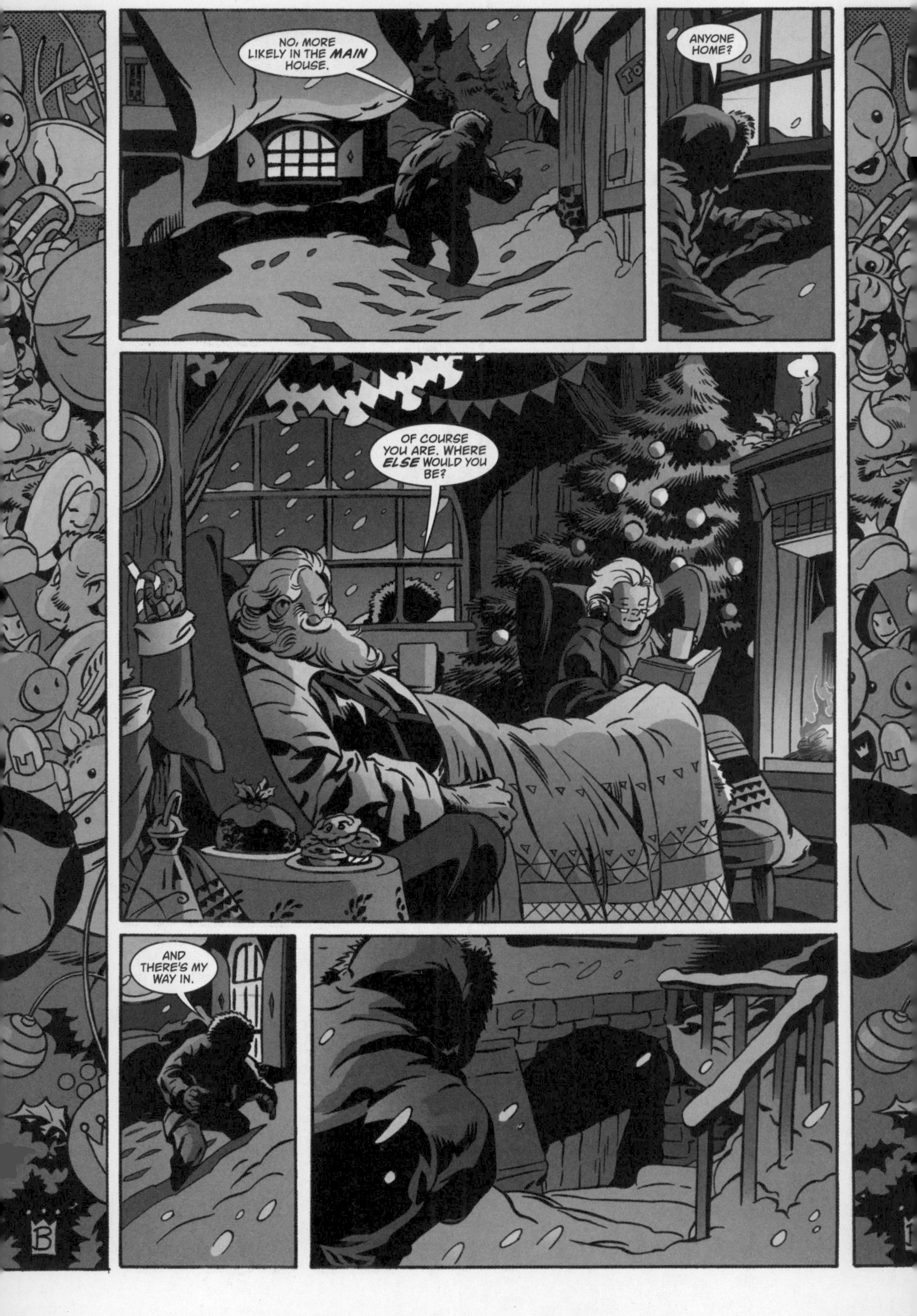
NO, MORE LIKELY IN THE MAIN HOUSE.
ANYONE HOME?
OF COURSE YOU ARE. WHERE ELSE WOULD YOU BE?
AND THERE'S MY WAY IN.

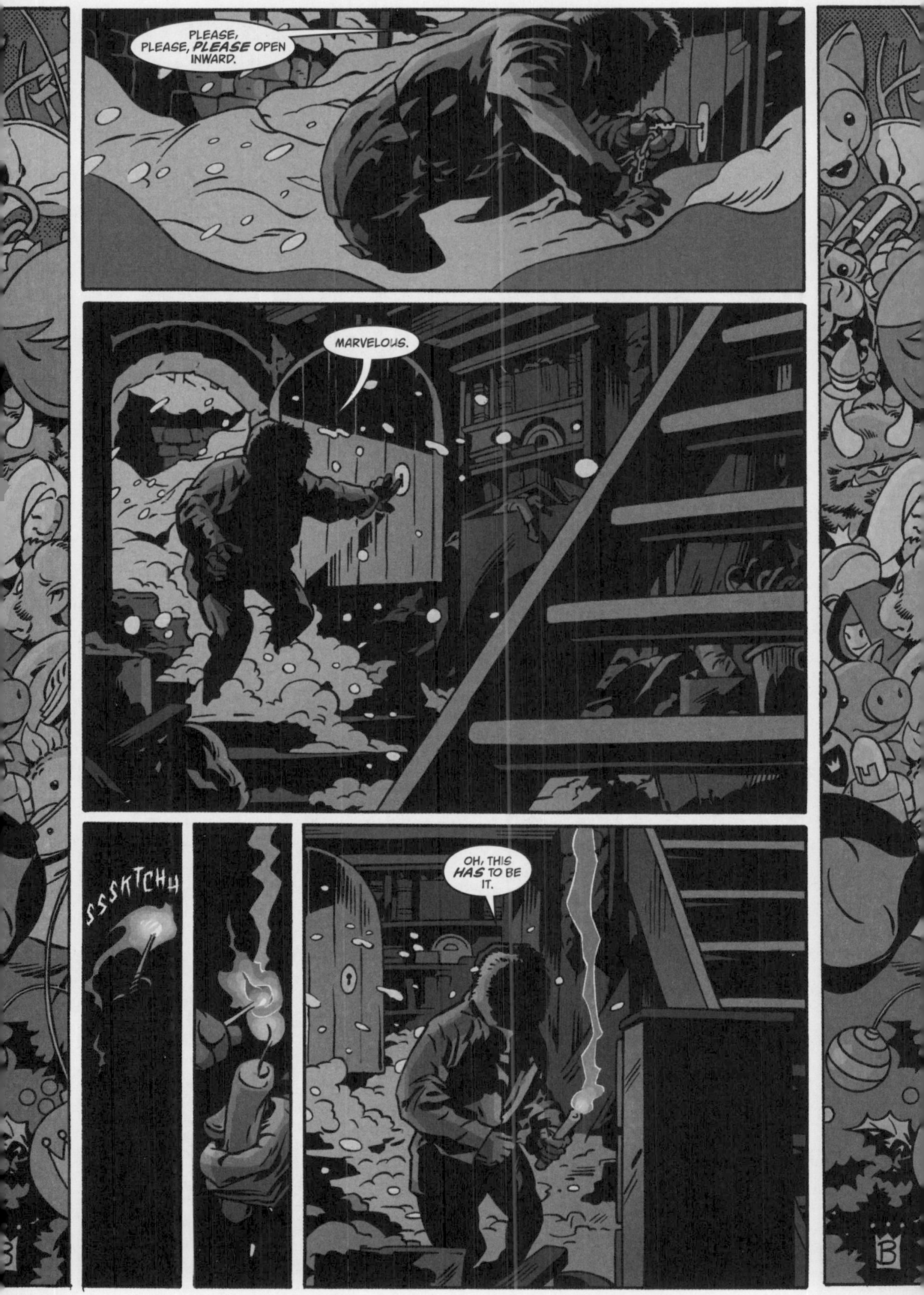
PLEASE, PLEASE, PLEASE OPEN INWARD.
MARVELOUS.
SSSKTCHH
OH, THIS HAS TO BE IT.

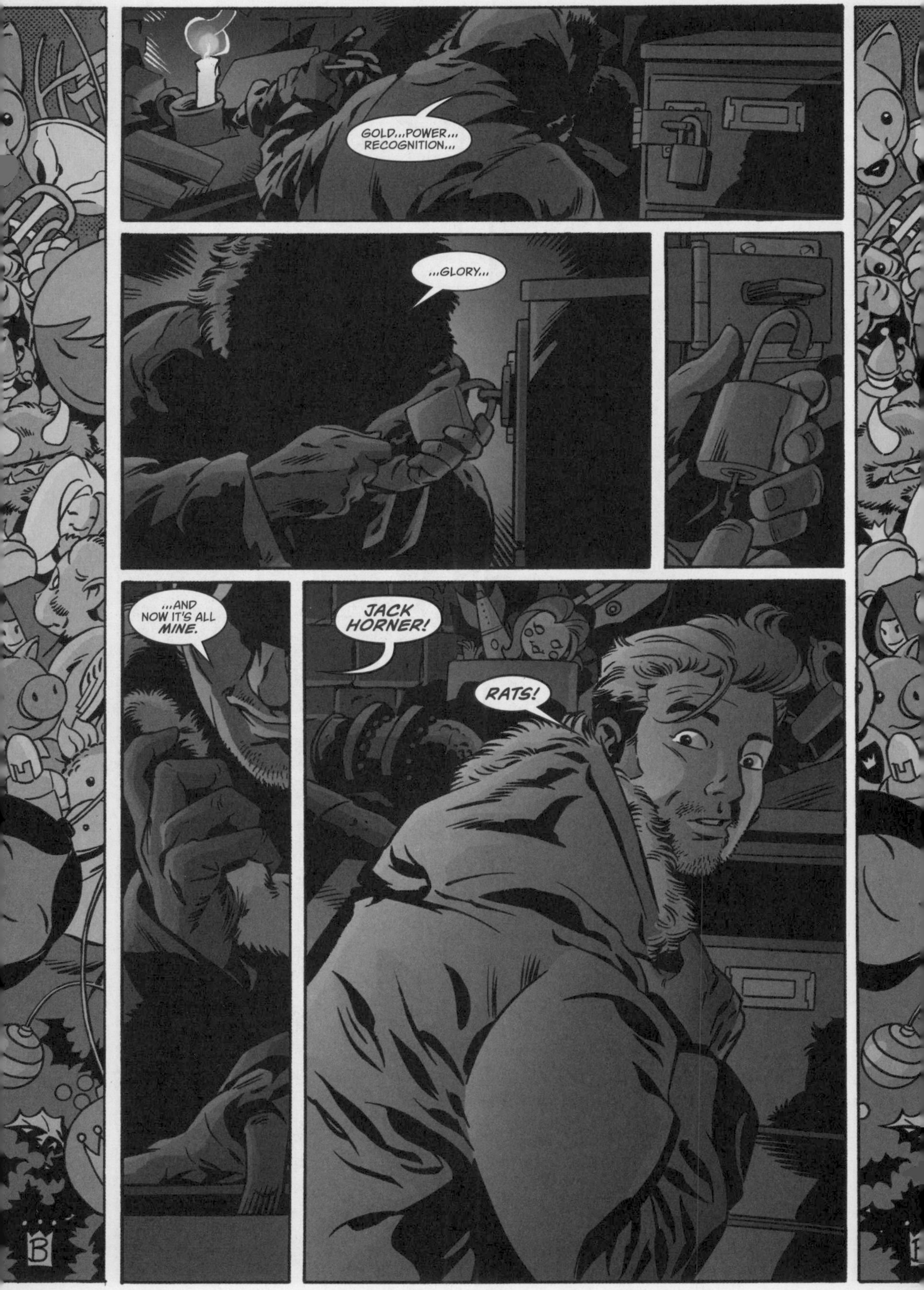
GOLD...POWER... RECOGNITION...
...GLORY...
...AND NOW IT'S ALL MINE.
JACK HORNER!
RATS!

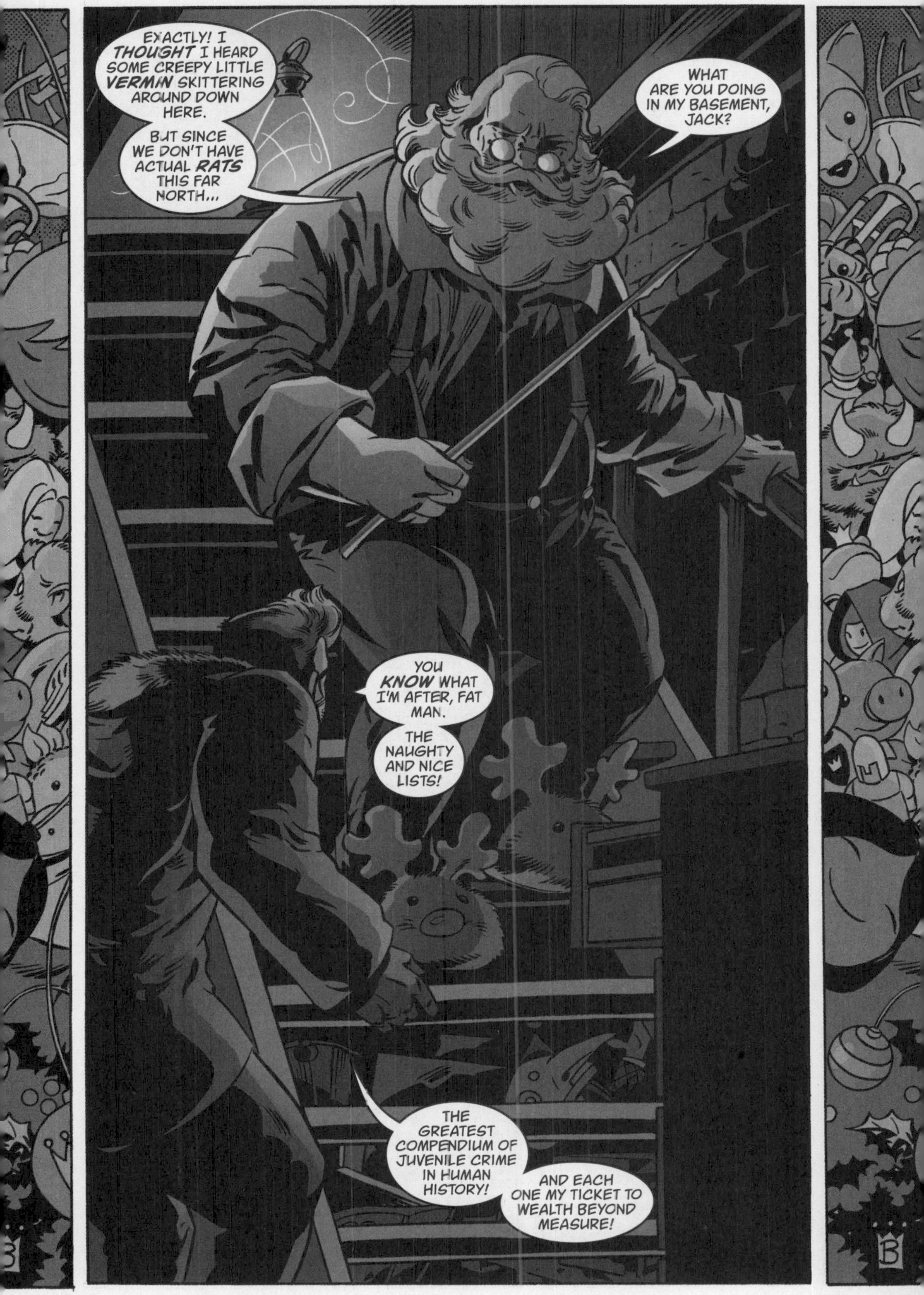
EXACTLY! I THOUGHT I HEARD SOME CREEPY LITTLE VERMIN SKITTERING AROUND DOWN HERE.
BUT SINCE WE DON'T HAVE ACTUAL RATS THIS FAR NORTH...
WHAT ARE YOU DOING IN MY BASEMENT, JACK?
YOU KNOW WHAT I'M AFTER, FAT MAN.
THE NAUGHTY AND NICE LISTS!
THE GREATEST COMPENDIUM OF JUVENILE CRIME IN HUMAN HISTORY!
AND EACH ONE MY TICKET TO WEALTH BEYOND MEASURE!

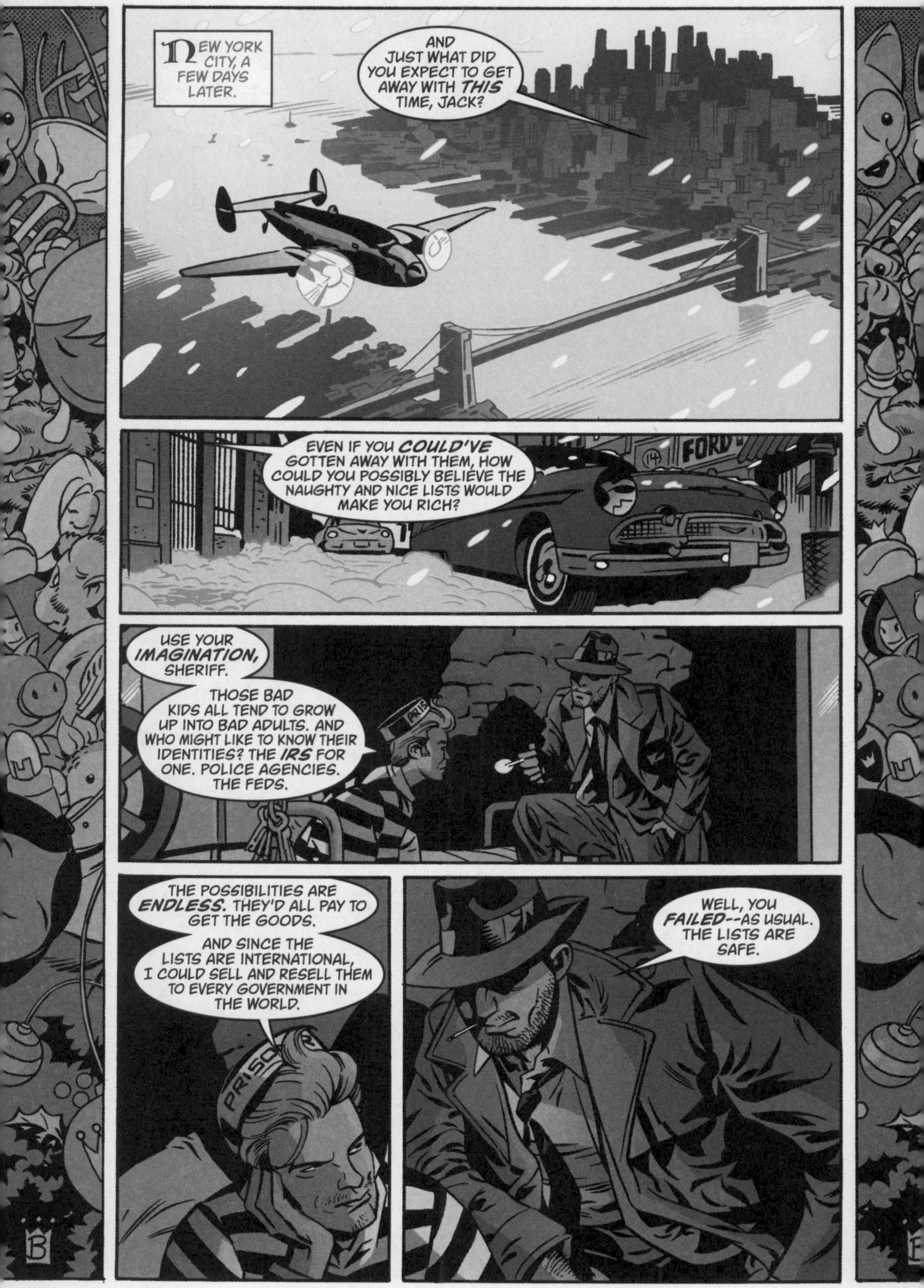
NEW YORK CITY, A FEW DAYS LATER.
AND JUST WHAT DID YOU EXPECT TO GET AWAY WITH THIS TIME, JACK?
EVEN IF YOU COULD'VE GOTTEN AWAY WITH THEM, HOW COULD YOU POSSIBLY BELIEVE THE NAUGHTY AND NICE LISTS WOULD MAKE YOU RICH?
FORD
USE YOUR IMAGINATION, SHERIFF.
THOSE BAD KIDS ALL TEND TO GROW UP INTO BAD ADULTS. AND WHO MIGHT LIKE TO KNOW THEIR IDENTITIES? THE IRS FOR ONE. POLICE AGENCIES. THE FEDS.
THE POSSIBILITIES ARE ENDLESS. THEY'D ALL PAY TO GET THE GOODS.
AND SINCE THE LISTS ARE INTERNATIONAL, I COULD SELL AND RESELL THEM TO EVERY GOVERNMENT IN THE WORLD.
WELL, YOU FAILED--AS USUAL. THE LISTS ARE SAFE.

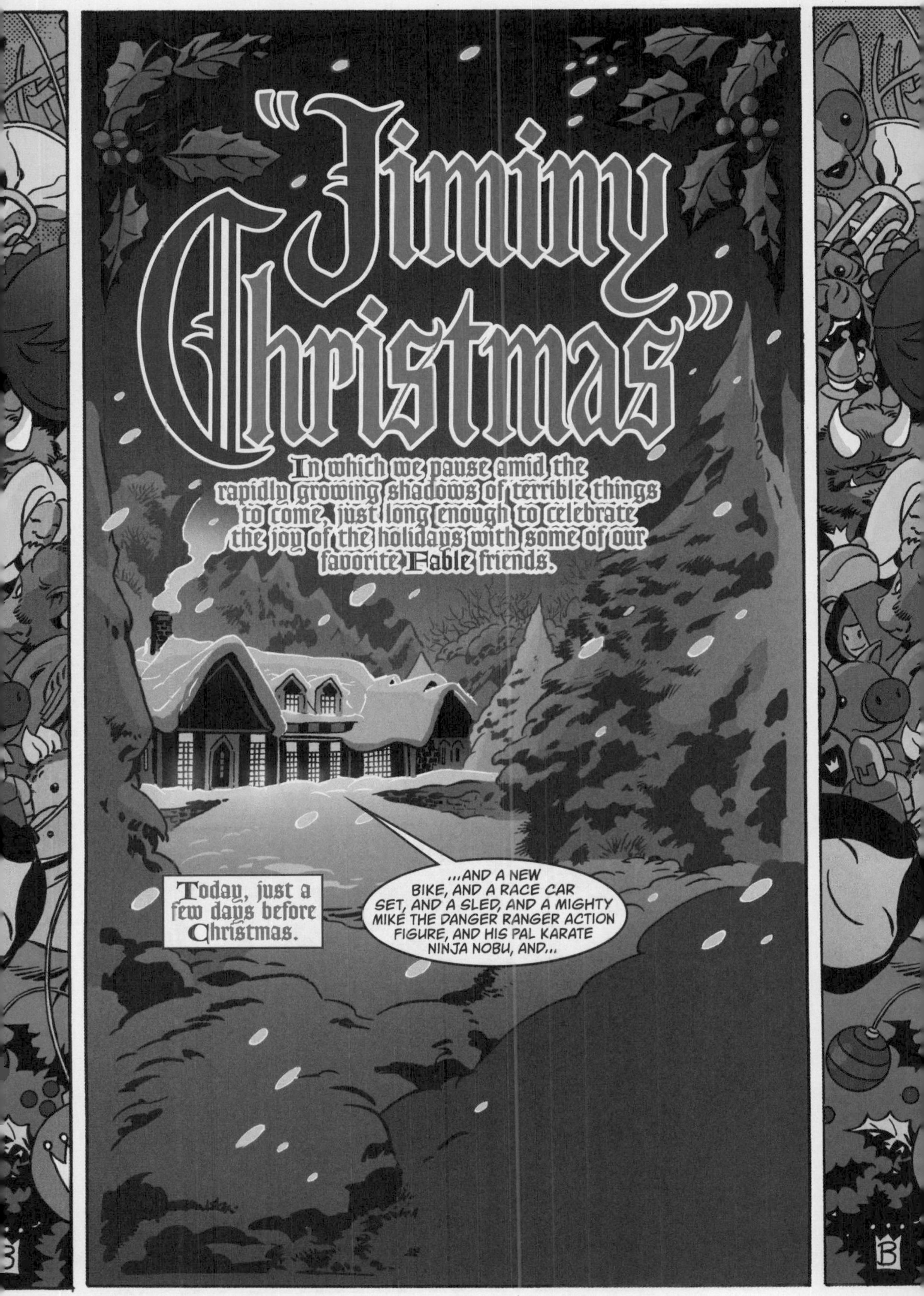
"Jiminy Christmas"
In which we pause amid the rapidly growing shadows of terrible things to come, just long enough to celebrate the joy of the holidays with some of our favorite Fable friends.
Today, just a few days before Christmas.
...AND A NEW BIKE, AND A RACE CAR SET, AND A SLED, AND A MIGHTY MIKE THE DANGER RANGER ACTION FIGURE, AND HIS PAL KARATE NINJA NOBU, AND...

Chapter Two — Wolf Manor

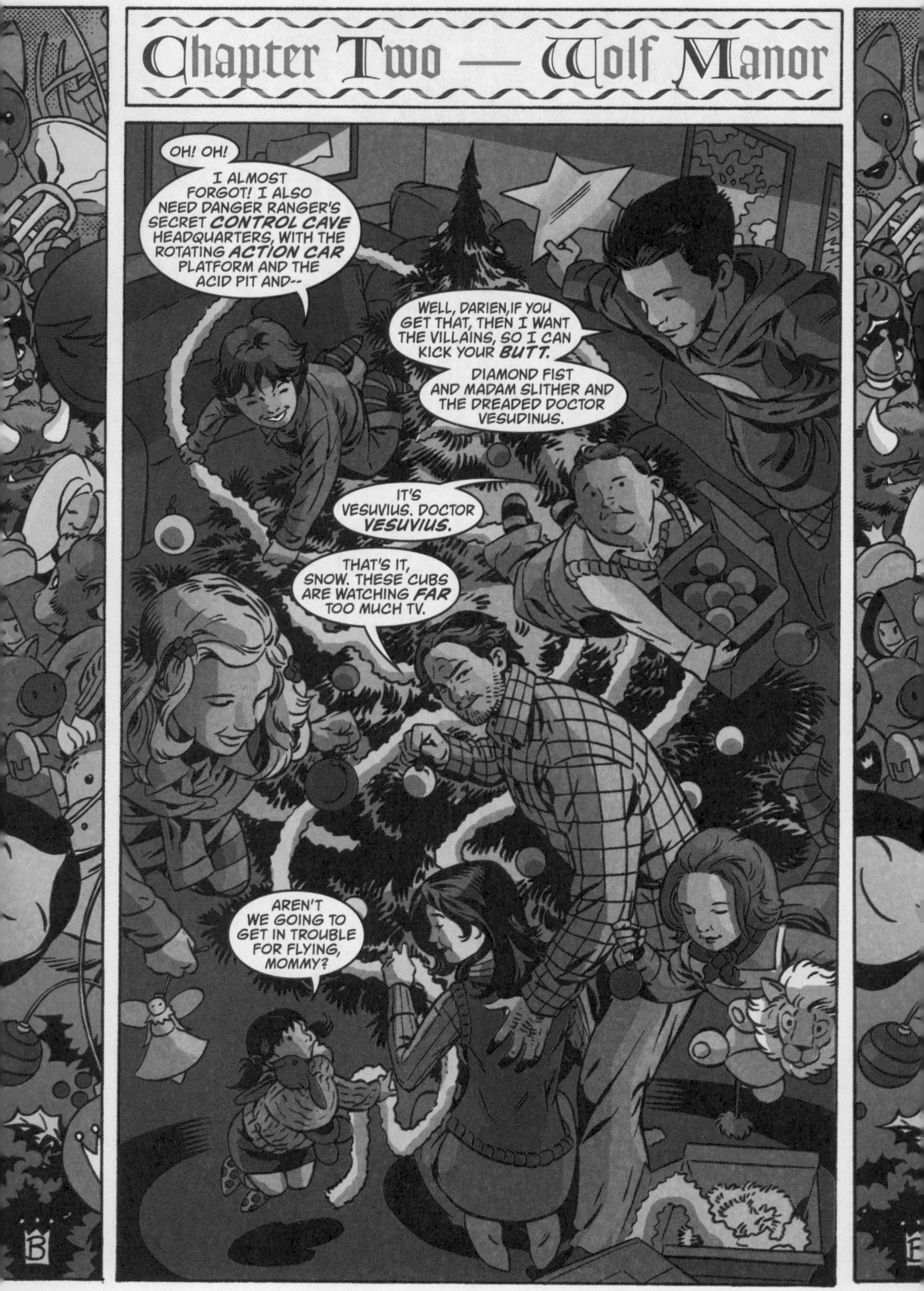
OH! OH!
I ALMOST FORGOT! I ALSO NEED DANGER RANGER'S SECRET CONTROL CAVE HEADQUARTERS, WITH THE ROTATING ACTION CAR PLATFORM AND THE ACID PIT AND--
WELL, DARIEN, IF YOU GET THAT, THEN I WANT THE VILLAINS, SO I CAN KICK YOUR BUTT.
DIAMOND FIST AND MADAM SLITHER AND THE DREADED DOCTOR VESUDINUS.
IT'S VESUVIUS. DOCTOR VESUVIUS.
THAT'S IT, SNOW. THESE CUBS ARE WATCHING FAR TOO MUCH TV.
AREN'T WE GOING TO GET IN TROUBLE FOR FLYING, MOMMY?

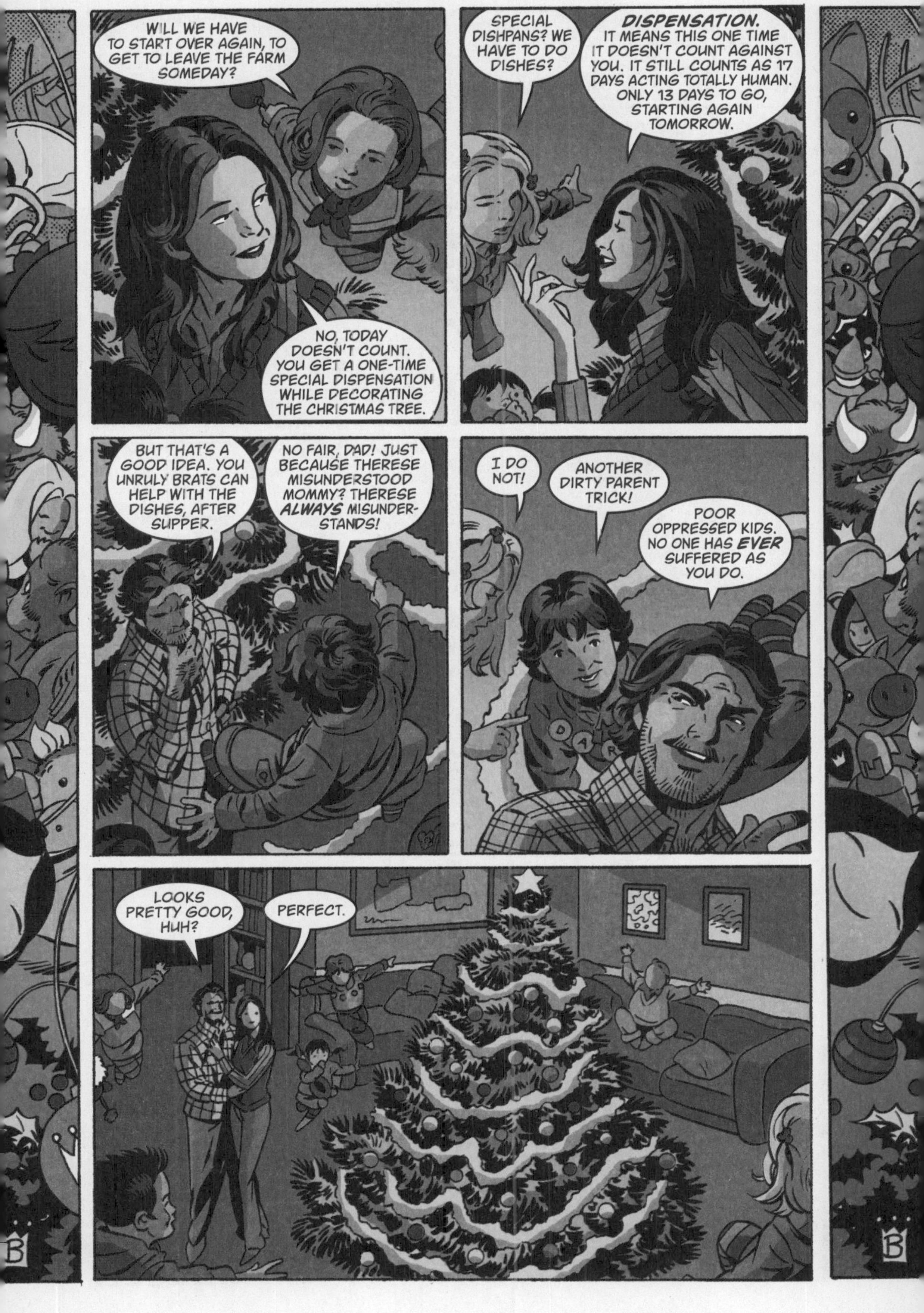
WILL WE HAVE TO START OVER AGAIN, TO GET TO LEAVE THE FARM SOMEDAY?
NO, TODAY DOESN'T COUNT. YOU GET A ONE-TIME SPECIAL DISPENSATION WHILE DECORATING THE CHRISTMAS TREE.
SPECIAL DISHPANS? WE HAVE TO DO DISHES?
DISPENSATION. IT MEANS THIS ONE TIME IT DOESN'T COUNT AGAINST YOU. IT STILL COUNTS AS 17 DAYS ACTING TOTALLY HUMAN. ONLY 13 DAYS TO GO, STARTING AGAIN TOMORROW.
BUT THAT'S A GOOD IDEA. YOU UNRULY BRATS CAN HELP WITH THE DISHES, AFTER SUPPER.
NO FAIR, DAD! JUST BECAUSE THERESE MISUNDERSTOOD MOMMY? THERESE ALWAYS MISUNDERSTANDS!
I DO NOT!
ANOTHER DIRTY PARENT TRICK!
POOR OPPRESSED KIDS. NO ONE HAS EVER SUFFERED AS YOU DO.
LOOKS PRETTY GOOD, HUH?
PERFECT.

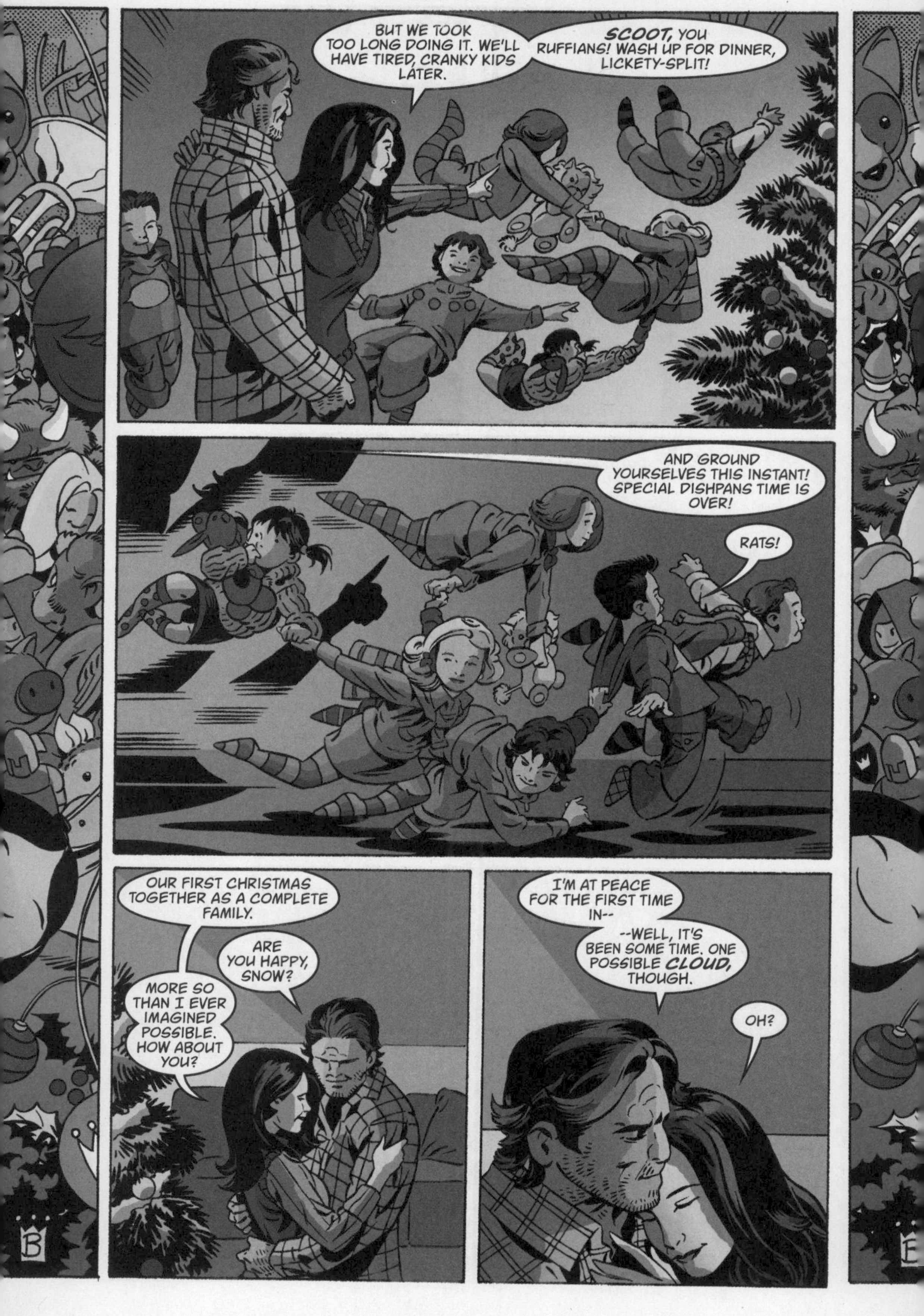

BUT WE TOOK TOO LONG DOING IT. WE'LL HAVE TIRED, CRANKY KIDS LATER.
SCOOT, YOU RUFFIANS! WASH UP FOR DINNER, LICKETY-SPLIT!
AND GROUND YOURSELVES THIS INSTANT! SPECIAL DISHPANS TIME IS OVER!
RATS!
OUR FIRST CHRISTMAS TOGETHER AS A COMPLETE FAMILY.
ARE YOU HAPPY, SNOW?
MORE SO THAN I EVER IMAGINED POSSIBLE. HOW ABOUT YOU?
I'M AT PEACE FOR THE FIRST TIME IN--
--WELL, IT'S BEEN SOME TIME. ONE POSSIBLE CLOUD, THOUGH.
OH?

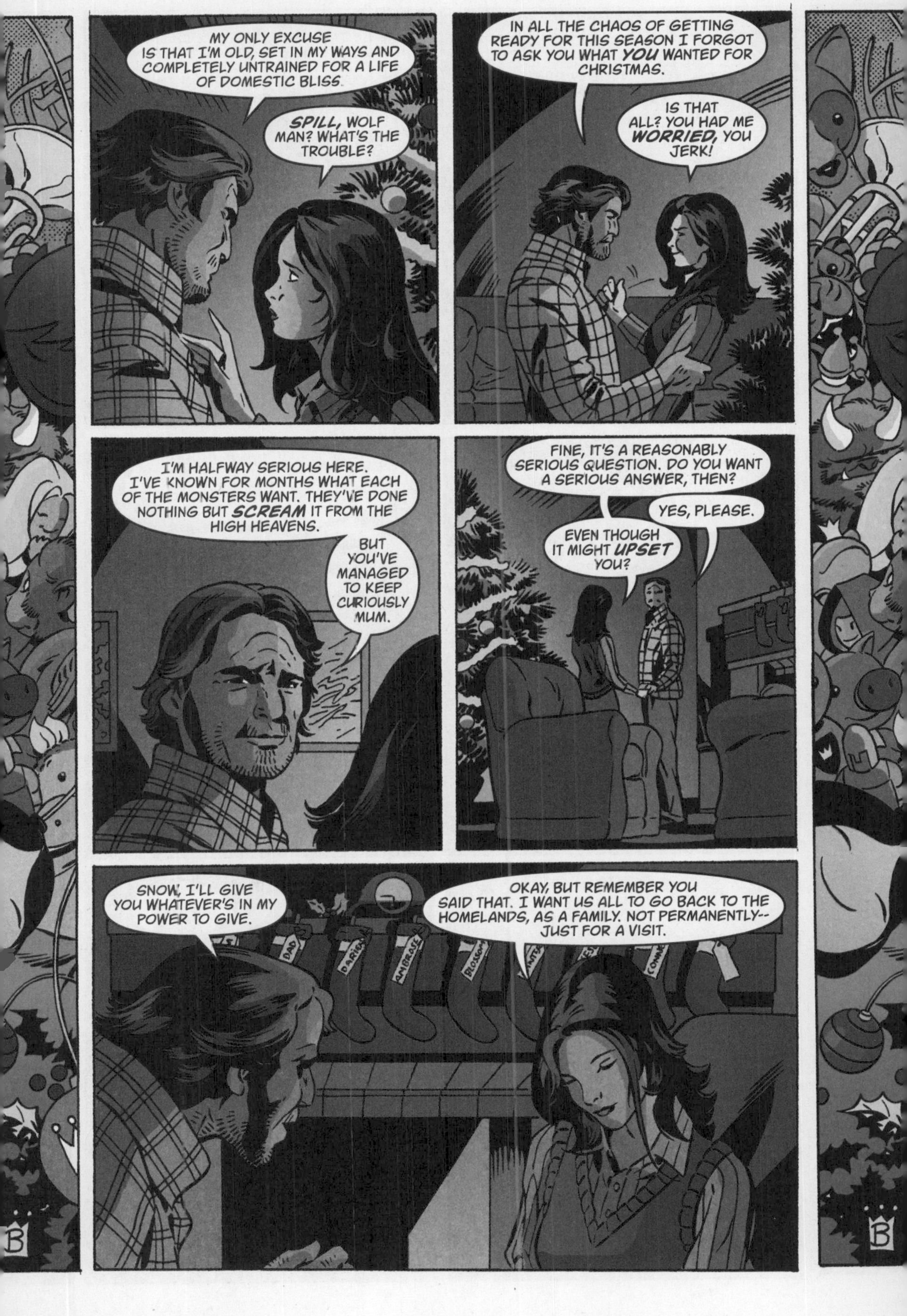
MY ONLY EXCUSE IS THAT I'M OLD, SET IN MY WAYS AND COMPLETELY UNTRAINED FOR A LIFE OF DOMESTIC BLISS.
SPILL, WOLF MAN? WHAT'S THE TROUBLE?
IN ALL THE CHAOS OF GETTING READY FOR THIS SEASON I FORGOT TO ASK YOU WHAT YOU WANTED FOR CHRISTMAS.
IS THAT ALL? YOU HAD ME WORRIED, YOU JERK!
I'M HALFWAY SERIOUS HERE. I'VE KNOWN FOR MONTHS WHAT EACH OF THE MONSTERS WANT. THEY'VE DONE NOTHING BUT SCREAM IT FROM THE HIGH HEAVENS.
BUT YOU'VE MANAGED TO KEEP CURIOUSLY MUM.
FINE, IT'S A REASONABLY SERIOUS QUESTION. DO YOU WANT A SERIOUS ANSWER, THEN?
YES, PLEASE.
EVEN THOUGH IT MIGHT UPSET YOU?
SNOW, I'LL GIVE YOU WHATEVER'S IN MY POWER TO GIVE.
OKAY, BUT REMEMBER YOU SAID THAT. I WANT US ALL TO GO BACK TO THE HOMELANDS, AS A FAMILY. NOT PERMANENTLY-- JUST FOR A VISIT.

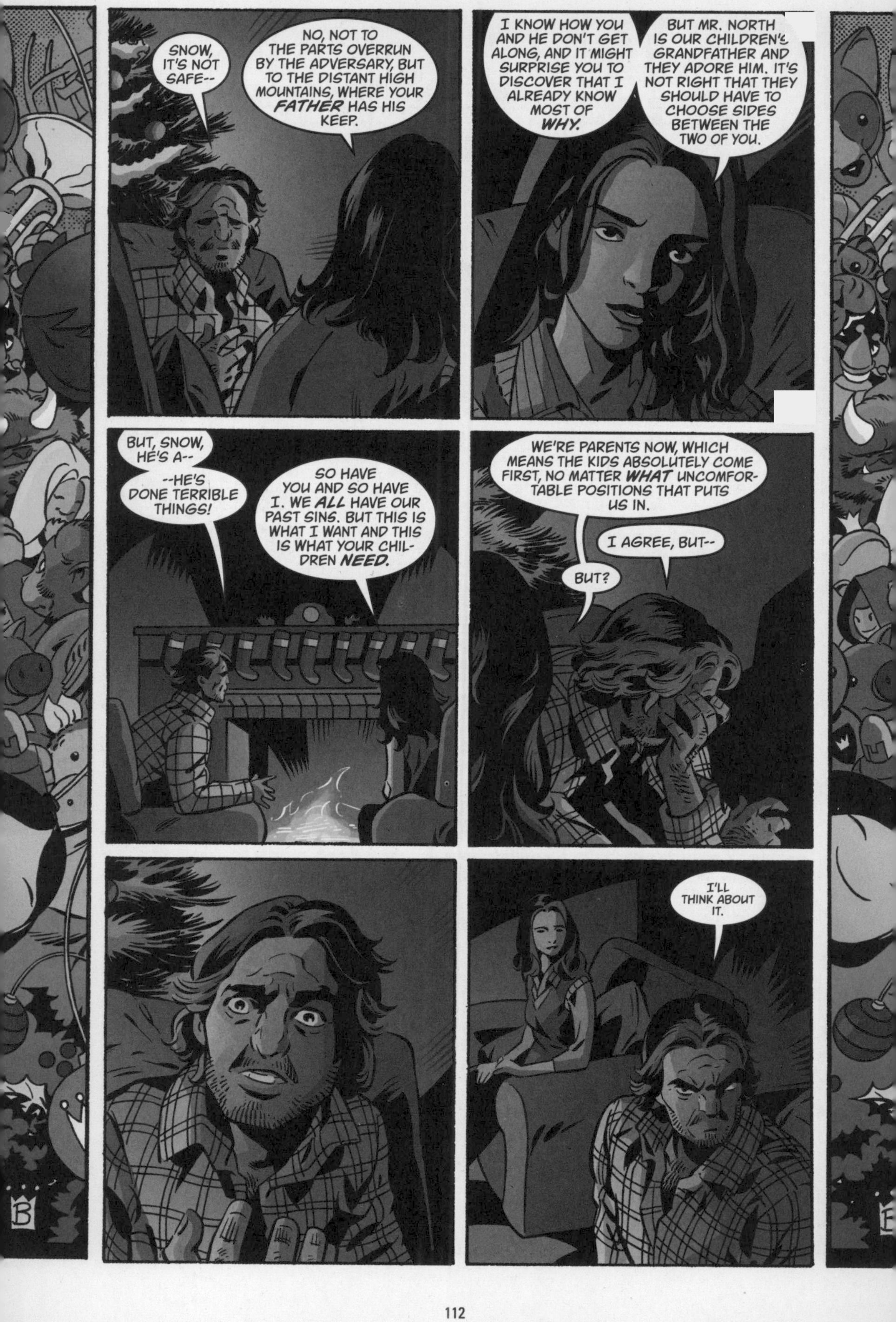
SNOW, IT'S NOT SAFE--
NO, NOT TO THE PARTS OVERRUN BY THE ADVERSARY, BUT TO THE DISTANT HIGH MOUNTAINS, WHERE YOUR FATHER HAS HIS KEEP.
I KNOW HOW YOU AND HE DON'T GET ALONG, AND IT MIGHT SURPRISE YOU TO DISCOVER THAT I ALREADY KNOW MOST OF WHY.
BUT MR. NORTH IS OUR CHILDREN'S GRANDFATHER AND THEY ADORE HIM. IT'S NOT RIGHT THAT THEY SHOULD HAVE TO CHOOSE SIDES BETWEEN THE TWO OF YOU.
BUT, SNOW, HE'S A--
--HE'S DONE TERRIBLE THINGS!
SO HAVE YOU AND SO HAVE I. WE ALL HAVE OUR PAST SINS. BUT THIS IS WHAT I WANT AND THIS IS WHAT YOUR CHILDREN NEED.
WE'RE PARENTS NOW, WHICH MEANS THE KIDS ABSOLUTELY COME FIRST, NO MATTER WHAT UNCOMFORTABLE POSITIONS THAT PUTS US IN.
I AGREE, BUT--
BUT?
I'LL THINK ABOUT IT.

Chapter Three — The Rug

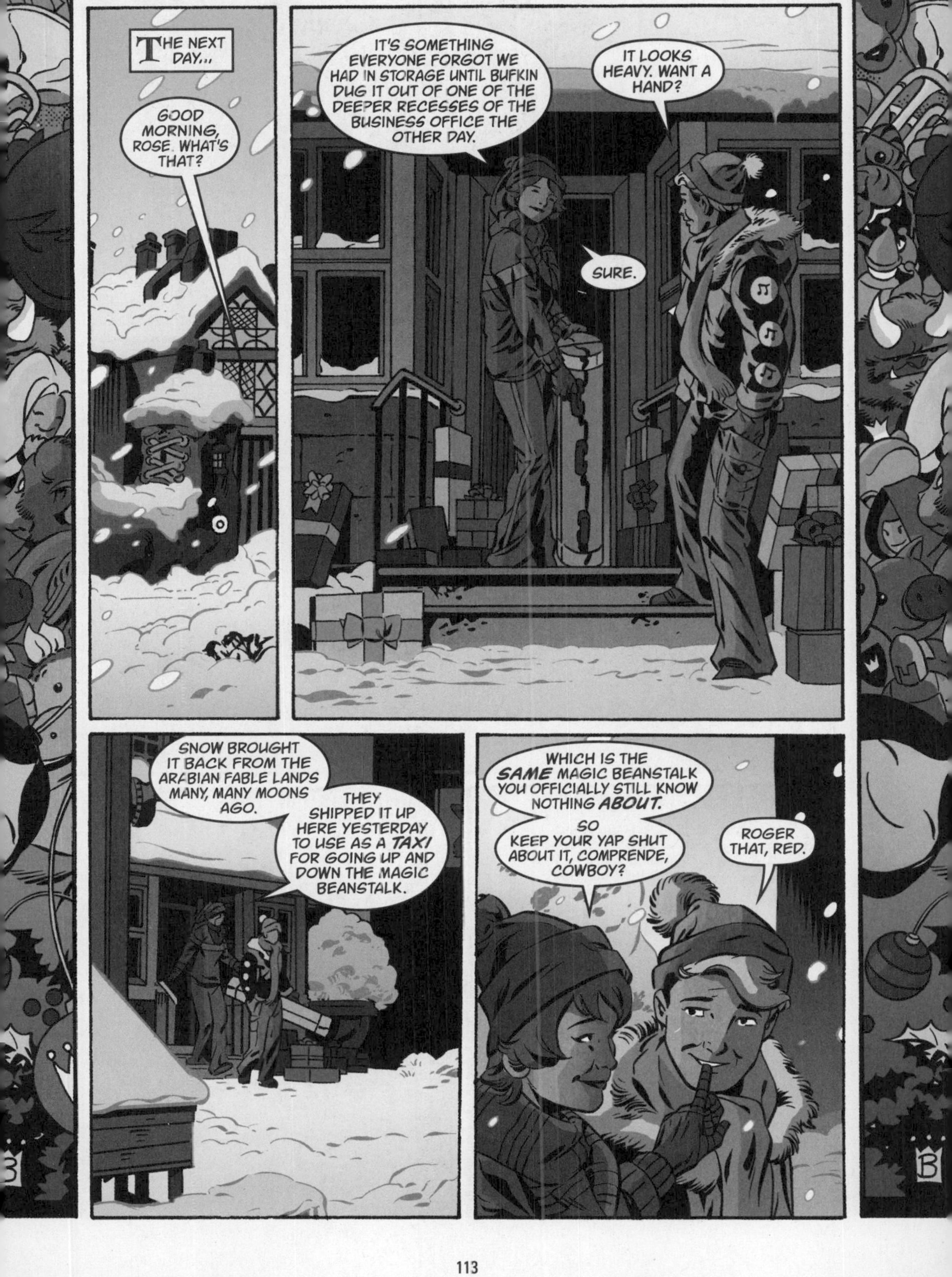

THE NEXT DAY...
GOOD MORNING, ROSE. WHAT'S THAT?
IT'S SOMETHING EVERYONE FORGOT WE HAD IN STORAGE UNTIL BUFKIN DUG IT OUT OF ONE OF THE DEEPER RECESSES OF THE BUSINESS OFFICE THE OTHER DAY.
IT LOOKS HEAVY. WANT A HAND?
SURE.
SNOW BROUGHT IT BACK FROM THE ARABIAN FABLE LANDS MANY, MANY MOONS AGO.
THEY SHIPPED IT UP HERE YESTERDAY TO USE AS A TAXI FOR GOING UP AND DOWN THE MAGIC BEANSTALK.
WHICH IS THE SAME MAGIC BEANSTALK YOU OFFICIALLY STILL KNOW NOTHING ABOUT.
SO KEEP YOUR YAP SHUT ABOUT IT, COMPRENDE, COWBOY?
ROGER THAT, RED.

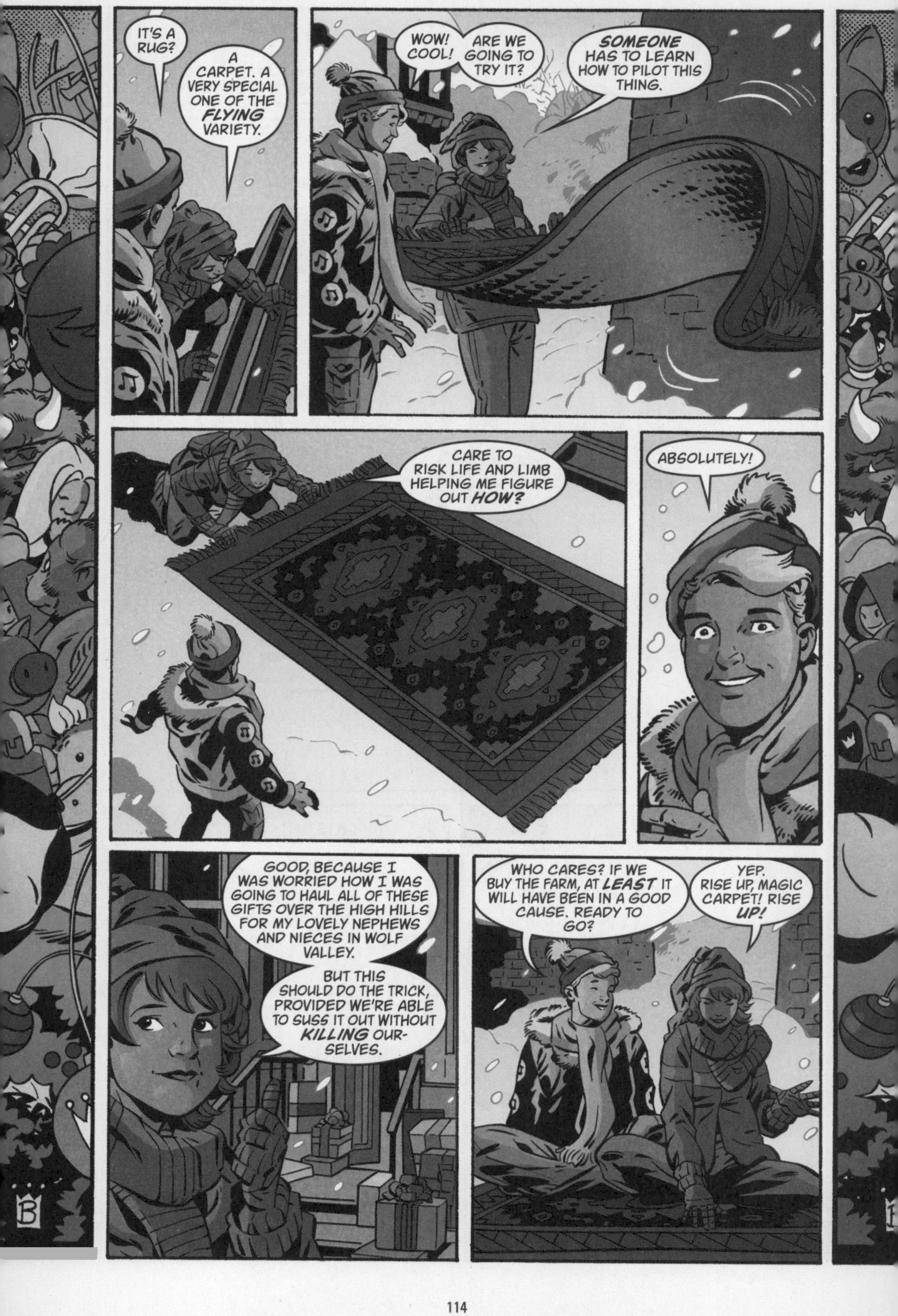
IT'S A RUG?
A CARPET. A VERY SPECIAL ONE OF THE FLYING VARIETY.
WOW! COOL!
ARE WE GOING TO TRY IT?
SOMEONE HAS TO LEARN HOW TO PILOT THIS THING.
CARE TO RISK LIFE AND LIMB HELPING ME FIGURE OUT HOW?
ABSOLUTELY!
GOOD, BECAUSE I WAS WORRIED HOW I WAS GOING TO HAUL ALL OF THESE GIFTS OVER THE HIGH HILLS FOR MY LOVELY NEPHEWS AND NIECES IN WOLF VALLEY.
BUT THIS SHOULD DO THE TRICK, PROVIDED WE'RE ABLE TO SUSS IT OUT WITHOUT KILLING OUR-SELVES.
WHO CARES? IF WE BUY THE FARM, AT LEAST IT WILL HAVE BEEN IN A GOOD CAUSE. READY TO GO?
YEP. RISE UP, MAGIC CARPET! RISE UP!

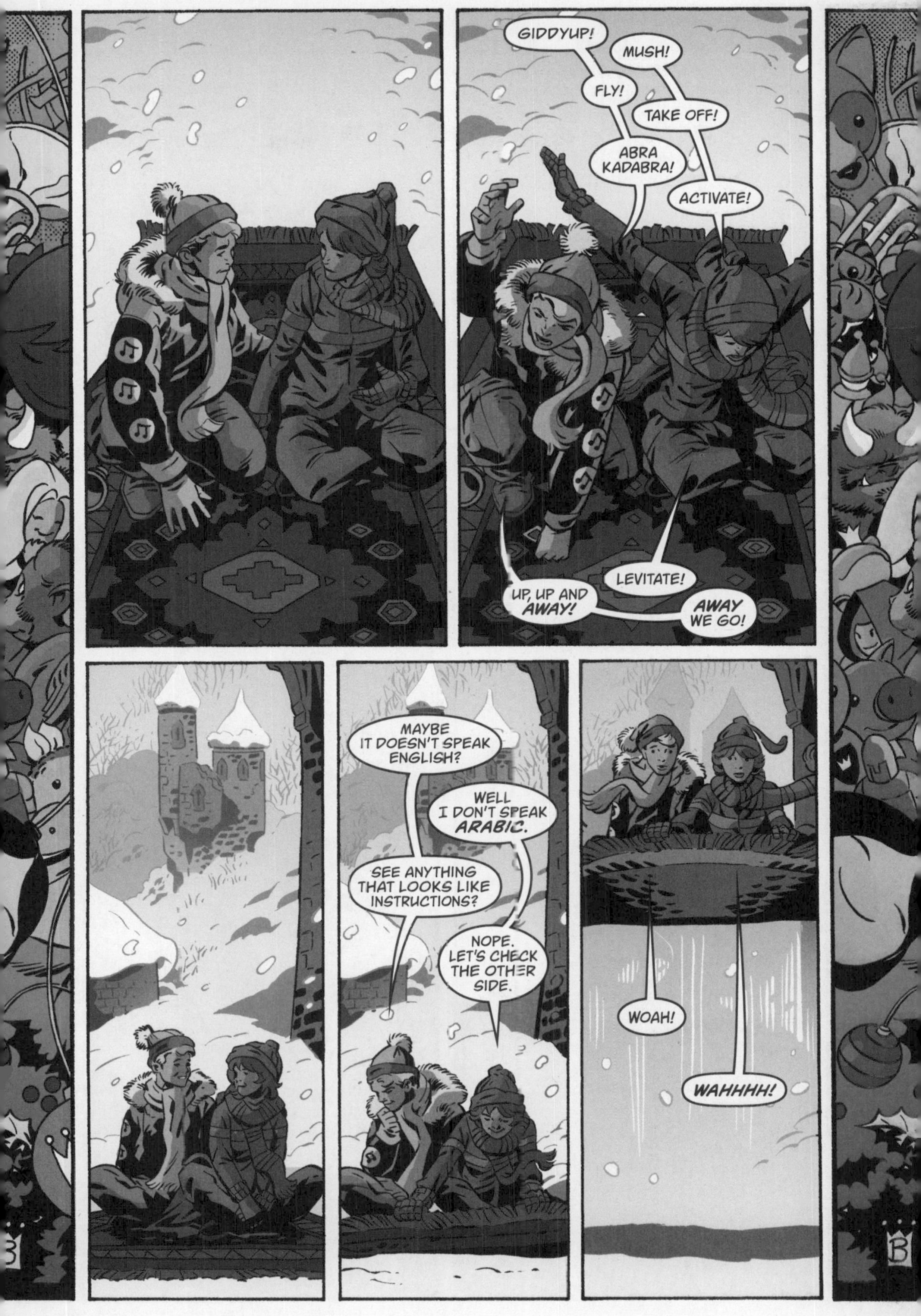
GIDDYUP!
MUSH!
FLY!
TAKE OFF!
ABRA KADABRA!
ACTIVATE!
LEVITATE!
UP, UP AND AWAY!
AWAY WE GO!
MAYBE IT DOESN'T SPEAK ENGLISH?
WELL I DON'T SPEAK ARABIC.
SEE ANYTHING THAT LOOKS LIKE INSTRUCTIONS?
NOPE. LET'S CHECK THE OTHER SIDE.
WOAH!
WAHHHH!

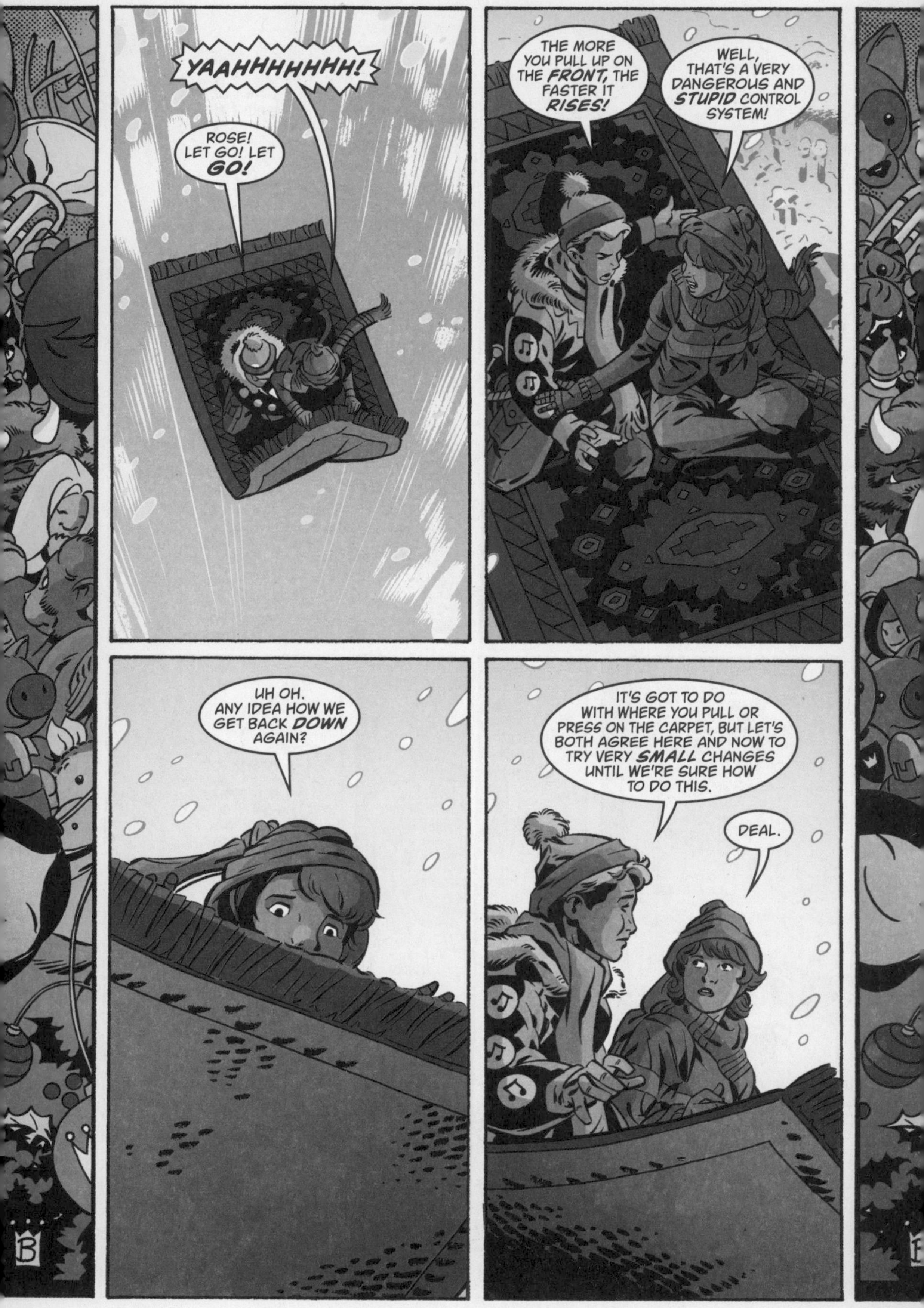
YAAHHHHHHH!
ROSE! LET GO! LET GO!
THE MORE YOU PULL UP ON THE FRONT, THE FASTER IT RISES!
WELL, THAT'S A VERY DANGEROUS AND STUPID CONTROL SYSTEM!
UH OH. ANY IDEA HOW WE GET BACK DOWN AGAIN?
IT'S GOT TO DO WITH WHERE YOU PULL OR PRESS ON THE CARPET, BUT LET'S BOTH AGREE HERE AND NOW TO TRY VERY SMALL CHANGES UNTIL WE'RE SURE HOW TO DO THIS.
DEAL.

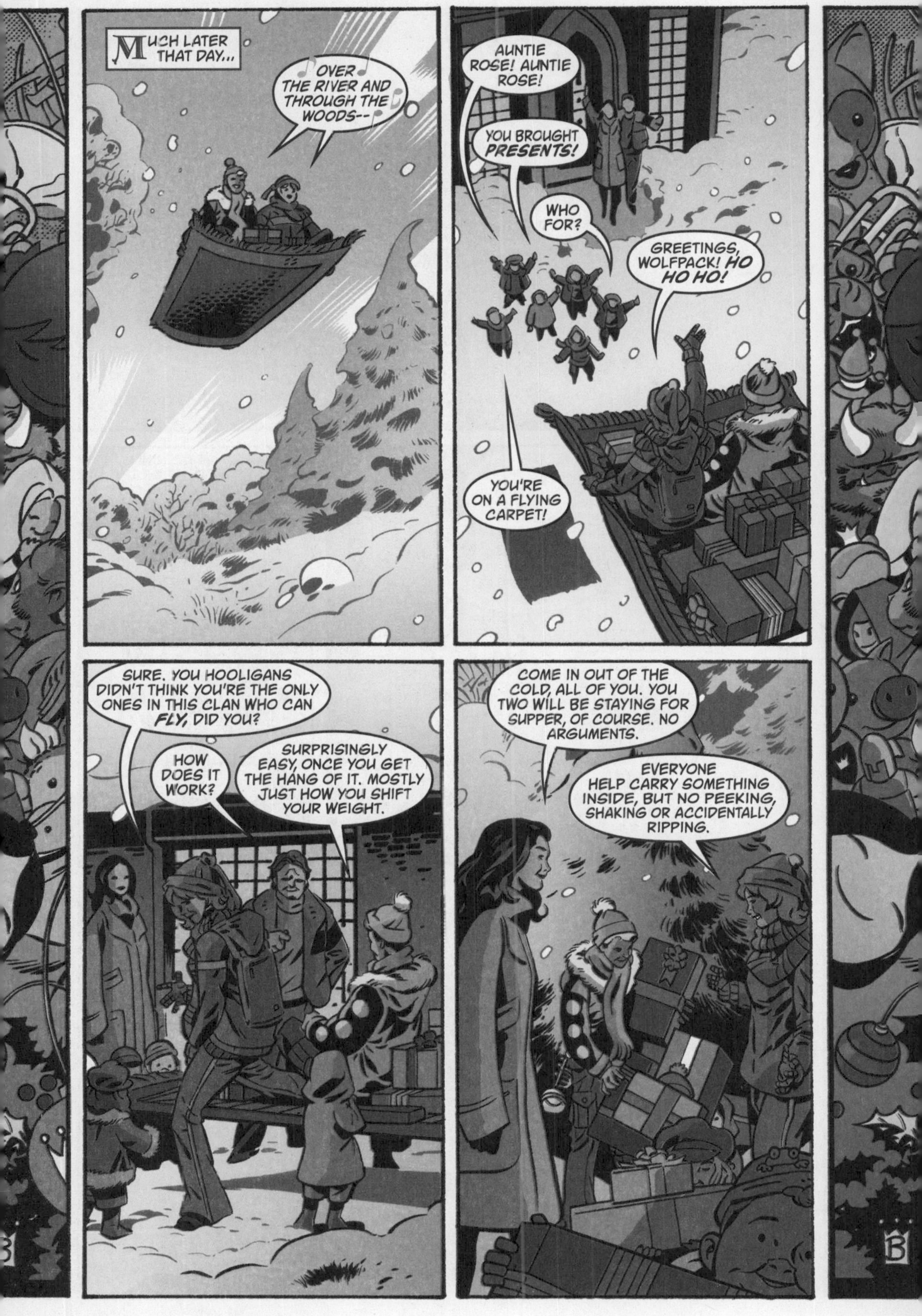
MUCH LATER THAT DAY...
OVER THE RIVER AND THROUGH THE WOODS--
AUNTIE ROSE! AUNTIE ROSE!
YOU BROUGHT PRESENTS!
WHO FOR?
GREETINGS, WOLFPACK! HO HO HO!
YOU'RE ON A FLYING CARPET!
SURE. YOU HOOLIGANS DIDN'T THINK YOU'RE THE ONLY ONES IN THIS CLAN WHO CAN FLY, DID YOU?
HOW DOES IT WORK?
SURPRISINGLY EASY, ONCE YOU GET THE HANG OF IT. MOSTLY JUST HOW YOU SHIFT YOUR WEIGHT.
COME IN OUT OF THE COLD, ALL OF YOU. YOU TWO WILL BE STAYING FOR SUPPER, OF COURSE. NO ARGUMENTS.
EVERYONE HELP CARRY SOMETHING INSIDE, BUT NO PEEKING, SHAKING OR ACCIDENTALLY RIPPING.

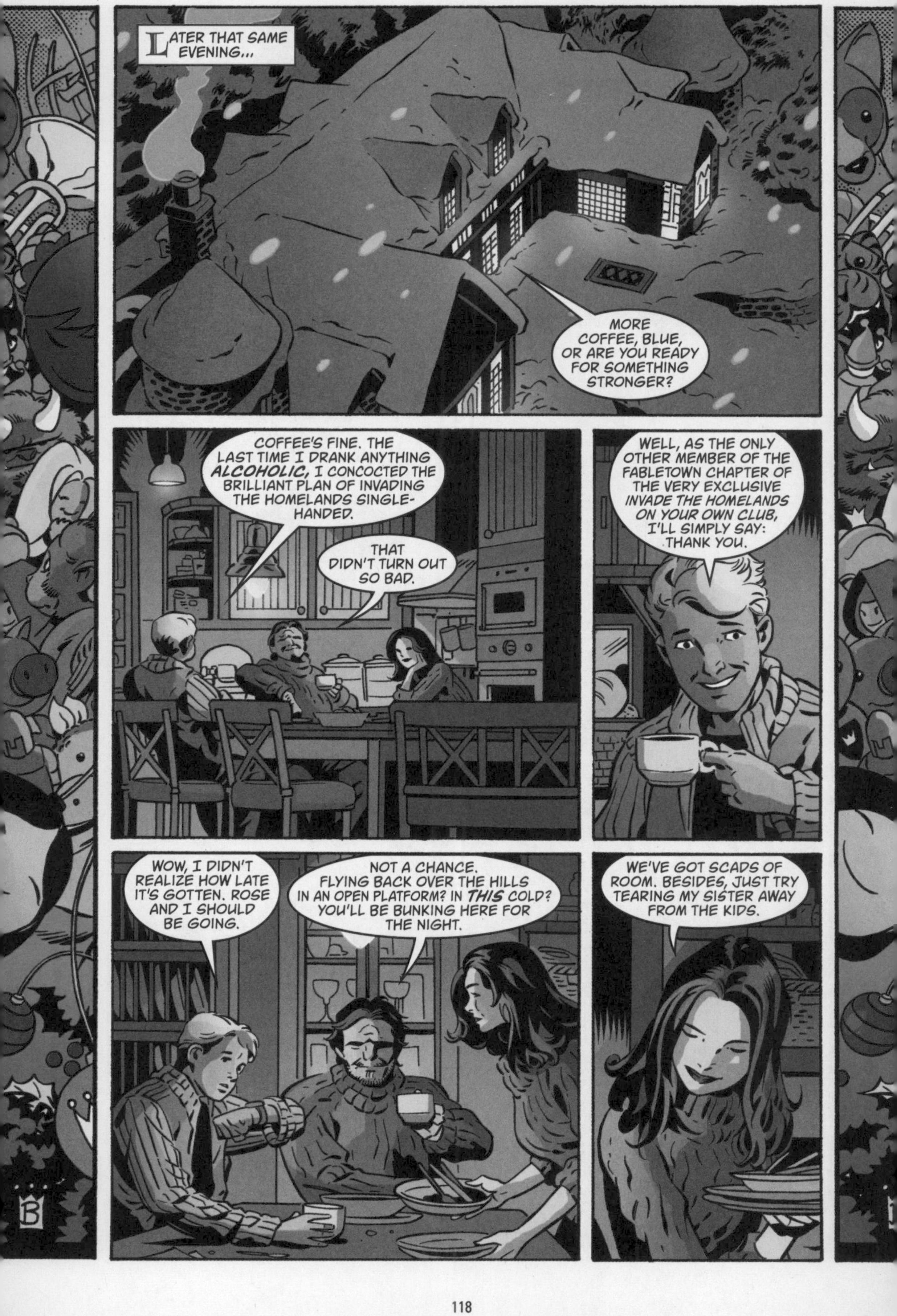
LATER THAT SAME EVENING...
MORE COFFEE, BLUE, OR ARE YOU READY FOR SOMETHING STRONGER?
COFFEE'S FINE. THE LAST TIME I DRANK ANYTHING *ALCOHOLIC*, I CONCOCTED THE BRILLIANT PLAN OF INVADING THE HOMELANDS SINGLE-HANDED.
THAT DIDN'T TURN OUT SO BAD.
WELL, AS THE ONLY OTHER MEMBER OF THE FABLETOWN CHAPTER OF THE VERY EXCLUSIVE *INVADE THE HOMELANDS ON YOUR OWN CLUB*, I'LL SIMPLY SAY: THANK YOU.
WOW, I DIDN'T REALIZE HOW LATE IT'S GOTTEN. ROSE AND I SHOULD BE GOING.
NOT A CHANCE. FLYING BACK OVER THE HILLS IN AN OPEN PLATFORM? IN *THIS* COLD? YOU'LL BE BUNKING HERE FOR THE NIGHT.
WE'VE GOT SCADS OF ROOM. BESIDES, JUST TRY TEARING MY SISTER AWAY FROM THE KIDS.

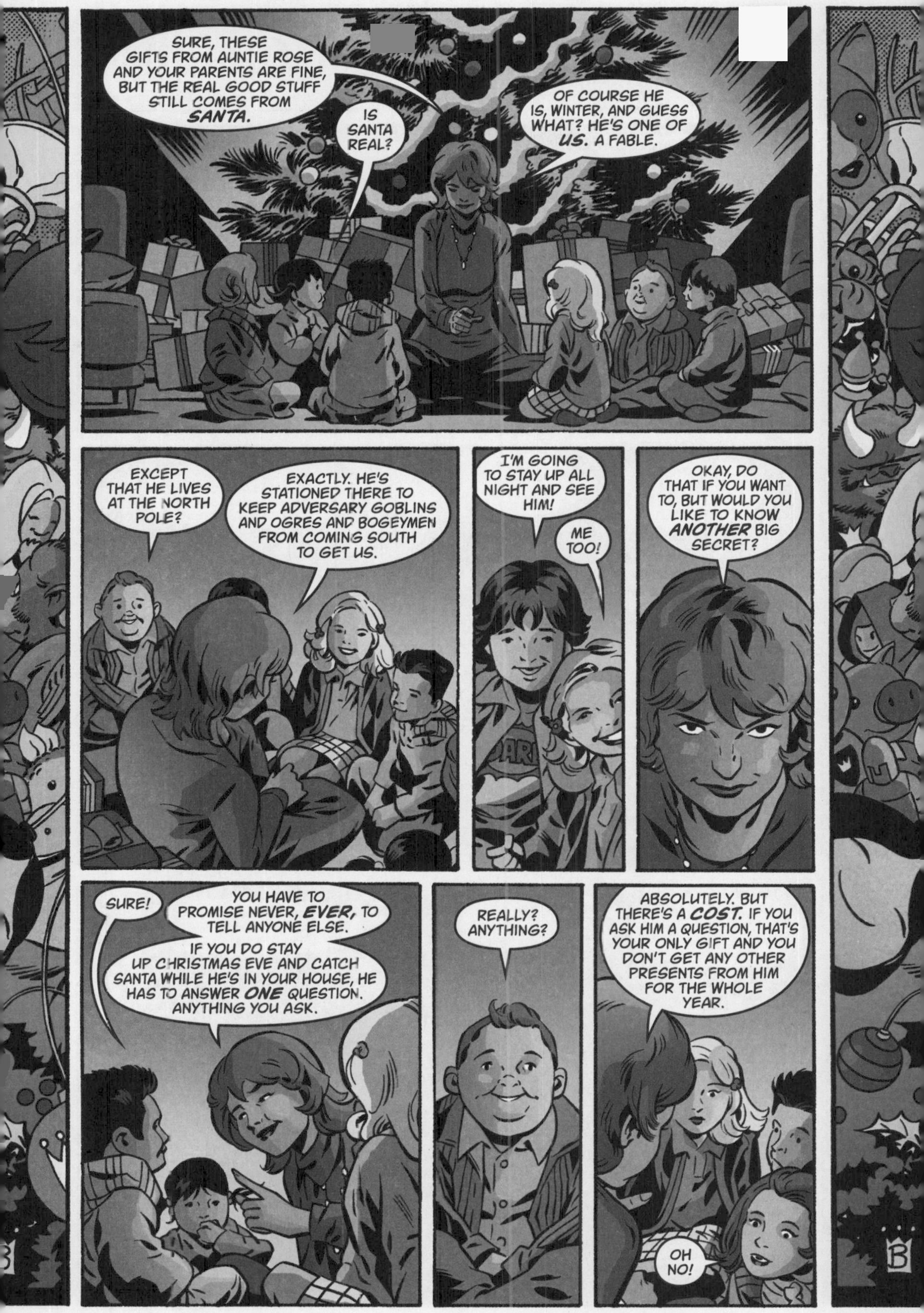
SURE, THESE GIFTS FROM AUNTIE ROSE AND YOUR PARENTS ARE FINE, BUT THE REAL GOOD STUFF STILL COMES FROM SANTA.
IS SANTA REAL?
OF COURSE HE IS, WINTER, AND GUESS WHAT? HE'S ONE OF US. A FABLE.
EXCEPT THAT HE LIVES AT THE NORTH POLE?
EXACTLY. HE'S STATIONED THERE TO KEEP ADVERSARY GOBLINS AND OGRES AND BOGEYMEN FROM COMING SOUTH TO GET US.
I'M GOING TO STAY UP ALL NIGHT AND SEE HIM!
ME TOO!
OKAY, DO THAT IF YOU WANT TO, BUT WOULD YOU LIKE TO KNOW ANOTHER BIG SECRET?
SURE!
YOU HAVE TO PROMISE NEVER, EVER, TO TELL ANYONE ELSE.
IF YOU DO STAY UP CHRISTMAS EVE AND CATCH SANTA WHILE HE'S IN YOUR HOUSE, HE HAS TO ANSWER ONE QUESTION. ANYTHING YOU ASK.
REALLY? ANYTHING?
ABSOLUTELY. BUT THERE'S A COST. IF YOU ASK HIM A QUESTION, THAT'S YOUR ONLY GIFT AND YOU DON'T GET ANY OTHER PRESENTS FROM HIM FOR THE WHOLE YEAR.
OH NO!

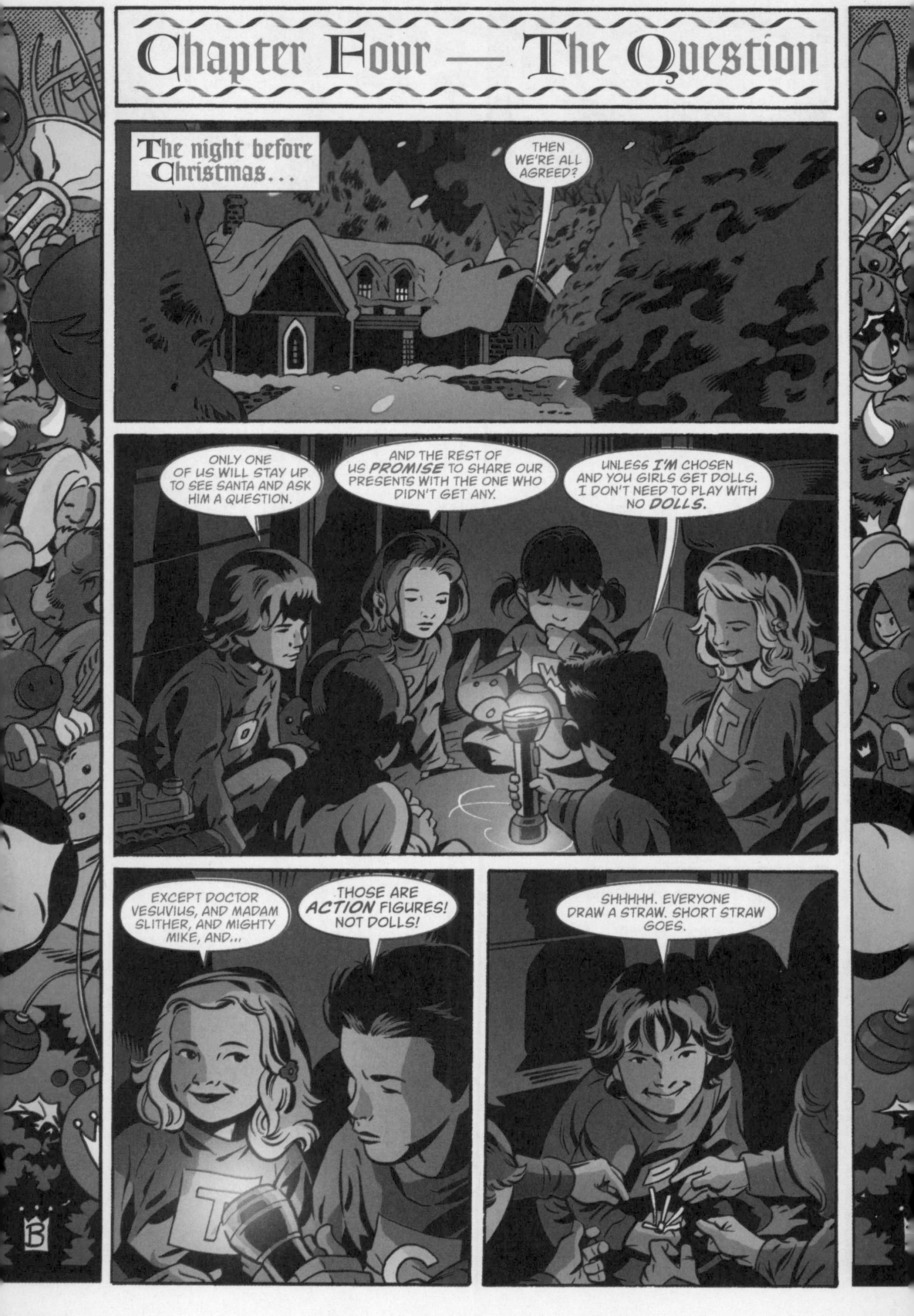
Chapter Four — The Question
The night before Christmas...
THEN WE'RE ALL AGREED?
ONLY ONE OF US WILL STAY UP TO SEE SANTA AND ASK HIM A QUESTION.
AND THE REST OF US PROMISE TO SHARE OUR PRESENTS WITH THE ONE WHO DIDN'T GET ANY.
UNLESS I'M CHOSEN AND YOU GIRLS GET DOLLS. I DON'T NEED TO PLAY WITH NO DOLLS.
EXCEPT DOCTOR VESUVIUS, AND MADAM SLITHER, AND MIGHTY MIKE, AND...
THOSE ARE ACTION FIGURES! NOT DOLLS!
SHHHHH. EVERYONE DRAW A STRAW. SHORT STRAW GOES.

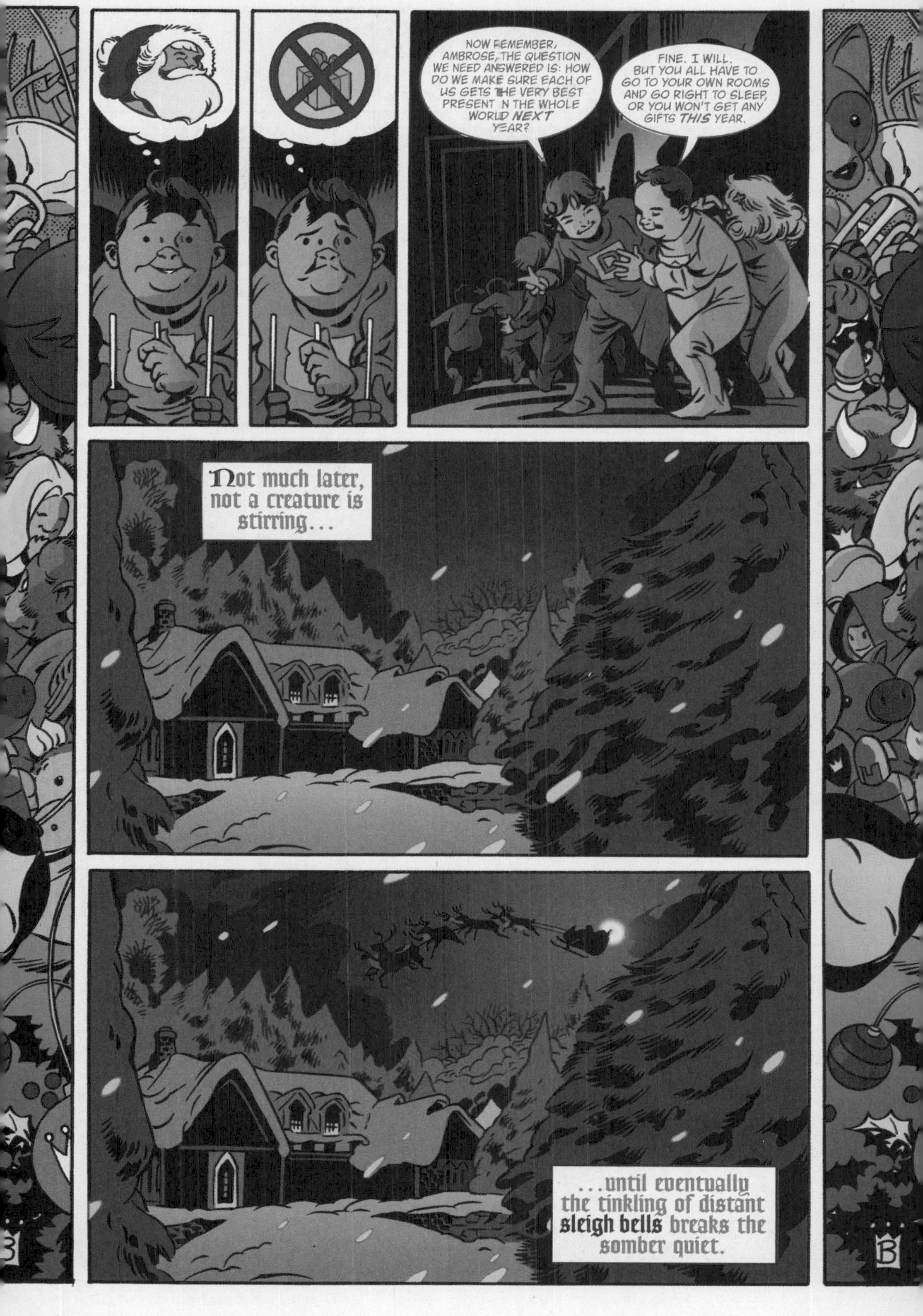
NOW REMEMBER, AMBROSE, THE QUESTION WE NEED ANSWERED IS: HOW DO WE MAKE SURE EACH OF US GETS THE VERY BEST PRESENT IN THE WHOLE WORLD NEXT YEAR?
FINE. I WILL. BUT YOU ALL HAVE TO GO TO YOUR OWN ROOMS AND GO RIGHT TO SLEEP, OR YOU WON'T GET ANY GIFTS THIS YEAR.
Not much later, not a creature is stirring...
...until eventually the tinkling of distant sleigh bells breaks the somber quiet.

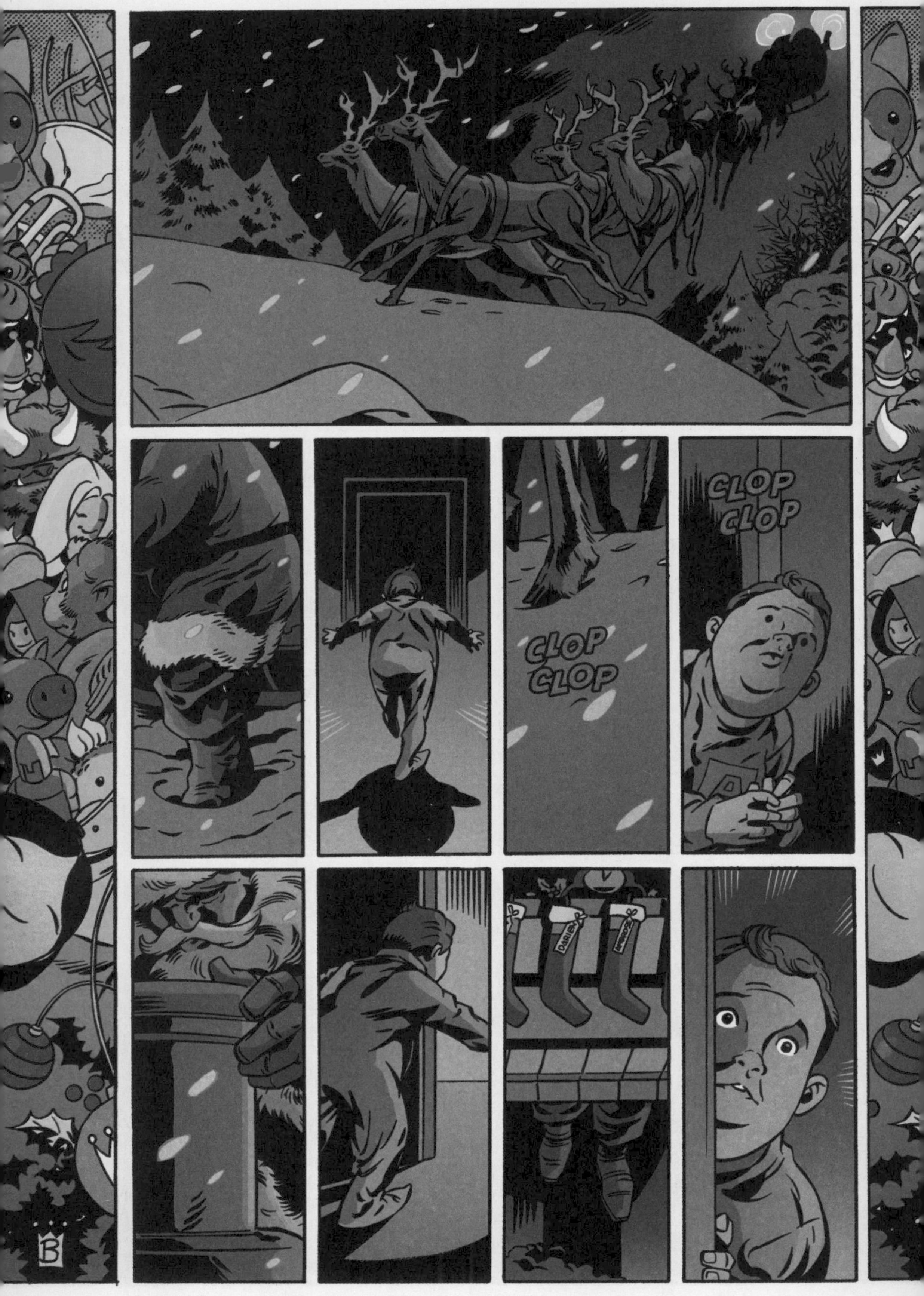
CLOP
CLOP
CLOP
CLOP
DARIEN

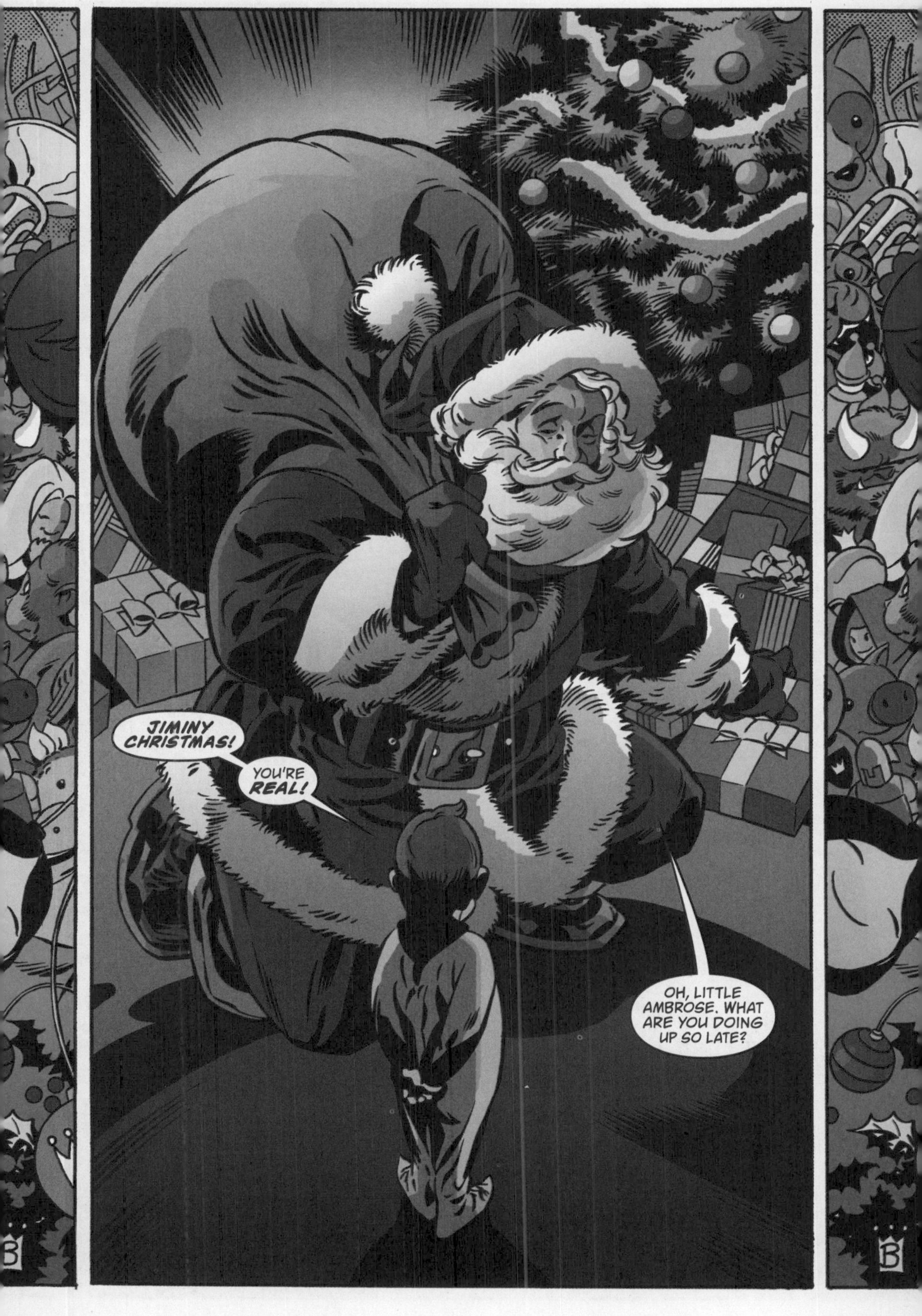

JIMINY CHRISTMAS!
YOU'RE REAL!
OH, LITTLE AMBROSE. WHAT ARE YOU DOING UP SO LATE?

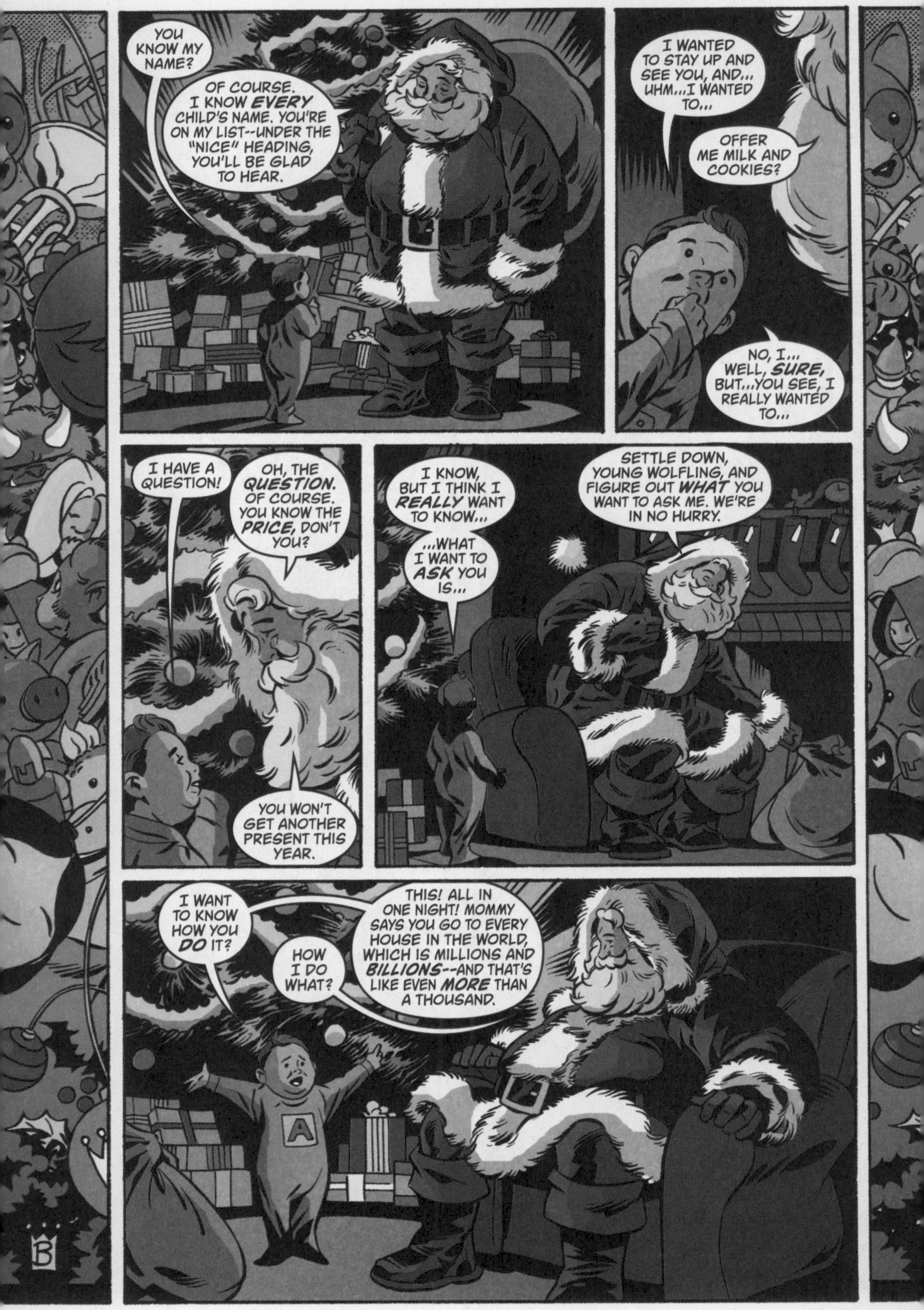
YOU KNOW MY NAME?
OF COURSE. I KNOW EVERY CHILD'S NAME. YOU'RE ON MY LIST--UNDER THE "NICE" HEADING, YOU'LL BE GLAD TO HEAR.
I WANTED TO STAY UP AND SEE YOU, AND... UHM...I WANTED TO...
OFFER ME MILK AND COOKIES?
NO, I... WELL, SURE, BUT...YOU SEE, I REALLY WANTED TO...
I HAVE A QUESTION!
OH, THE QUESTION. OF COURSE. YOU KNOW THE PRICE, DON'T YOU?
YOU WON'T GET ANOTHER PRESENT THIS YEAR.
I KNOW, BUT I THINK I REALLY WANT TO KNOW...
...WHAT I WANT TO ASK YOU IS...
SETTLE DOWN, YOUNG WOLFLING, AND FIGURE OUT WHAT YOU WANT TO ASK ME. WE'RE IN NO HURRY.
I WANT TO KNOW HOW YOU DO IT?
HOW I DO WHAT?
THIS! ALL IN ONE NIGHT! MOMMY SAYS YOU GO TO EVERY HOUSE IN THE WORLD, WHICH IS MILLIONS AND BILLIONS--AND THAT'S LIKE EVEN MORE THAN A THOUSAND.

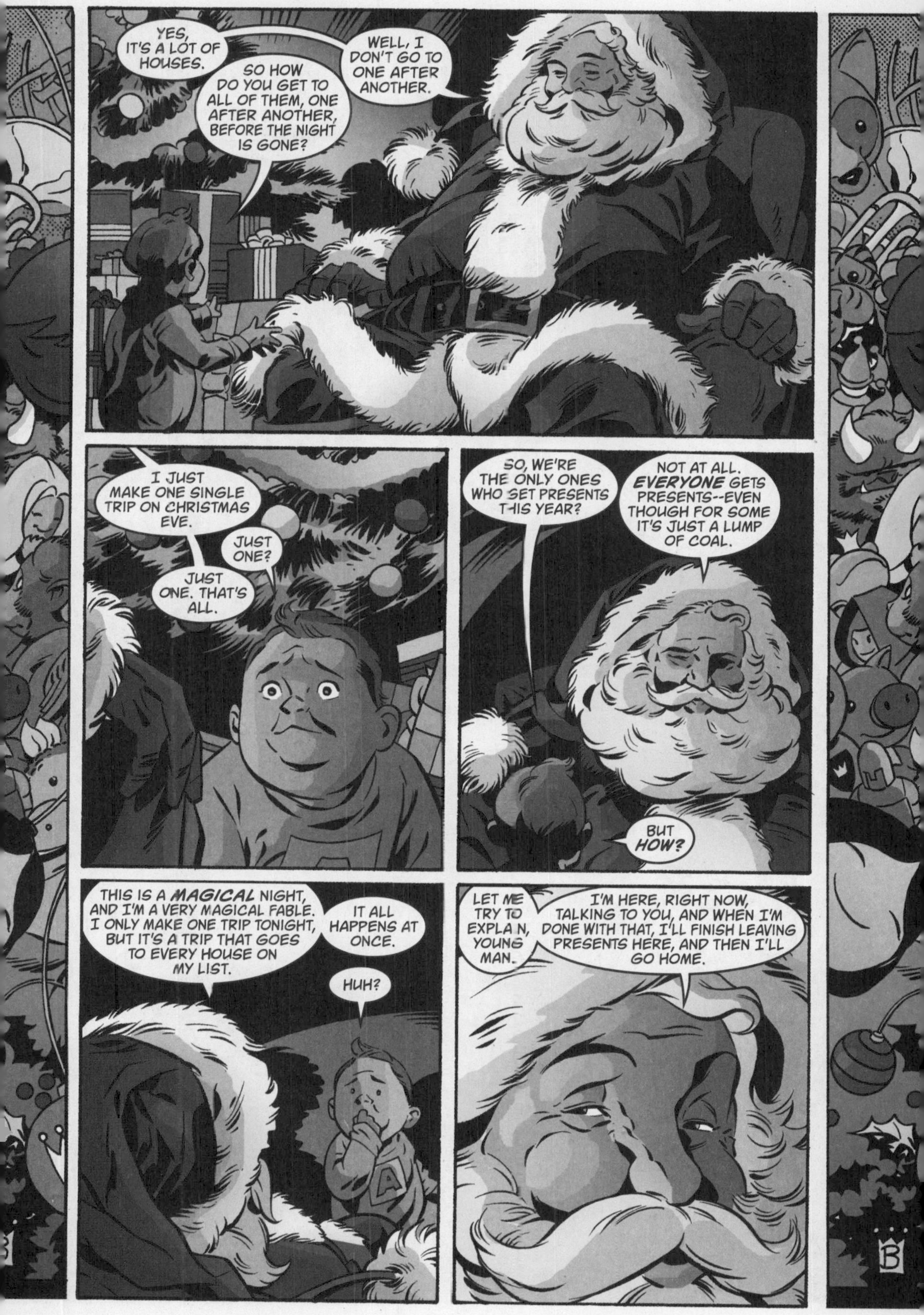
YES, IT'S A LOT OF HOUSES.
SO HOW DO YOU GET TO ALL OF THEM, ONE AFTER ANOTHER, BEFORE THE NIGHT IS GONE?
WELL, I DON'T GO TO ONE AFTER ANOTHER.
I JUST MAKE ONE SINGLE TRIP ON CHRISTMAS EVE.
JUST ONE?
JUST ONE. THAT'S ALL.
SO, WE'RE THE ONLY ONES WHO GET PRESENTS THIS YEAR?
NOT AT ALL. EVERYONE GETS PRESENTS--EVEN THOUGH FOR SOME IT'S JUST A LUMP OF COAL.
BUT HOW?
THIS IS A MAGICAL NIGHT, AND I'M A VERY MAGICAL FABLE. I ONLY MAKE ONE TRIP TONIGHT, BUT IT'S A TRIP THAT GOES TO EVERY HOUSE ON MY LIST.
IT ALL HAPPENS AT ONCE.
HUH?
LET ME TRY TO EXPLAIN, YOUNG MAN.
I'M HERE, RIGHT NOW, TALKING TO YOU, AND WHEN I'M DONE WITH THAT, I'LL FINISH LEAVING PRESENTS HERE, AND THEN I'LL GO HOME.

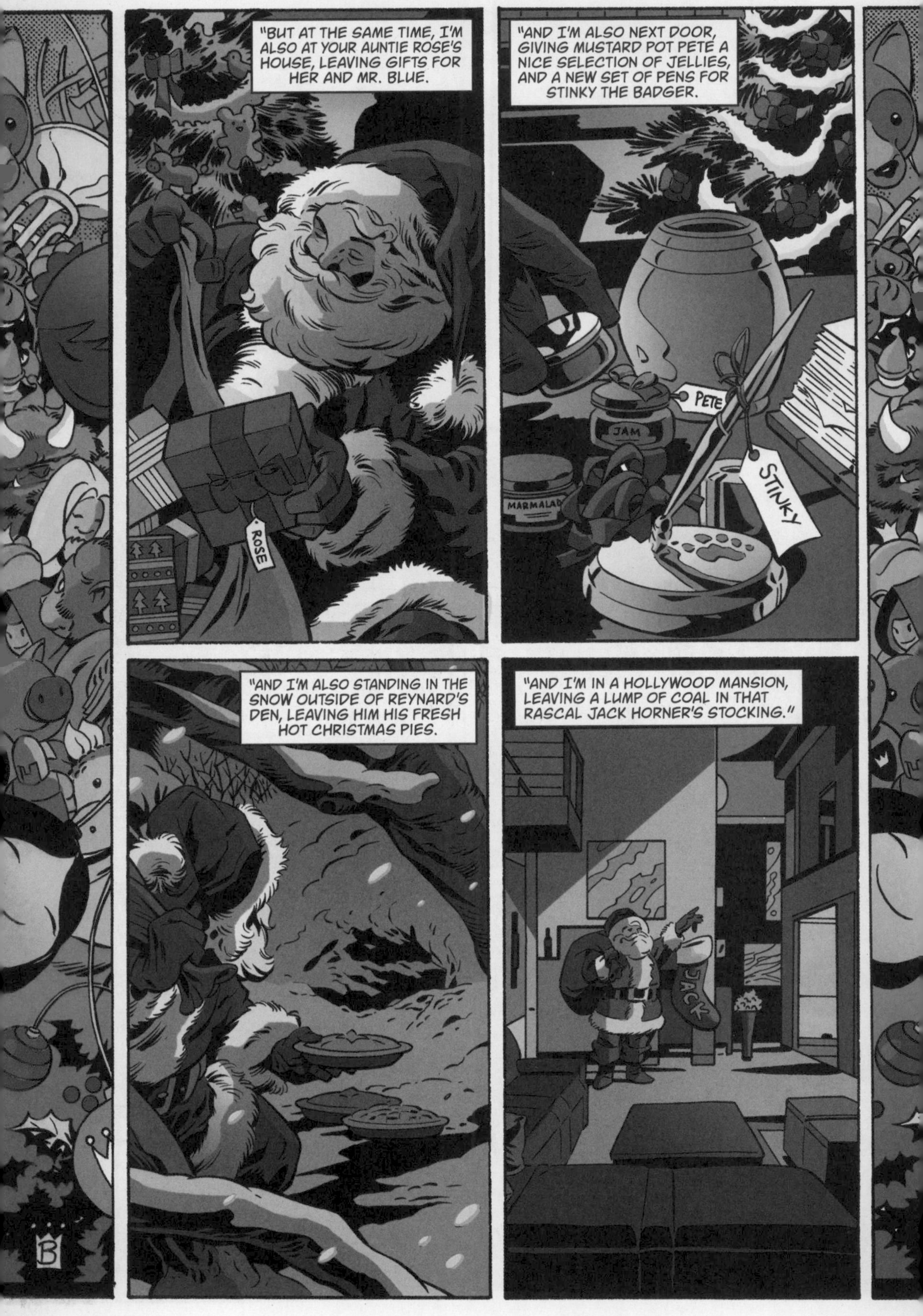
"BUT AT THE SAME TIME, I'M ALSO AT YOUR AUNTIE ROSE'S HOUSE, LEAVING GIFTS FOR HER AND MR. BLUE.
ROSE
"AND I'M ALSO NEXT DOOR, GIVING MUSTARD POT PETE A NICE SELECTION OF JELLIES, AND A NEW SET OF PENS FOR STINKY THE BADGER.
PETE
JAM
MARMALAD
STINKY
"AND I'M ALSO STANDING IN THE SNOW OUTSIDE OF REYNARD'S DEN, LEAVING HIM HIS FRESH HOT CHRISTMAS PIES.
"AND I'M IN A HOLLYWOOD MANSION, LEAVING A LUMP OF COAL IN THAT RASCAL JACK HORNER'S STOCKING."
JACK

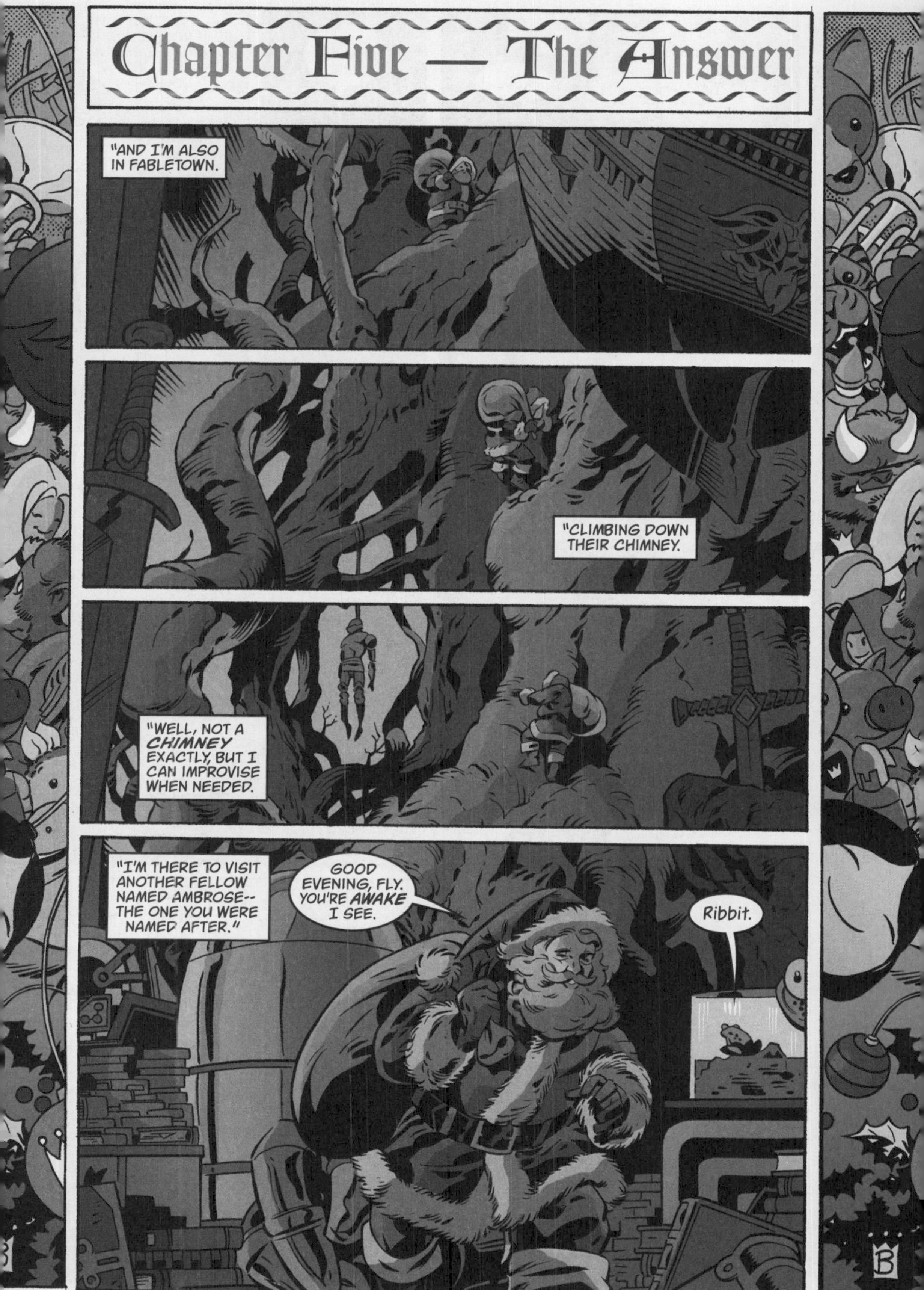
Chapter Five — The Answer
"AND I'M ALSO IN FABLETOWN.
"CLIMBING DOWN THEIR CHIMNEY.
"WELL, NOT A CHIMNEY EXACTLY, BUT I CAN IMPROVISE WHEN NEEDED.
"I'M THERE TO VISIT ANOTHER FELLOW NAMED AMBROSE-- THE ONE YOU WERE NAMED AFTER."
GOOD EVENING, FLY. YOU'RE AWAKE I SEE.
Ribbit.

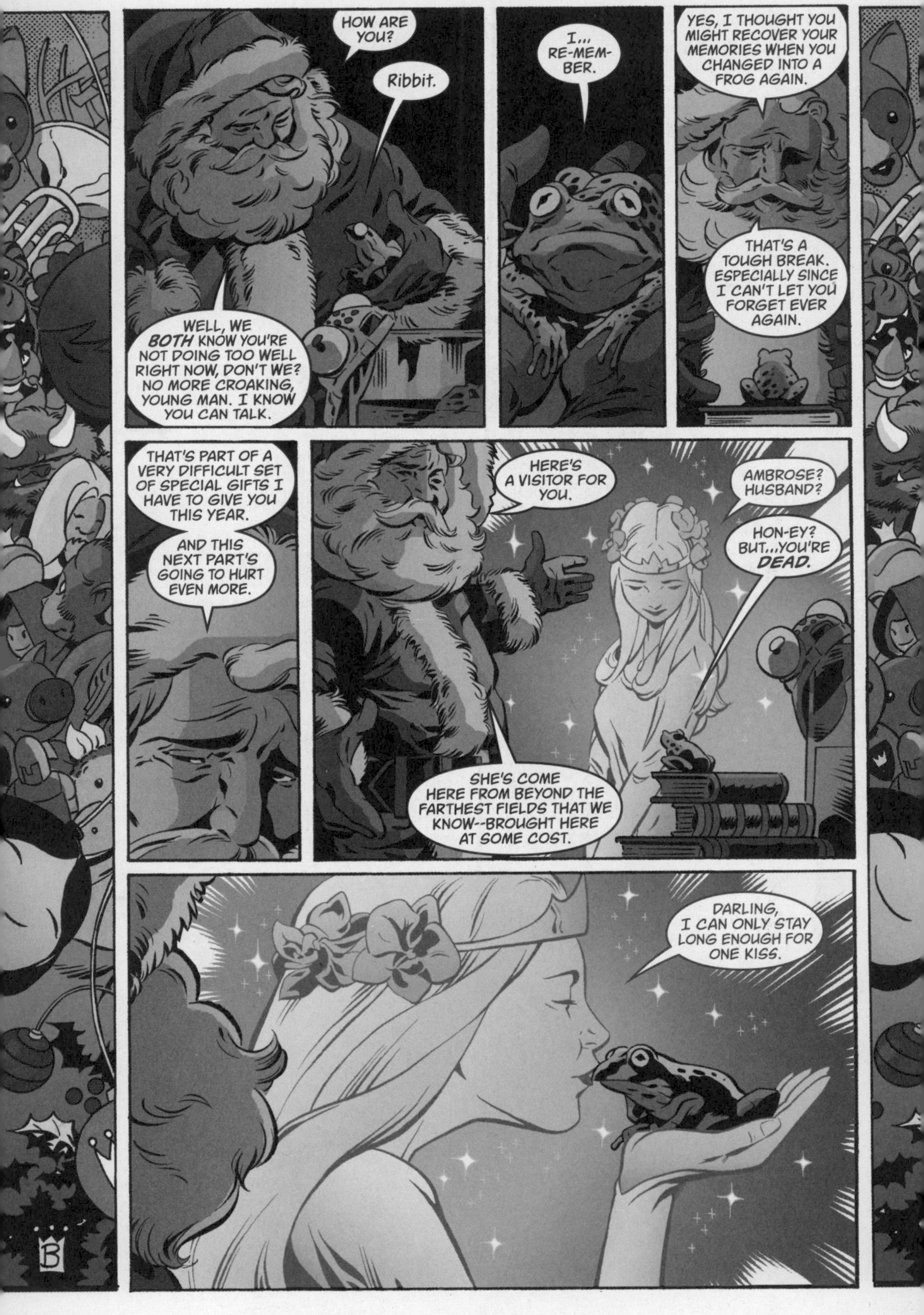

HOW ARE YOU?
Ribbit.
WELL, WE BOTH KNOW YOU'RE NOT DOING TOO WELL RIGHT NOW, DON'T WE? NO MORE CROAKING, YOUNG MAN. I KNOW YOU CAN TALK.
I... RE-MEM-BER.
YES, I THOUGHT YOU MIGHT RECOVER YOUR MEMORIES WHEN YOU CHANGED INTO A FROG AGAIN.
THAT'S A TOUGH BREAK. ESPECIALLY SINCE I CAN'T LET YOU FORGET EVER AGAIN.
THAT'S PART OF A VERY DIFFICULT SET OF SPECIAL GIFTS I HAVE TO GIVE YOU THIS YEAR.
AND THIS NEXT PART'S GOING TO HURT EVEN MORE.
HERE'S A VISITOR FOR YOU.
AMBROSE? HUSBAND?
HON-EY? BUT...YOU'RE DEAD.
SHE'S COME HERE FROM BEYOND THE FARTHEST FIELDS THAT WE KNOW--BROUGHT HERE AT SOME COST.
DARLING, I CAN ONLY STAY LONG ENOUGH FOR ONE KISS.

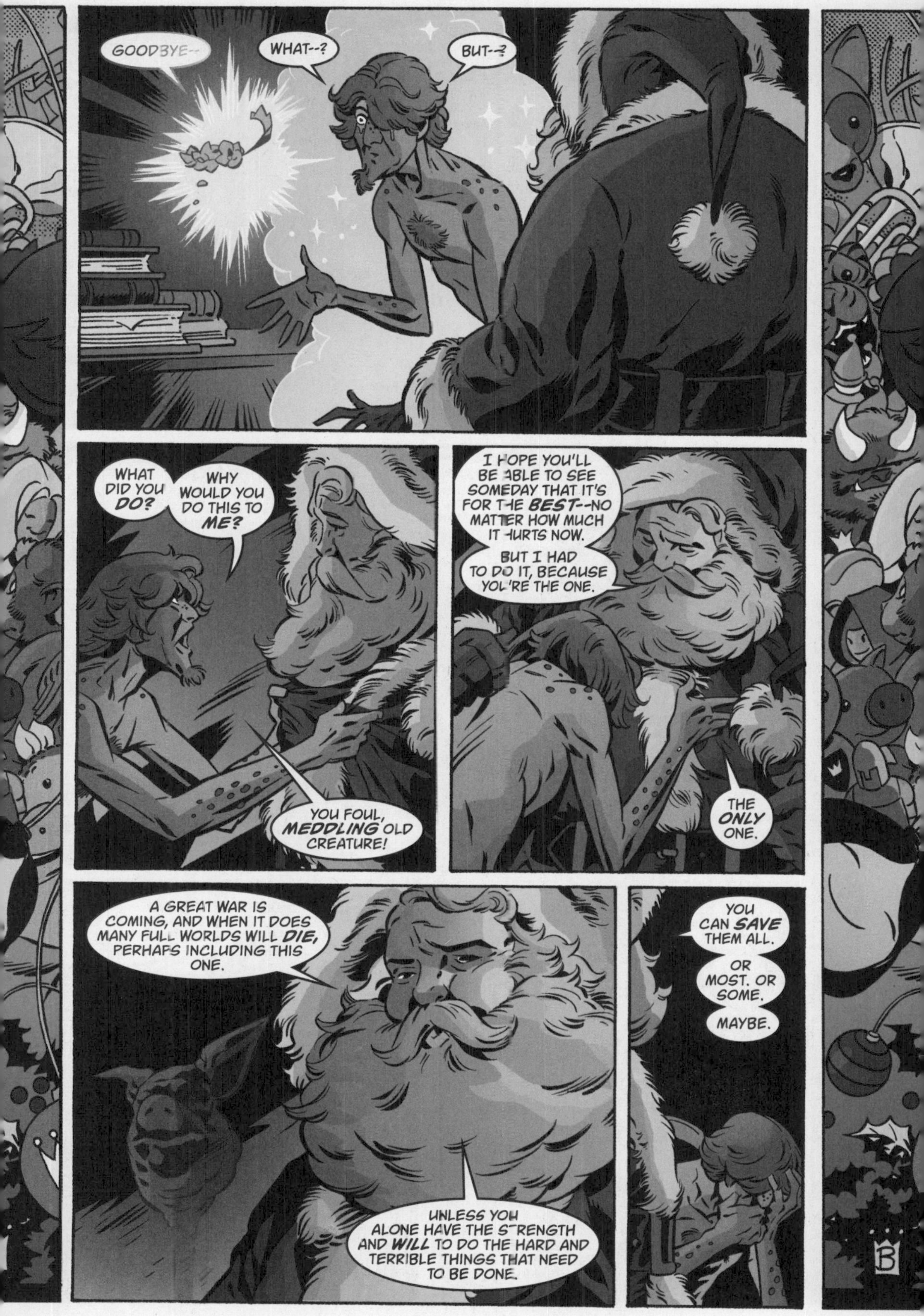
GOODBYE--
WHAT--?
BUT--?
WHAT DID YOU DO?
WHY WOULD YOU DO THIS TO ME?
YOU FOUL, MEDDLING OLD CREATURE!
I HOPE YOU'LL BE ABLE TO SEE SOMEDAY THAT IT'S FOR THE BEST--NO MATTER HOW MUCH IT HURTS NOW.
BUT I HAD TO DO IT, BECAUSE YOU'RE THE ONE.
THE ONLY ONE.
A GREAT WAR IS COMING, AND WHEN IT DOES MANY FULL WORLDS WILL DIE, PERHAPS INCLUDING THIS ONE.
UNLESS YOU ALONE HAVE THE STRENGTH AND WILL TO DO THE HARD AND TERRIBLE THINGS THAT NEED TO BE DONE.
YOU CAN SAVE THEM ALL.
OR MOST. OR SOME.
MAYBE.

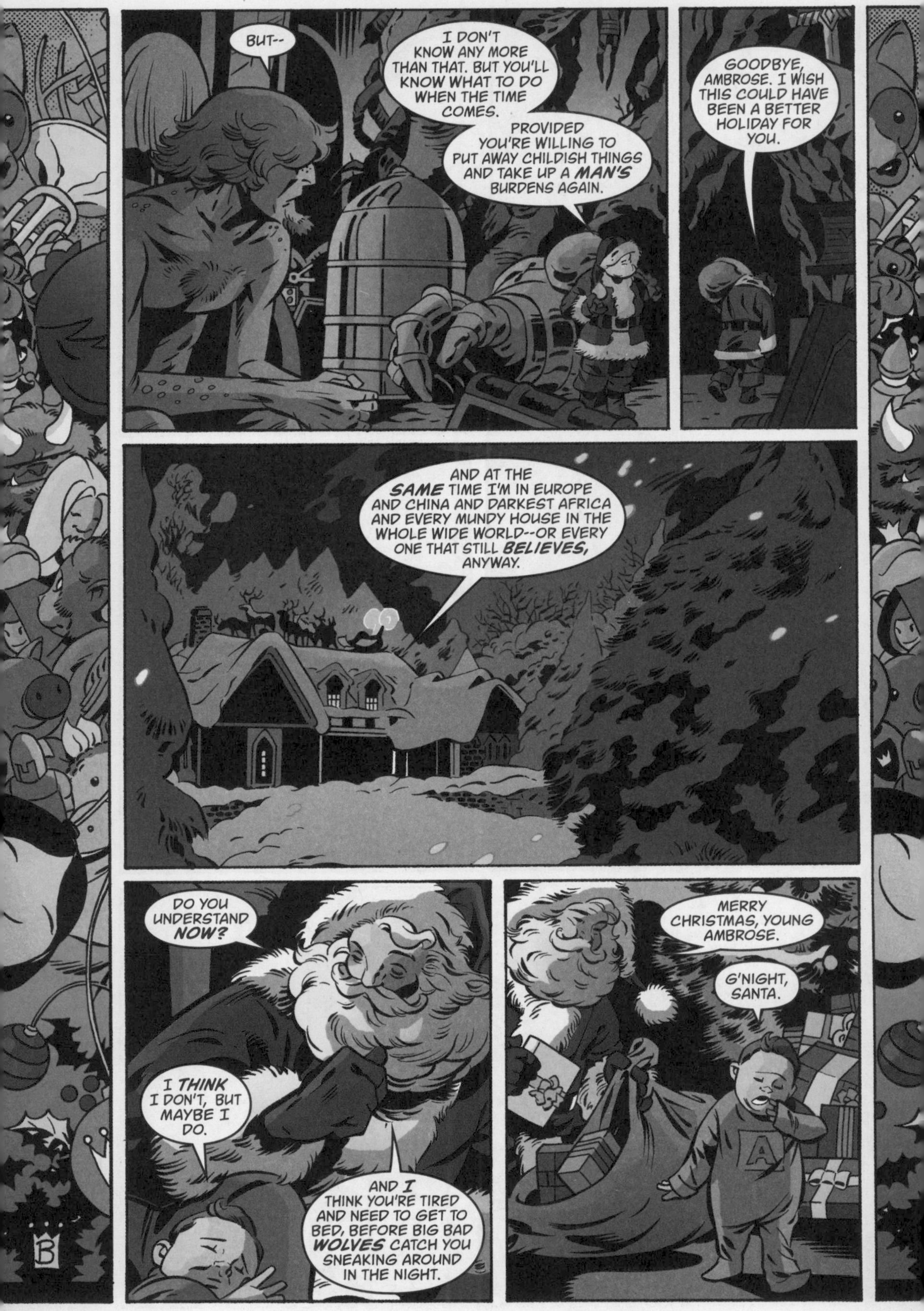
BUT--
I DON'T KNOW ANY MORE THAN THAT. BUT YOU'LL KNOW WHAT TO DO WHEN THE TIME COMES.
PROVIDED YOU'RE WILLING TO PUT AWAY CHILDISH THINGS AND TAKE UP A MAN'S BURDENS AGAIN.
GOODBYE, AMBROSE. I WISH THIS COULD HAVE BEEN A BETTER HOLIDAY FOR YOU.
AND AT THE SAME TIME I'M IN EUROPE AND CHINA AND DARKEST AFRICA AND EVERY MUNDY HOUSE IN THE WHOLE WIDE WORLD--OR EVERY ONE THAT STILL BELIEVES, ANYWAY.
DO YOU UNDERSTAND NOW?
I THINK I DON'T, BUT MAYBE I DO.
AND I THINK YOU'RE TIRED AND NEED TO GET TO BED, BEFORE BIG BAD WOLVES CATCH YOU SNEAKING AROUND IN THE NIGHT.
MERRY CHRISTMAS, YOUNG AMBROSE.
G'NIGHT, SANTA.

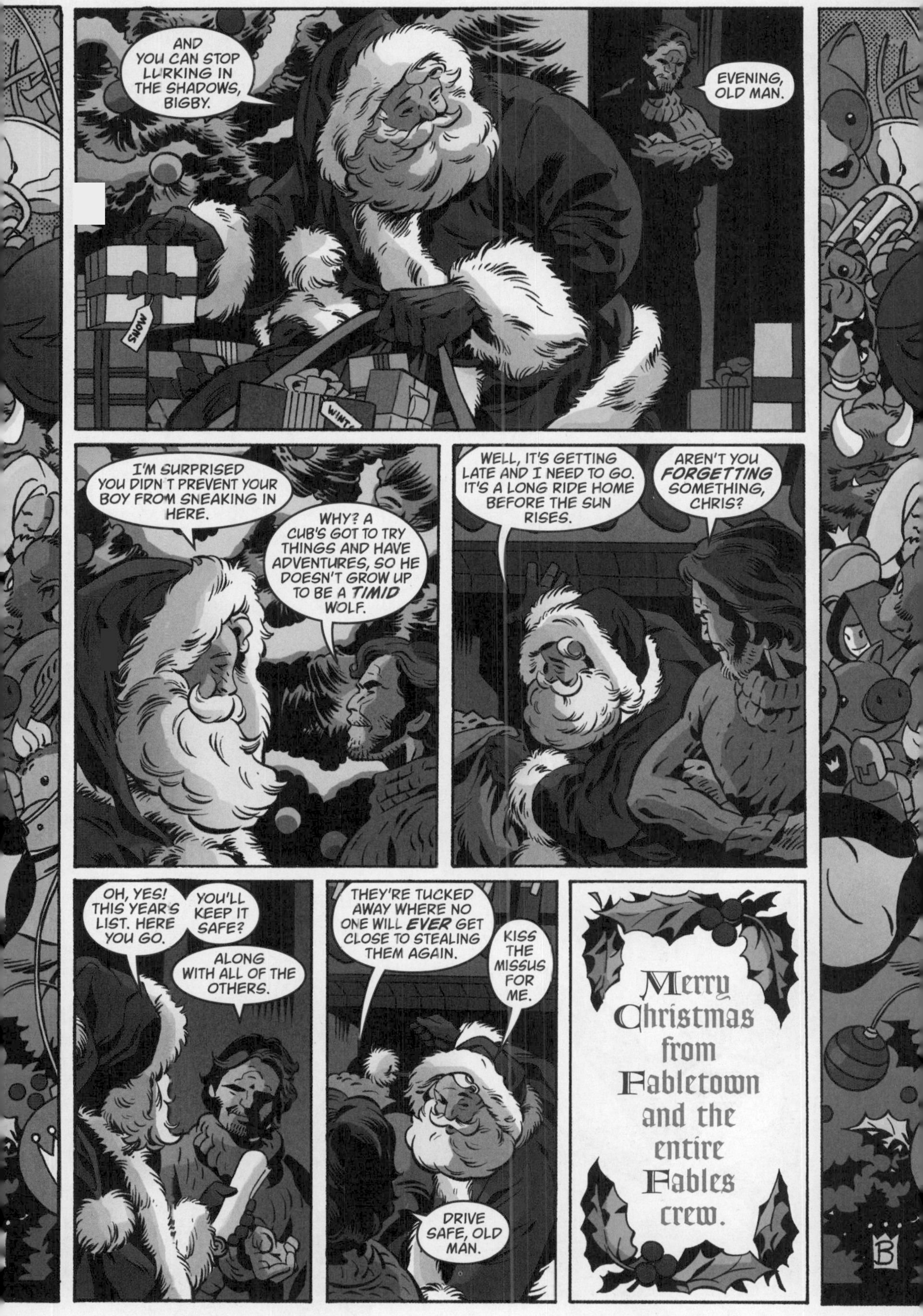
AND YOU CAN STOP LURKING IN THE SHADOWS, BIGBY.
EVENING, OLD MAN.
SNOW
WINT
I'M SURPRISED YOU DIDN'T PREVENT YOUR BOY FROM SNEAKING IN HERE.
WHY? A CUB'S GOT TO TRY THINGS AND HAVE ADVENTURES, SO HE DOESN'T GROW UP TO BE A *TIMID* WOLF.
WELL, IT'S GETTING LATE AND I NEED TO GO. IT'S A LONG RIDE HOME BEFORE THE SUN RISES.
AREN'T YOU *FORGETTING* SOMETHING, CHRIS?
OH, YES! THIS YEAR'S LIST. HERE YOU GO.
YOU'LL KEEP IT SAFE?
ALONG WITH ALL OF THE OTHERS.
THEY'RE TUCKED AWAY WHERE NO ONE WILL *EVER* GET CLOSE TO STEALING THEM AGAIN.
KISS THE MISSUS FOR ME.
DRIVE SAFE, OLD MAN.
Merry Christmas from Fabletown and the entire Fables crew.

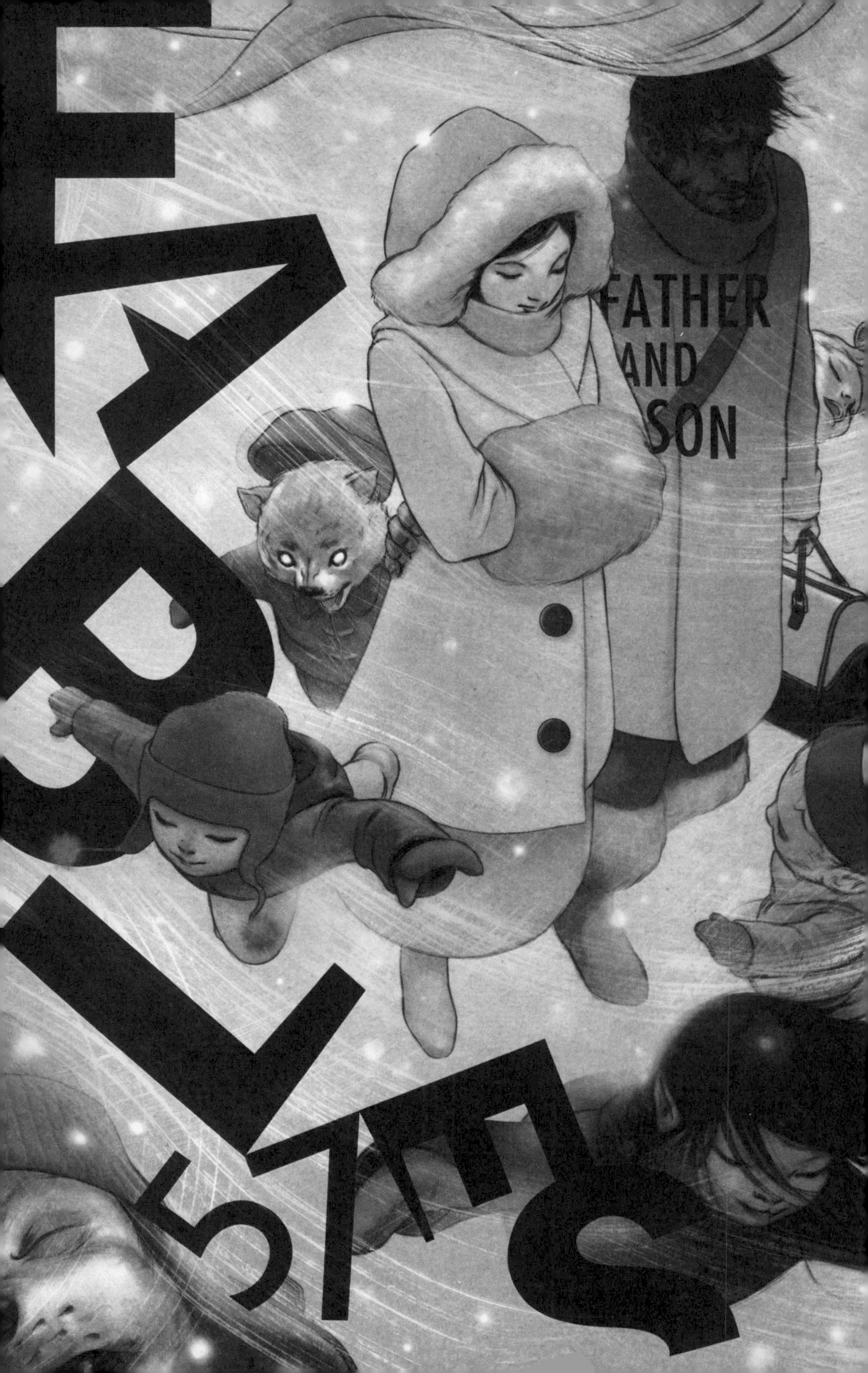
FATHER
AND
SON

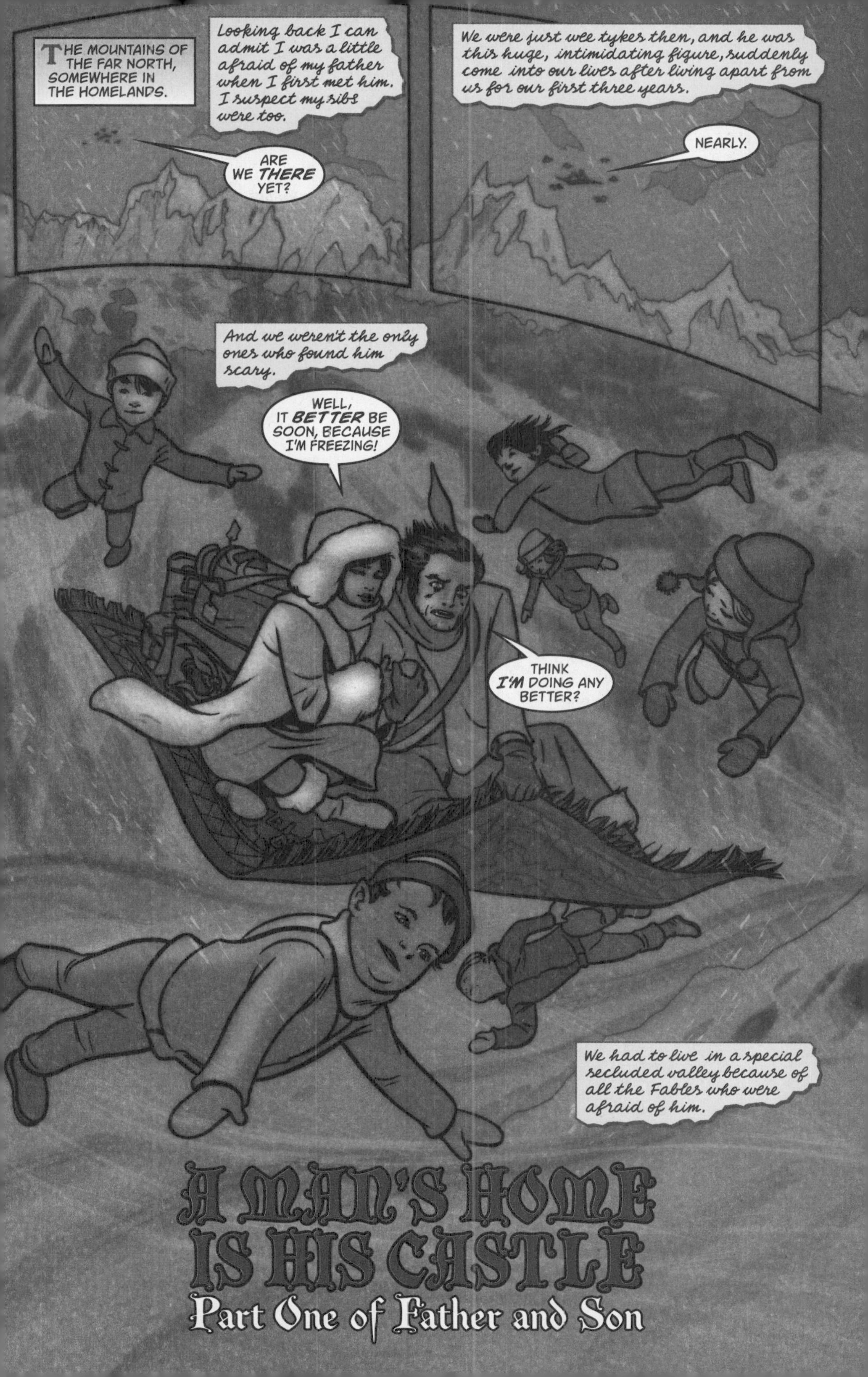
THE MOUNTAINS OF THE FAR NORTH, SOMEWHERE IN THE HOMELANDS.
Looking back I can admit I was a little afraid of my father when I first met him. I suspect my sibs were too.
ARE WE THERE YET?
We were just wee tykes then, and he was this huge, intimidating figure, suddenly come into our lives after living apart from us for our first three years.
NEARLY.
And we weren't the only ones who found him scary.
WELL, IT BETTER BE SOON, BECAUSE I'M FREEZING!
THINK I'M DOING ANY BETTER?
We had to live in a special secluded valley because of all the Fables who were afraid of him.
A MAN'S HOME IS HIS CASTLE
Part One of Father and Son

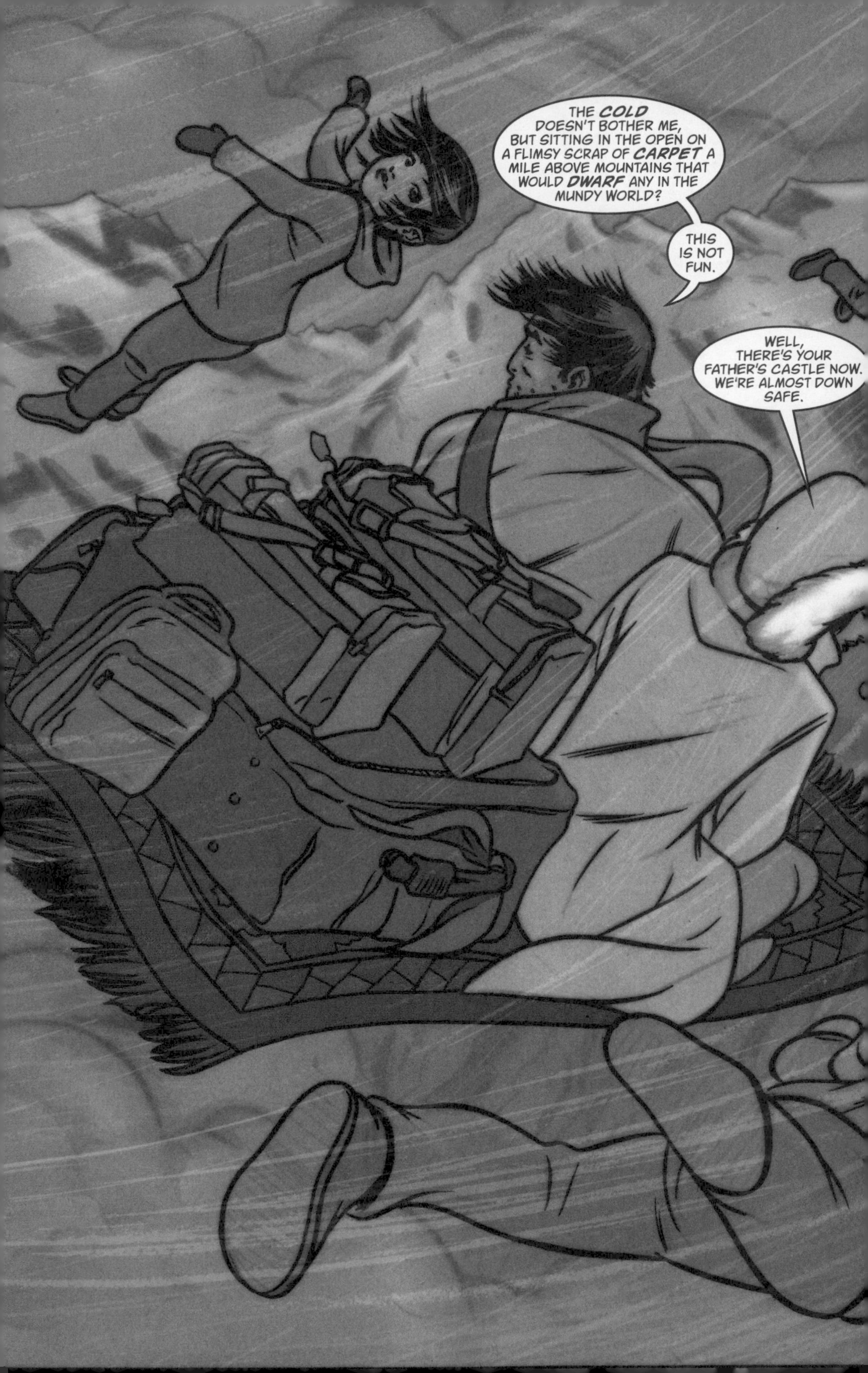
THE COLD DOESN'T BOTHER ME, BUT SITTING IN THE OPEN ON A FLIMSY SCRAP OF CARPET A MILE ABOVE MOUNTAINS THAT WOULD DWARF ANY IN THE MUNDY WORLD?
THIS IS NOT FUN.
WELL, THERE'S YOUR FATHER'S CASTLE NOW. WE'RE ALMOST DOWN SAFE.

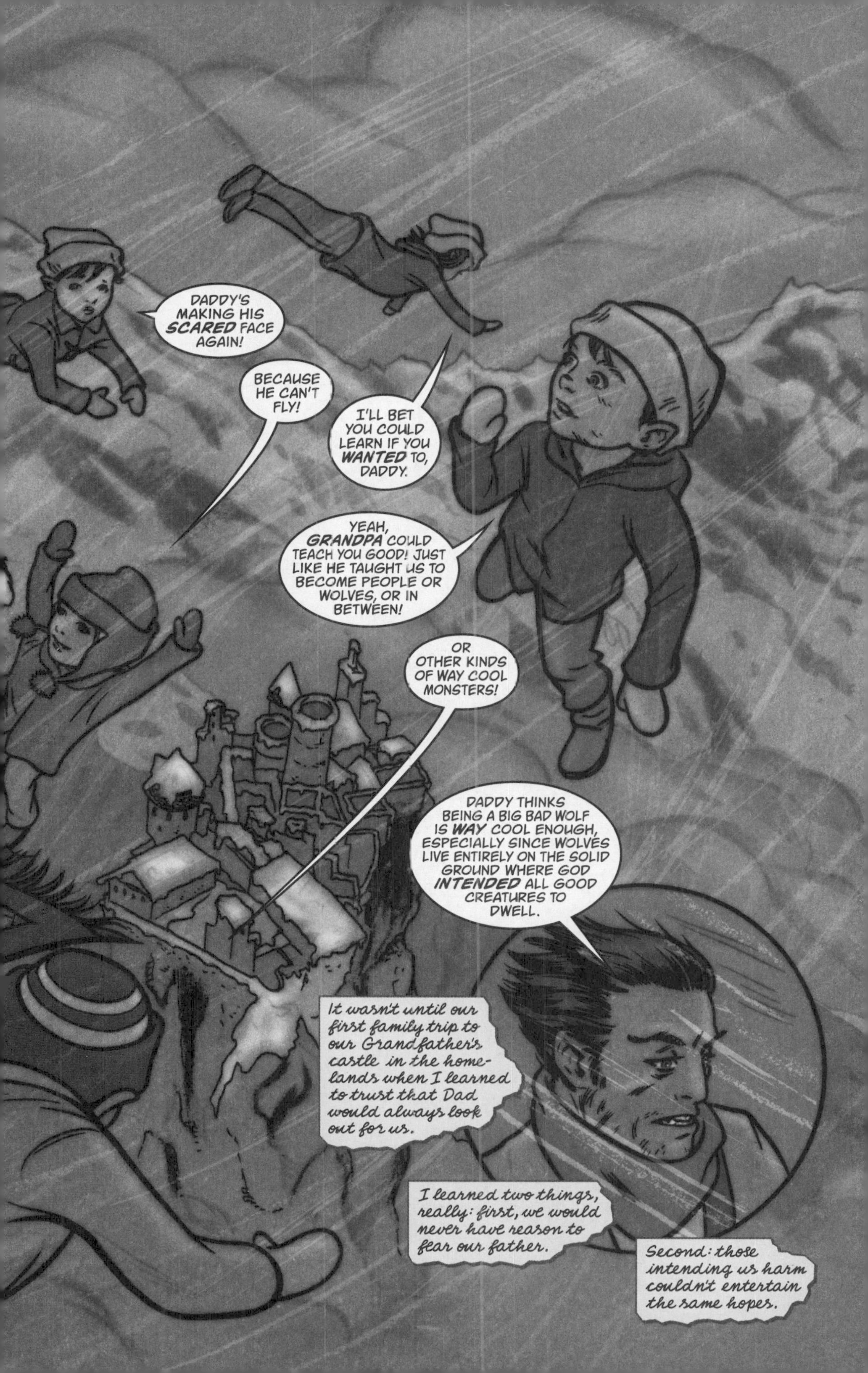

DADDY'S MAKING HIS SCARED FACE AGAIN!
BECAUSE HE CAN'T FLY!
I'LL BET YOU COULD LEARN IF YOU WANTED TO, DADDY.
YEAH, GRANDPA COULD TEACH YOU GOOD! JUST LIKE HE TAUGHT US TO BECOME PEOPLE OR WOLVES, OR IN BETWEEN!
OR OTHER KINDS OF WAY COOL MONSTERS!
DADDY THINKS BEING A BIG BAD WOLF IS WAY COOL ENOUGH, ESPECIALLY SINCE WOLVES LIVE ENTIRELY ON THE SOLID GROUND WHERE GOD INTENDED ALL GOOD CREATURES TO DWELL.
It wasn't until our first family trip to our Grandfather's castle in the homelands when I learned to trust that Dad would always look out for us.
I learned two things, really: first, we would never have reason to fear our father.
Second: those intending us harm couldn't entertain the same hopes.

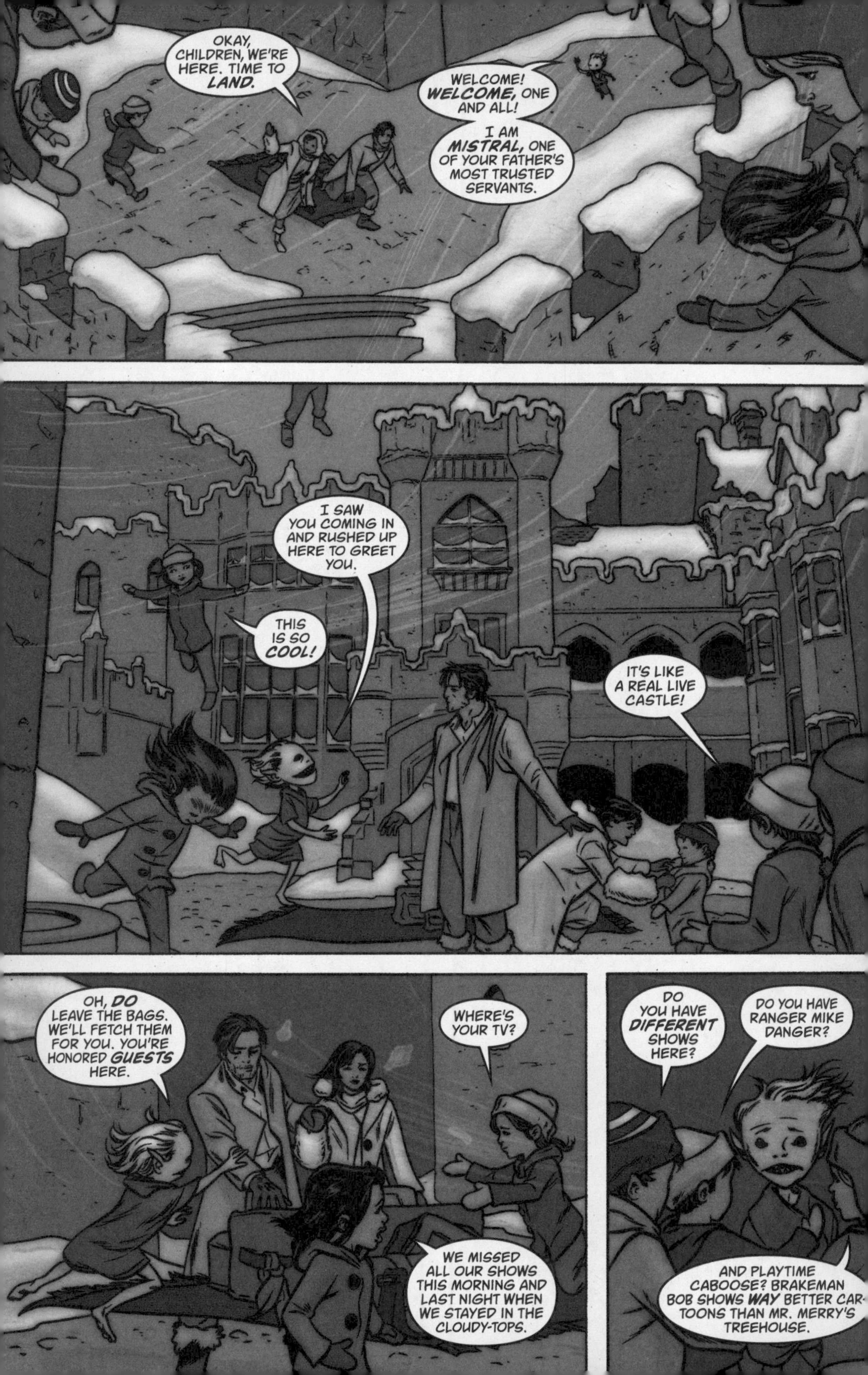
OKAY, CHILDREN, WE'RE HERE. TIME TO LAND.
WELCOME! WELCOME, ONE AND ALL!
I AM MISTRAL, ONE OF YOUR FATHER'S MOST TRUSTED SERVANTS.
I SAW YOU COMING IN AND RUSHED UP HERE TO GREET YOU.
THIS IS SO COOL!
IT'S LIKE A REAL LIVE CASTLE!
OH, DO LEAVE THE BAGS. WE'LL FETCH THEM FOR YOU. YOU'RE HONORED GUESTS HERE.
WHERE'S YOUR TV?
WE MISSED ALL OUR SHOWS THIS MORNING AND LAST NIGHT WHEN WE STAYED IN THE CLOUDY-TOPS.
DO YOU HAVE DIFFERENT SHOWS HERE?
DO YOU HAVE RANGER MIKE DANGER?
AND PLAYTIME CABOOSE? BRAKEMAN BOB SHOWS WAY BETTER CARTOONS THAN MR. MERRY'S TREEHOUSE.

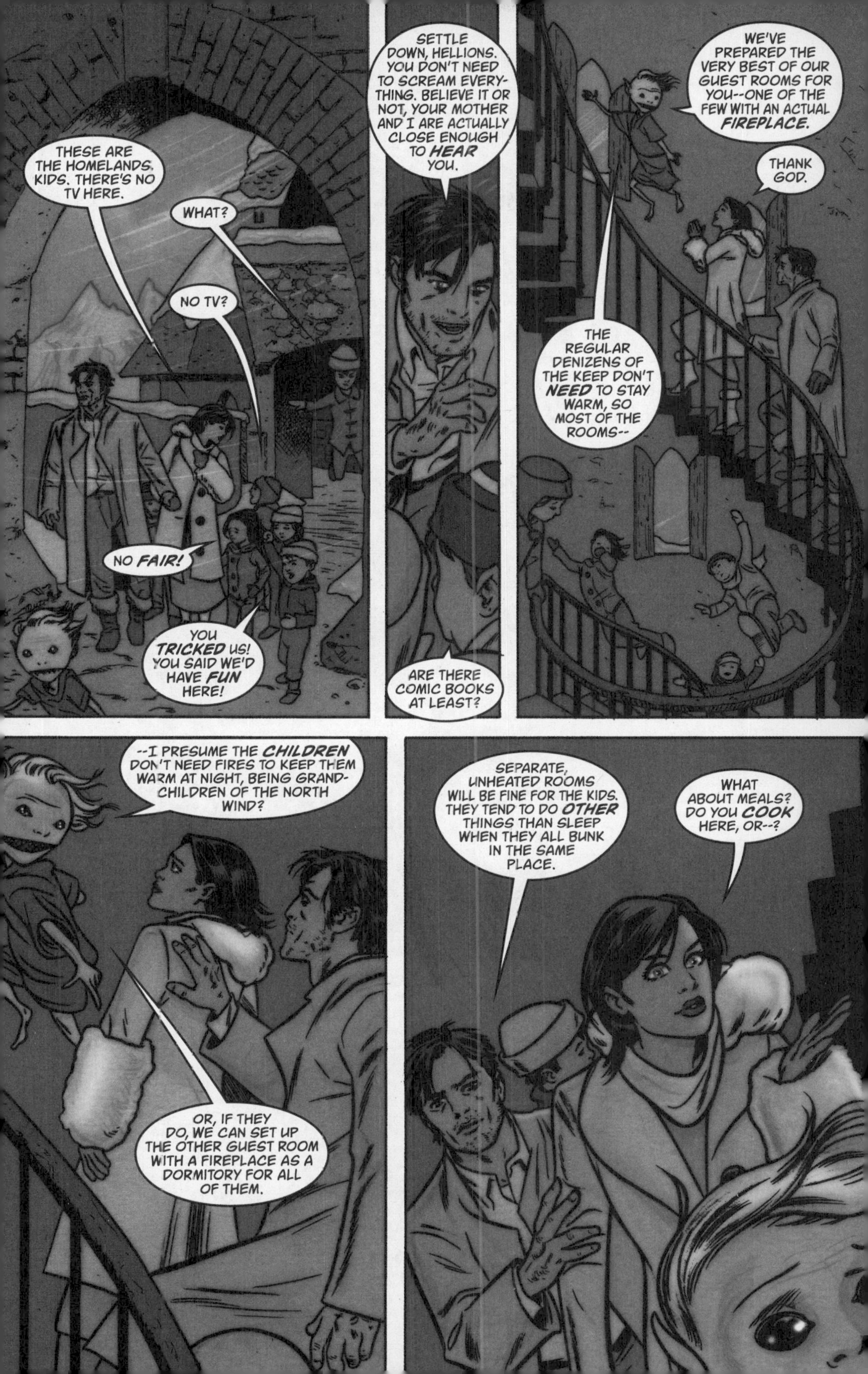
THESE ARE THE HOMELANDS, KIDS. THERE'S NO TV HERE.
WHAT?
NO TV?
NO FAIR!
YOU TRICKED US! YOU SAID WE'D HAVE FUN HERE!
SETTLE DOWN, HELLIONS. YOU DON'T NEED TO SCREAM EVERYTHING. BELIEVE IT OR NOT, YOUR MOTHER AND I ARE ACTUALLY CLOSE ENOUGH TO HEAR YOU.
ARE THERE COMIC BOOKS AT LEAST?
WE'VE PREPARED THE VERY BEST OF OUR GUEST ROOMS FOR YOU--ONE OF THE FEW WITH AN ACTUAL FIREPLACE.
THANK GOD.
THE REGULAR DENIZENS OF THE KEEP DON'T NEED TO STAY WARM, SO MOST OF THE ROOMS--
--I PRESUME THE CHILDREN DON'T NEED FIRES TO KEEP THEM WARM AT NIGHT, BEING GRANDCHILDREN OF THE NORTH WIND?
OR, IF THEY DO, WE CAN SET UP THE OTHER GUEST ROOM WITH A FIREPLACE AS A DORMITORY FOR ALL OF THEM.
SEPARATE, UNHEATED ROOMS WILL BE FINE FOR THE KIDS. THEY TEND TO DO OTHER THINGS THAN SLEEP WHEN THEY ALL BUNK IN THE SAME PLACE.
WHAT ABOUT MEALS? DO YOU COOK HERE, OR--?

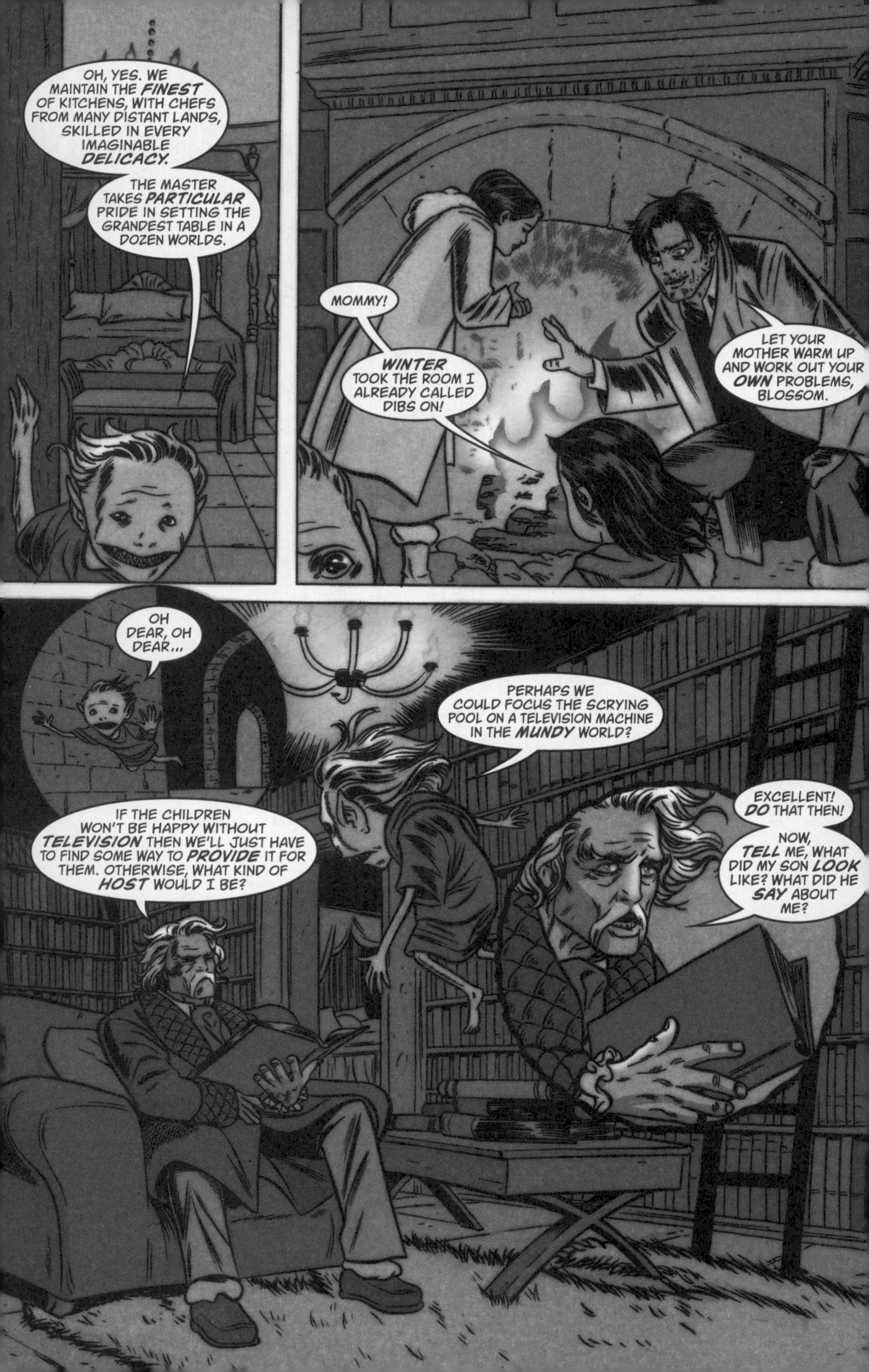
OH, YES. WE MAINTAIN THE FINEST OF KITCHENS, WITH CHEFS FROM MANY DISTANT LANDS, SKILLED IN EVERY IMAGINABLE DELICACY.
THE MASTER TAKES PARTICULAR PRIDE IN SETTING THE GRANDEST TABLE IN A DOZEN WORLDS.
MOMMY!
WINTER TOOK THE ROOM I ALREADY CALLED DIBS ON!
LET YOUR MOTHER WARM UP AND WORK OUT YOUR OWN PROBLEMS, BLOSSOM.
OH DEAR, OH DEAR...
PERHAPS WE COULD FOCUS THE SCRYING POOL ON A TELEVISION MACHINE IN THE MUNDY WORLD?
IF THE CHILDREN WON'T BE HAPPY WITHOUT TELEVISION THEN WE'LL JUST HAVE TO FIND SOME WAY TO PROVIDE IT FOR THEM. OTHERWISE, WHAT KIND OF HOST WOULD I BE?
EXCELLENT! DO THAT THEN!
NOW, TELL ME, WHAT DID MY SON LOOK LIKE? WHAT DID HE SAY ABOUT ME?

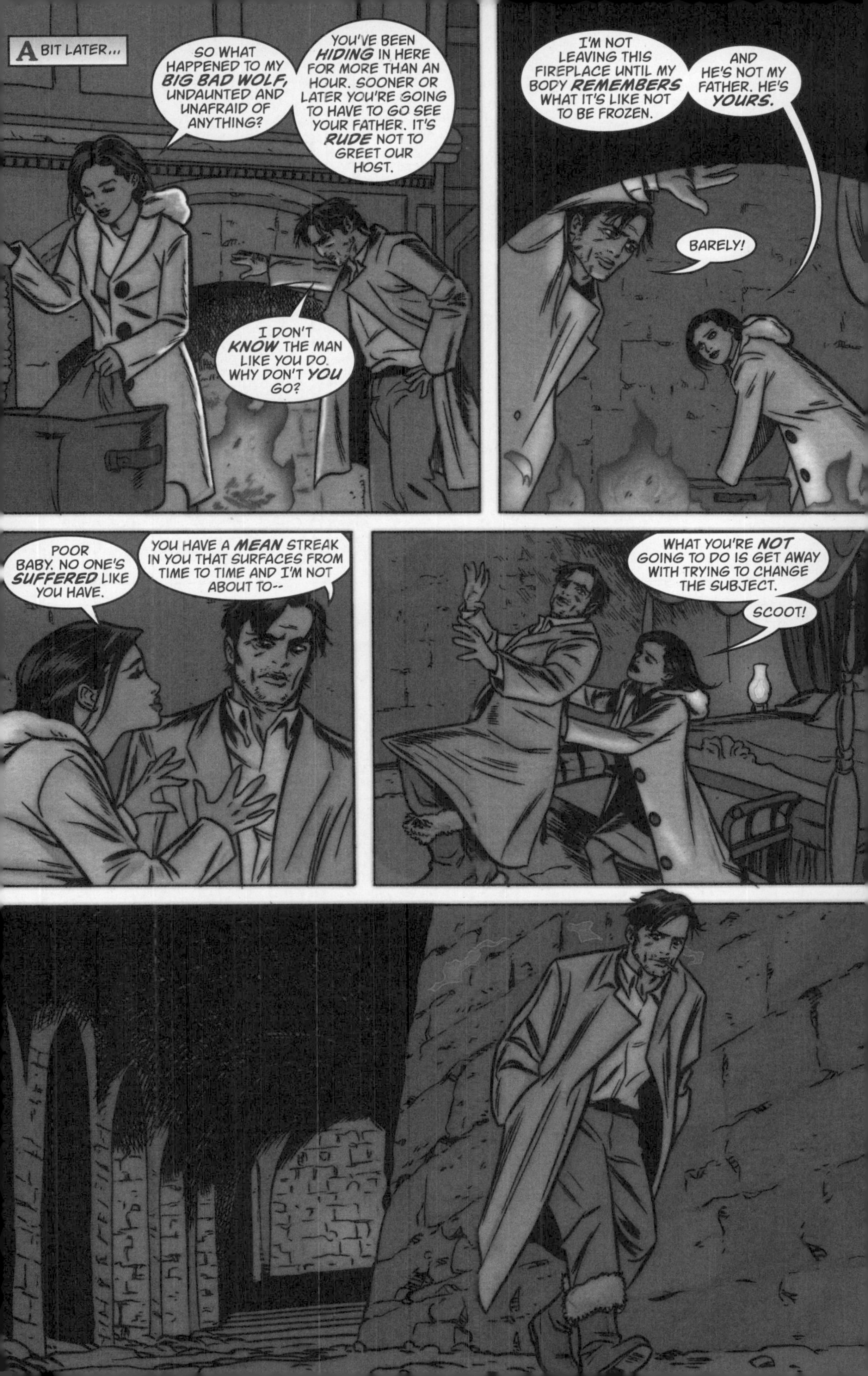
A BIT LATER...
SO WHAT HAPPENED TO MY BIG BAD WOLF, UNDAUNTED AND UNAFRAID OF ANYTHING?
YOU'VE BEEN HIDING IN HERE FOR MORE THAN AN HOUR. SOONER OR LATER YOU'RE GOING TO HAVE TO GO SEE YOUR FATHER. IT'S RUDE NOT TO GREET OUR HOST.
I DON'T KNOW THE MAN LIKE YOU DO. WHY DON'T YOU GO?
I'M NOT LEAVING THIS FIREPLACE UNTIL MY BODY REMEMBERS WHAT IT'S LIKE NOT TO BE FROZEN.
AND HE'S NOT MY FATHER. HE'S YOURS.
BARELY!
POOR BABY. NO ONE'S SUFFERED LIKE YOU HAVE.
YOU HAVE A MEAN STREAK IN YOU THAT SURFACES FROM TIME TO TIME AND I'M NOT ABOUT TO--
WHAT YOU'RE NOT GOING TO DO IS GET AWAY WITH TRYING TO CHANGE THE SUBJECT.
SCOOT!

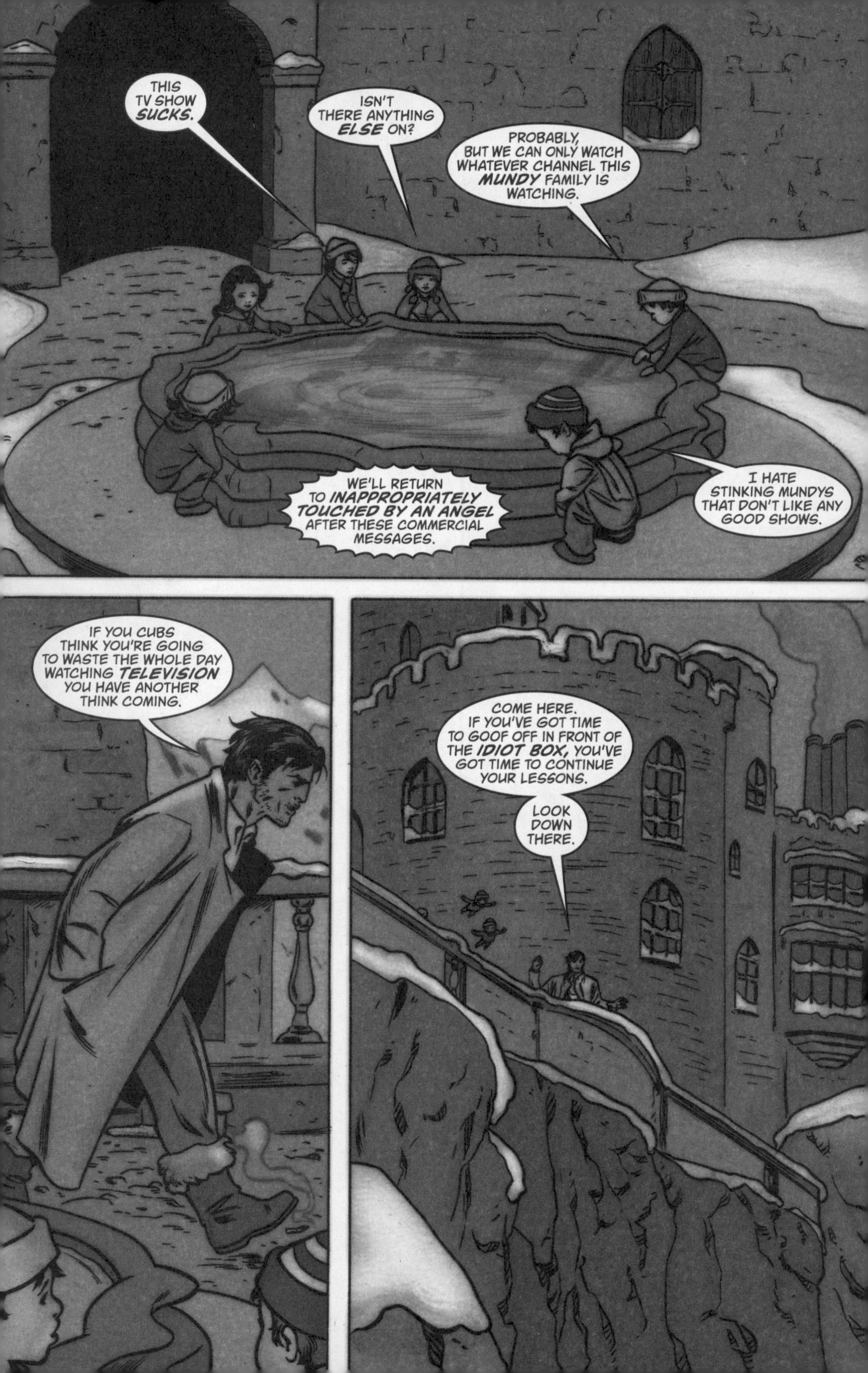
THIS TV SHOW SUCKS.
ISN'T THERE ANYTHING ELSE ON?
PROBABLY, BUT WE CAN ONLY WATCH WHATEVER CHANNEL THIS MUNDY FAMILY IS WATCHING.
WE'LL RETURN TO INAPPROPRIATELY TOUCHED BY AN ANGEL AFTER THESE COMMERCIAL MESSAGES.
I HATE STINKING MUNDYS THAT DON'T LIKE ANY GOOD SHOWS.
IF YOU CUBS THINK YOU'RE GOING TO WASTE THE WHOLE DAY WATCHING TELEVISION YOU HAVE ANOTHER THINK COMING.
COME HERE. IF YOU'VE GOT TIME TO GOOF OFF IN FRONT OF THE IDIOT BOX, YOU'VE GOT TIME TO CONTINUE YOUR LESSONS.
LOOK DOWN THERE.

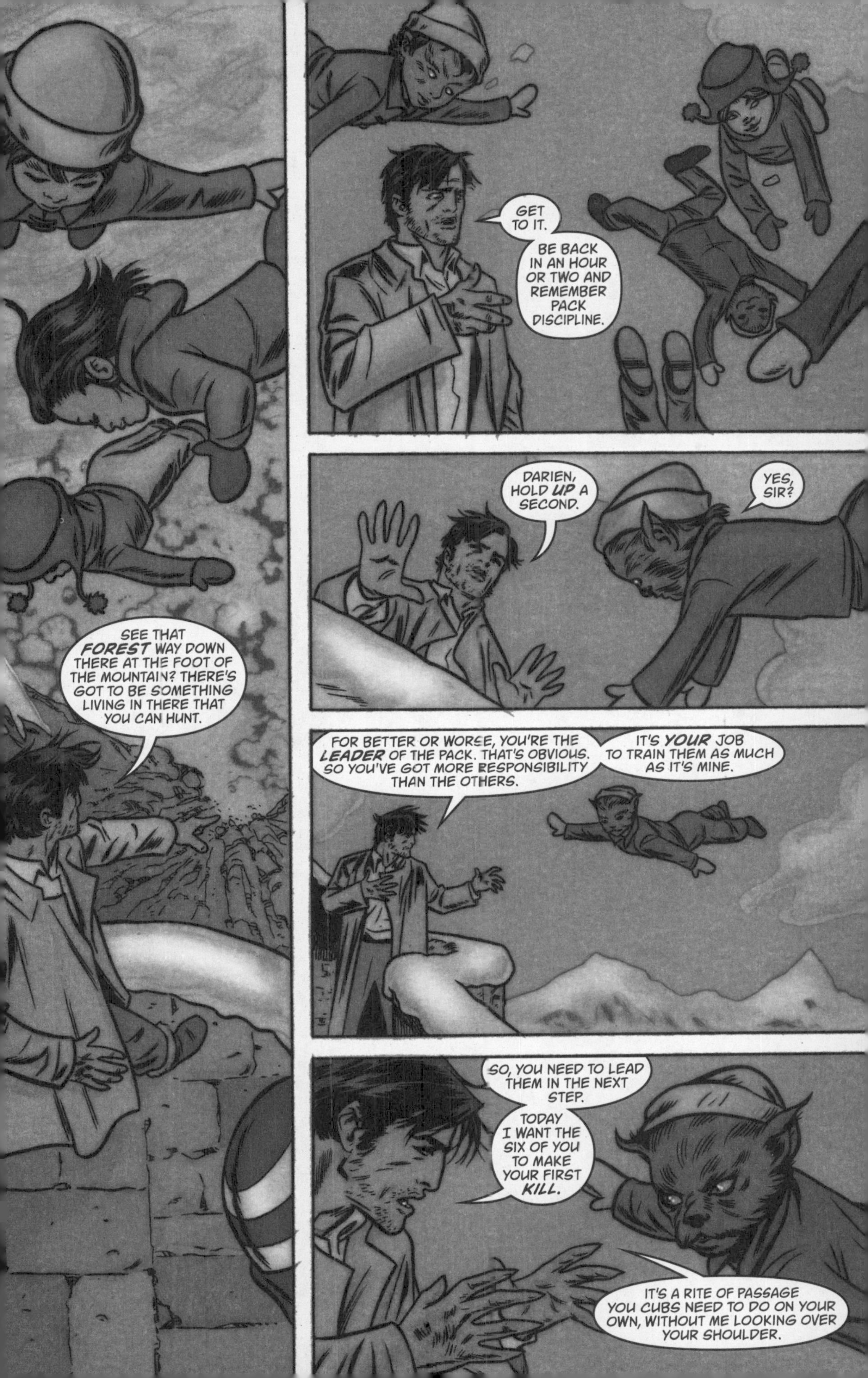
GET TO IT.
BE BACK IN AN HOUR OR TWO AND REMEMBER PACK DISCIPLINE.
SEE THAT FOREST WAY DOWN THERE AT THE FOOT OF THE MOUNTAIN? THERE'S GOT TO BE SOMETHING LIVING IN THERE THAT YOU CAN HUNT.
DARIEN, HOLD UP A SECOND.
YES, SIR?
FOR BETTER OR WORSE, YOU'RE THE LEADER OF THE PACK. THAT'S OBVIOUS. SO YOU'VE GOT MORE RESPONSIBILITY THAN THE OTHERS.
IT'S YOUR JOB TO TRAIN THEM AS MUCH AS IT'S MINE.
SO, YOU NEED TO LEAD THEM IN THE NEXT STEP.
TODAY I WANT THE SIX OF YOU TO MAKE YOUR FIRST KILL.
IT'S A RITE OF PASSAGE YOU CUBS NEED TO DO ON YOUR OWN, WITHOUT ME LOOKING OVER YOUR SHOULDER.

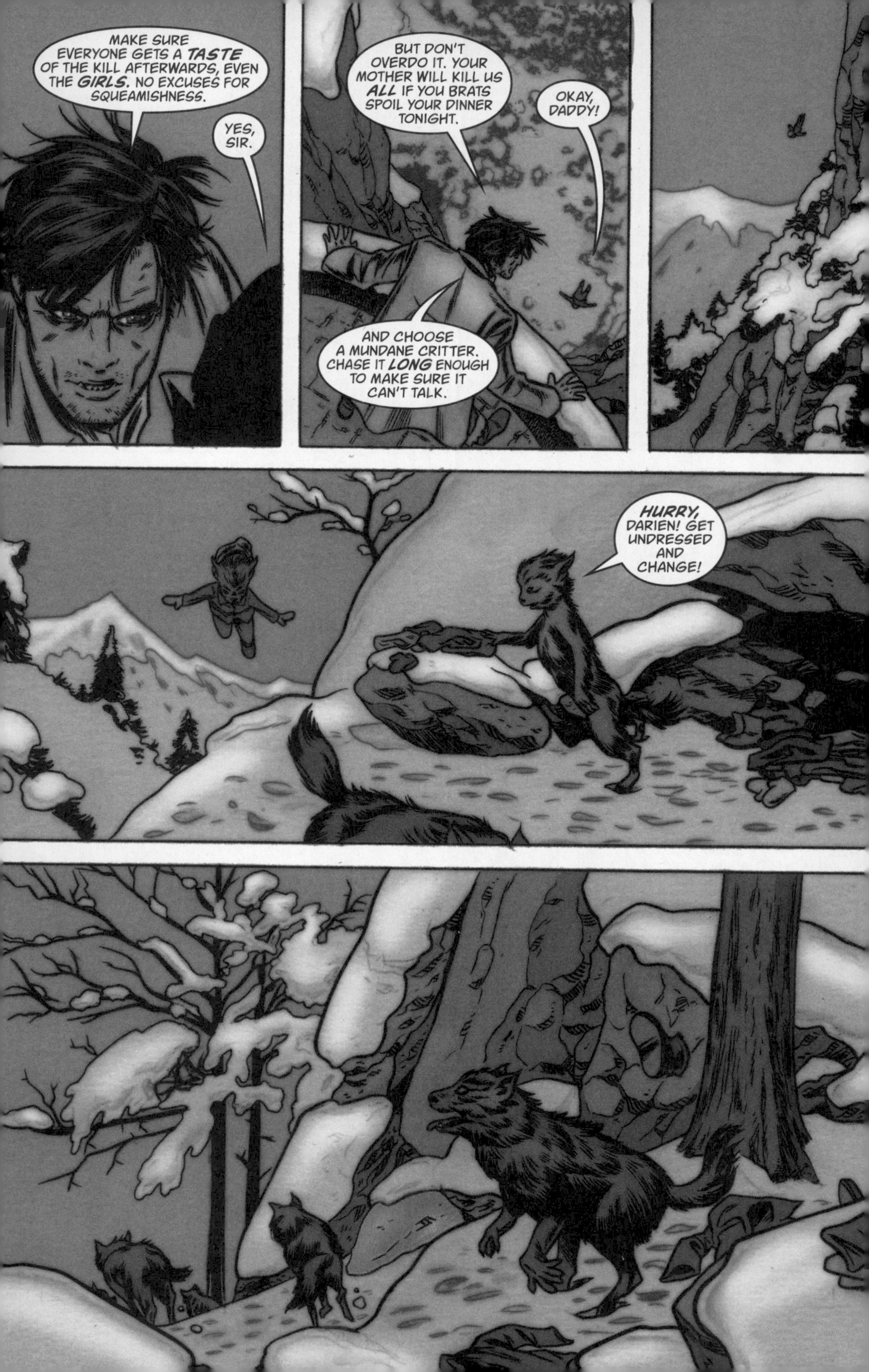
MAKE SURE EVERYONE GETS A TASTE OF THE KILL AFTERWARDS, EVEN THE GIRLS. NO EXCUSES FOR SQUEAMISHNESS.
YES, SIR.
BUT DON'T OVERDO IT. YOUR MOTHER WILL KILL US ALL IF YOU BRATS SPOIL YOUR DINNER TONIGHT.
OKAY, DADDY!
AND CHOOSE A MUNDANE CRITTER. CHASE IT LONG ENOUGH TO MAKE SURE IT CAN'T TALK.
HURRY, DARIEN! GET UNDRESSED AND CHANGE!

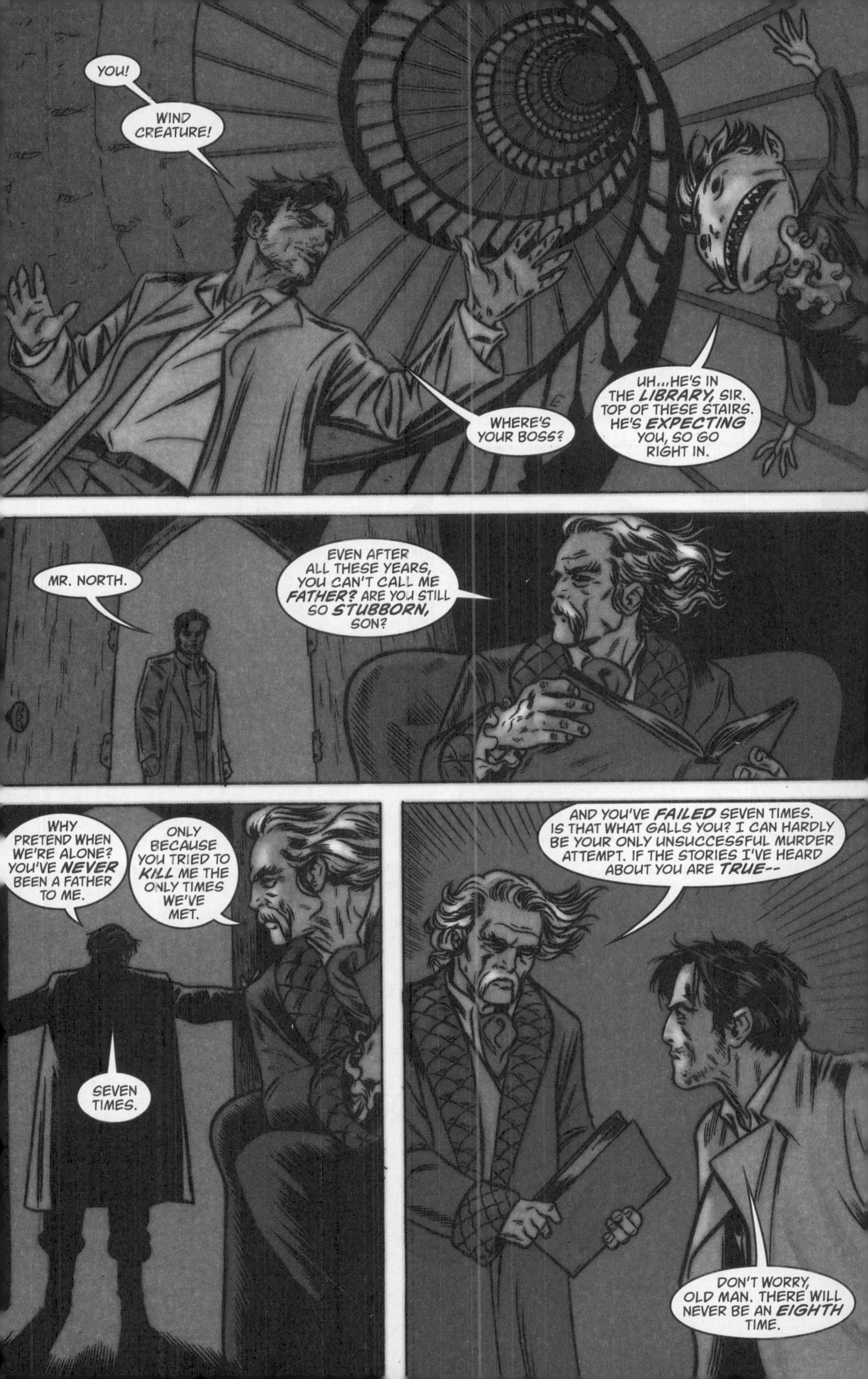
YOU!
WIND CREATURE!
WHERE'S YOUR BOSS?
UH...HE'S IN THE LIBRARY, SIR. TOP OF THESE STAIRS. HE'S EXPECTING YOU, SO GO RIGHT IN.
MR. NORTH.
EVEN AFTER ALL THESE YEARS, YOU CAN'T CALL ME FATHER? ARE YOU STILL SO STUBBORN, SON?
WHY PRETEND WHEN WE'RE ALONE? YOU'VE NEVER BEEN A FATHER TO ME.
ONLY BECAUSE YOU TRIED TO KILL ME THE ONLY TIMES WE'VE MET.
SEVEN TIMES.
AND YOU'VE FAILED SEVEN TIMES. IS THAT WHAT GALLS YOU? I CAN HARDLY BE YOUR ONLY UNSUCCESSFUL MURDER ATTEMPT. IF THE STORIES I'VE HEARD ABOUT YOU ARE TRUE--
DON'T WORRY, OLD MAN. THERE WILL NEVER BE AN EIGHTH TIME.

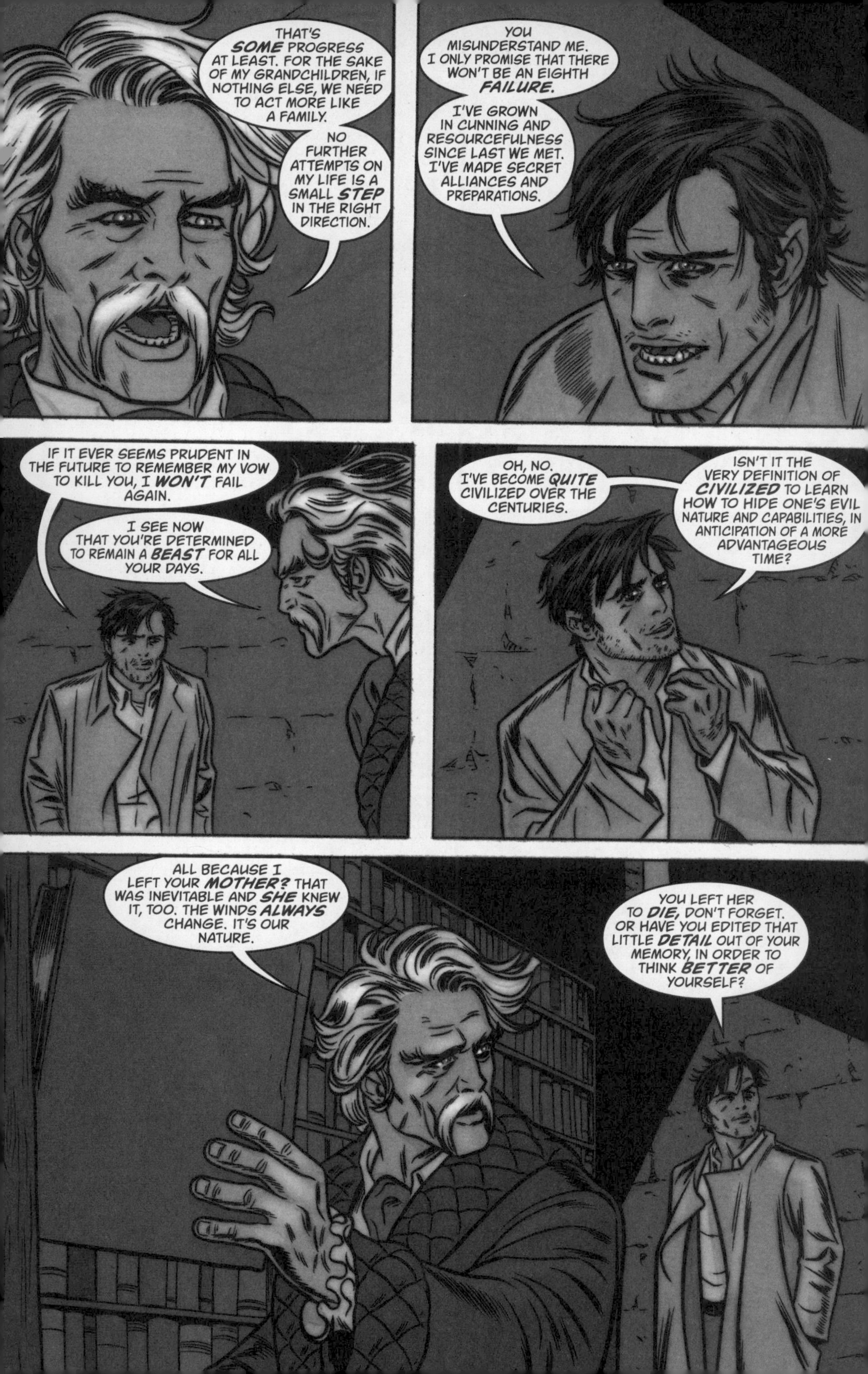

THAT'S SOME PROGRESS AT LEAST. FOR THE SAKE OF MY GRANDCHILDREN, IF NOTHING ELSE, WE NEED TO ACT MORE LIKE A FAMILY.
NO FURTHER ATTEMPTS ON MY LIFE IS A SMALL STEP IN THE RIGHT DIRECTION.
YOU MISUNDERSTAND ME. I ONLY PROMISE THAT THERE WON'T BE AN EIGHTH FAILURE.
I'VE GROWN IN CUNNING AND RESOURCEFULNESS SINCE LAST WE MET. I'VE MADE SECRET ALLIANCES AND PREPARATIONS.
IF IT EVER SEEMS PRUDENT IN THE FUTURE TO REMEMBER MY VOW TO KILL YOU, I WON'T FAIL AGAIN.
I SEE NOW THAT YOU'RE DETERMINED TO REMAIN A BEAST FOR ALL YOUR DAYS.
OH, NO. I'VE BECOME QUITE CIVILIZED OVER THE CENTURIES.
ISN'T IT THE VERY DEFINITION OF CIVILIZED TO LEARN HOW TO HIDE ONE'S EVIL NATURE AND CAPABILITIES, IN ANTICIPATION OF A MORE ADVANTAGEOUS TIME?
ALL BECAUSE I LEFT YOUR MOTHER? THAT WAS INEVITABLE AND SHE KNEW IT, TOO. THE WINDS ALWAYS CHANGE. IT'S OUR NATURE.
YOU LEFT HER TO DIE, DON'T FORGET. OR HAVE YOU EDITED THAT LITTLE DETAIL OUT OF YOUR MEMORY, IN ORDER TO THINK BETTER OF YOURSELF?

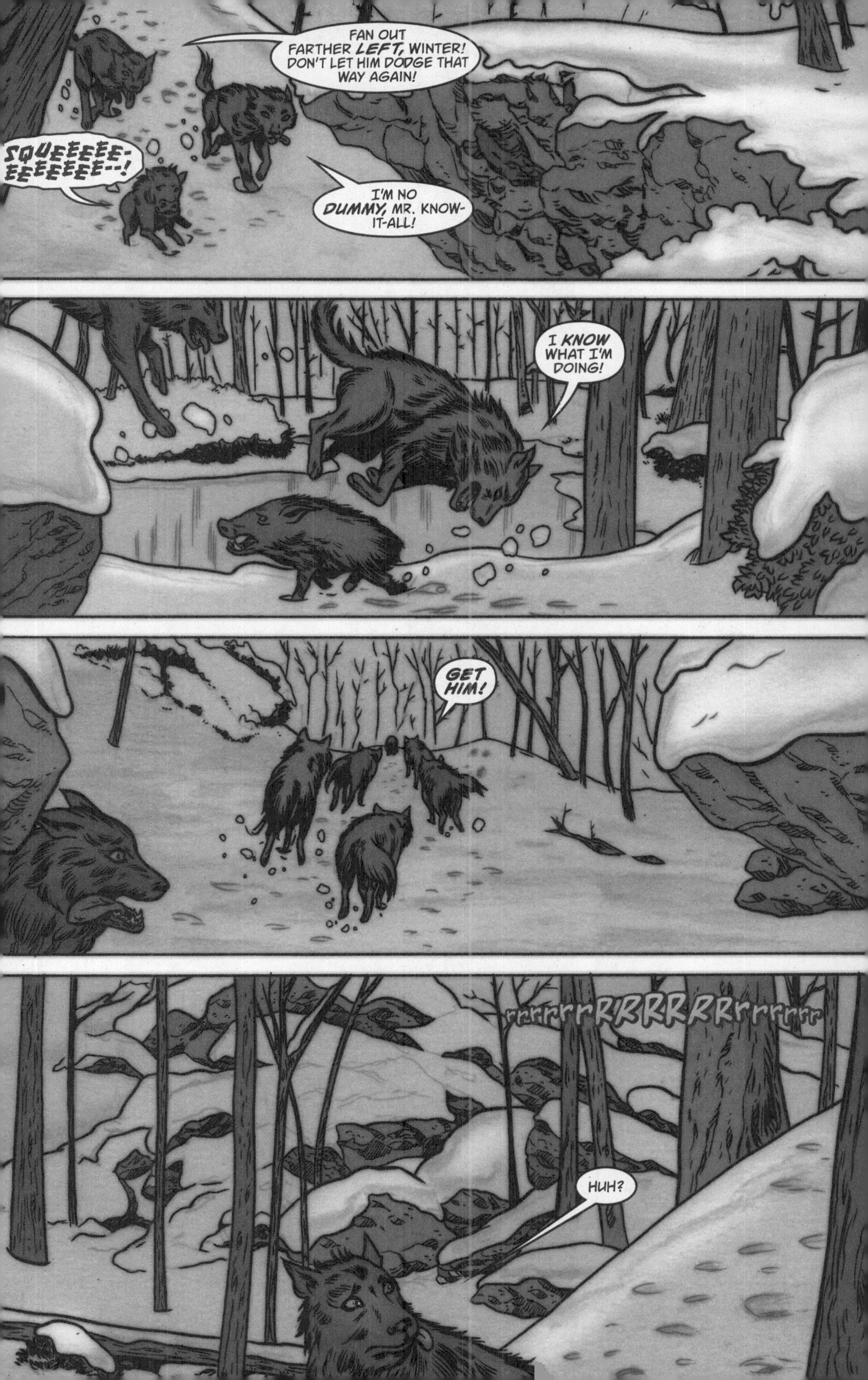
FAN OUT FARTHER LEFT, WINTER! DON'T LET HIM DODGE THAT WAY AGAIN!
SQUEEEEEE-EEEEEEE--!
I'M NO DUMMY, MR. KNOW-IT-ALL!
I KNOW WHAT I'M DOING!
GET HIM!
rrrrrrRRRRRRrrrrrrr
HUH?

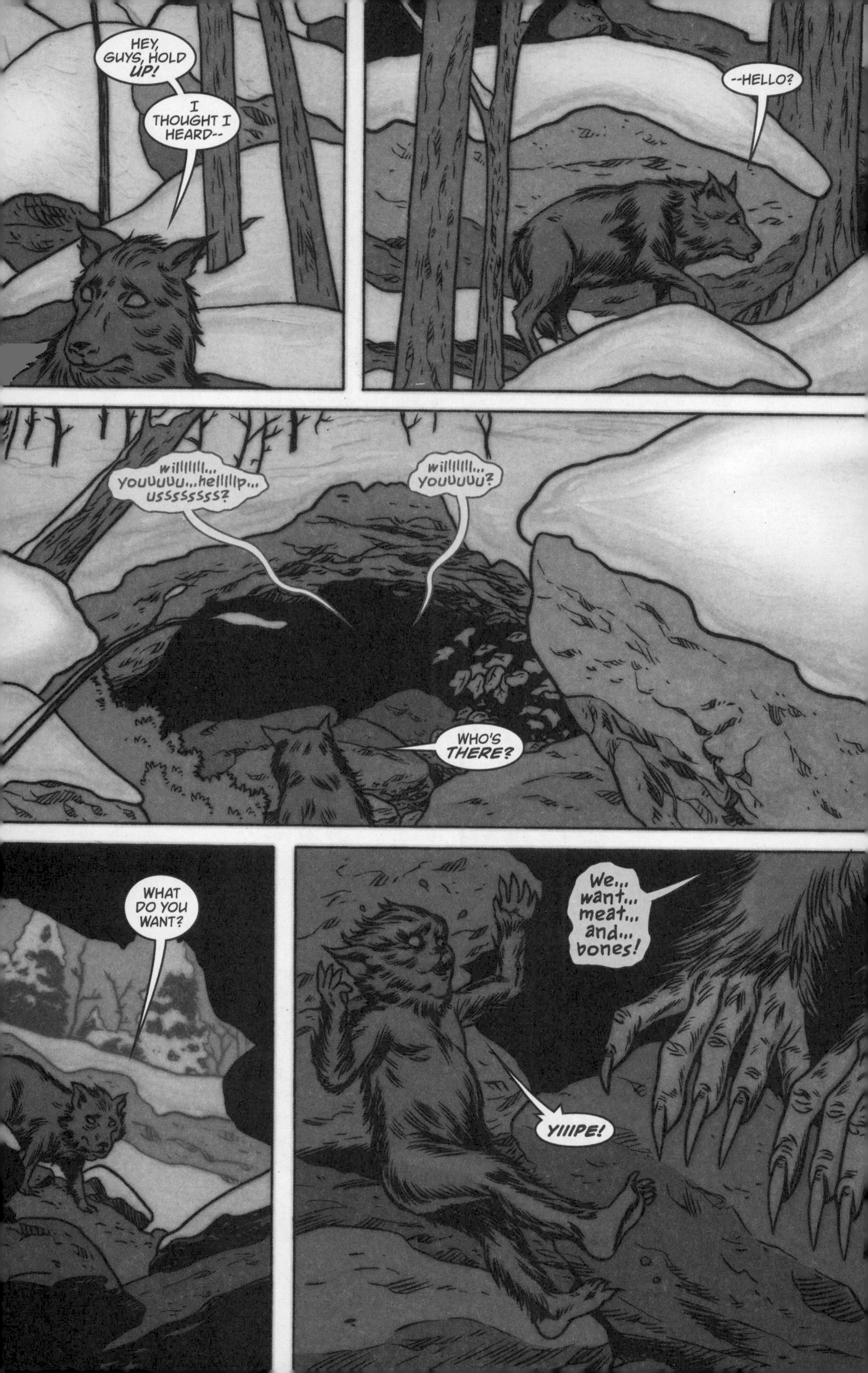
HEY, GUYS, HOLD *UP!*
I THOUGHT I HEARD--
--HELLO?
willlllll... youuuuu...hellllp... usssssssss?
willllll... youuuuu?
WHO'S *THERE?*
WHAT DO YOU WANT?
We... want... meat... and... bones!
YIIIPE!

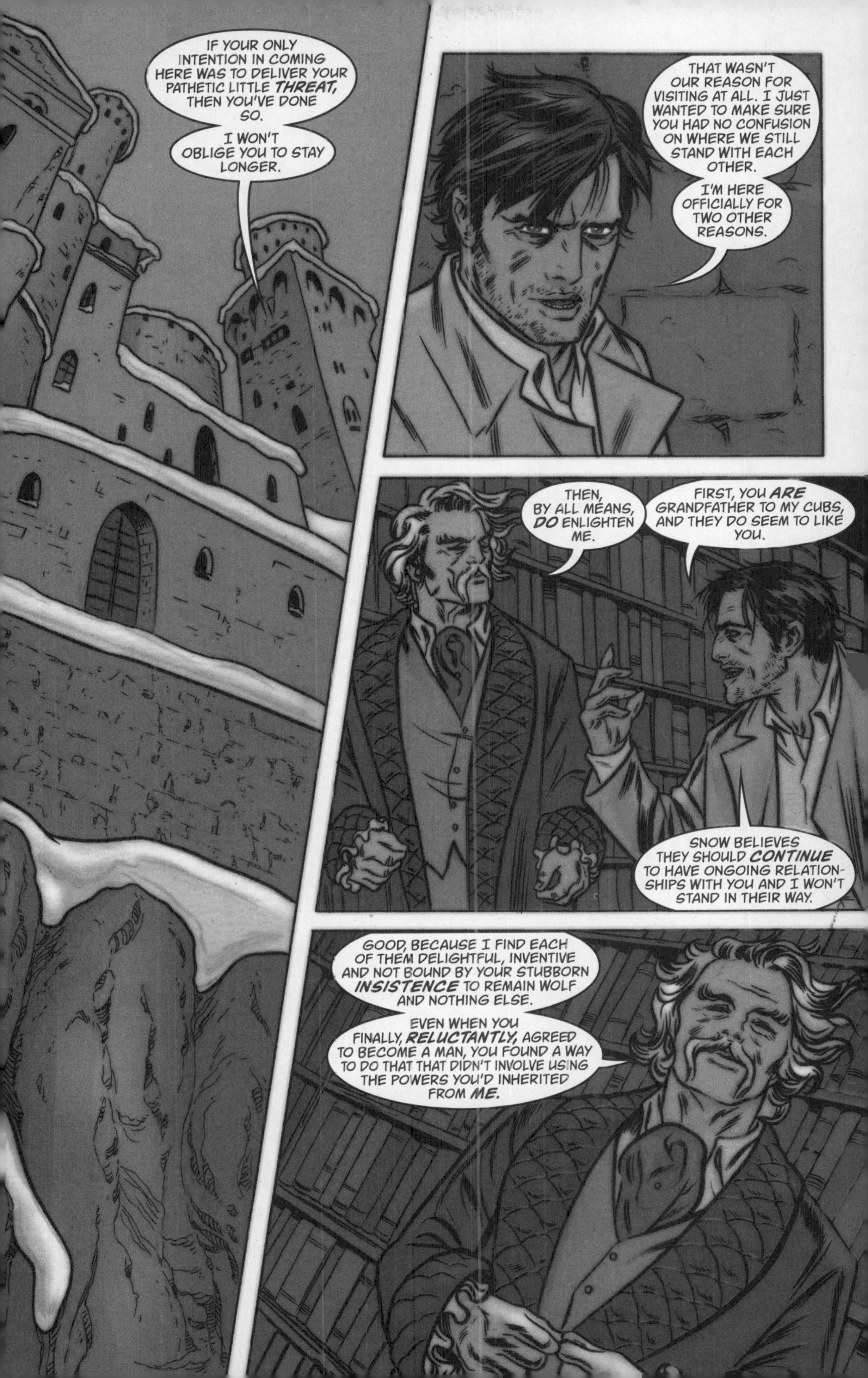
IF YOUR ONLY INTENTION IN COMING HERE WAS TO DELIVER YOUR PATHETIC LITTLE *THREAT,* THEN YOU'VE DONE SO.
I WON'T OBLIGE YOU TO STAY LONGER.
THAT WASN'T OUR REASON FOR VISITING AT ALL. I JUST WANTED TO MAKE SURE YOU HAD NO CONFUSION ON WHERE WE STILL STAND WITH EACH OTHER.
I'M HERE OFFICIALLY FOR TWO OTHER REASONS.
THEN, BY ALL MEANS, ***DO*** ENLIGHTEN ME.
FIRST, YOU ***ARE*** GRANDFATHER TO MY CUBS, AND THEY DO SEEM TO LIKE YOU.
SNOW BELIEVES THEY SHOULD ***CONTINUE*** TO HAVE ONGOING RELATION-SHIPS WITH YOU AND I WON'T STAND IN THEIR WAY.
GOOD, BECAUSE I FIND EACH OF THEM DELIGHTFUL, INVENTIVE AND NOT BOUND BY YOUR STUBBORN ***INSISTENCE*** TO REMAIN WOLF AND NOTHING ELSE.
EVEN WHEN YOU FINALLY, ***RELUCTANTLY,*** AGREED TO BECOME A MAN, YOU FOUND A WAY TO DO THAT THAT DIDN'T INVOLVE USING THE POWERS YOU'D INHERITED FROM ***ME.***

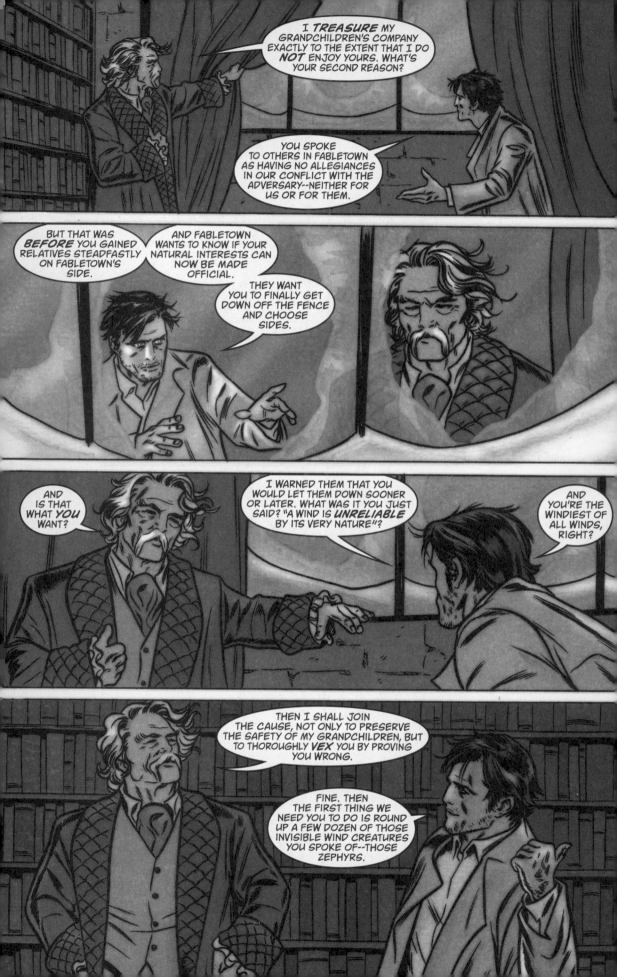

I *TREASURE* MY GRANDCHILDREN'S COMPANY EXACTLY TO THE EXTENT THAT I DO *NOT* ENJOY YOURS. WHAT'S YOUR SECOND REASON?

YOU SPOKE TO OTHERS IN FABLETOWN AS HAVING NO ALLEGIANCES IN OUR CONFLICT WITH THE ADVERSARY--NEITHER FOR US OR FOR THEM.

BUT THAT WAS *BEFORE* YOU GAINED RELATIVES STEADFASTLY ON FABLETOWN'S SIDE.

AND FABLETOWN WANTS TO KNOW IF YOUR NATURAL INTERESTS CAN NOW BE MADE OFFICIAL.

THEY WANT YOU TO FINALLY GET DOWN OFF THE FENCE AND CHOOSE SIDES.

AND IS THAT WHAT *YOU* WANT?

I WARNED THEM THAT YOU WOULD LET THEM DOWN SOONER OR LATER. WHAT WAS IT YOU JUST SAID? "A WIND IS *UNRELIABLE* BY ITS VERY NATURE"?

AND YOU'RE THE WINDIEST OF ALL WINDS, RIGHT?

THEN I SHALL JOIN THE CAUSE, NOT ONLY TO PRESERVE THE SAFETY OF MY GRANDCHILDREN, BUT TO THOROUGHLY *VEX* YOU BY PROVING YOU WRONG.

FINE. THEN THE FIRST THING WE NEED YOU TO DO IS ROUND UP A FEW DOZEN OF THOSE INVISIBLE WIND CREATURES YOU SPOKE OF--THOSE ZEPHYRS.

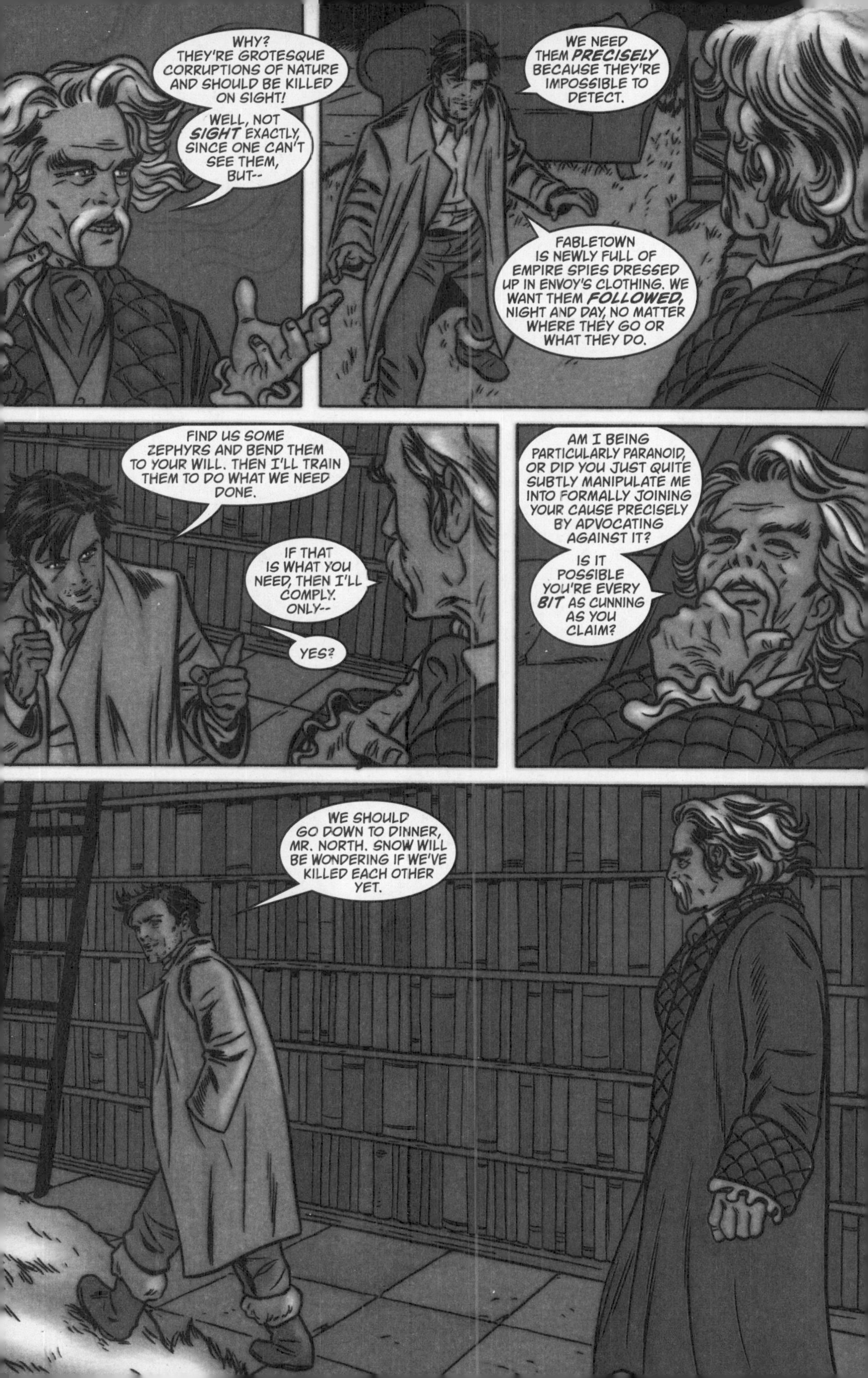

WHY? THEY'RE GROTESQUE CORRUPTIONS OF NATURE AND SHOULD BE KILLED ON SIGHT!
WELL, NOT SIGHT EXACTLY, SINCE ONE CAN'T SEE THEM, BUT--
WE NEED THEM PRECISELY BECAUSE THEY'RE IMPOSSIBLE TO DETECT.
FABLETOWN IS NEWLY FULL OF EMPIRE SPIES DRESSED UP IN ENVOY'S CLOTHING. WE WANT THEM FOLLOWED, NIGHT AND DAY, NO MATTER WHERE THEY GO OR WHAT THEY DO.
FIND US SOME ZEPHYRS AND BEND THEM TO YOUR WILL. THEN I'LL TRAIN THEM TO DO WHAT WE NEED DONE.
IF THAT IS WHAT YOU NEED, THEN I'LL COMPLY. ONLY--
YES?
AM I BEING PARTICULARLY PARANOID, OR DID YOU JUST QUITE SUBTLY MANIPULATE ME INTO FORMALLY JOINING YOUR CAUSE PRECISELY BY ADVOCATING AGAINST IT?
IS IT POSSIBLE YOU'RE EVERY BIT AS CUNNING AS YOU CLAIM?
WE SHOULD GO DOWN TO DINNER, MR. NORTH. SNOW WILL BE WONDERING IF WE'VE KILLED EACH OTHER YET.

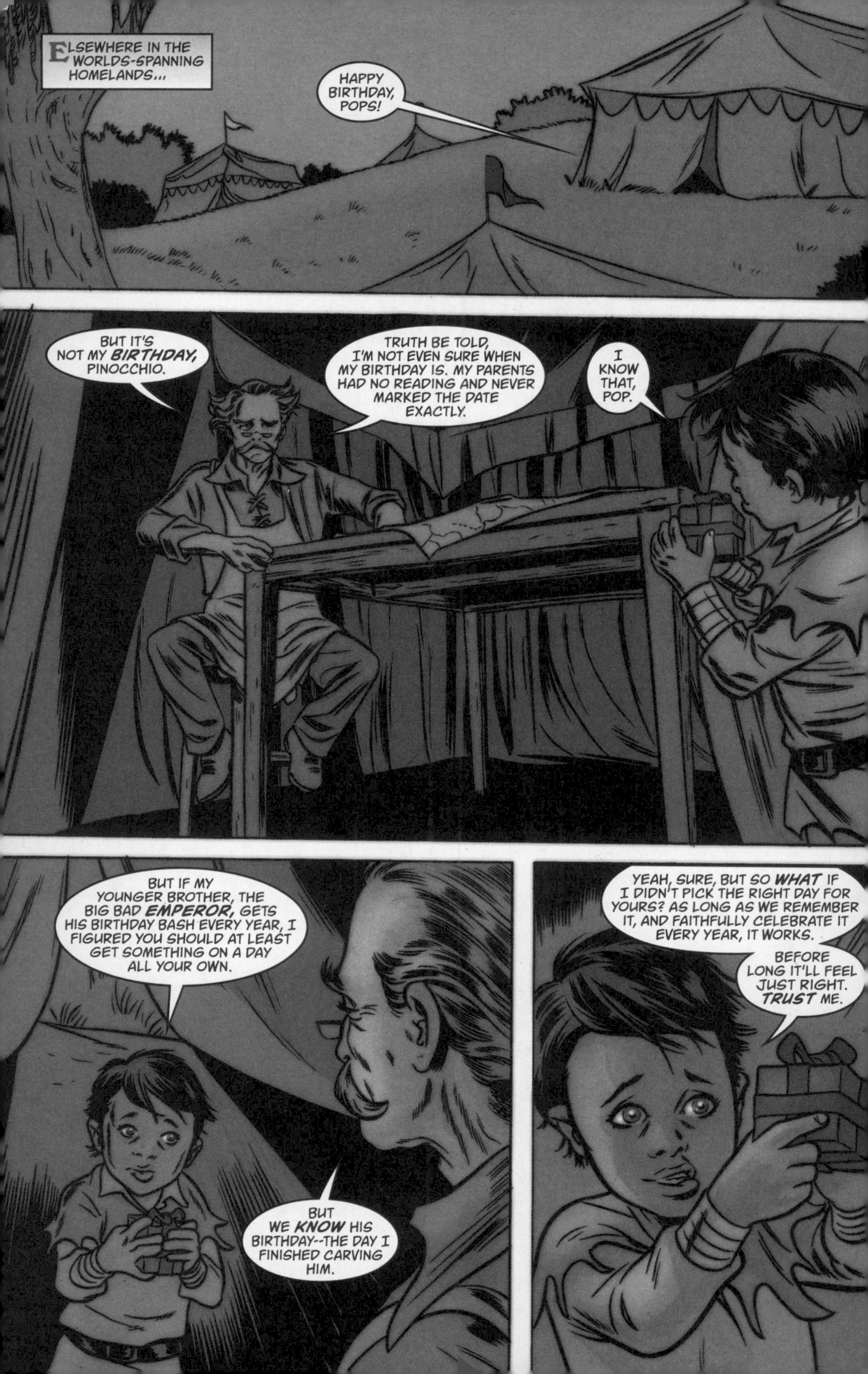
ELSEWHERE IN THE WORLDS-SPANNING HOMELANDS...
HAPPY BIRTHDAY, POPS!
BUT IT'S NOT MY BIRTHDAY, PINOCCHIO.
TRUTH BE TOLD, I'M NOT EVEN SURE WHEN MY BIRTHDAY IS. MY PARENTS HAD NO READING AND NEVER MARKED THE DATE EXACTLY.
I KNOW THAT, POP.
BUT IF MY YOUNGER BROTHER, THE BIG BAD EMPEROR, GETS HIS BIRTHDAY BASH EVERY YEAR, I FIGURED YOU SHOULD AT LEAST GET SOMETHING ON A DAY ALL YOUR OWN.
BUT WE KNOW HIS BIRTHDAY--THE DAY I FINISHED CARVING HIM.
YEAH, SURE, BUT SO WHAT IF I DIDN'T PICK THE RIGHT DAY FOR YOURS? AS LONG AS WE REMEMBER IT, AND FAITHFULLY CELEBRATE IT EVERY YEAR, IT WORKS.
BEFORE LONG IT'LL FEEL JUST RIGHT. TRUST ME.

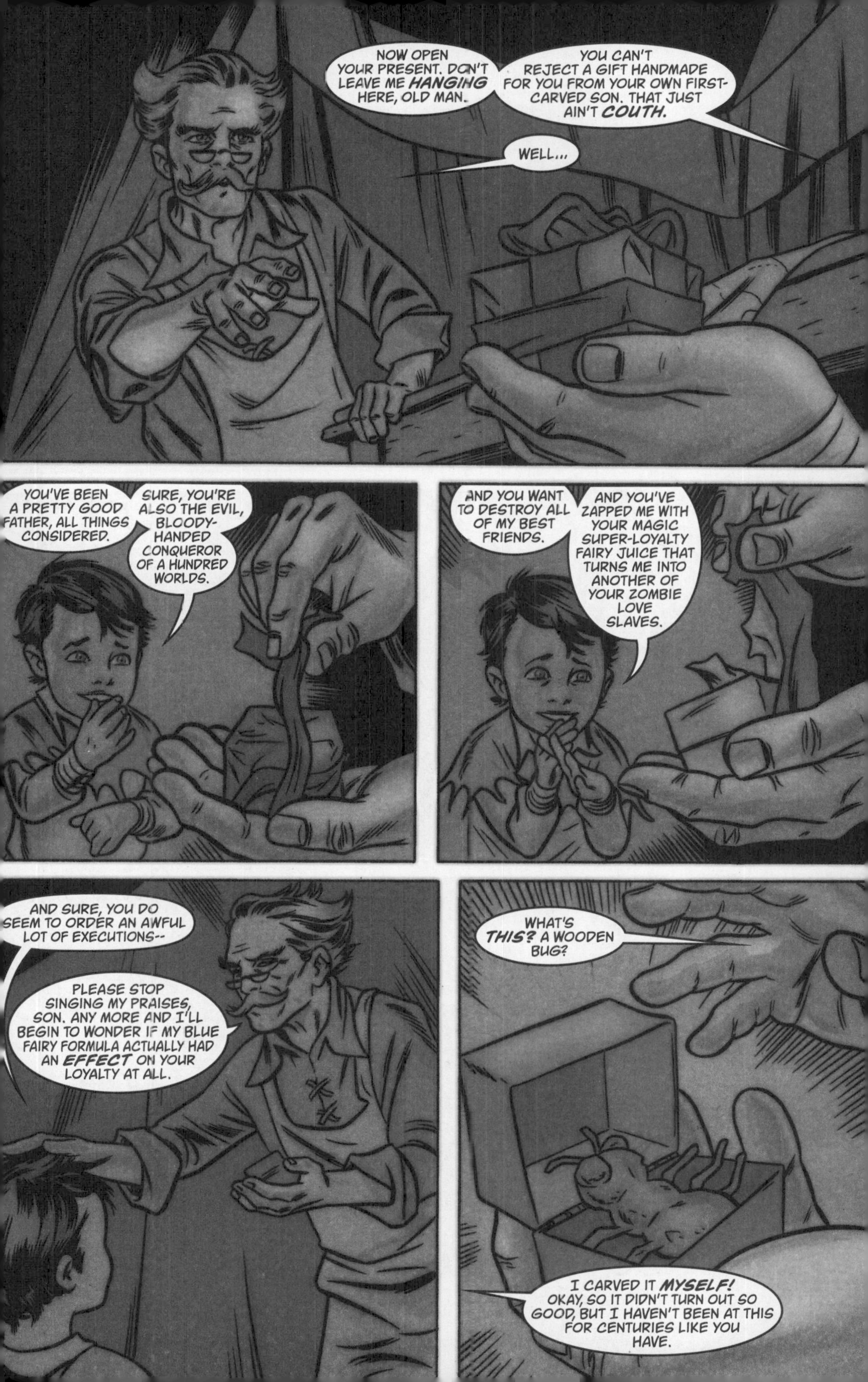

NOW OPEN YOUR PRESENT. DON'T LEAVE ME HANGING HERE, OLD MAN.
YOU CAN'T REJECT A GIFT HANDMADE FOR YOU FROM YOUR OWN FIRST-CARVED SON. THAT JUST AIN'T COUTH.
WELL...
YOU'VE BEEN A PRETTY GOOD FATHER, ALL THINGS CONSIDERED.
SURE, YOU'RE ALSO THE EVIL, BLOODY-HANDED CONQUEROR OF A HUNDRED WORLDS.
AND YOU WANT TO DESTROY ALL OF MY BEST FRIENDS.
AND YOU'VE ZAPPED ME WITH YOUR MAGIC SUPER-LOYALTY FAIRY JUICE THAT TURNS ME INTO ANOTHER OF YOUR ZOMBIE LOVE SLAVES.
AND SURE, YOU DO SEEM TO ORDER AN AWFUL LOT OF EXECUTIONS--
PLEASE STOP SINGING MY PRAISES, SON. ANY MORE AND I'LL BEGIN TO WONDER IF MY BLUE FAIRY FORMULA ACTUALLY HAD AN EFFECT ON YOUR LOYALTY AT ALL.
WHAT'S THIS? A WOODEN BUG?
I CARVED IT MYSELF! OKAY, SO IT DIDN'T TURN OUT SO GOOD, BUT I HAVEN'T BEEN AT THIS FOR CENTURIES LIKE YOU HAVE.

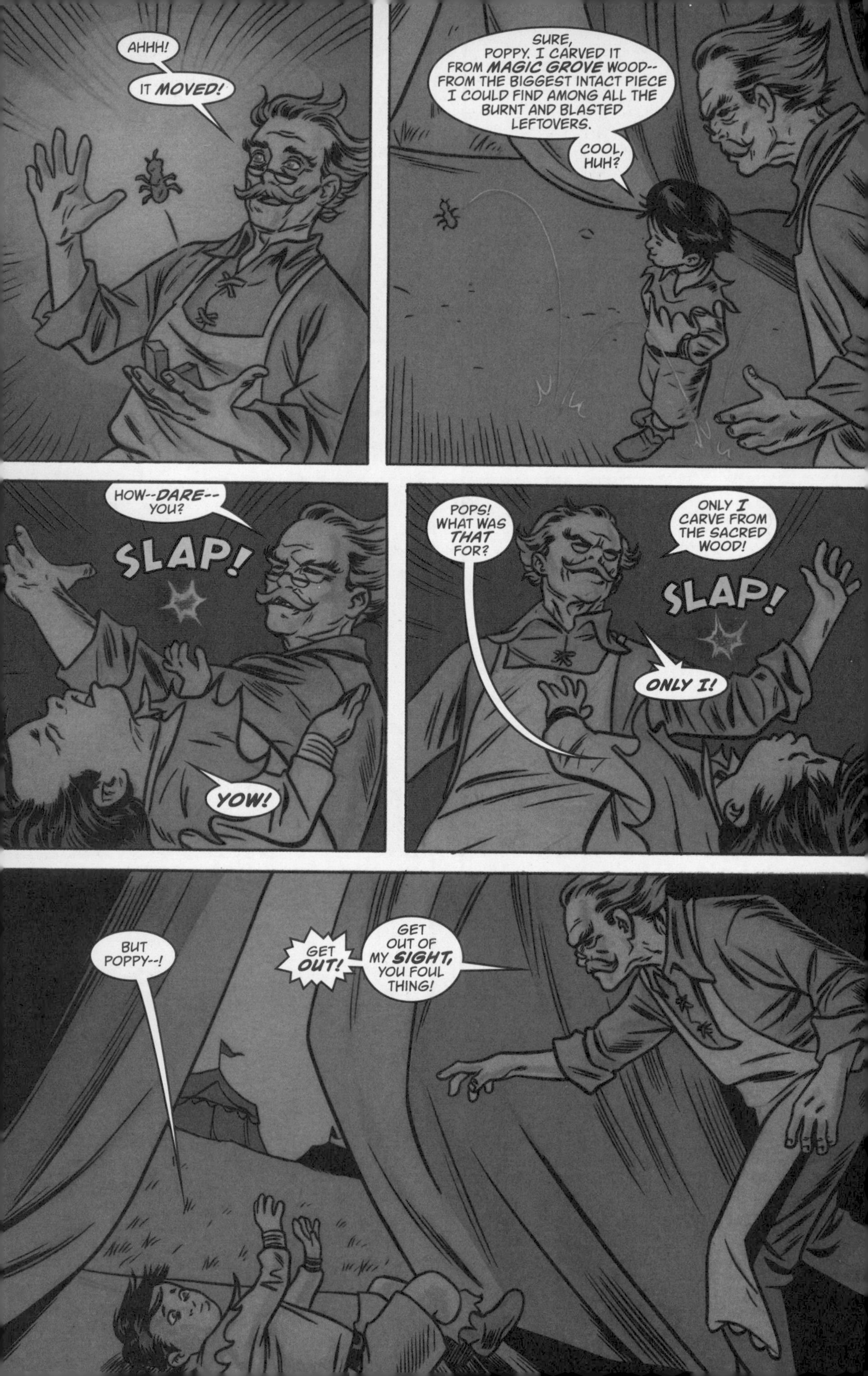
AHHH!
IT MOVED!
SURE, POPPY. I CARVED IT FROM MAGIC GROVE WOOD-- FROM THE BIGGEST INTACT PIECE I COULD FIND AMONG ALL THE BURNT AND BLASTED LEFTOVERS.
COOL, HUH?
HOW--DARE--YOU?
SLAP!
YOW!
POPS! WHAT WAS THAT FOR?
ONLY I CARVE FROM THE SACRED WOOD!
SLAP!
ONLY I!
BUT POPPY--!
GET OUT!
GET OUT OF MY SIGHT, YOU FOUL THING!

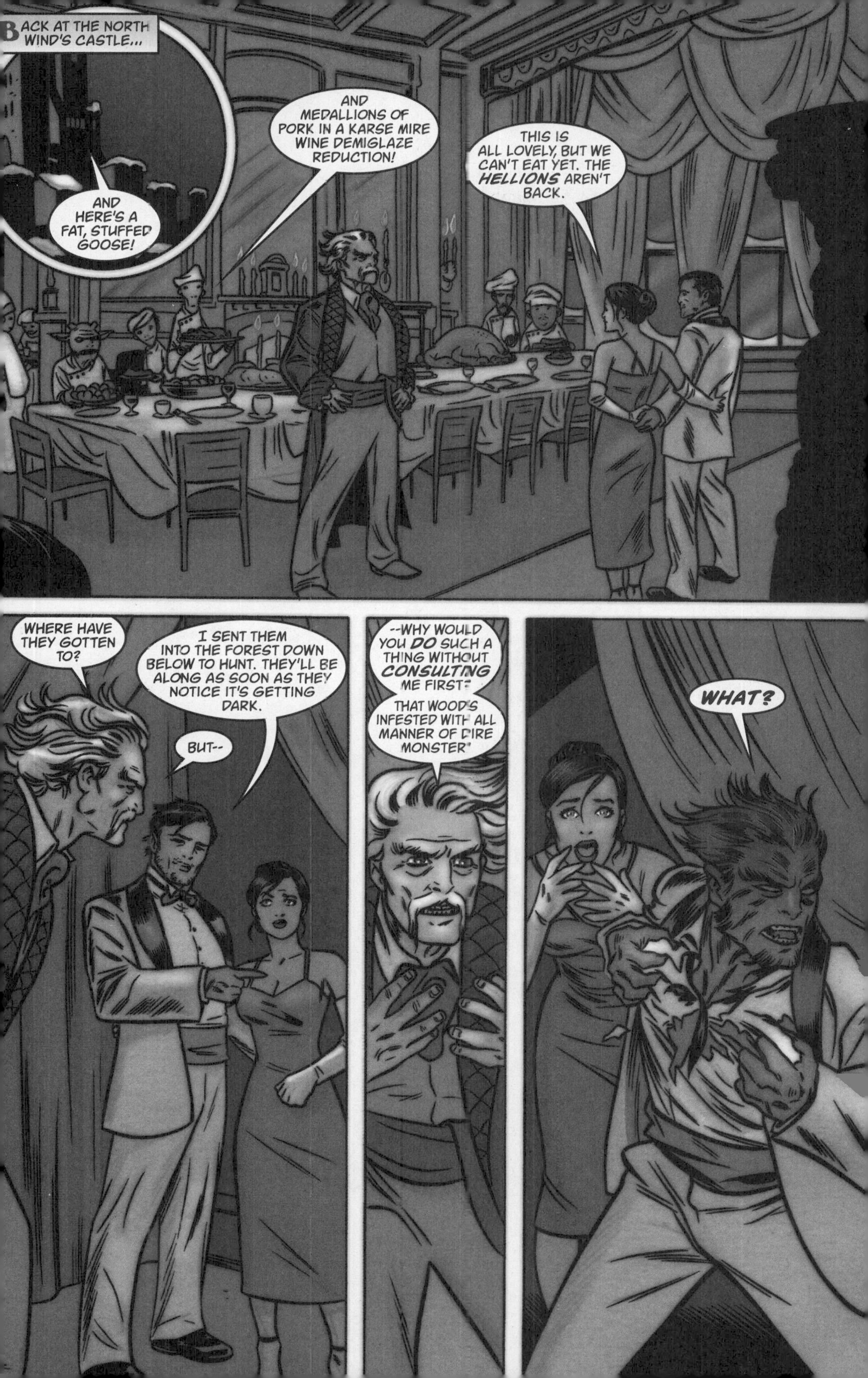
BACK AT THE NORTH WIND'S CASTLE...
AND HERE'S A FAT, STUFFED GOOSE!
AND MEDALLIONS OF PORK IN A KARSE MIRE WINE DEMIGLAZE REDUCTION!
THIS IS ALL LOVELY, BUT WE CAN'T EAT YET. THE HELLIONS AREN'T BACK.
WHERE HAVE THEY GOTTEN TO?
I SENT THEM INTO THE FOREST DOWN BELOW TO HUNT. THEY'LL BE ALONG AS SOON AS THEY NOTICE IT'S GETTING DARK.
BUT--
--WHY WOULD YOU DO SUCH A THING WITHOUT CONSULTING ME FIRST?
THAT WOOD'S INFESTED WITH ALL MANNER OF DIRE MONSTER
WHAT?

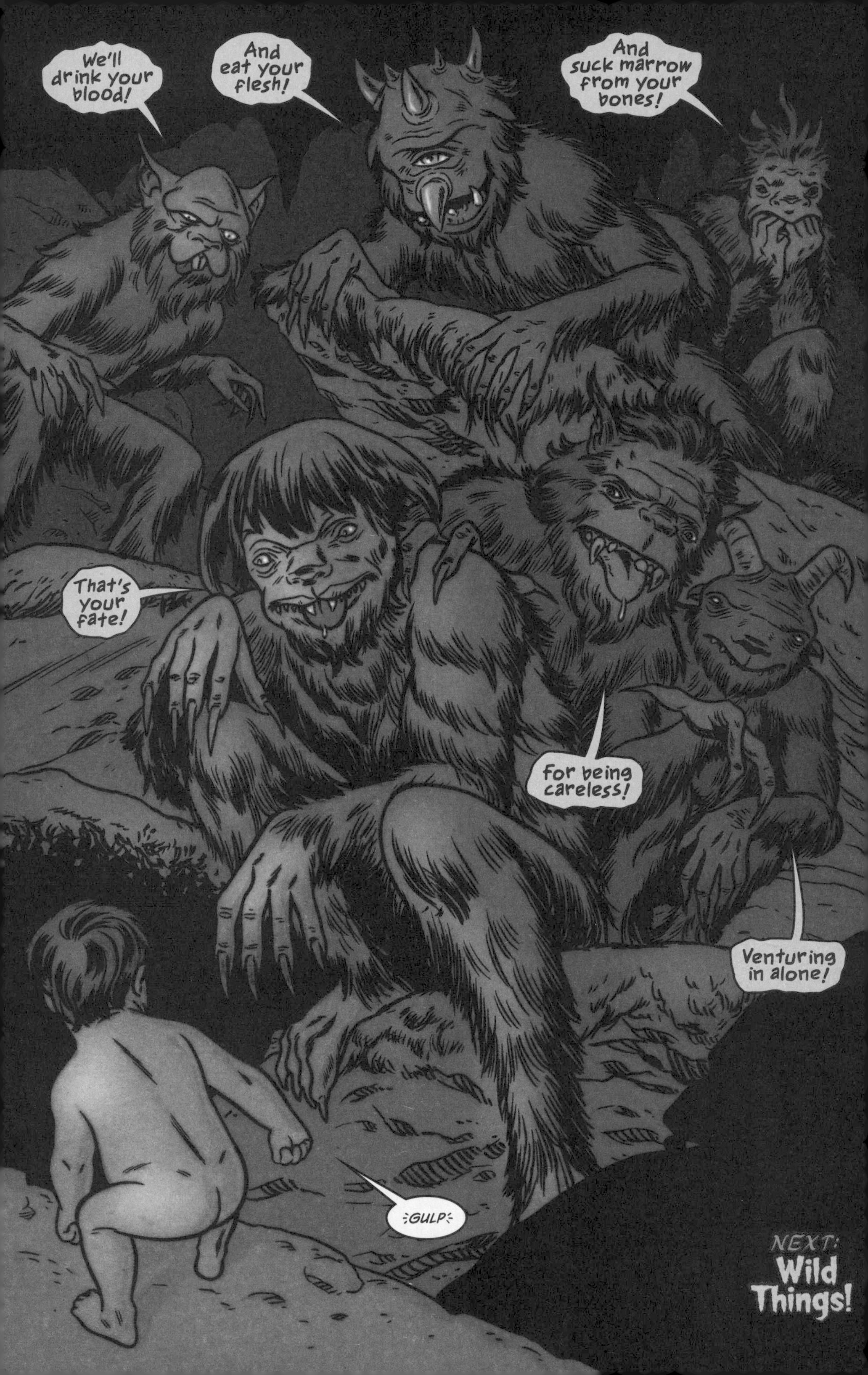
We'll drink your blood!
And eat your flesh!
And suck marrow from your bones!
That's your fate!
For being careless!
Venturing in alone!
GULP
NEXT: Wild Things!

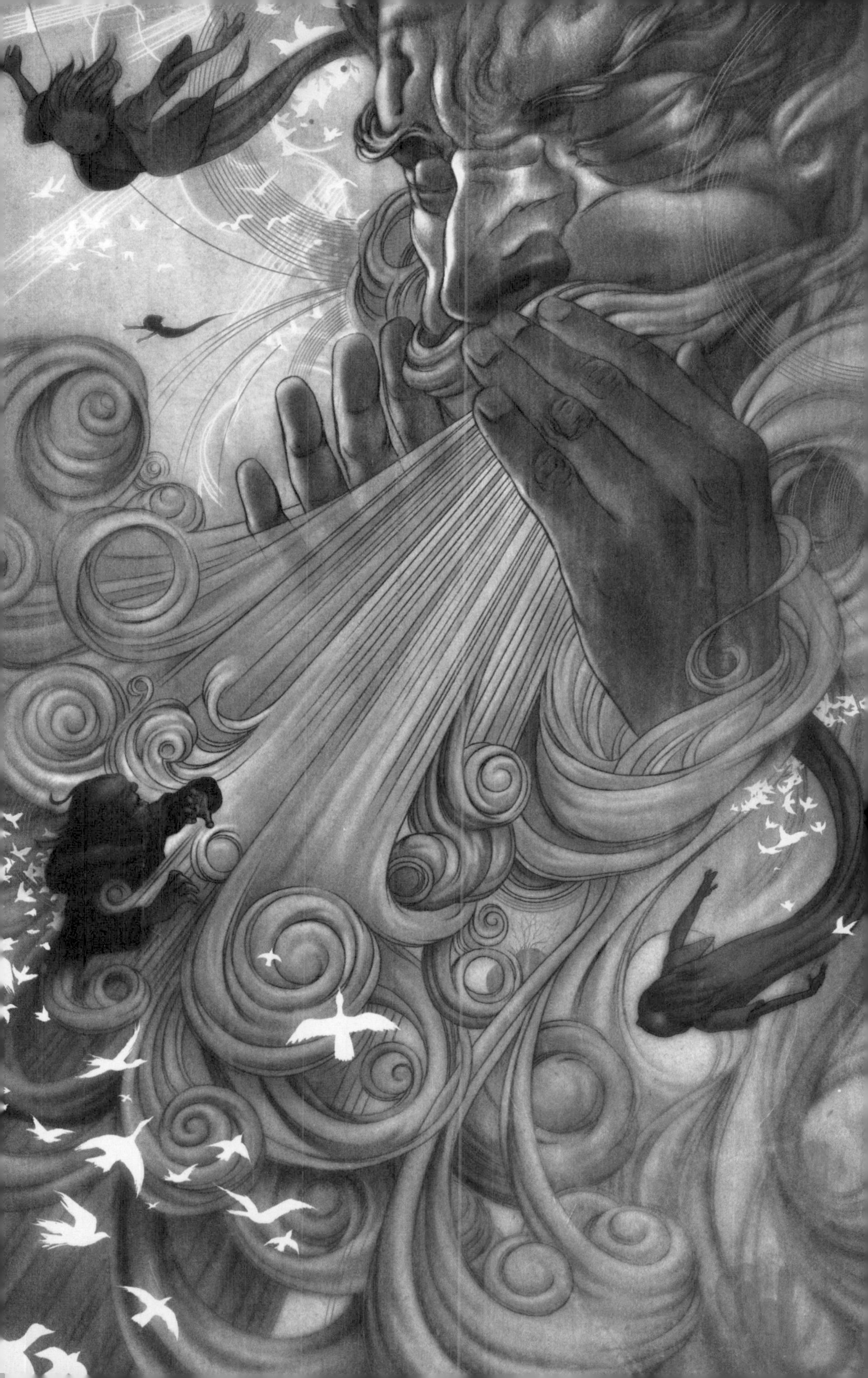

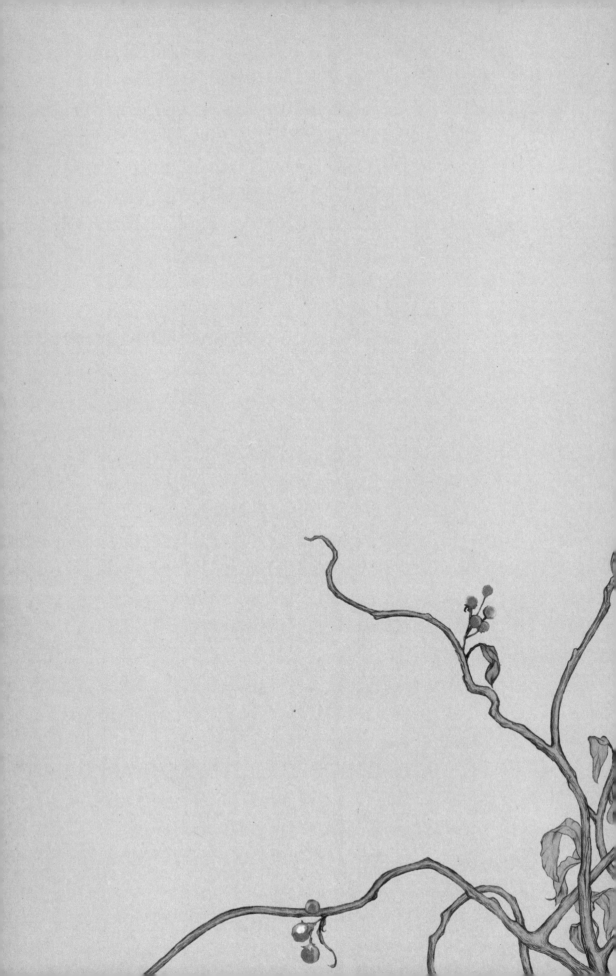

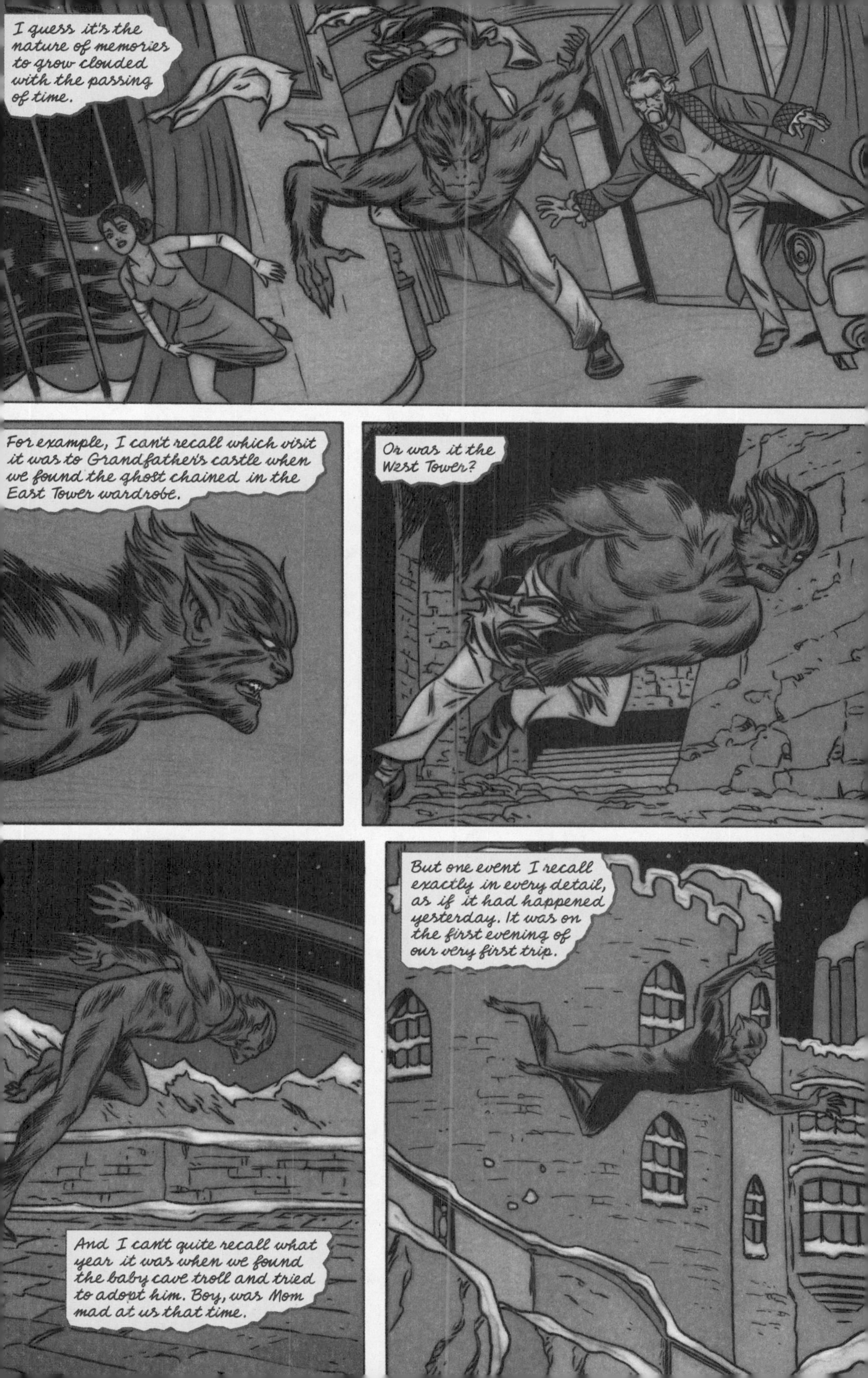
I guess it's the nature of memories to grow clouded with the passing of time.
For example, I can't recall which visit it was to Grandfather's castle when we found the ghost chained in the East Tower wardrobe.
Or was it the West Tower?
And I can't quite recall what year it was when we found the baby cave troll and tried to adopt him. Boy, was Mom mad at us that time.
But one event I recall exactly in every detail, as if it had happened yesterday. It was on the first evening of our very first trip.

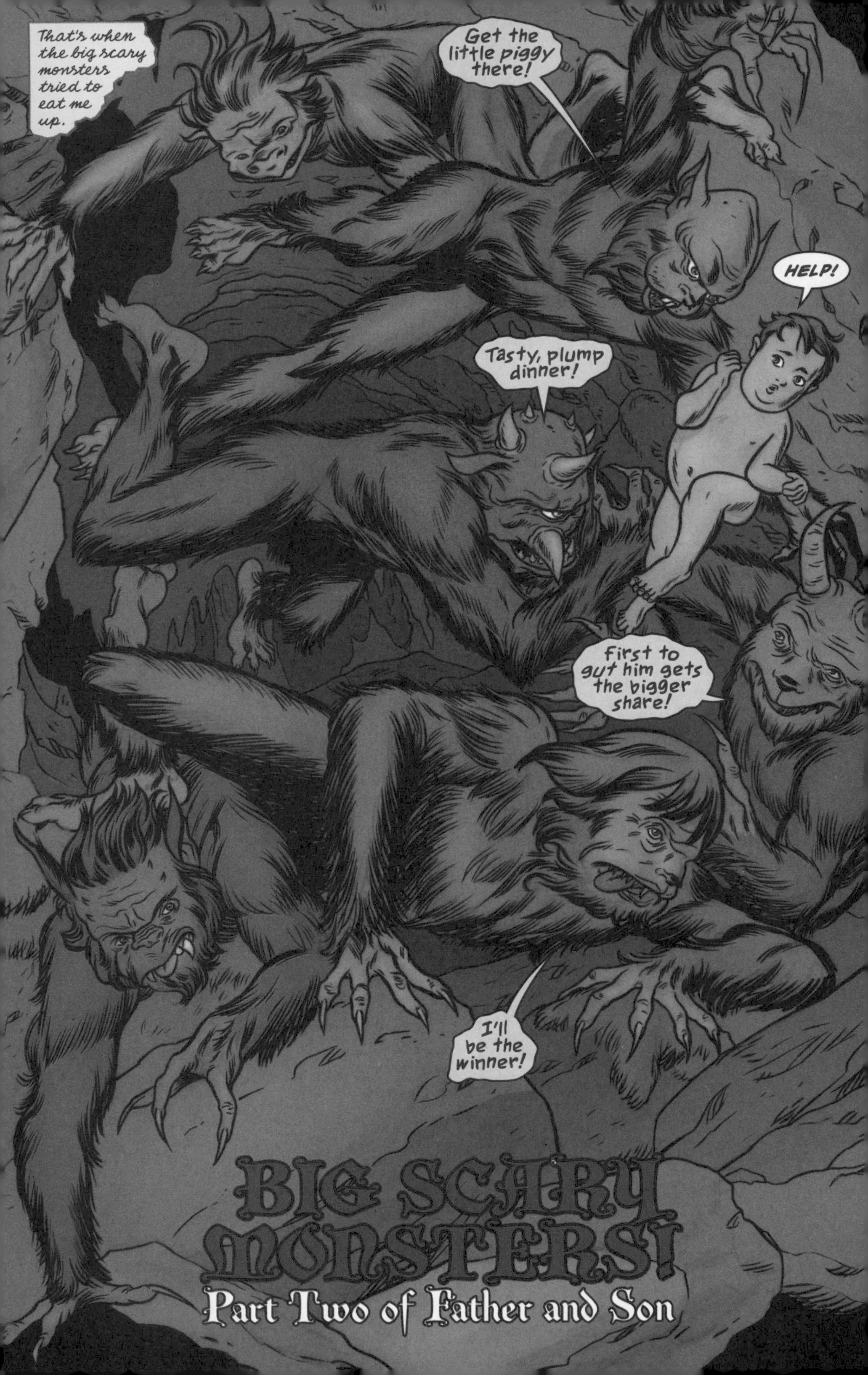
That's when the big scary monsters tried to eat me up.
Get the little piggy there!
HELP!
Tasty, plump dinner!
First to gut him gets the bigger share!
I'll be the winner!
BIG SCARY MONSTERS!
Part Two of Father and Son

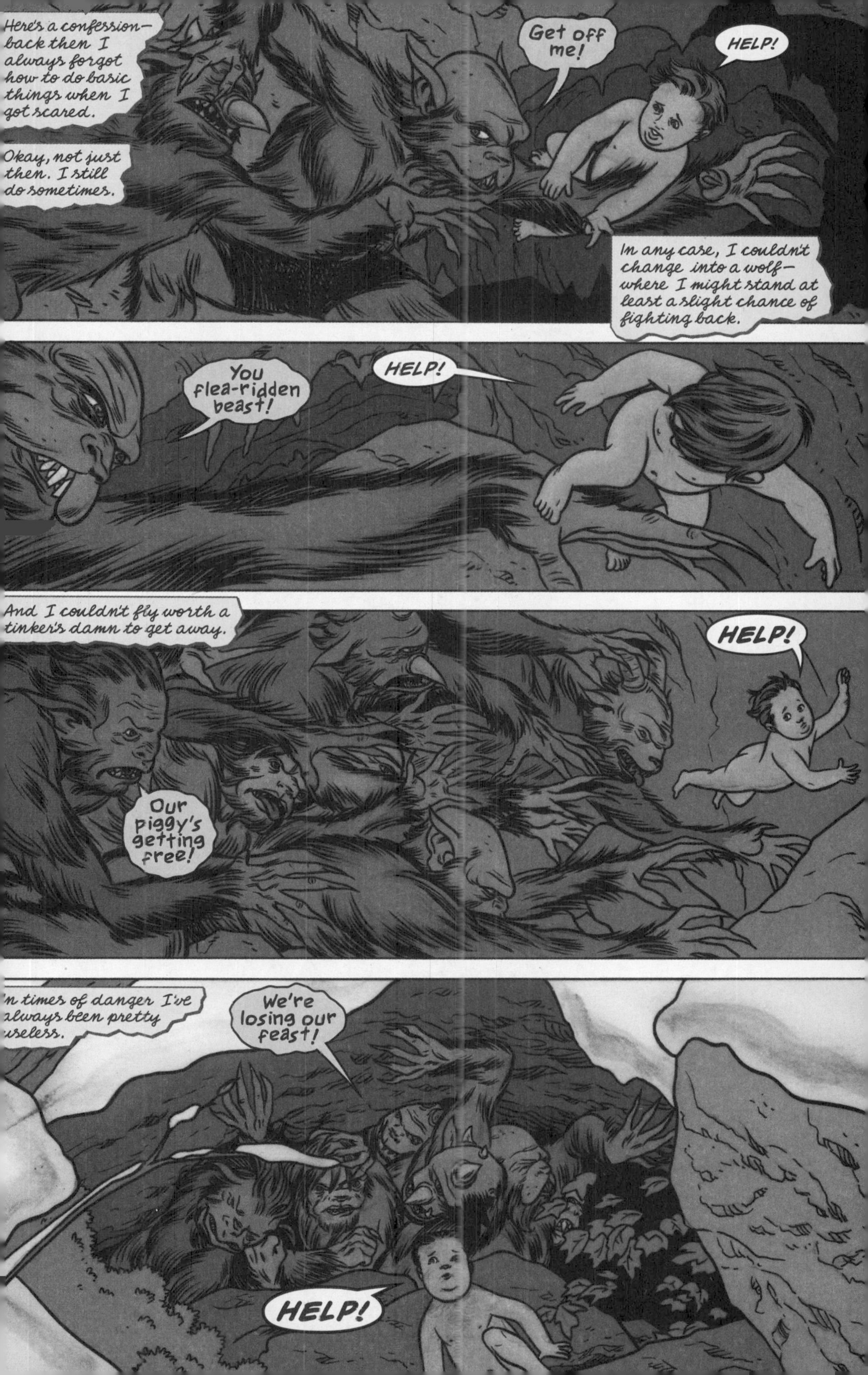
Here's a confession—back then I always forgot how to do basic things when I got scared.
Okay, not just then. I still do sometimes.
Get off me!
HELP!
In any case, I couldn't change into a wolf—where I might stand at least a slight chance of fighting back.
You flea-ridden beast!
HELP!
And I couldn't fly worth a tinker's damn to get away.
HELP!
Our piggy's getting free!
n times of danger I've lways been pretty seless.
We're losing our feast!
HELP!

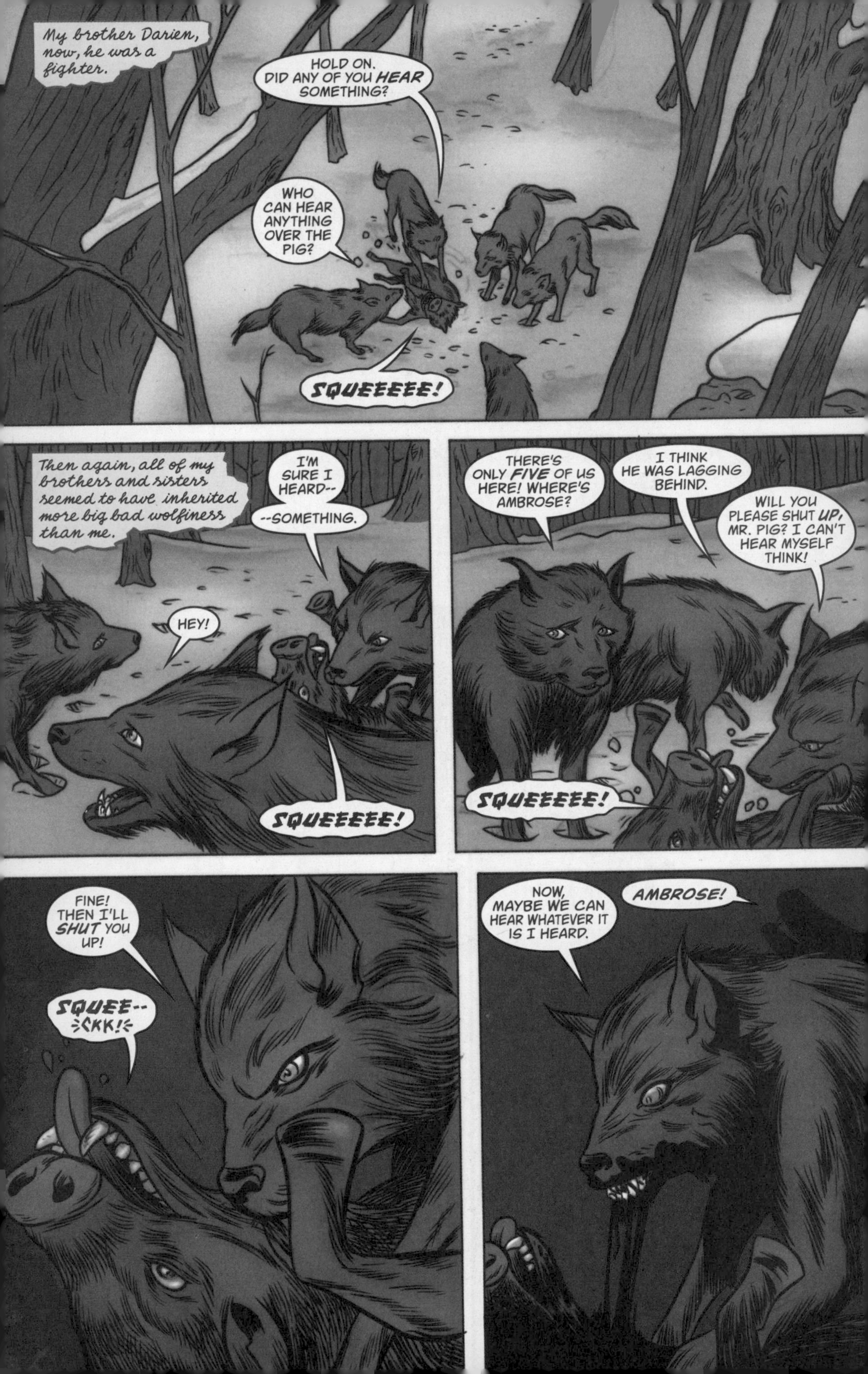

My brother Darien, now, he was a fighter.
HOLD ON. DID ANY OF YOU HEAR SOMETHING?
WHO CAN HEAR ANYTHING OVER THE PIG?
SQUEEEEEE!
Then again, all of my brothers and sisters seemed to have inherited more big bad wolfiness than me.
I'M SURE I HEARD--
--SOMETHING.
HEY!
SQUEEEEEE!
THERE'S ONLY FIVE OF US HERE! WHERE'S AMBROSE?
I THINK HE WAS LAGGING BEHIND.
WILL YOU PLEASE SHUT UP, MR. PIG? I CAN'T HEAR MYSELF THINK!
SQUEEEEEE!
FINE! THEN I'LL SHUT YOU UP!
SQUEE-- CKK!
NOW, MAYBE WE CAN HEAR WHATEVER IT IS I HEARD.
AMBROSE!

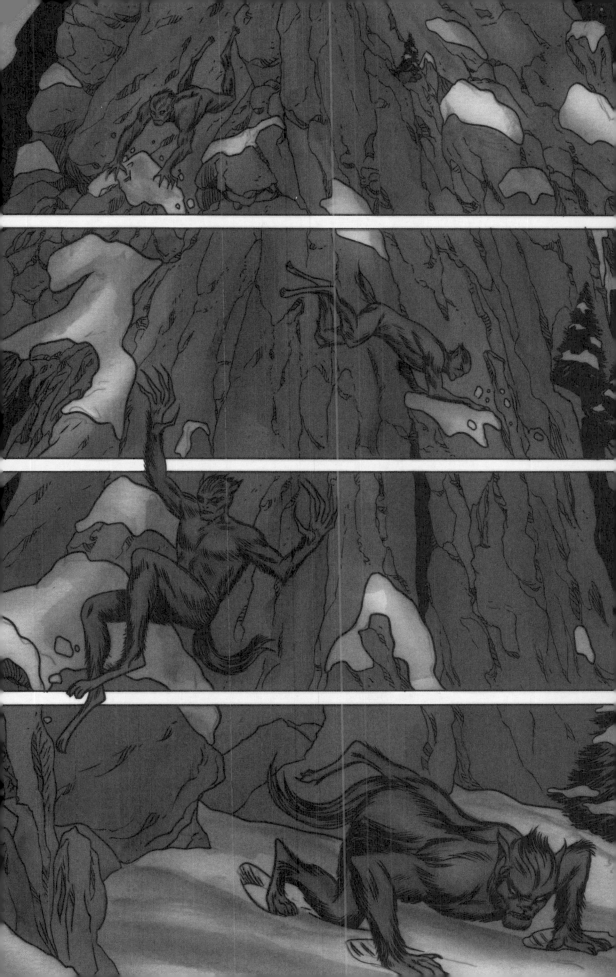

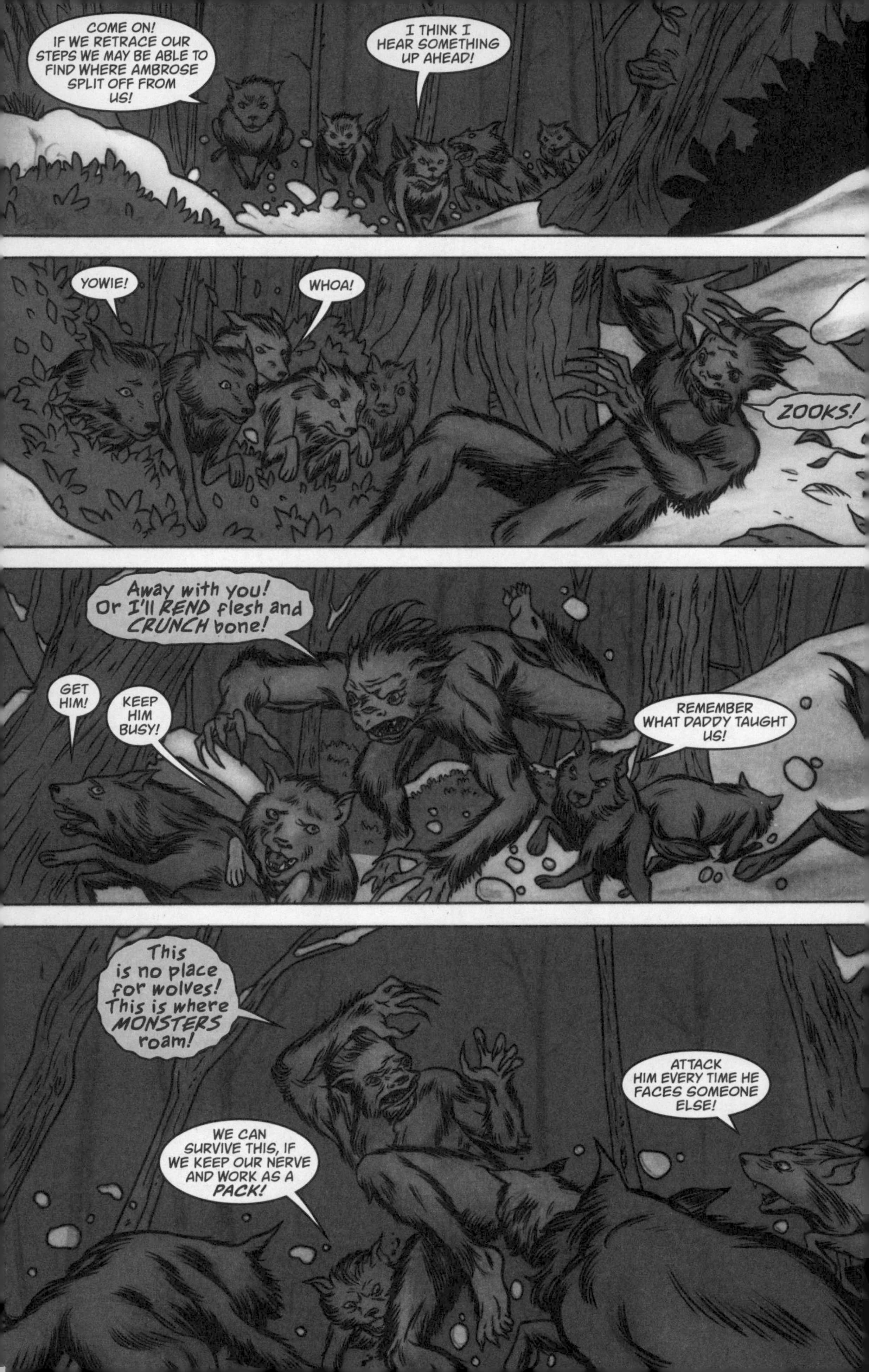
COME ON! IF WE RETRACE OUR STEPS WE MAY BE ABLE TO FIND WHERE AMBROSE SPLIT OFF FROM US!
I THINK I HEAR SOMETHING UP AHEAD!
YOWIE!
WHOA!
ZOOKS!
Away with you! Or I'll REND flesh and CRUNCH bone!
GET HIM!
KEEP HIM BUSY!
REMEMBER WHAT DADDY TAUGHT US!
This is no place for wolves! This is where MONSTERS roam!
ATTACK HIM EVERY TIME HE FACES SOMEONE ELSE!
WE CAN SURVIVE THIS, IF WE KEEP OUR NERVE AND WORK AS A PACK!

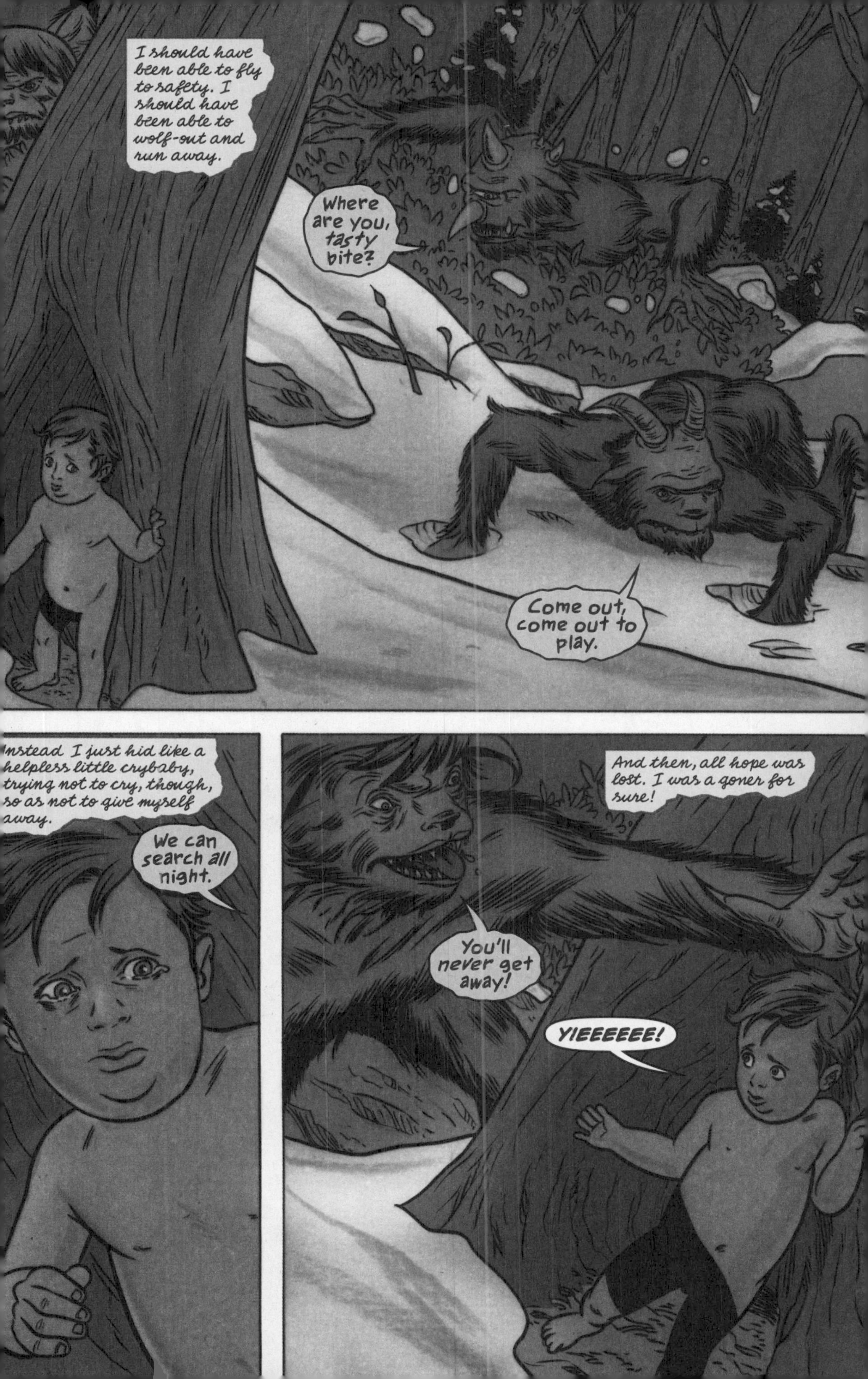
I should have been able to fly to safety. I should have been able to wolf-out and run away.
Where are you, tasty bite?
Come out, come out to play.
Instead I just hid like a helpless little crybaby, trying not to cry, though, so as not to give myself away.
We can search all night.
And then, all hope was lost. I was a goner for sure!
You'll never get away!
YIEEEEEE!

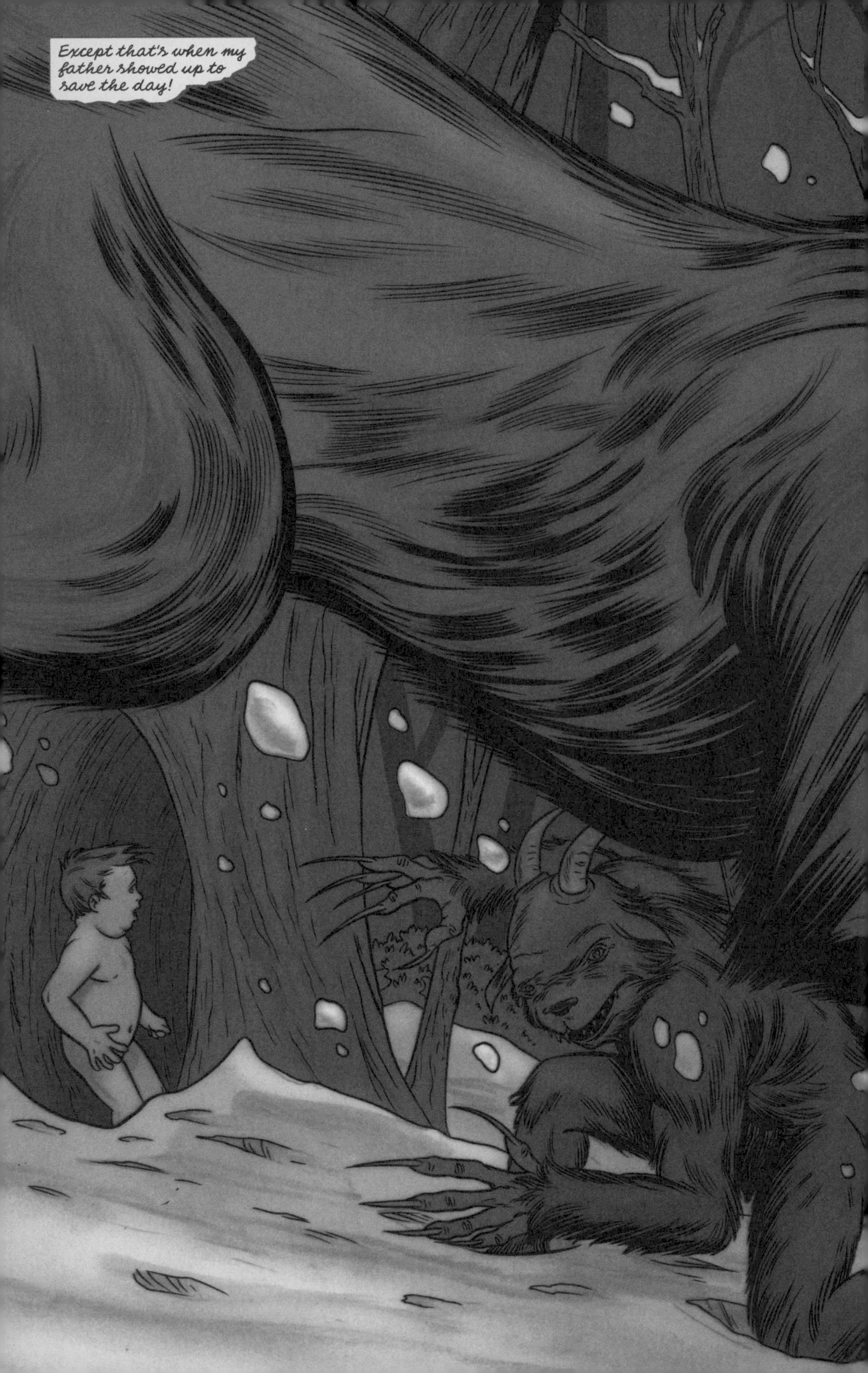
Except that's when my father showed up to save the day!

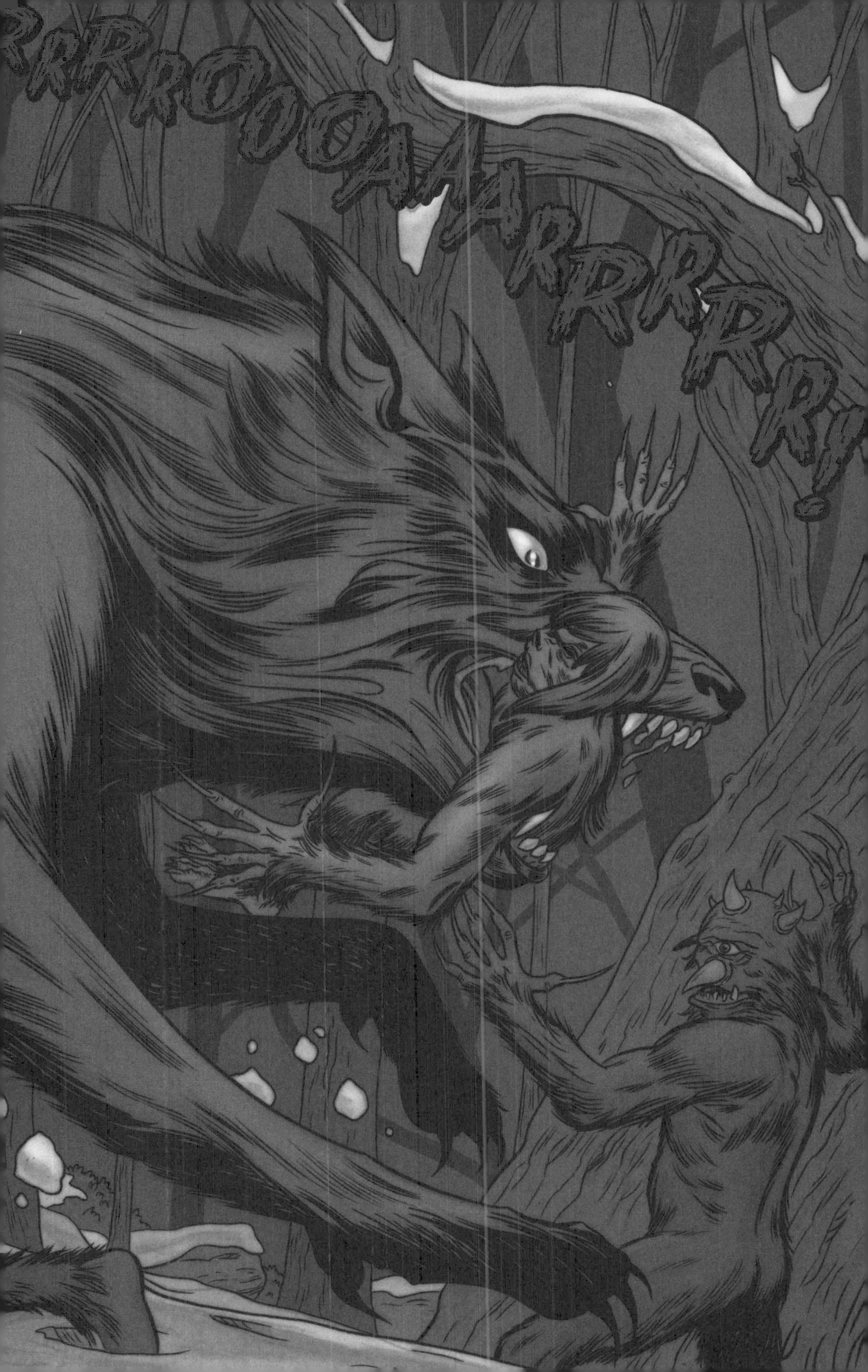
RRRROOOOAARRRRRR!

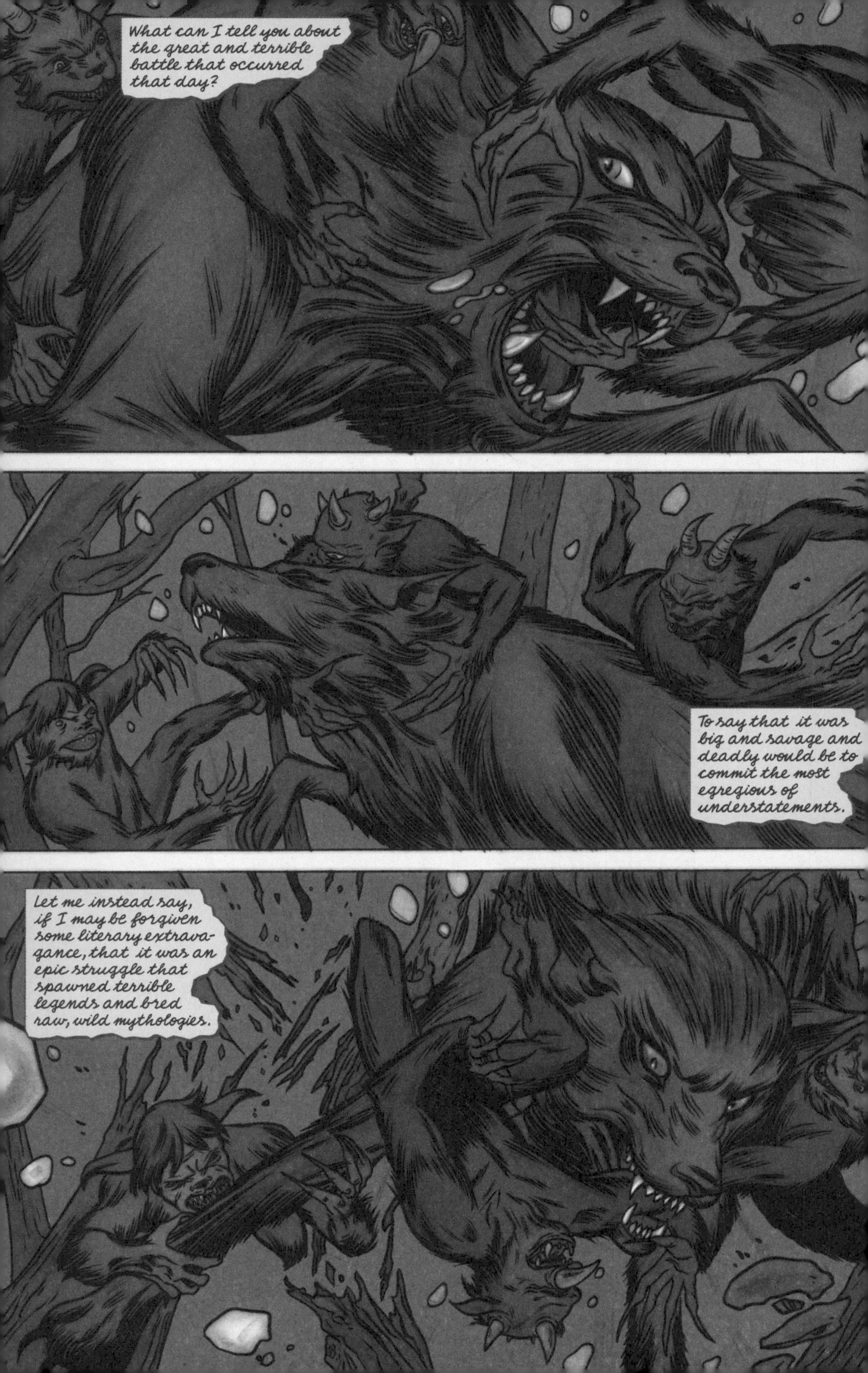
What can I tell you about the great and terrible battle that occurred that day?
To say that it was big and savage and deadly would be to commit the most egregious of understatements.
Let me instead say, if I may be forgiven some literary extravagance, that it was an epic struggle that spawned terrible legends and bred raw, wild mythologies.

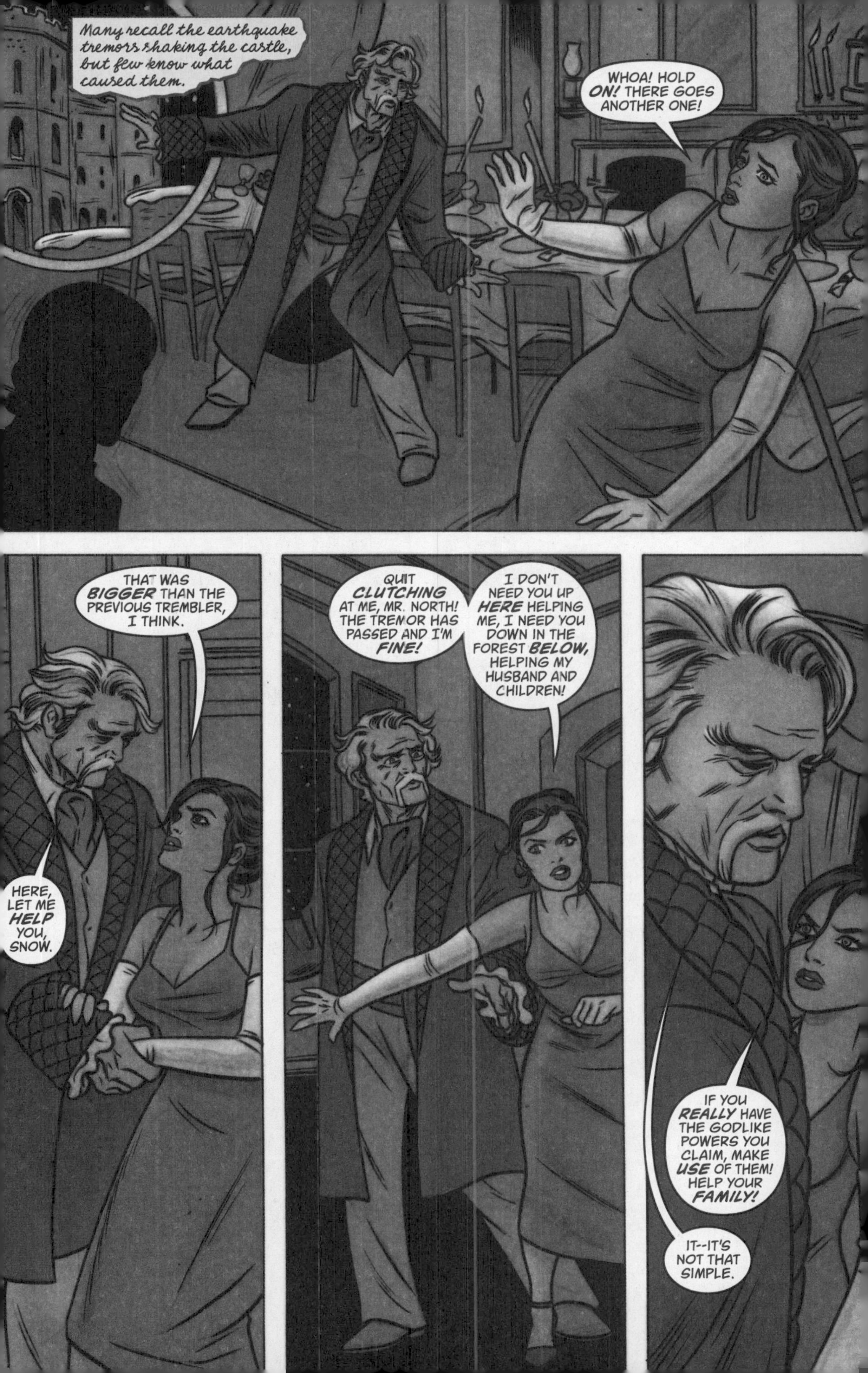
Many recall the earthquake tremors shaking the castle, but few know what caused them.
WHOA! HOLD ON! THERE GOES ANOTHER ONE!
THAT WAS BIGGER THAN THE PREVIOUS TREMBLER, I THINK.
HERE, LET ME HELP YOU, SNOW.
QUIT CLUTCHING AT ME, MR. NORTH! THE TREMOR HAS PASSED AND I'M FINE!
I DON'T NEED YOU UP HERE HELPING ME, I NEED YOU DOWN IN THE FOREST BELOW, HELPING MY HUSBAND AND CHILDREN!
IF YOU REALLY HAVE THE GODLIKE POWERS YOU CLAIM, MAKE USE OF THEM! HELP YOUR FAMILY!
IT--IT'S NOT THAT SIMPLE.

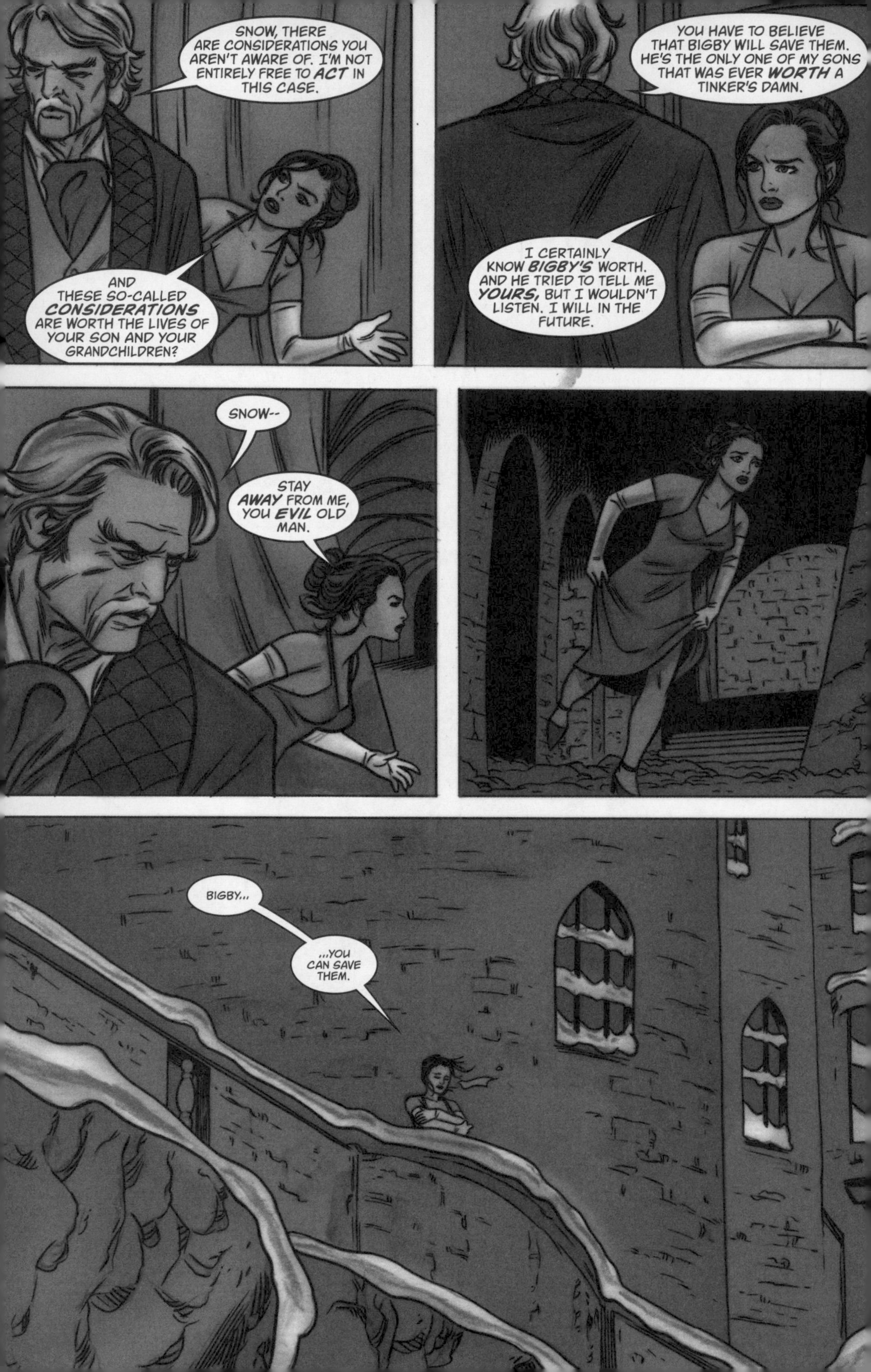
SNOW, THERE ARE CONSIDERATIONS YOU AREN'T AWARE OF. I'M NOT ENTIRELY FREE TO ACT IN THIS CASE.
AND THESE SO-CALLED CONSIDERATIONS ARE WORTH THE LIVES OF YOUR SON AND YOUR GRANDCHILDREN?
YOU HAVE TO BELIEVE THAT BIGBY WILL SAVE THEM. HE'S THE ONLY ONE OF MY SONS THAT WAS EVER WORTH A TINKER'S DAMN.
I CERTAINLY KNOW BIGBY'S WORTH. AND HE TRIED TO TELL ME YOURS, BUT I WOULDN'T LISTEN. I WILL IN THE FUTURE.
SNOW--
STAY AWAY FROM ME, YOU EVIL OLD MAN.
BIGBY...
...YOU CAN SAVE THEM.

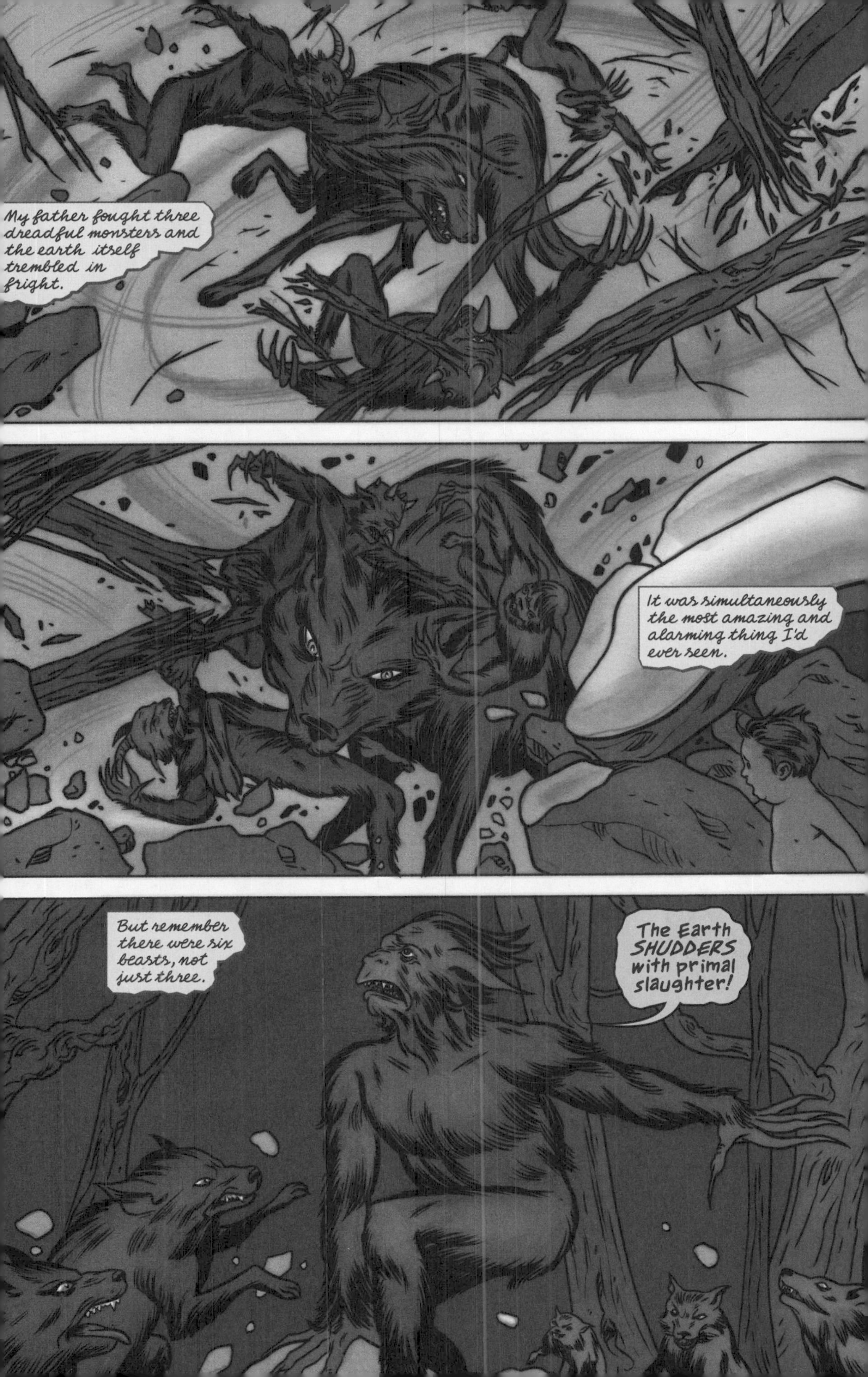
My father fought three dreadful monsters and the earth itself trembled in fright.
It was simultaneously the most amazing and alarming thing I'd ever seen.
But remember there were six beasts, not just three.
The Earth SHUDDERS with primal slaughter!

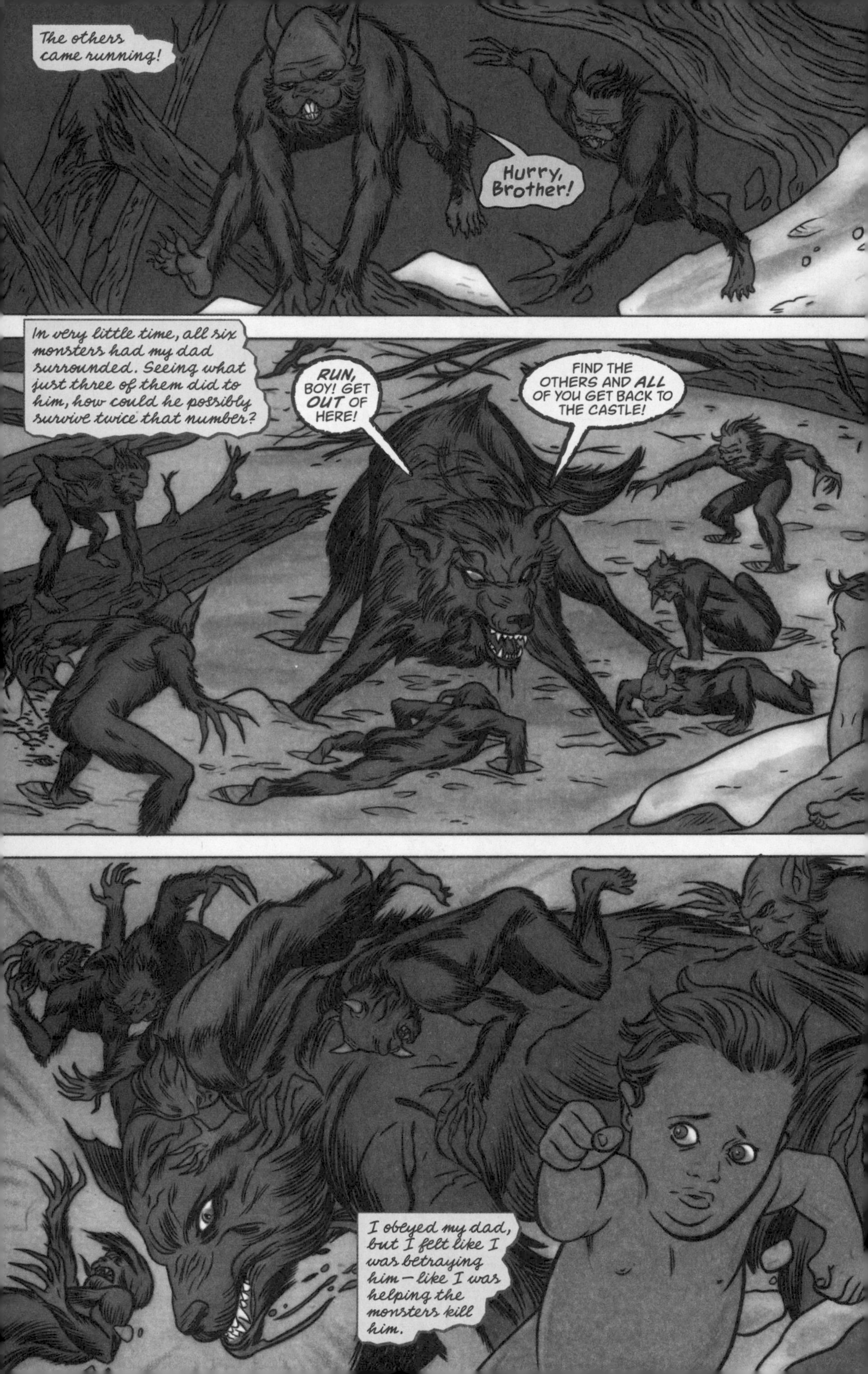

The others came running!
Hurry, Brother!
In very little time, all six monsters had my dad surrounded. Seeing what just three of them did to him, how could he possibly survive twice that number?
RUN, BOY! GET OUT OF HERE!
FIND THE OTHERS AND ALL OF YOU GET BACK TO THE CASTLE!
I obeyed my dad, but I felt like I was betraying him—like I was helping the monsters kill him.

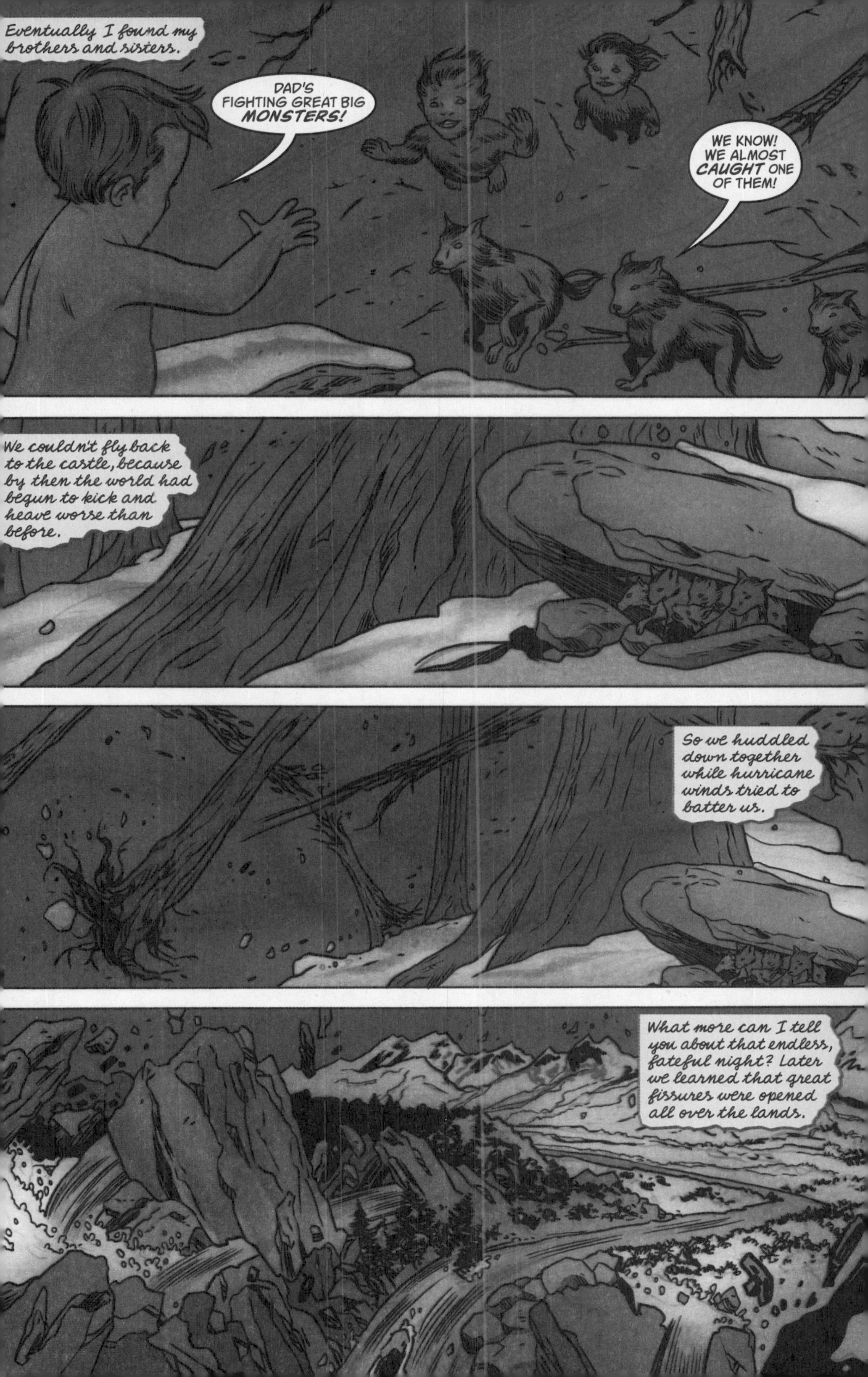

Eventually I found my brothers and sisters.
DAD'S FIGHTING GREAT BIG MONSTERS!
WE KNOW! WE ALMOST CAUGHT ONE OF THEM!
We couldn't fly back to the castle, because by then the world had begun to kick and heave worse than before.
So we huddled down together while hurricane winds tried to batter us.
What more can I tell you about that endless, fateful night? Later we learned that great fissures were opened all over the lands.

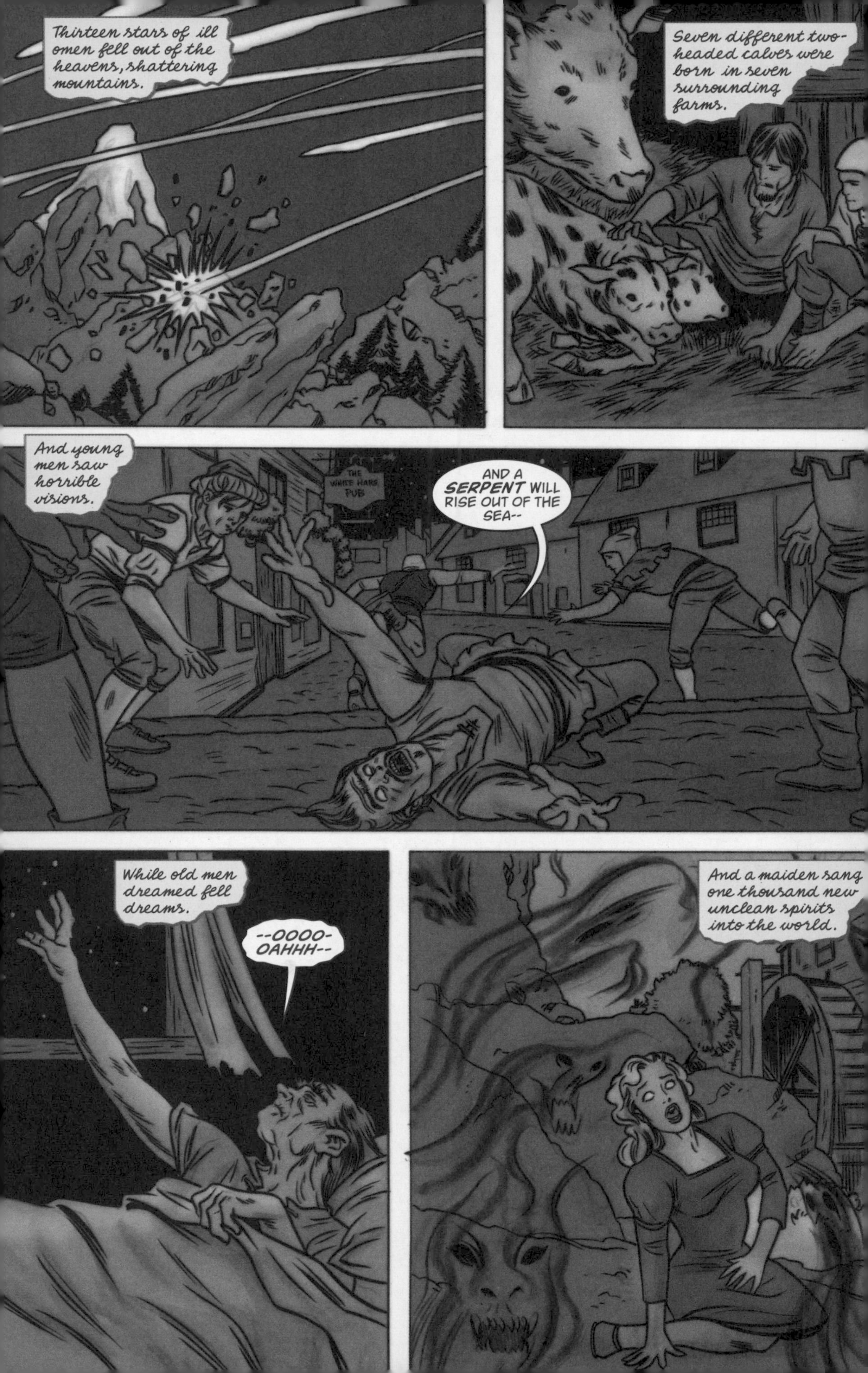
Thirteen stars of ill omen fell out of the heavens, shattering mountains.
Seven different two-headed calves were born in seven surrounding farms.
And young men saw horrible visions.
THE WHITE HART PUB
AND A SERPENT WILL RISE OUT OF THE SEA--
While old men dreamed fell dreams.
--OOOO-OAHHH--
And a maiden sang one thousand new unclean spirits into the world.

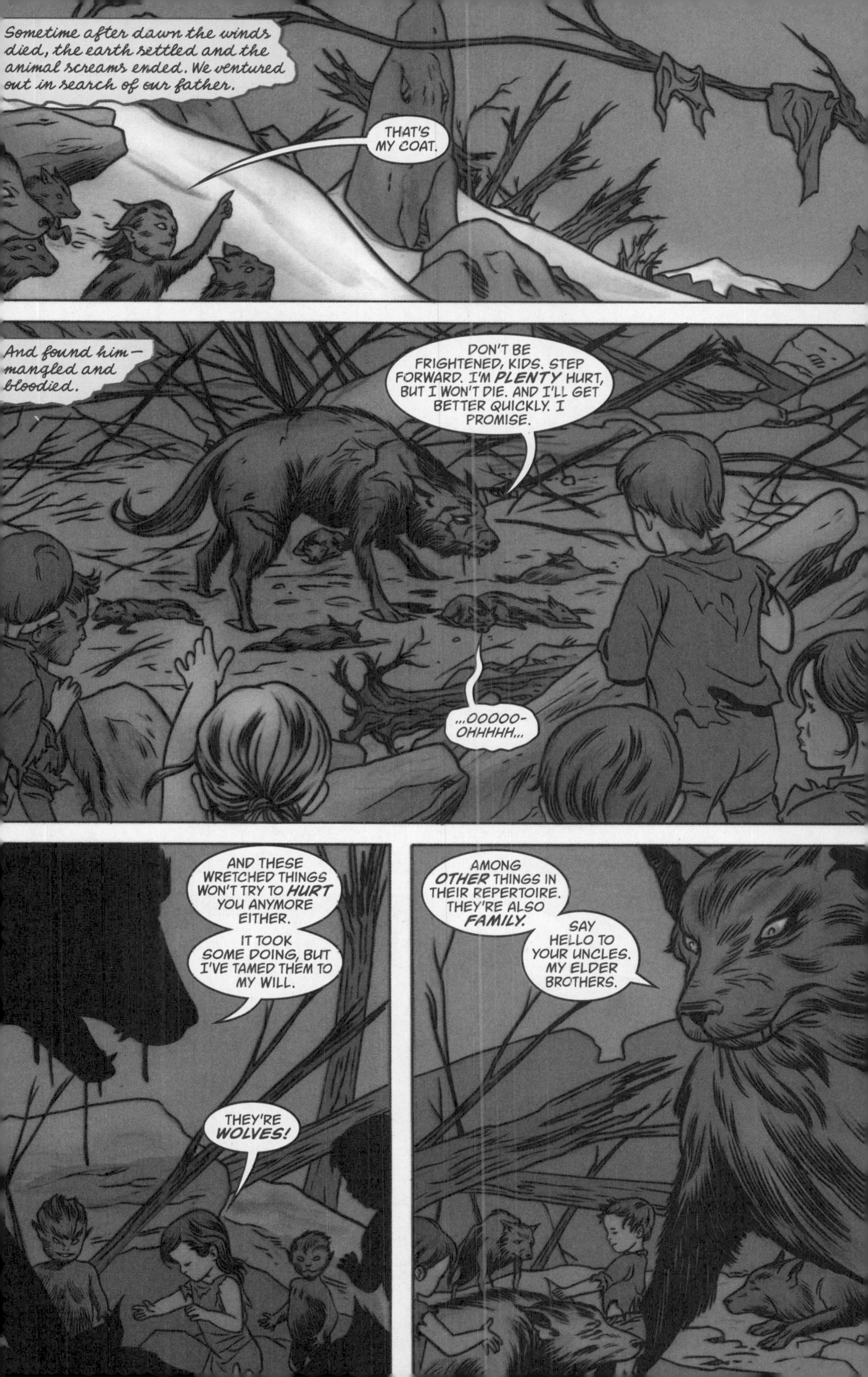
Sometime after dawn the winds died, the earth settled and the animal screams ended. We ventured out in search of our father.
THAT'S MY COAT.
And found him— mangled and bloodied.
DON'T BE FRIGHTENED, KIDS. STEP FORWARD. I'M PLENTY HURT, BUT I WON'T DIE. AND I'LL GET BETTER QUICKLY. I PROMISE.
...OOOOO-OHHHHH...
AND THESE WRETCHED THINGS WON'T TRY TO HURT YOU ANYMORE EITHER.
IT TOOK SOME DOING, BUT I'VE TAMED THEM TO MY WILL.
THEY'RE WOLVES!
AMONG OTHER THINGS IN THEIR REPERTOIRE. THEY'RE ALSO FAMILY.
SAY HELLO TO YOUR UNCLES. MY ELDER BROTHERS.

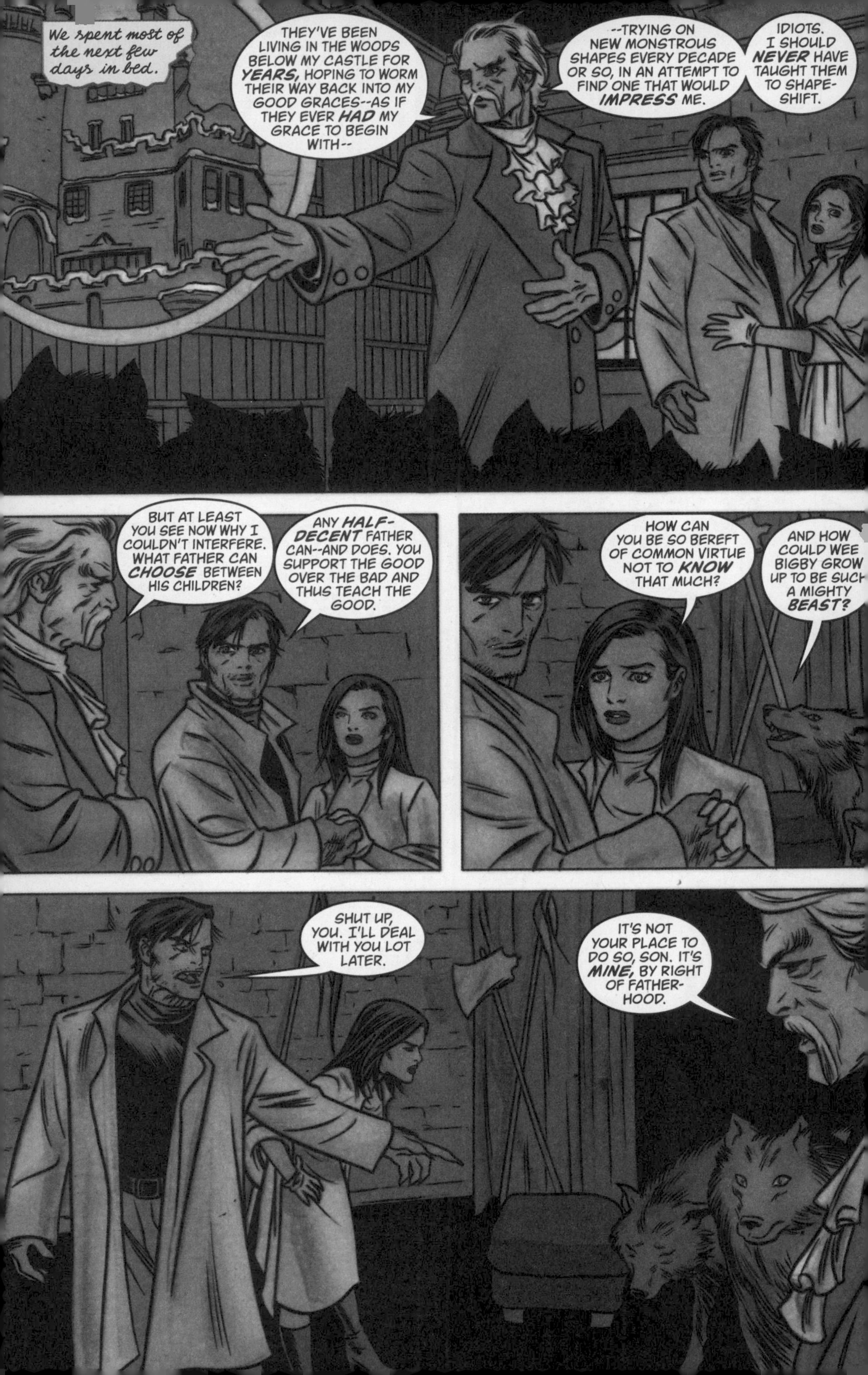
We spent most of the next few days in bed.
THEY'VE BEEN LIVING IN THE WOODS BELOW MY CASTLE FOR YEARS, HOPING TO WORM THEIR WAY BACK INTO MY GOOD GRACES--AS IF THEY EVER HAD MY GRACE TO BEGIN WITH--
--TRYING ON NEW MONSTROUS SHAPES EVERY DECADE OR SO, IN AN ATTEMPT TO FIND ONE THAT WOULD IMPRESS ME.
IDIOTS. I SHOULD NEVER HAVE TAUGHT THEM TO SHAPE-SHIFT.
BUT AT LEAST YOU SEE NOW WHY I COULDN'T INTERFERE. WHAT FATHER CAN CHOOSE BETWEEN HIS CHILDREN?
ANY HALF-DECENT FATHER CAN--AND DOES. YOU SUPPORT THE GOOD OVER THE BAD AND THUS TEACH THE GOOD.
HOW CAN YOU BE SO BEREFT OF COMMON VIRTUE NOT TO KNOW THAT MUCH?
AND HOW COULD WEE BIGBY GROW UP TO BE SUCH A MIGHTY BEAST?
SHUT UP, YOU. I'LL DEAL WITH YOU LOT LATER.
IT'S NOT YOUR PLACE TO DO SO, SON. IT'S MINE, BY RIGHT OF FATHER-HOOD.

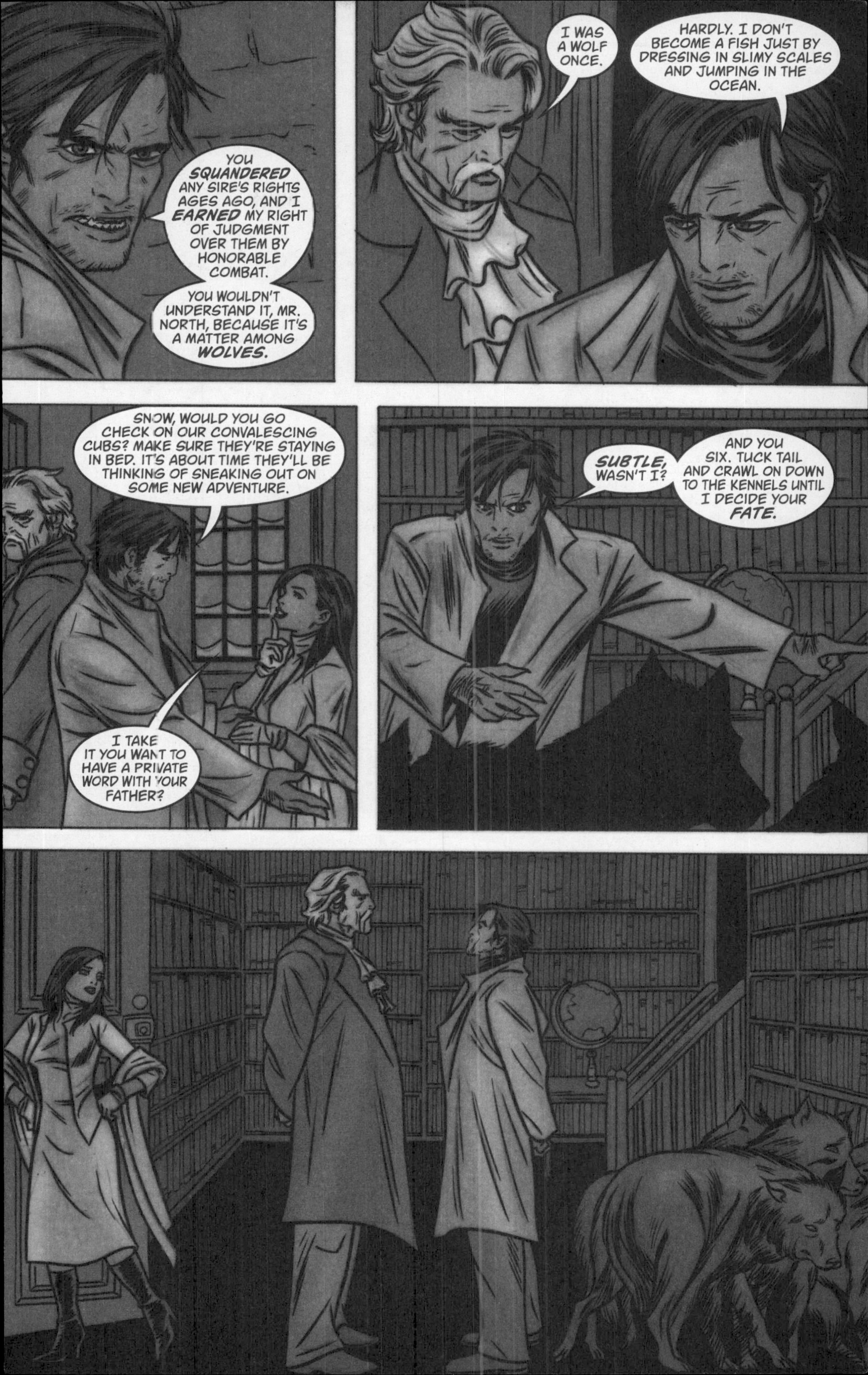
YOU **SQUANDERED** ANY SIRE'S RIGHTS AGES AGO, AND I **EARNED** MY RIGHT OF JUDGMENT OVER THEM BY HONORABLE COMBAT.
YOU WOULDN'T UNDERSTAND IT, MR. NORTH, BECAUSE IT'S A MATTER AMONG **WOLVES**.
I WAS A WOLF ONCE.
HARDLY. I DON'T BECOME A FISH JUST BY DRESSING IN SLIMY SCALES AND JUMPING IN THE OCEAN.
SNOW, WOULD YOU GO CHECK ON OUR CONVALESCING CUBS? MAKE SURE THEY'RE STAYING IN BED. IT'S ABOUT TIME THEY'LL BE THINKING OF SNEAKING OUT ON SOME NEW ADVENTURE.
I TAKE IT YOU WANT TO HAVE A PRIVATE WORD WITH YOUR FATHER?
SUBTLE, WASN'T I?
AND YOU SIX. TUCK TAIL AND CRAWL ON DOWN TO THE KENNELS UNTIL I DECIDE YOUR **FATE**.

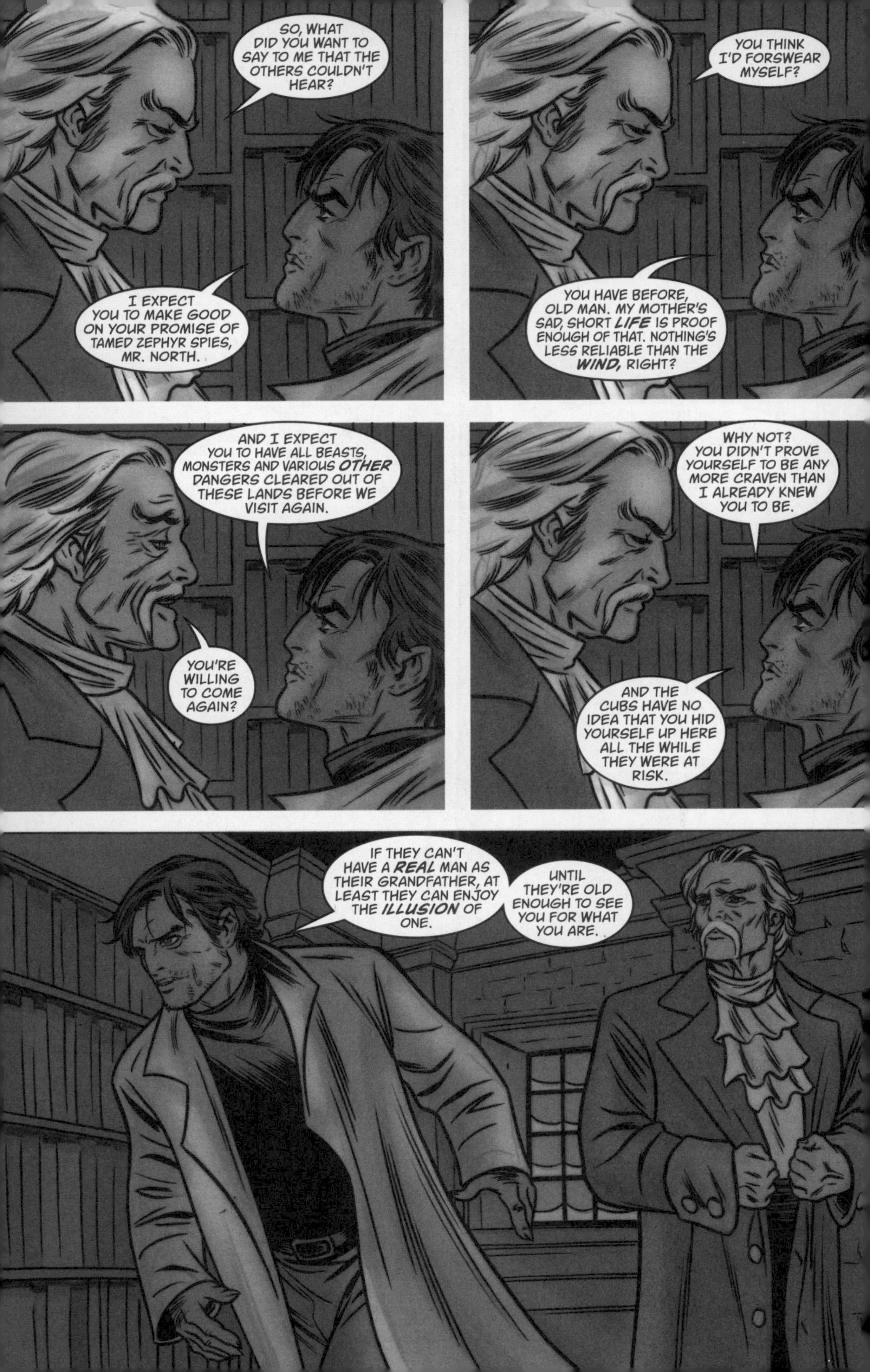
SO, WHAT DID YOU WANT TO SAY TO ME THAT THE OTHERS COULDN'T HEAR?
I EXPECT YOU TO MAKE GOOD ON YOUR PROMISE OF TAMED ZEPHYR SPIES, MR. NORTH.
YOU THINK I'D FORSWEAR MYSELF?
YOU HAVE BEFORE, OLD MAN. MY MOTHER'S SAD, SHORT LIFE IS PROOF ENOUGH OF THAT. NOTHING'S LESS RELIABLE THAN THE WIND, RIGHT?
AND I EXPECT YOU TO HAVE ALL BEASTS, MONSTERS AND VARIOUS OTHER DANGERS CLEARED OUT OF THESE LANDS BEFORE WE VISIT AGAIN.
YOU'RE WILLING TO COME AGAIN?
WHY NOT? YOU DIDN'T PROVE YOURSELF TO BE ANY MORE CRAVEN THAN I ALREADY KNEW YOU TO BE.
AND THE CUBS HAVE NO IDEA THAT YOU HID YOURSELF UP HERE ALL THE WHILE THEY WERE AT RISK.
IF THEY CAN'T HAVE A REAL MAN AS THEIR GRANDFATHER, AT LEAST THEY CAN ENJOY THE ILLUSION OF ONE.
UNTIL THEY'RE OLD ENOUGH TO SEE YOU FOR WHAT YOU ARE.

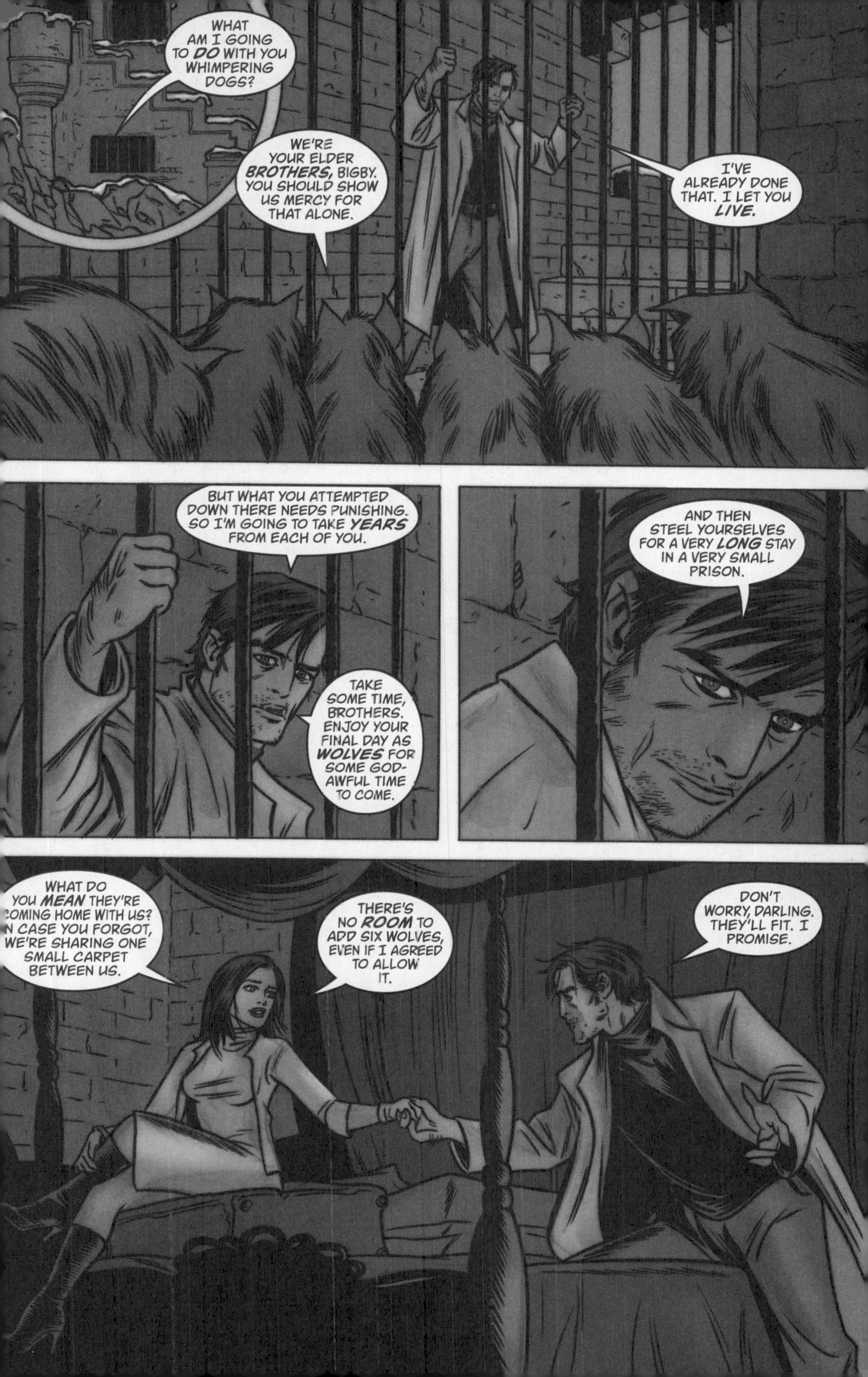

WHAT AM I GOING TO DO WITH YOU WHIMPERING DOGS?
WE'RE YOUR ELDER BROTHERS, BIGBY. YOU SHOULD SHOW US MERCY FOR THAT ALONE.
I'VE ALREADY DONE THAT. I LET YOU LIVE.
BUT WHAT YOU ATTEMPTED DOWN THERE NEEDS PUNISHING. SO I'M GOING TO TAKE YEARS FROM EACH OF YOU.
TAKE SOME TIME, BROTHERS. ENJOY YOUR FINAL DAY AS WOLVES FOR SOME GOD-AWFUL TIME TO COME.
AND THEN STEEL YOURSELVES FOR A VERY LONG STAY IN A VERY SMALL PRISON.
WHAT DO YOU MEAN THEY'RE COMING HOME WITH US? IN CASE YOU FORGOT, WE'RE SHARING ONE SMALL CARPET BETWEEN US.
THERE'S NO ROOM TO ADD SIX WOLVES, EVEN IF I AGREED TO ALLOW IT.
DON'T WORRY, DARLING. THEY'LL FIT. I PROMISE.

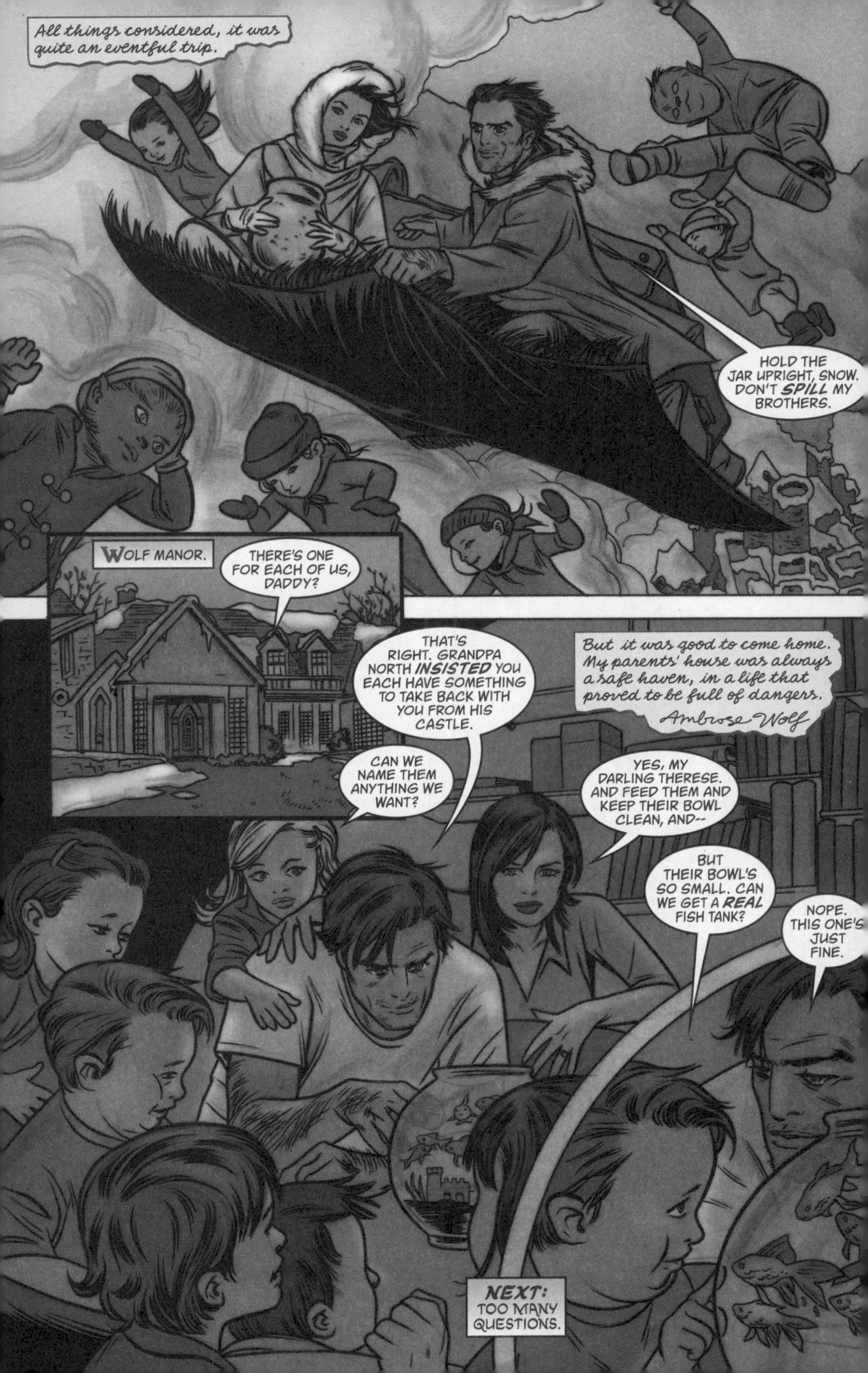
All things considered, it was quite an eventful trip.
HOLD THE JAR UPRIGHT, SNOW. DON'T SPILL MY BROTHERS.
WOLF MANOR.
THERE'S ONE FOR EACH OF US, DADDY?
THAT'S RIGHT. GRANDPA NORTH INSISTED YOU EACH HAVE SOMETHING TO TAKE BACK WITH YOU FROM HIS CASTLE.
But it was good to come home. My parents' house was always a safe haven, in a life that proved to be full of dangers.
Ambrose Wolf
CAN WE NAME THEM ANYTHING WE WANT?
YES, MY DARLING THERESE. AND FEED THEM AND KEEP THEIR BOWL CLEAN, AND--
BUT THEIR BOWL'S SO SMALL. CAN WE GET A REAL FISH TANK?
NOPE. THIS ONE'S JUST FINE.
NEXT: TOO MANY QUESTIONS.

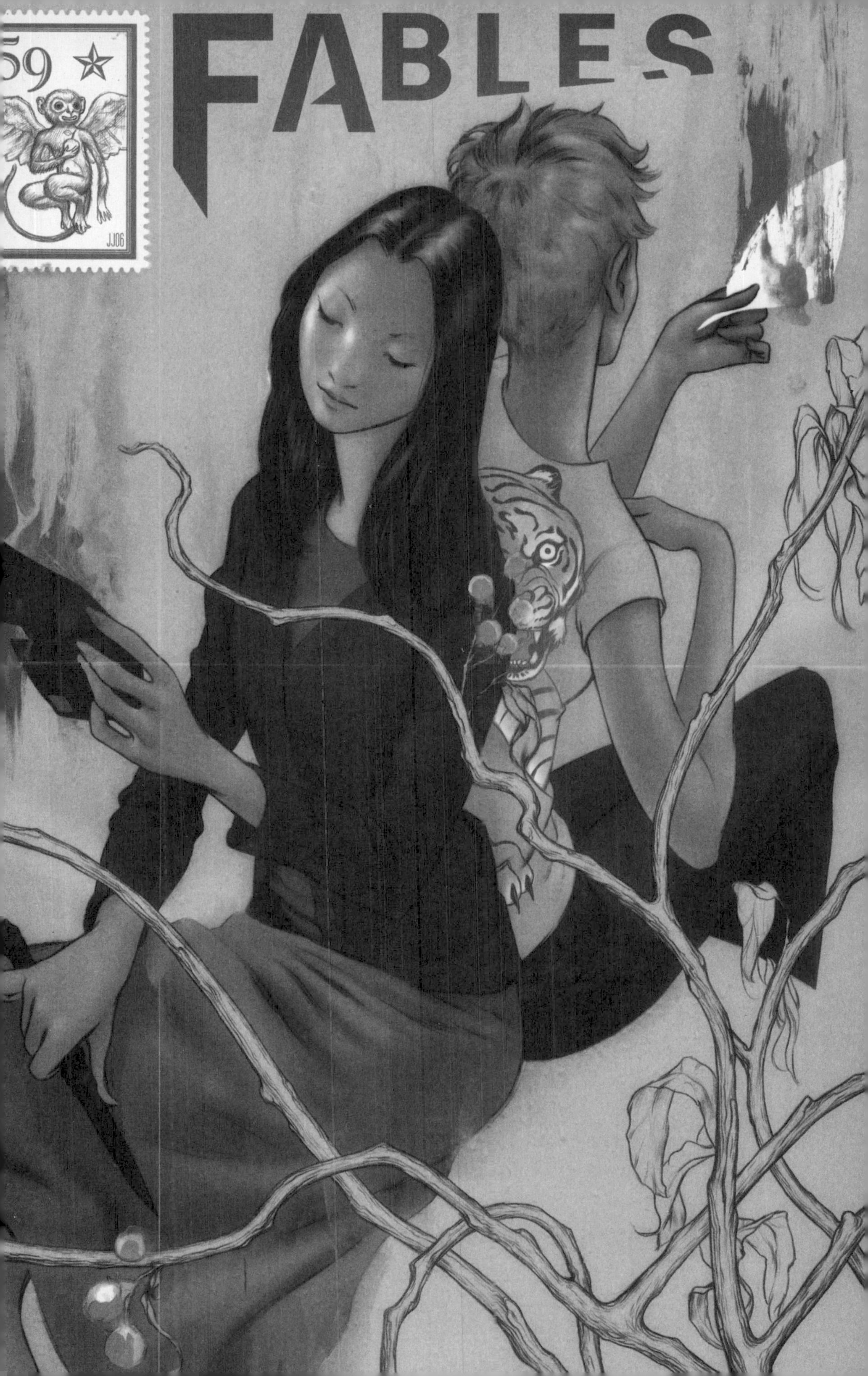
FABLES
59
JJ06

Burning Questions

In which we take a break from our gathering storm of troubles, tumults and dangers to dwell for just a small time on a modest cluster of heretofore unanswered, albeit humble, mysteries.

All of the stories were written by Bill Willingham
at the command of various readers.
Lettering by Todd Klein - Coloring by Lee Loughridge
Cover by James Jean - Assistant Editor: Angela Rufino
Editor: Shelly Bond
And the stories, in order of appearance, were illustrated by
M. K. Perker   Jim Rugg
Mark Buckingham   Andrew Pepoy
Joëlle Jones   D'Israeli
Jill Thompson   David Lapham
John K. Snyder III   Eric Shanower
Barry Kitson

By way of introduction, this issue answers questions posed by our loyal, imaginative and, above all, inquisitive readers. The questions were strictly limited to inquiries about past events in the fifty-plus issues of Fables published to date. Some questions couldn't be used, of course, for diverse reasons. In many cases the same, or similar, questions were asked by multiple readers (in which case the first reader to ask received credit for it). Also, in many cases, readers asked questions that were already slated to be important parts of upcoming stories. After filtering out those that couldn't be used, there were still far too many submissions than could possibly fit into this slim single issue, even after reducing the list to only the most excellent of the excellent. Thank you, everyone who participated. Since this issue started with you, this issue is dedicated to each and every one of you. Here then, for your amusement and edification, are our answers to the eleven questions that best inspired our elite cadre of assembled talents.

Eduardo Blake of Buenos Aires, Argentina asks:

Did Hakim ever manage to get a regular job?

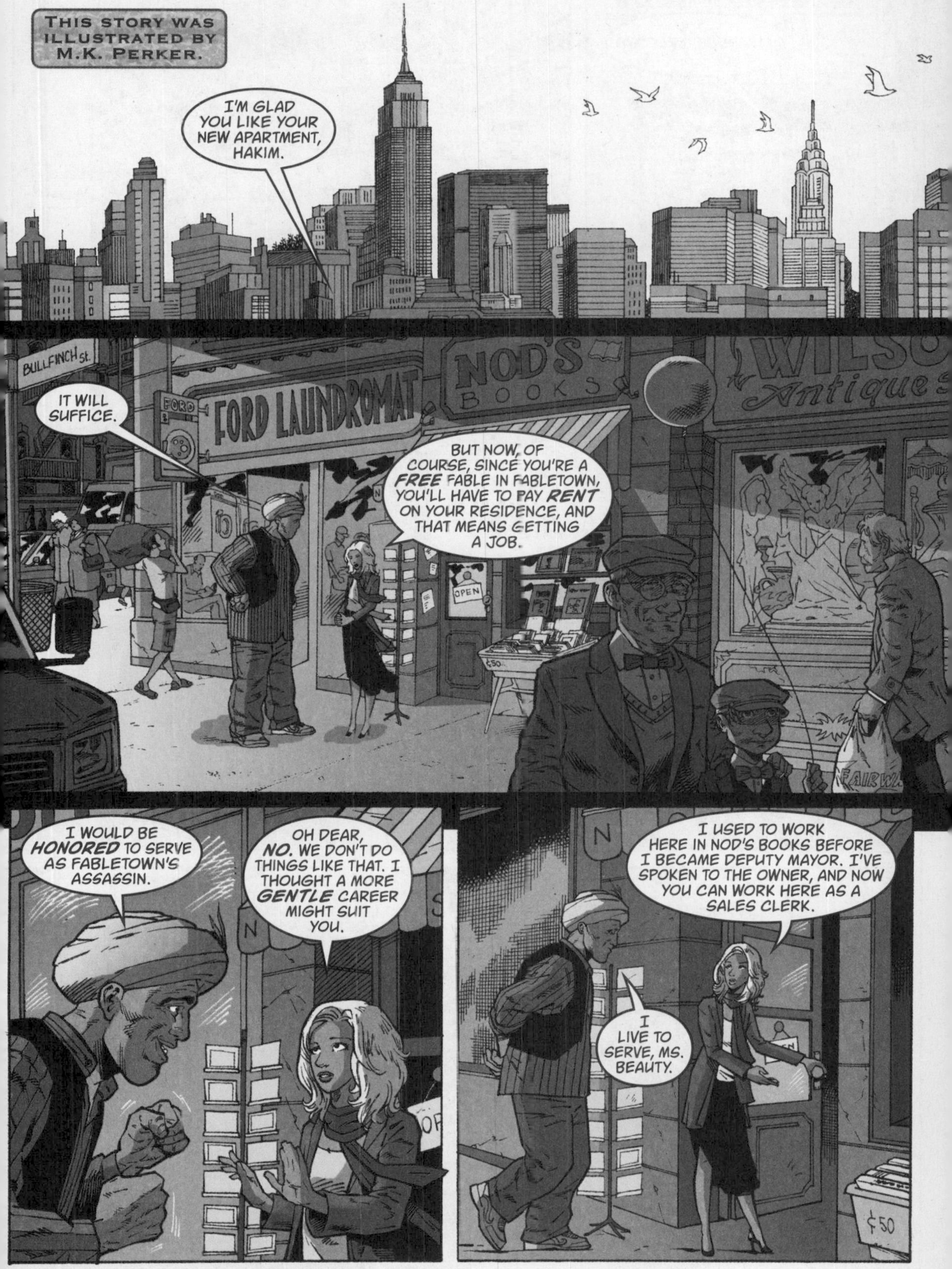
THIS STORY WAS ILLUSTRATED BY M.K. PERKER.
I'M GLAD YOU LIKE YOUR NEW APARTMENT, HAKIM.
BULLFINCH St.
FORD LAUNDROMAT
NOD'S BOOKS
WILSO Antiques
IT WILL SUFFICE.
BUT NOW, OF COURSE, SINCE YOU'RE A FREE FABLE IN FABLETOWN, YOU'LL HAVE TO PAY RENT ON YOUR RESIDENCE, AND THAT MEANS GETTING A JOB.
OPEN
I WOULD BE HONORED TO SERVE AS FABLETOWN'S ASSASSIN.
OH DEAR, NO. WE DON'T DO THINGS LIKE THAT. I THOUGHT A MORE GENTLE CAREER MIGHT SUIT YOU.
I USED TO WORK HERE IN NOD'S BOOKS BEFORE I BECAME DEPUTY MAYOR. I'VE SPOKEN TO THE OWNER, AND NOW YOU CAN WORK HERE AS A SALES CLERK.
I LIVE TO SERVE, MS. BEAUTY.

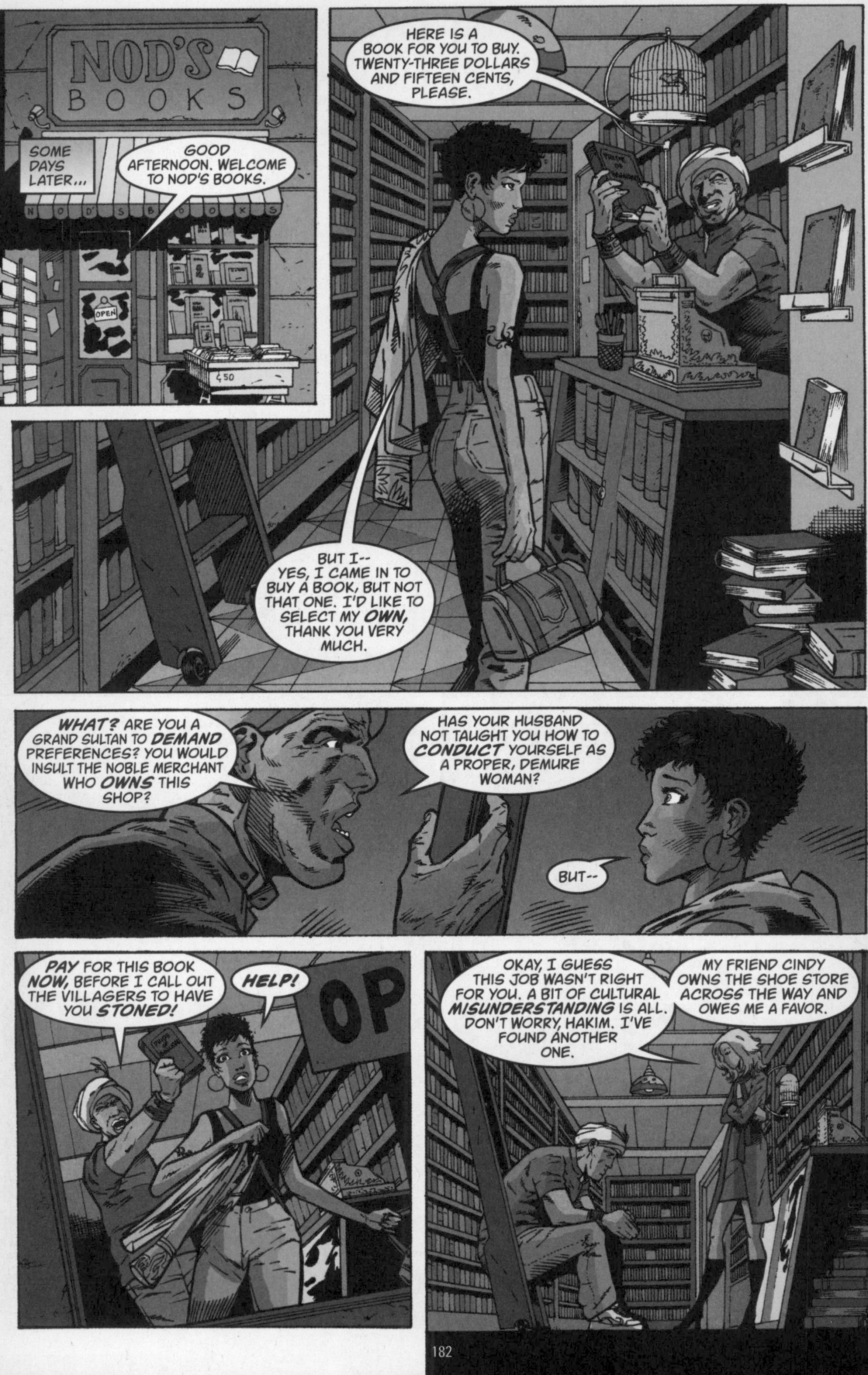
NOD'S BOOKS
SOME DAYS LATER...
GOOD AFTERNOON. WELCOME TO NOD'S BOOKS.
OPEN
N O D ' S B O O K S
HERE IS A BOOK FOR YOU TO BUY. TWENTY-THREE DOLLARS AND FIFTEEN CENTS, PLEASE.
BUT I-- YES, I CAME IN TO BUY A BOOK, BUT NOT THAT ONE. I'D LIKE TO SELECT MY OWN, THANK YOU VERY MUCH.
WHAT? ARE YOU A GRAND SULTAN TO DEMAND PREFERENCES? YOU WOULD INSULT THE NOBLE MERCHANT WHO OWNS THIS SHOP?
HAS YOUR HUSBAND NOT TAUGHT YOU HOW TO CONDUCT YOURSELF AS A PROPER, DEMURE WOMAN?
BUT--
PAY FOR THIS BOOK NOW, BEFORE I CALL OUT THE VILLAGERS TO HAVE YOU STONED!
HELP!
OP
OKAY, I GUESS THIS JOB WASN'T RIGHT FOR YOU. A BIT OF CULTURAL MISUNDERSTANDING IS ALL. DON'T WORRY, HAKIM. I'VE FOUND ANOTHER ONE.
MY FRIEND CINDY OWNS THE SHOE STORE ACROSS THE WAY AND OWES ME A FAVOR.

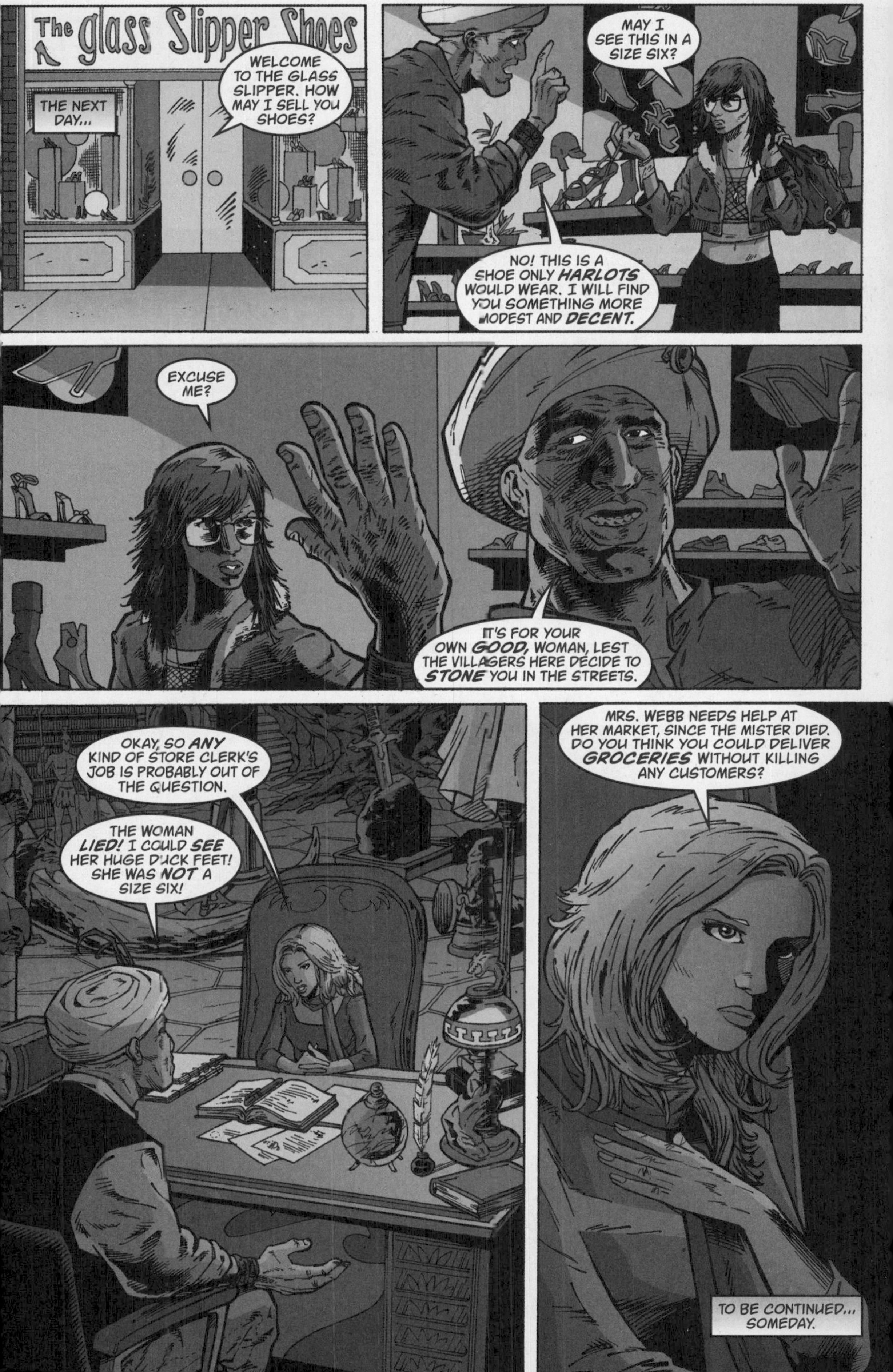

The glass Slipper Shoes
THE NEXT DAY...
WELCOME TO THE GLASS SLIPPER. HOW MAY I SELL YOU SHOES?
MAY I SEE THIS IN A SIZE SIX?
NO! THIS IS A SHOE ONLY HARLOTS WOULD WEAR. I WILL FIND YOU SOMETHING MORE MODEST AND DECENT.
EXCUSE ME?
IT'S FOR YOUR OWN GOOD, WOMAN, LEST THE VILLAGERS HERE DECIDE TO STONE YOU IN THE STREETS.
OKAY, SO ANY KIND OF STORE CLERK'S JOB IS PROBABLY OUT OF THE QUESTION.
THE WOMAN LIED! I COULD SEE HER HUGE DUCK FEET! SHE WAS NOT A SIZE SIX!
MRS. WEBB NEEDS HELP AT HER MARKET, SINCE THE MISTER DIED. DO YOU THINK YOU COULD DELIVER GROCERIES WITHOUT KILLING ANY CUSTOMERS?
TO BE CONTINUED... SOMEDAY.

Christopher Maslanka of Howell, New Jersey asks:

How does Bufkin keep getting his hands on the liquor?

THIS STORY WAS ILLUSTRATED BY JIM RUGG.

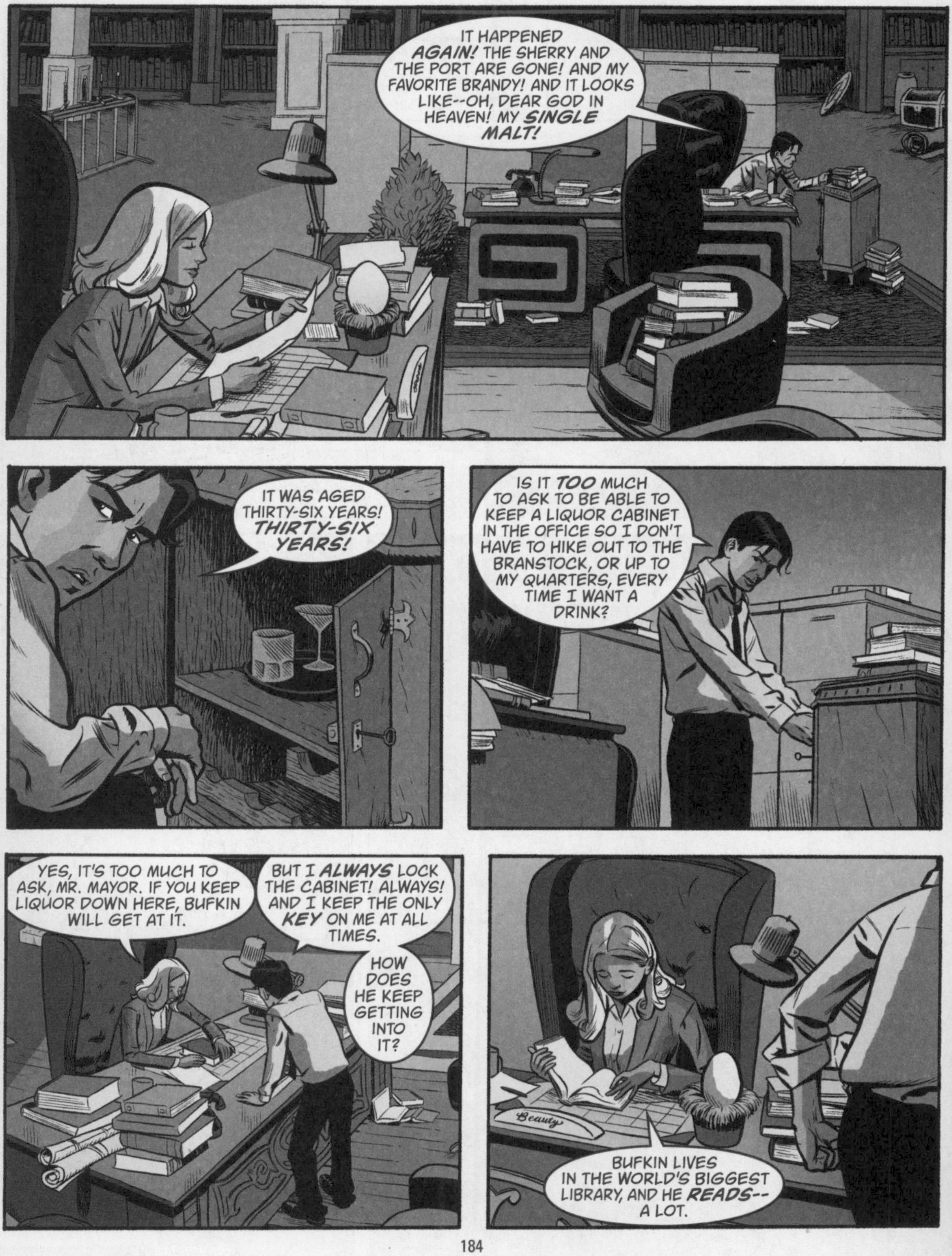
IT HAPPENED AGAIN! THE SHERRY AND THE PORT ARE GONE! AND MY FAVORITE BRANDY! AND IT LOOKS LIKE--OH, DEAR GOD IN HEAVEN! MY SINGLE MALT!
IT WAS AGED THIRTY-SIX YEARS! THIRTY-SIX YEARS!
IS IT TOO MUCH TO ASK TO BE ABLE TO KEEP A LIQUOR CABINET IN THE OFFICE SO I DON'T HAVE TO HIKE OUT TO THE BRANSTOCK, OR UP TO MY QUARTERS, EVERY TIME I WANT A DRINK?
YES, IT'S TOO MUCH TO ASK, MR. MAYOR. IF YOU KEEP LIQUOR DOWN HERE, BUFKIN WILL GET AT IT.
BUT I ALWAYS LOCK THE CABINET! ALWAYS! AND I KEEP THE ONLY KEY ON ME AT ALL TIMES.
HOW DOES HE KEEP GETTING INTO IT?
Beauty
BUFKIN LIVES IN THE WORLD'S BIGGEST LIBRARY, AND HE READS-- A LOT.

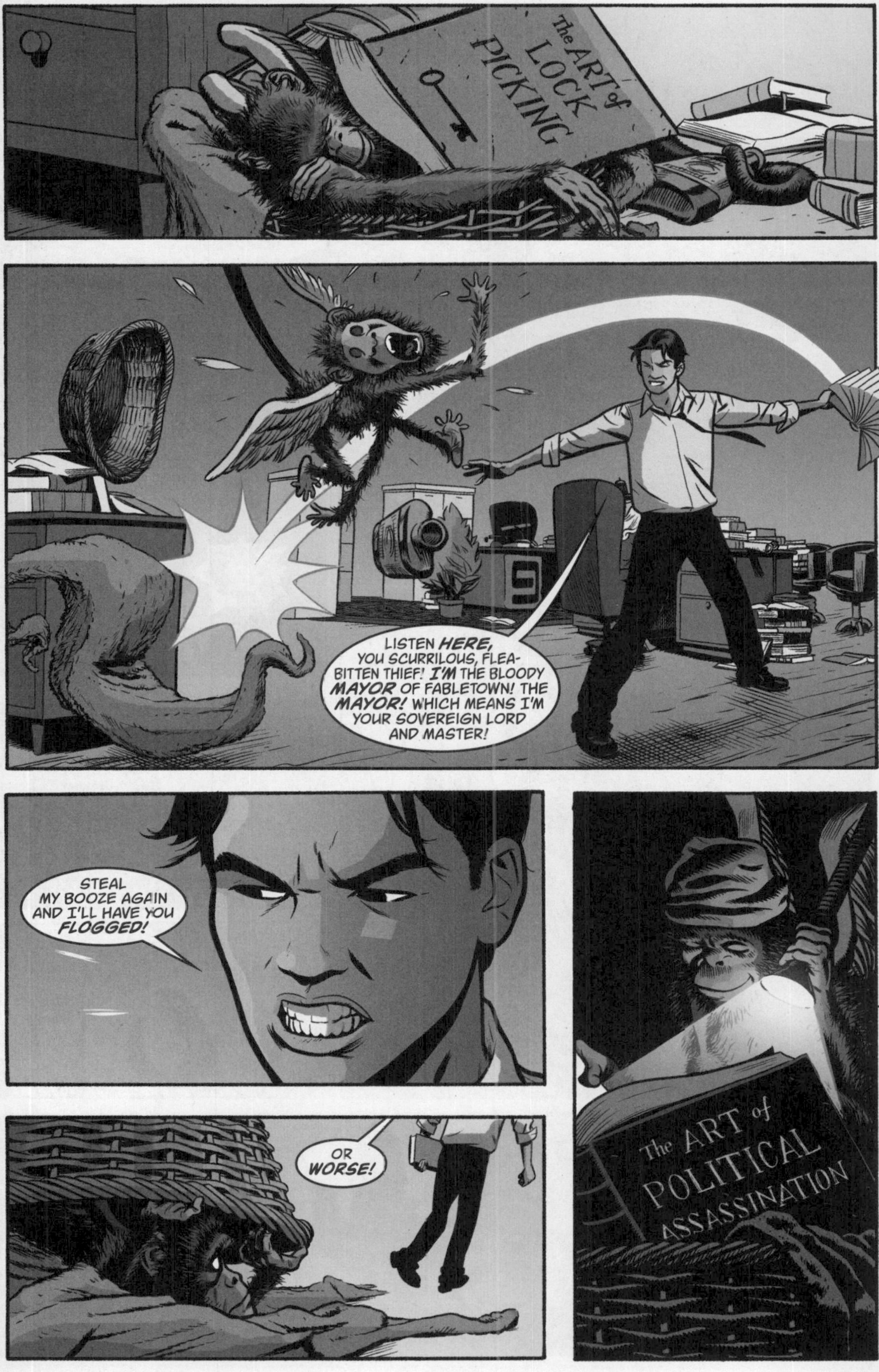
The ART of LOCK PICKING
LISTEN HERE, YOU SCURRILOUS, FLEA-BITTEN THIEF! I'M THE BLOODY MAYOR OF FABLETOWN! THE MAYOR! WHICH MEANS I'M YOUR SOVEREIGN LORD AND MASTER!
STEAL MY BOOZE AGAIN AND I'LL HAVE YOU FLOGGED!
OR WORSE!
The ART of POLITICAL ASSASSINATION

Ed Mayer of Plainfield, Illinois asks:

What is training like for a new member of the Mouse Police?

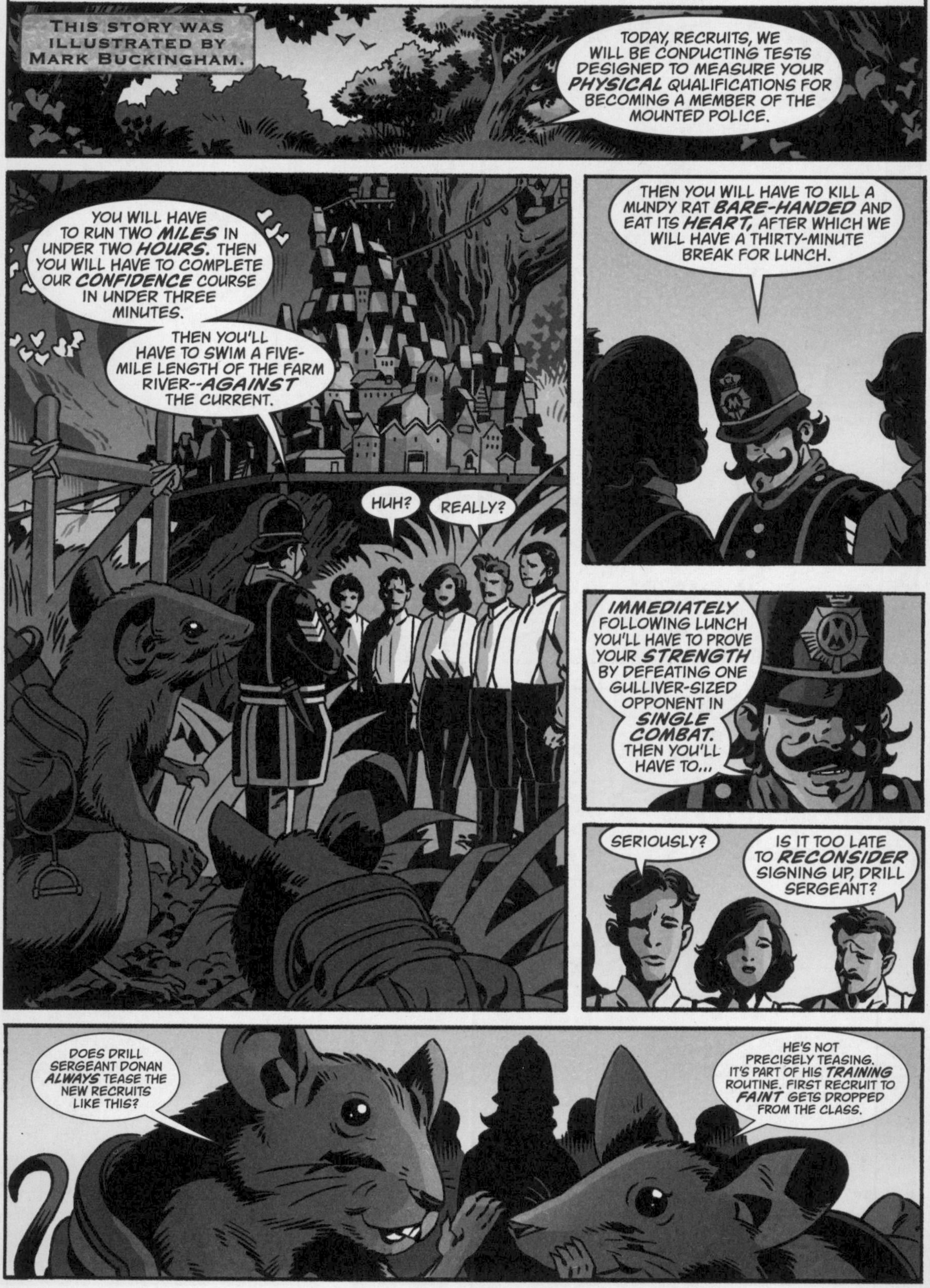
THIS STORY WAS ILLUSTRATED BY MARK BUCKINGHAM.
TODAY, RECRUITS, WE WILL BE CONDUCTING TESTS DESIGNED TO MEASURE YOUR PHYSICAL QUALIFICATIONS FOR BECOMING A MEMBER OF THE MOUNTED POLICE.
YOU WILL HAVE TO RUN TWO MILES IN UNDER TWO HOURS. THEN YOU WILL HAVE TO COMPLETE OUR CONFIDENCE COURSE IN UNDER THREE MINUTES.
THEN YOU'LL HAVE TO SWIM A FIVE-MILE LENGTH OF THE FARM RIVER--AGAINST THE CURRENT.
HUH?
REALLY?
THEN YOU WILL HAVE TO KILL A MUNDY RAT BARE-HANDED AND EAT ITS HEART, AFTER WHICH WE WILL HAVE A THIRTY-MINUTE BREAK FOR LUNCH.
IMMEDIATELY FOLLOWING LUNCH YOU'LL HAVE TO PROVE YOUR STRENGTH BY DEFEATING ONE GULLIVER-SIZED OPPONENT IN SINGLE COMBAT. THEN YOU'LL HAVE TO...
SERIOUSLY?
IS IT TOO LATE TO RECONSIDER SIGNING UP, DRILL SERGEANT?
DOES DRILL SERGEANT DONAN ALWAYS TEASE THE NEW RECRUITS LIKE THIS?
HE'S NOT PRECISELY TEASING. IT'S PART OF HIS TRAINING ROUTINE. FIRST RECRUIT TO FAINT GETS DROPPED FROM THE CLASS.

Tim Hotchkin of Saint Paul, Minnesota asks:

Did Jack leave anyone messages before he left Fabletown forever?

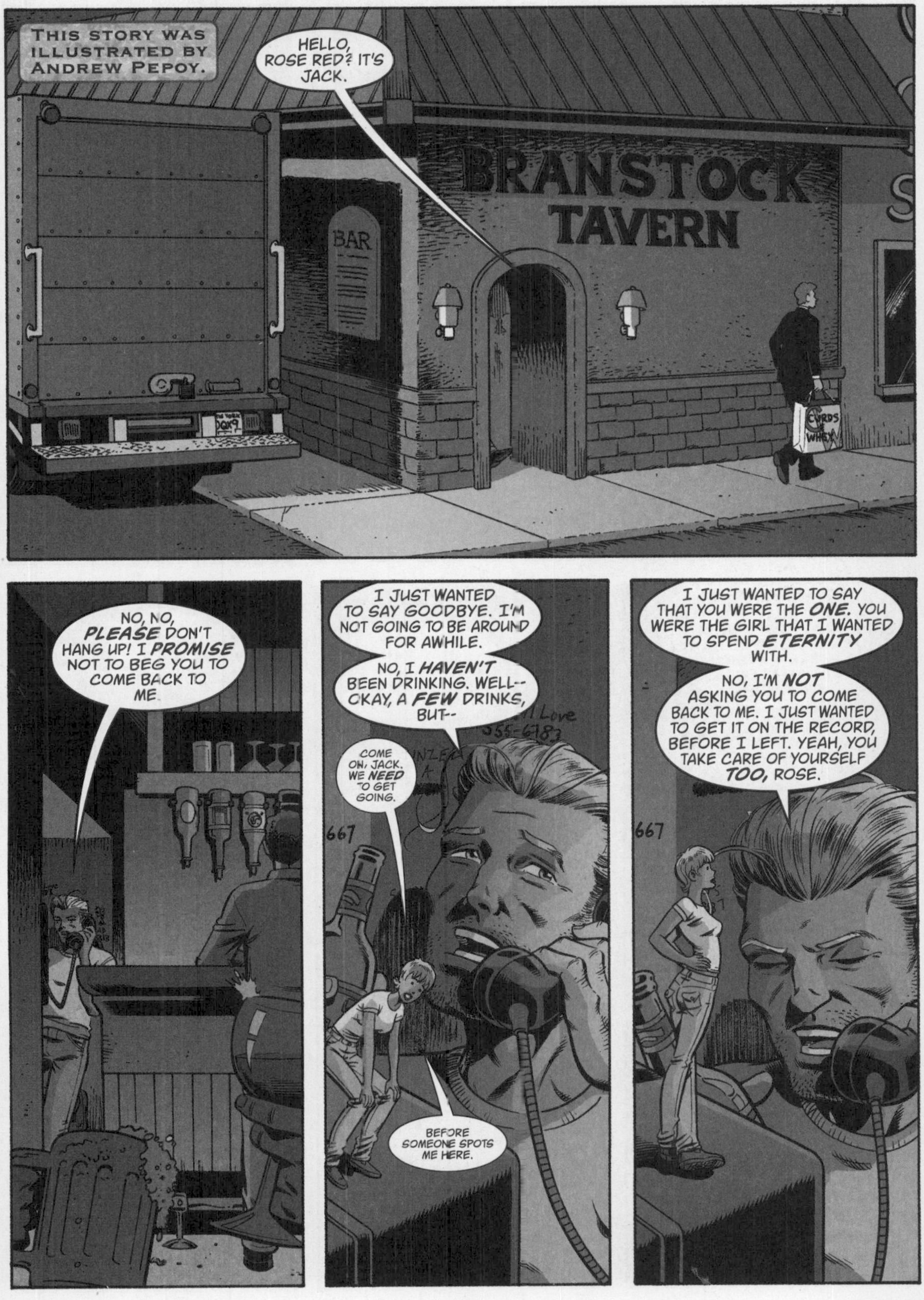
THIS STORY WAS ILLUSTRATED BY ANDREW PEPOY.
HELLO, ROSE RED? IT'S JACK.
BRANSTOCK TAVERN
BAR
NO, NO, PLEASE DON'T HANG UP! I PROMISE NOT TO BEG YOU TO COME BACK TO ME.
I JUST WANTED TO SAY GOODBYE. I'M NOT GOING TO BE AROUND FOR AWHILE.
NO, I HAVEN'T BEEN DRINKING. WELL-- OKAY, A FEW DRINKS, BUT--
COME ON, JACK. WE NEED TO GET GOING.
BEFORE SOMEONE SPOTS ME HERE.
I JUST WANTED TO SAY THAT YOU WERE THE ONE. YOU WERE THE GIRL THAT I WANTED TO SPEND ETERNITY WITH.
NO, I'M NOT ASKING YOU TO COME BACK TO ME. I JUST WANTED TO GET IT ON THE RECORD, BEFORE I LEFT. YEAH, YOU TAKE CARE OF YOURSELF TOO, ROSE.

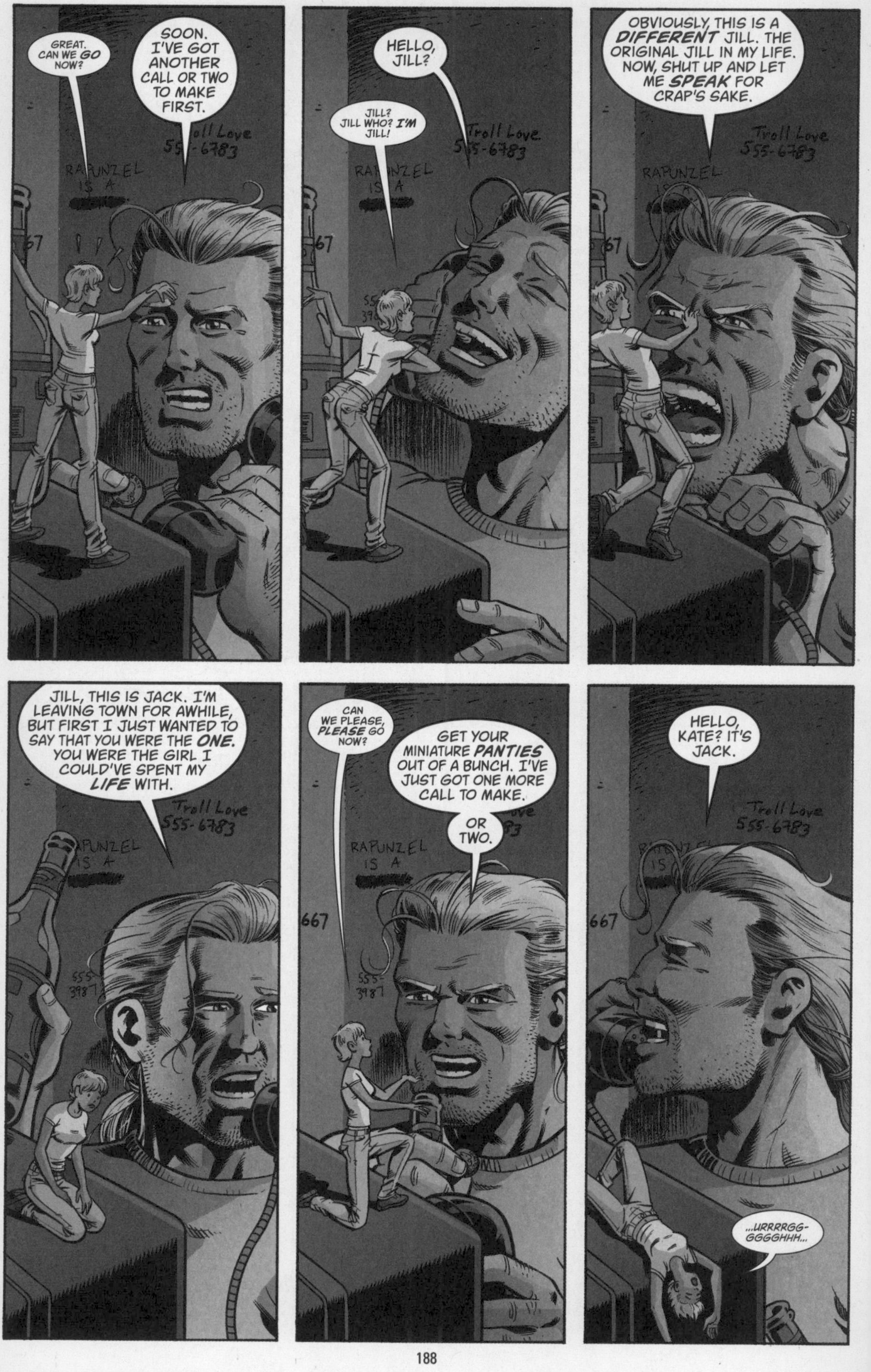
GREAT. CAN WE GO NOW?
SOON. I'VE GOT ANOTHER CALL OR TWO TO MAKE FIRST.
Troll Love 555-6783
RAPUNZEL IS A
HELLO, JILL?
JILL? JILL WHO? I'M JILL!
OBVIOUSLY, THIS IS A DIFFERENT JILL. THE ORIGINAL JILL IN MY LIFE. NOW, SHUT UP AND LET ME SPEAK FOR CRAP'S SAKE.
JILL, THIS IS JACK. I'M LEAVING TOWN FOR AWHILE, BUT FIRST I JUST WANTED TO SAY THAT YOU WERE THE ONE. YOU WERE THE GIRL I COULD'VE SPENT MY LIFE WITH.
CAN WE PLEASE, PLEASE GO NOW?
GET YOUR MINIATURE PANTIES OUT OF A BUNCH. I'VE JUST GOT ONE MORE CALL TO MAKE.
OR TWO.
HELLO, KATE? IT'S JACK.
...URRRRGG-GGGGHHH...

Duncan Berry of Burnley, England asks: How are the new Three Little Pigs adjusting to being pigs?

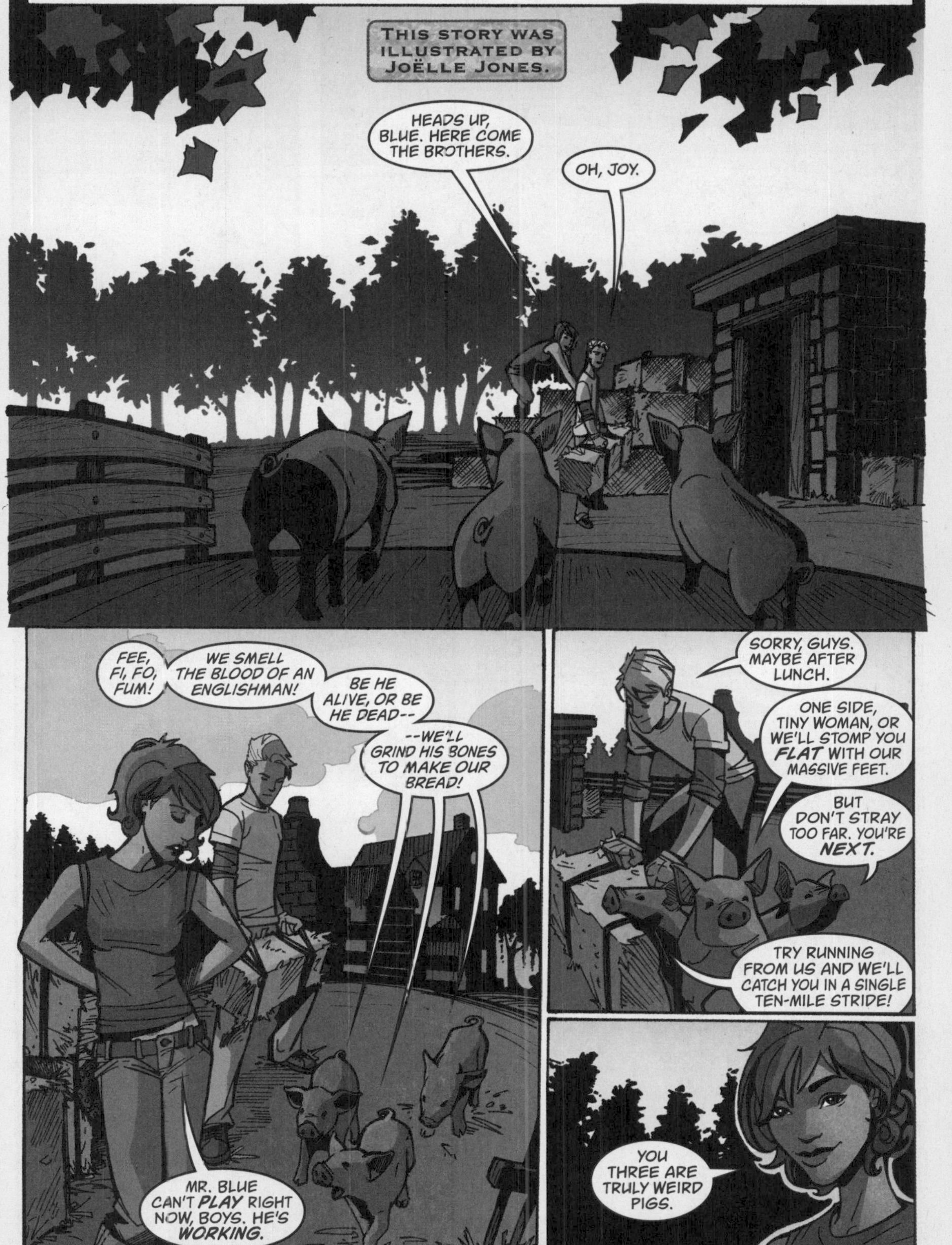
THIS STORY WAS ILLUSTRATED BY JOËLLE JONES.
HEADS UP, BLUE. HERE COME THE BROTHERS.
OH, JOY.
FEE, FI, FO, FUM!
WE SMELL THE BLOOD OF AN ENGLISHMAN!
BE HE ALIVE, OR BE HE DEAD--
--WE'LL GRIND HIS BONES TO MAKE OUR BREAD!
MR. BLUE CAN'T *PLAY* RIGHT NOW, BOYS. HE'S *WORKING.*
SORRY, GUYS. MAYBE AFTER LUNCH.
ONE SIDE, TINY WOMAN, OR WE'LL STOMP YOU *FLAT* WITH OUR MASSIVE FEET.
BUT DON'T STRAY TOO FAR. YOU'RE *NEXT.*
TRY RUNNING FROM US AND WE'LL CATCH YOU IN A SINGLE TEN-MILE STRIDE!
YOU THREE ARE TRULY WEIRD PIGS.

Colin Campbell of Malvern, Pennsylvania asks:

Besides Fly, who else has asked questions of the magic mirror?

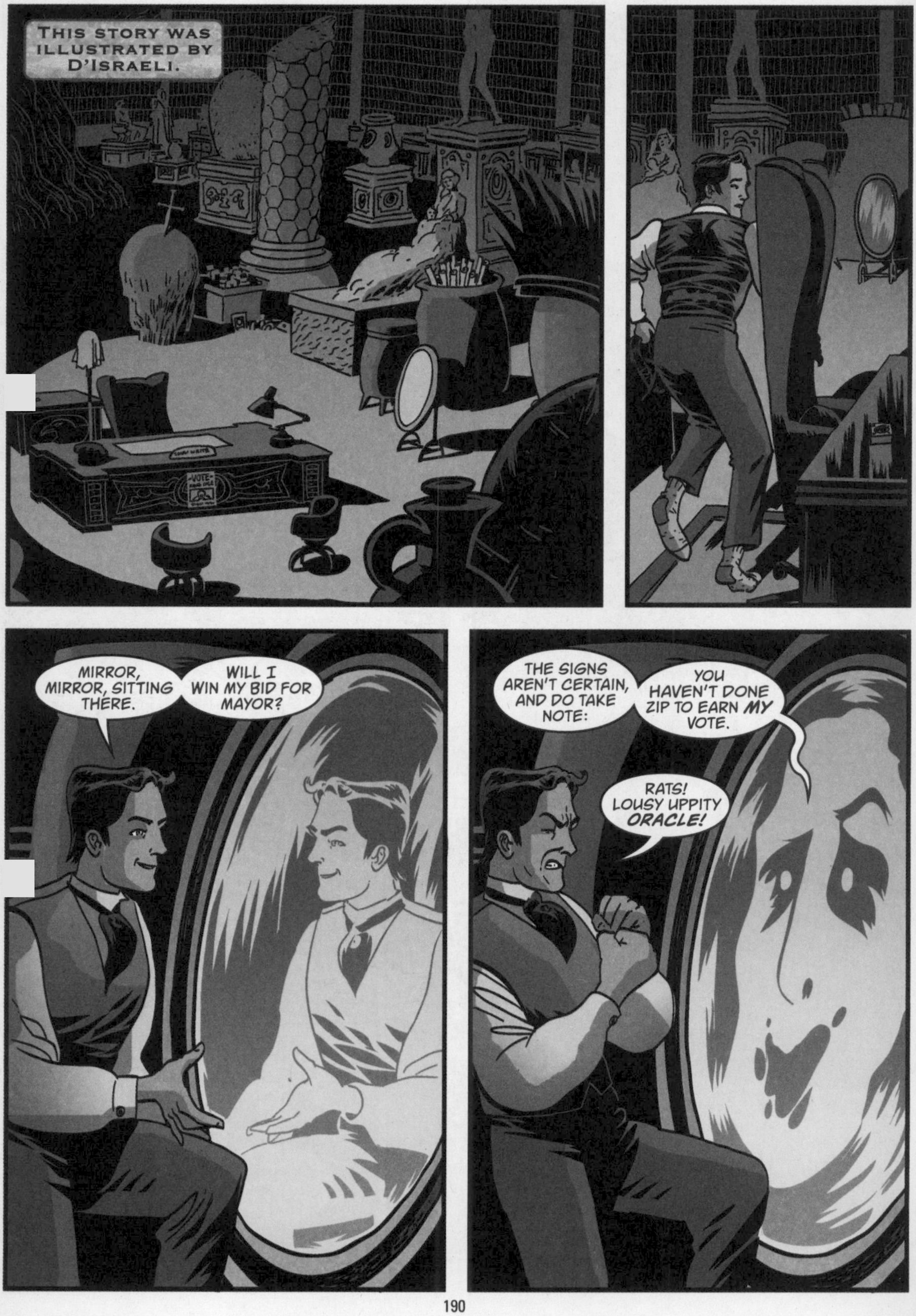

THIS STORY WAS ILLUSTRATED BY D'ISRAELI.
MIRROR, MIRROR, SITTING THERE.
WILL I WIN MY BID FOR MAYOR?
THE SIGNS AREN'T CERTAIN, AND DO TAKE NOTE:
YOU HAVEN'T DONE ZIP TO EARN MY VOTE.
RATS! LOUSY UPPITY ORACLE!

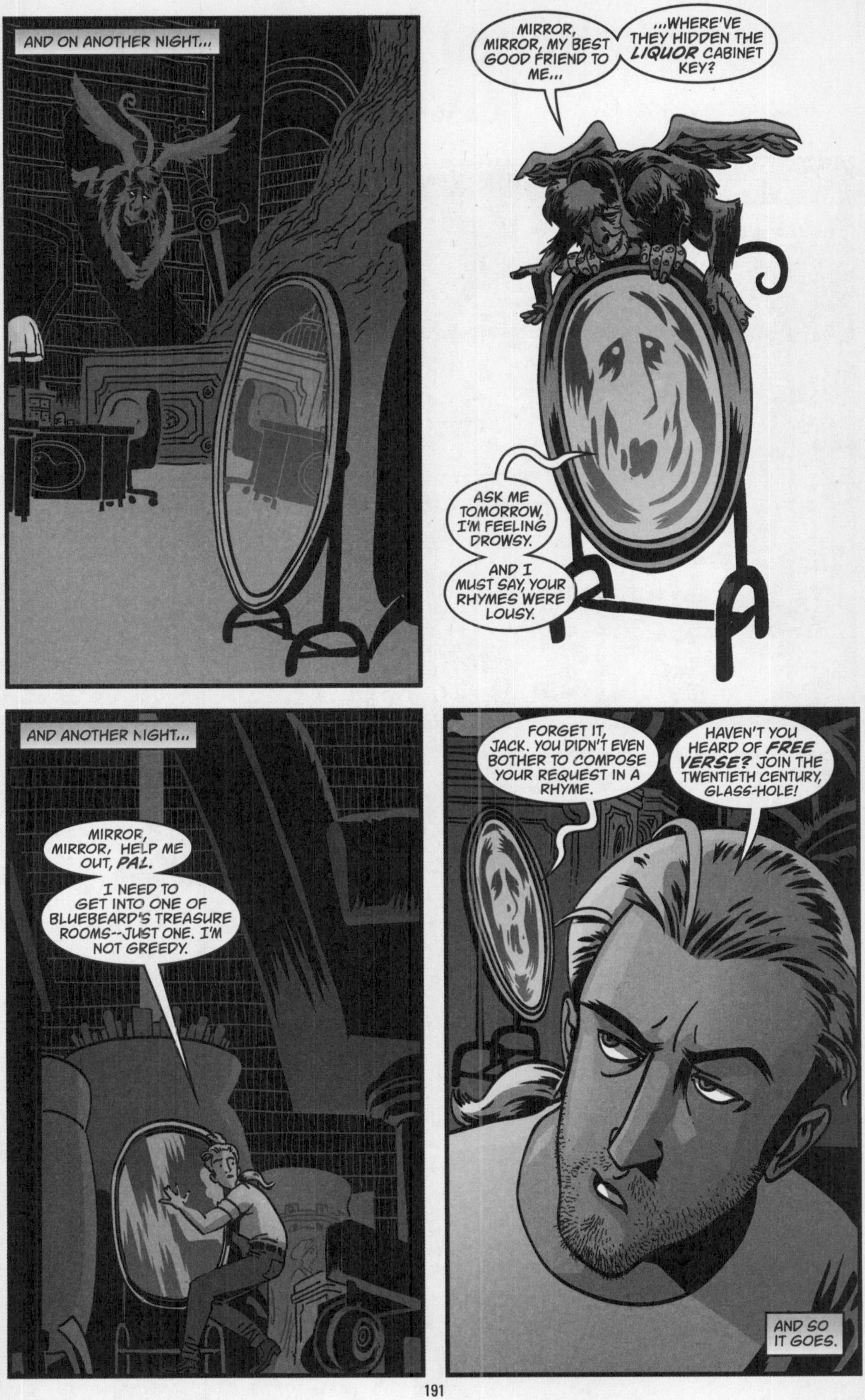
AND ON ANOTHER NIGHT...
MIRROR, MIRROR, MY BEST GOOD FRIEND TO ME...
...WHERE'VE THEY HIDDEN THE LIQUOR CABINET KEY?
ASK ME TOMORROW, I'M FEELING DROWSY.
AND I MUST SAY, YOUR RHYMES WERE LOUSY.
AND ANOTHER NIGHT...
MIRROR, MIRROR, HELP ME OUT, PAL.
I NEED TO GET INTO ONE OF BLUEBEARD'S TREASURE ROOMS--JUST ONE. I'M NOT GREEDY.
FORGET IT, JACK. YOU DIDN'T EVEN BOTHER TO COMPOSE YOUR REQUEST IN A RHYME.
HAVEN'T YOU HEARD OF FREE VERSE? JOIN THE TWENTIETH CENTURY, GLASS-HOLE!
AND SO IT GOES.

Brandon Cook of Huntington, West Virginia asks:

What is Boy Blue's favorite song?

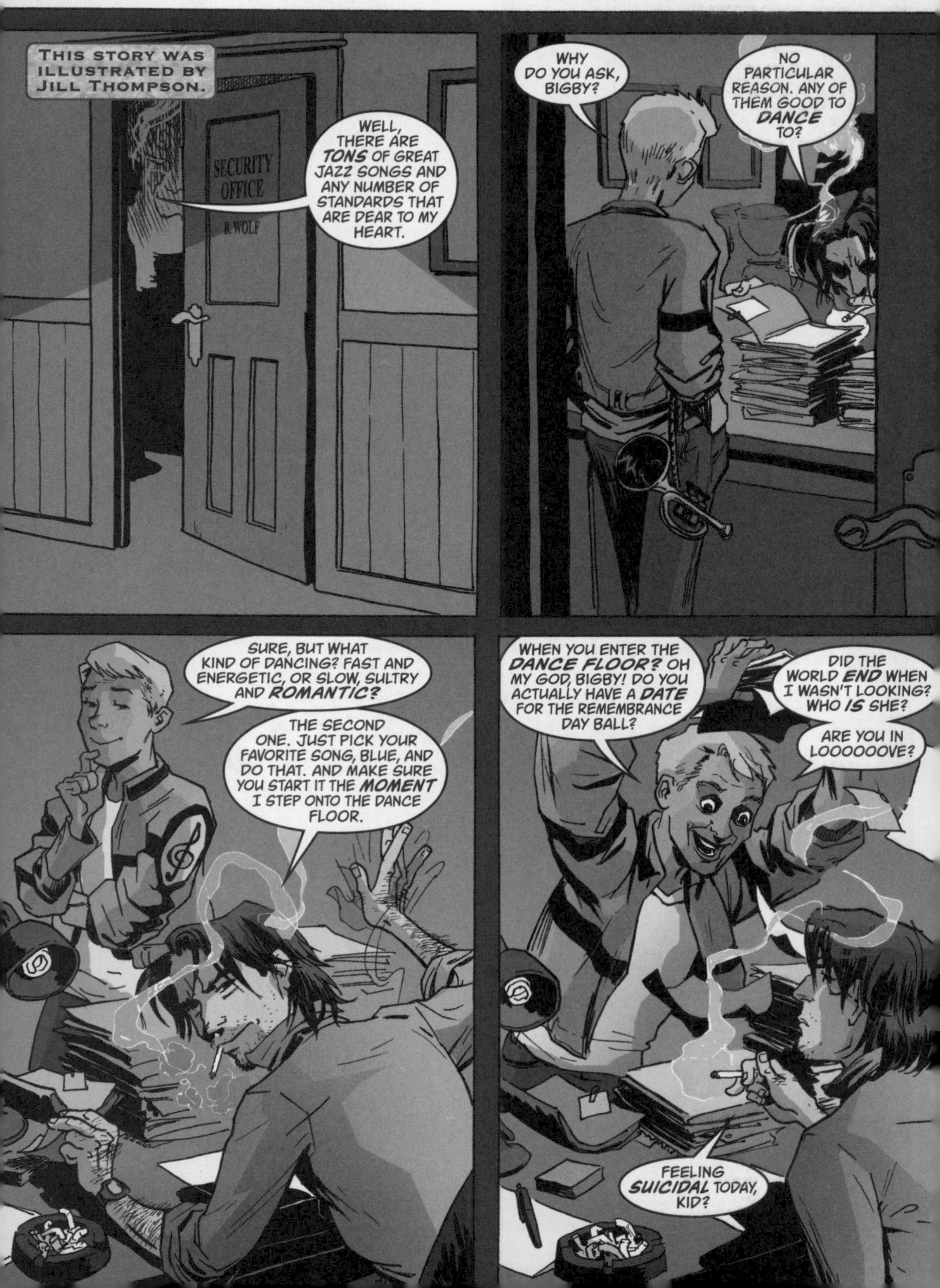
THIS STORY WAS ILLUSTRATED BY JILL THOMPSON.
SECURITY OFFICE
B. WOLF
WELL, THERE ARE TONS OF GREAT JAZZ SONGS AND ANY NUMBER OF STANDARDS THAT ARE DEAR TO MY HEART.
WHY DO YOU ASK, BIGBY?
NO PARTICULAR REASON. ANY OF THEM GOOD TO DANCE TO?
SURE, BUT WHAT KIND OF DANCING? FAST AND ENERGETIC, OR SLOW, SULTRY AND ROMANTIC?
THE SECOND ONE. JUST PICK YOUR FAVORITE SONG, BLUE, AND DO THAT. AND MAKE SURE YOU START IT THE MOMENT I STEP ONTO THE DANCE FLOOR.
WHEN YOU ENTER THE DANCE FLOOR? OH MY GOD, BIGBY! DO YOU ACTUALLY HAVE A DATE FOR THE REMEMBRANCE DAY BALL?
DID THE WORLD END WHEN I WASN'T LOOKING? WHO IS SHE?
ARE YOU IN LOOOOOOVE?
FEELING SUICIDAL TODAY, KID?

Tiana Krohn-Ching of Honolulu, Hawaii asks:

What song was playing when Snow and Bigby first danced together at the Remembrance Day Ball?

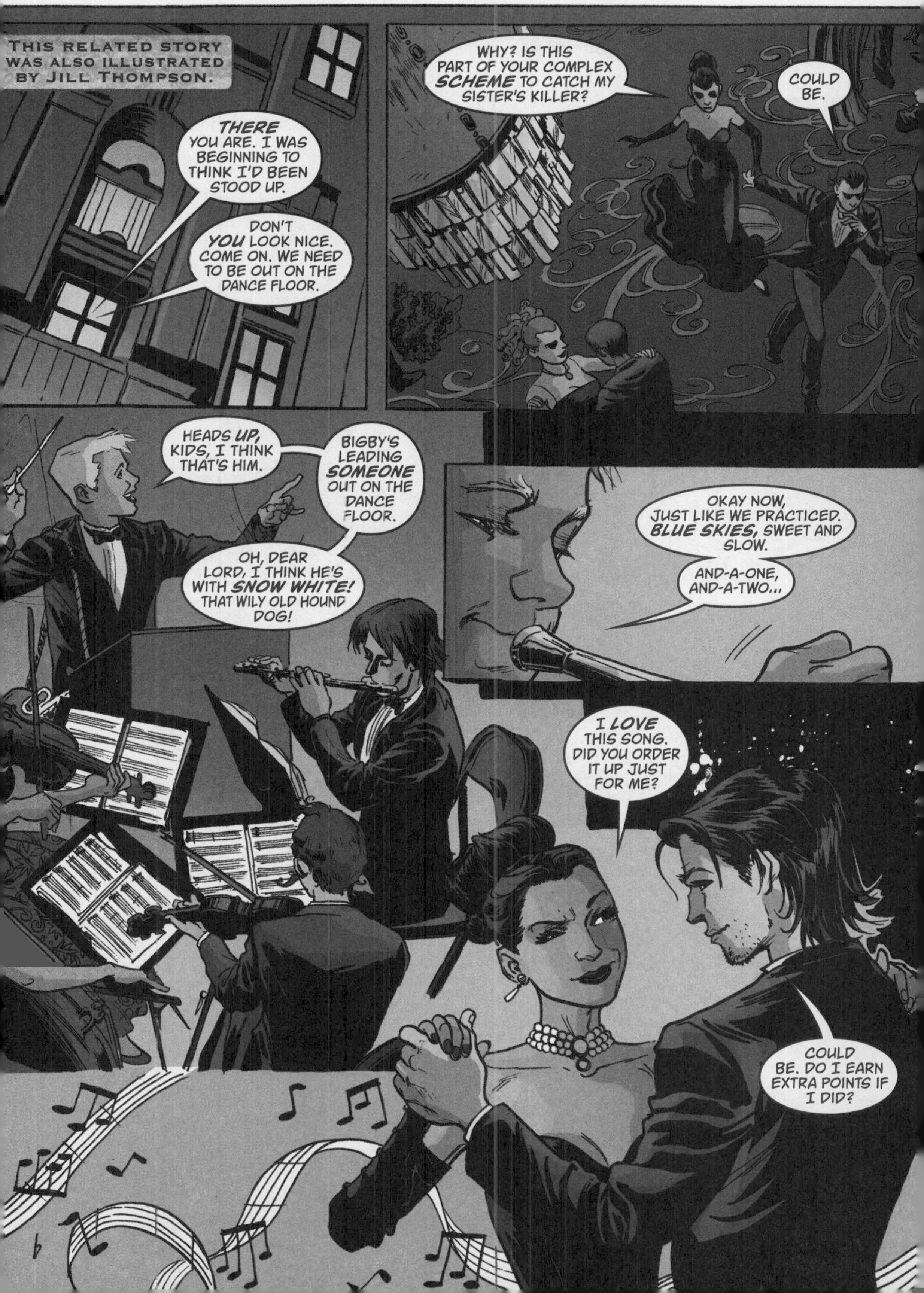

THIS RELATED STORY WAS ALSO ILLUSTRATED BY JILL THOMPSON.
THERE YOU ARE. I WAS BEGINNING TO THINK I'D BEEN STOOD UP.
DON'T YOU LOOK NICE. COME ON. WE NEED TO BE OUT ON THE DANCE FLOOR.
WHY? IS THIS PART OF YOUR COMPLEX SCHEME TO CATCH MY SISTER'S KILLER?
COULD BE.
HEADS UP, KIDS, I THINK THAT'S HIM.
BIGBY'S LEADING SOMEONE OUT ON THE DANCE FLOOR.
OH, DEAR LORD, I THINK HE'S WITH SNOW WHITE! THAT WILY OLD HOUND DOG!
OKAY NOW, JUST LIKE WE PRACTICED. BLUE SKIES, SWEET AND SLOW.
AND-A-ONE, AND-A-TWO...
I LOVE THIS SONG. DID YOU ORDER IT UP JUST FOR ME?
COULD BE. DO I EARN EXTRA POINTS IF I DID?

Jennifer Ferrell of San Diego, California asks:

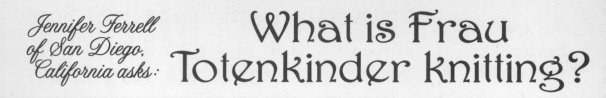

What is Frau Totenkinder knitting?

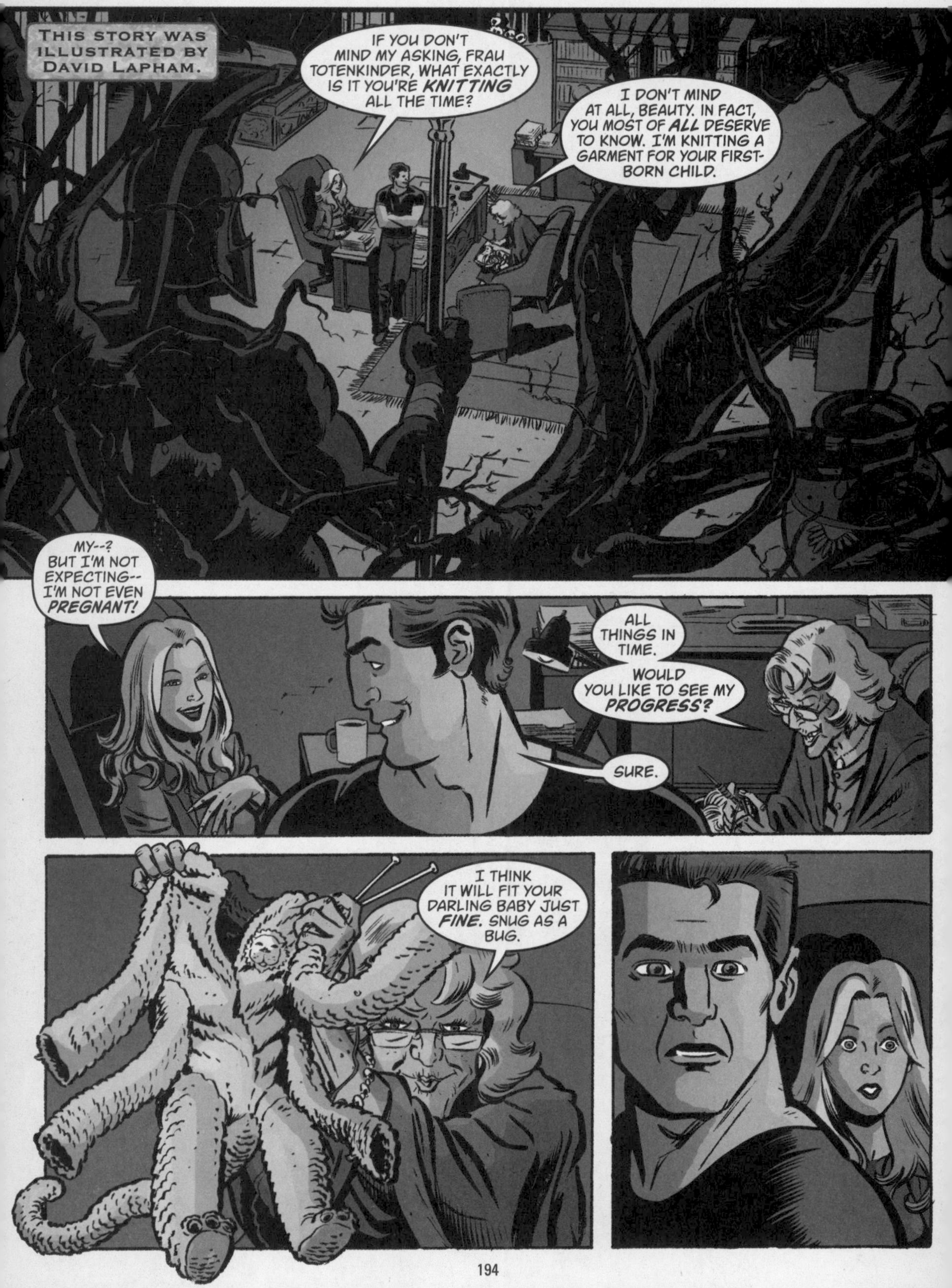
THIS STORY WAS ILLUSTRATED BY DAVID LAPHAM.
IF YOU DON'T MIND MY ASKING, FRAU TOTENKINDER, WHAT EXACTLY IS IT YOU'RE KNITTING ALL THE TIME?
I DON'T MIND AT ALL, BEAUTY. IN FACT, YOU MOST OF ALL DESERVE TO KNOW. I'M KNITTING A GARMENT FOR YOUR FIRST-BORN CHILD.
MY--? BUT I'M NOT EXPECTING-- I'M NOT EVEN PREGNANT!
ALL THINGS IN TIME.
WOULD YOU LIKE TO SEE MY PROGRESS?
SURE.
I THINK IT WILL FIT YOUR DARLING BABY JUST FINE. SNUG AS A BUG.

Paul Nolan of Southampton, U.K. asks: Who was Prince Charming's first love?

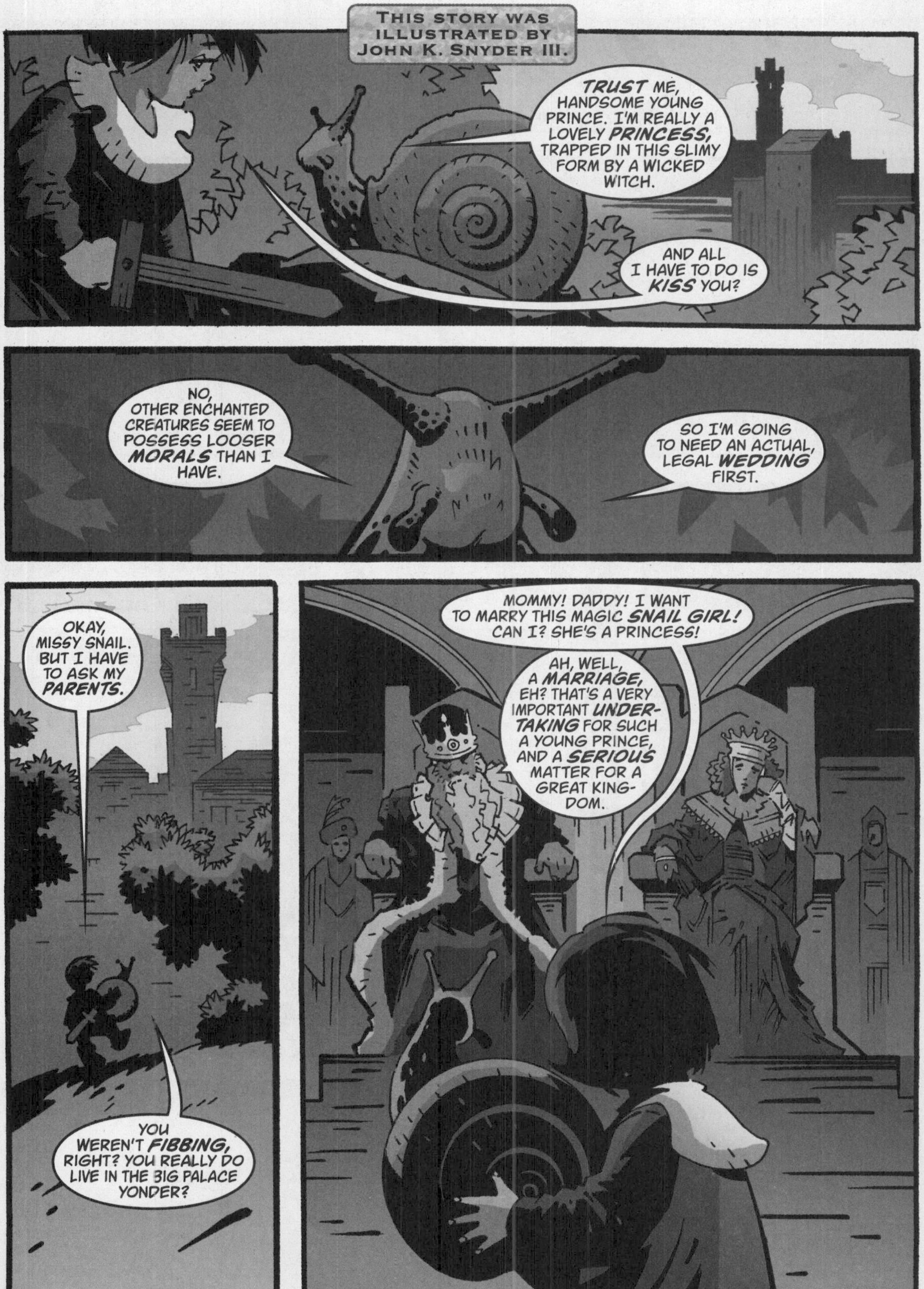

THIS STORY WAS ILLUSTRATED BY JOHN K. SNYDER III.
TRUST ME, HANDSOME YOUNG PRINCE. I'M REALLY A LOVELY PRINCESS, TRAPPED IN THIS SLIMY FORM BY A WICKED WITCH.
AND ALL I HAVE TO DO IS KISS YOU?
NO, OTHER ENCHANTED CREATURES SEEM TO POSSESS LOOSER MORALS THAN I HAVE.
SO I'M GOING TO NEED AN ACTUAL, LEGAL WEDDING FIRST.
OKAY, MISSY SNAIL. BUT I HAVE TO ASK MY PARENTS.
YOU WEREN'T FIBBING, RIGHT? YOU REALLY DO LIVE IN THE BIG PALACE YONDER?
MOMMY! DADDY! I WANT TO MARRY THIS MAGIC SNAIL GIRL! CAN I? SHE'S A PRINCESS!
AH, WELL, A MARRIAGE, EH? THAT'S A VERY IMPORTANT UNDERTAKING FOR SUCH A YOUNG PRINCE, AND A SERIOUS MATTER FOR A GREAT KINGDOM.

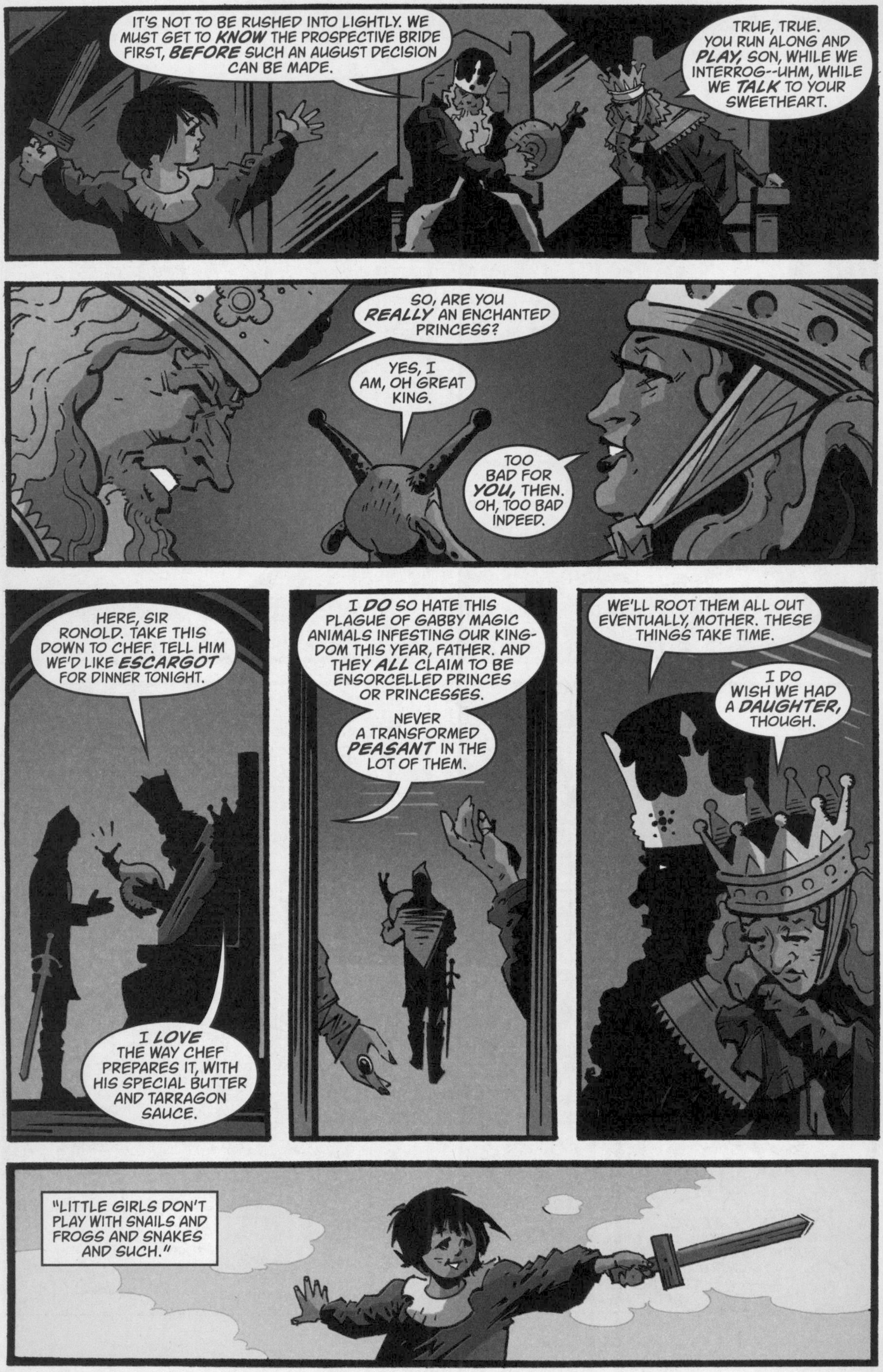
IT'S NOT TO BE RUSHED INTO LIGHTLY. WE MUST GET TO KNOW THE PROSPECTIVE BRIDE FIRST, BEFORE SUCH AN AUGUST DECISION CAN BE MADE.
TRUE, TRUE. YOU RUN ALONG AND PLAY, SON, WHILE WE INTERROG--UHM, WHILE WE TALK TO YOUR SWEETHEART.
SO, ARE YOU REALLY AN ENCHANTED PRINCESS?
YES, I AM, OH GREAT KING.
TOO BAD FOR YOU, THEN. OH, TOO BAD INDEED.
HERE, SIR RONOLD. TAKE THIS DOWN TO CHEF. TELL HIM WE'D LIKE ESCARGOT FOR DINNER TONIGHT.
I LOVE THE WAY CHEF PREPARES IT, WITH HIS SPECIAL BUTTER AND TARRAGON SAUCE.
I DO SO HATE THIS PLAGUE OF GABBY MAGIC ANIMALS INFESTING OUR KINGDOM THIS YEAR, FATHER. AND THEY ALL CLAIM TO BE ENSORCELLED PRINCES OR PRINCESSES.
NEVER A TRANSFORMED PEASANT IN THE LOT OF THEM.
WE'LL ROOT THEM ALL OUT EVENTUALLY, MOTHER. THESE THINGS TAKE TIME.
I DO WISH WE HAD A DAUGHTER, THOUGH.
"LITTLE GIRLS DON'T PLAY WITH SNAILS AND FROGS AND SNAKES AND SUCH."

Angela Rufino of Philadelphia, Pennsylvania asks:

How many romantic conquests has Prince Charming had?

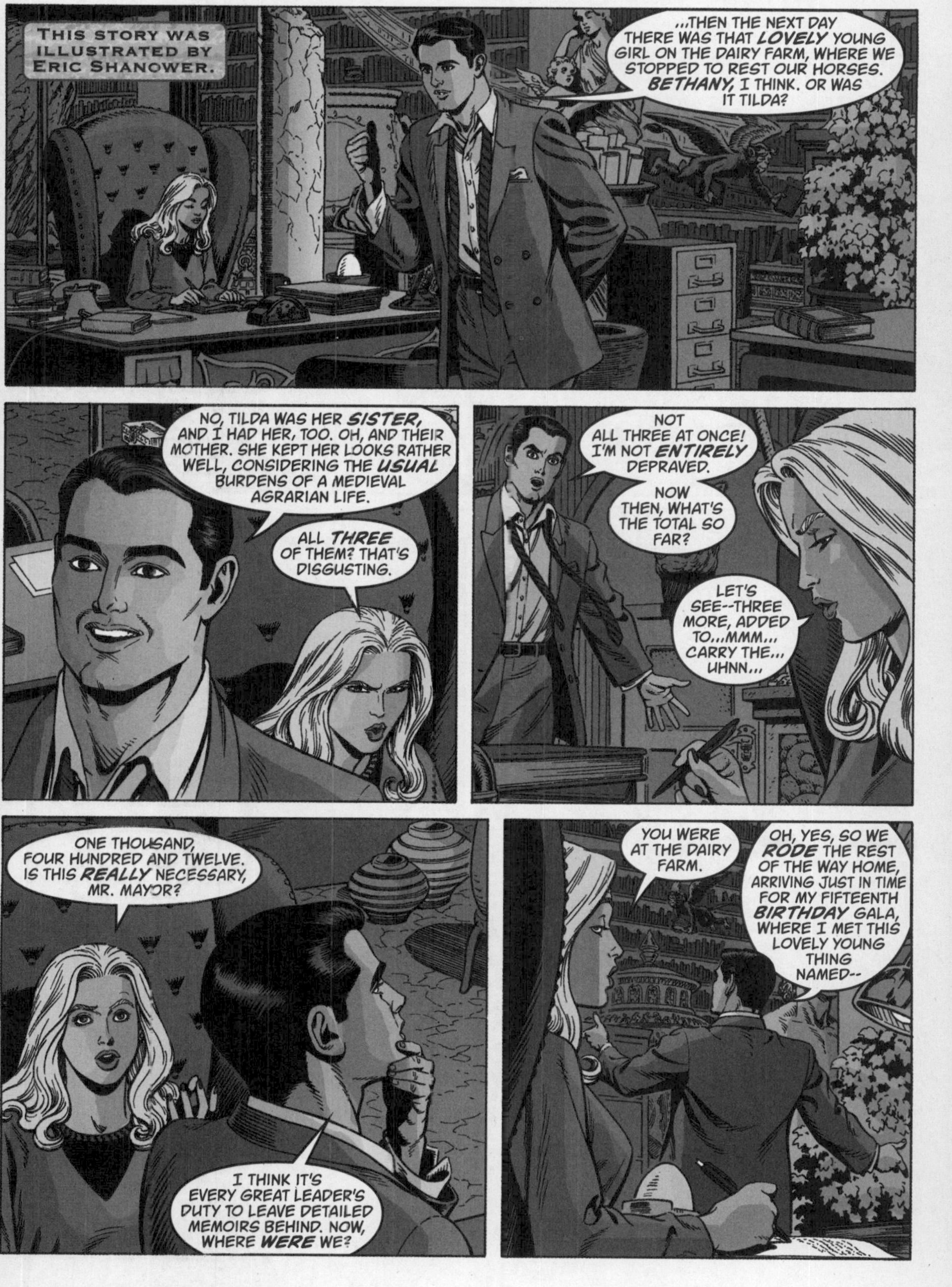
THIS STORY WAS ILLUSTRATED BY ERIC SHANOWER.
...THEN THE NEXT DAY THERE WAS THAT LOVELY YOUNG GIRL ON THE DAIRY FARM, WHERE WE STOPPED TO REST OUR HORSES. BETHANY, I THINK. OR WAS IT TILDA?
NO, TILDA WAS HER SISTER, AND I HAD HER, TOO. OH, AND THEIR MOTHER. SHE KEPT HER LOOKS RATHER WELL, CONSIDERING THE USUAL BURDENS OF A MEDIEVAL AGRARIAN LIFE.
ALL THREE OF THEM? THAT'S DISGUSTING.
NOT ALL THREE AT ONCE! I'M NOT ENTIRELY DEPRAVED.
NOW THEN, WHAT'S THE TOTAL SO FAR?
LET'S SEE--THREE MORE, ADDED TO...MMM... CARRY THE... UHNN...
ONE THOUSAND, FOUR HUNDRED AND TWELVE. IS THIS REALLY NECESSARY, MR. MAYOR?
I THINK IT'S EVERY GREAT LEADER'S DUTY TO LEAVE DETAILED MEMOIRS BEHIND. NOW, WHERE WERE WE?
YOU WERE AT THE DAIRY FARM.
OH, YES, SO WE RODE THE REST OF THE WAY HOME, ARRIVING JUST IN TIME FOR MY FIFTEENTH BIRTHDAY GALA, WHERE I MET THIS LOVELY YOUNG THING NAMED--

Shelly Bond of New York, New York asks: **Who caught the bouquet at Snow White's wedding?**

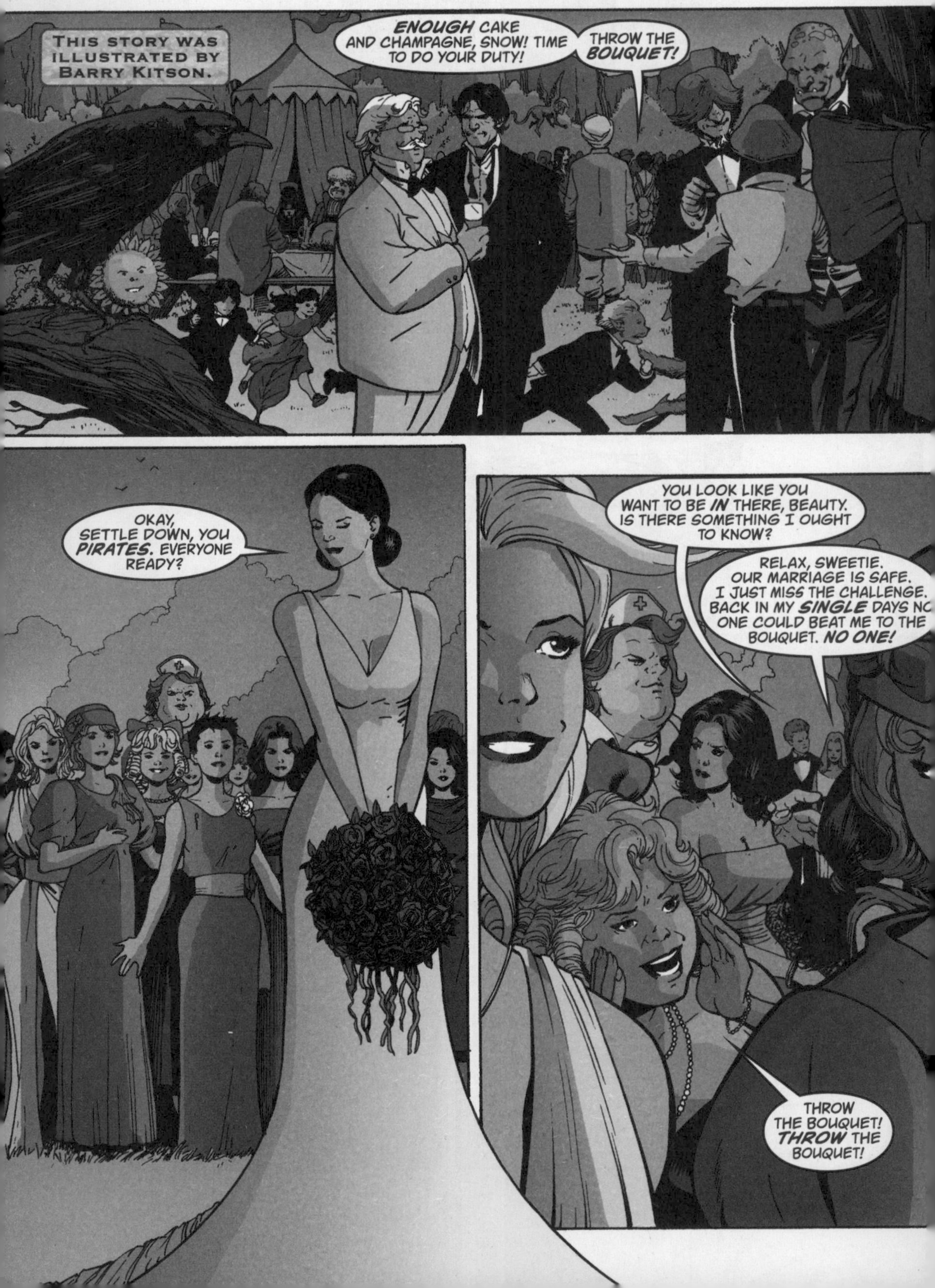
THIS STORY WAS ILLUSTRATED BY BARRY KITSON.
ENOUGH CAKE AND CHAMPAGNE, SNOW! TIME TO DO YOUR DUTY!
THROW THE BOUQUET!
OKAY, SETTLE DOWN, YOU PIRATES. EVERYONE READY?
YOU LOOK LIKE YOU WANT TO BE IN THERE, BEAUTY. IS THERE SOMETHING I OUGHT TO KNOW?
RELAX, SWEETIE. OUR MARRIAGE IS SAFE. I JUST MISS THE CHALLENGE. BACK IN MY SINGLE DAYS NO ONE COULD BEAT ME TO THE BOUQUET. NO ONE!
THROW THE BOUQUET! THROW THE BOUQUET!

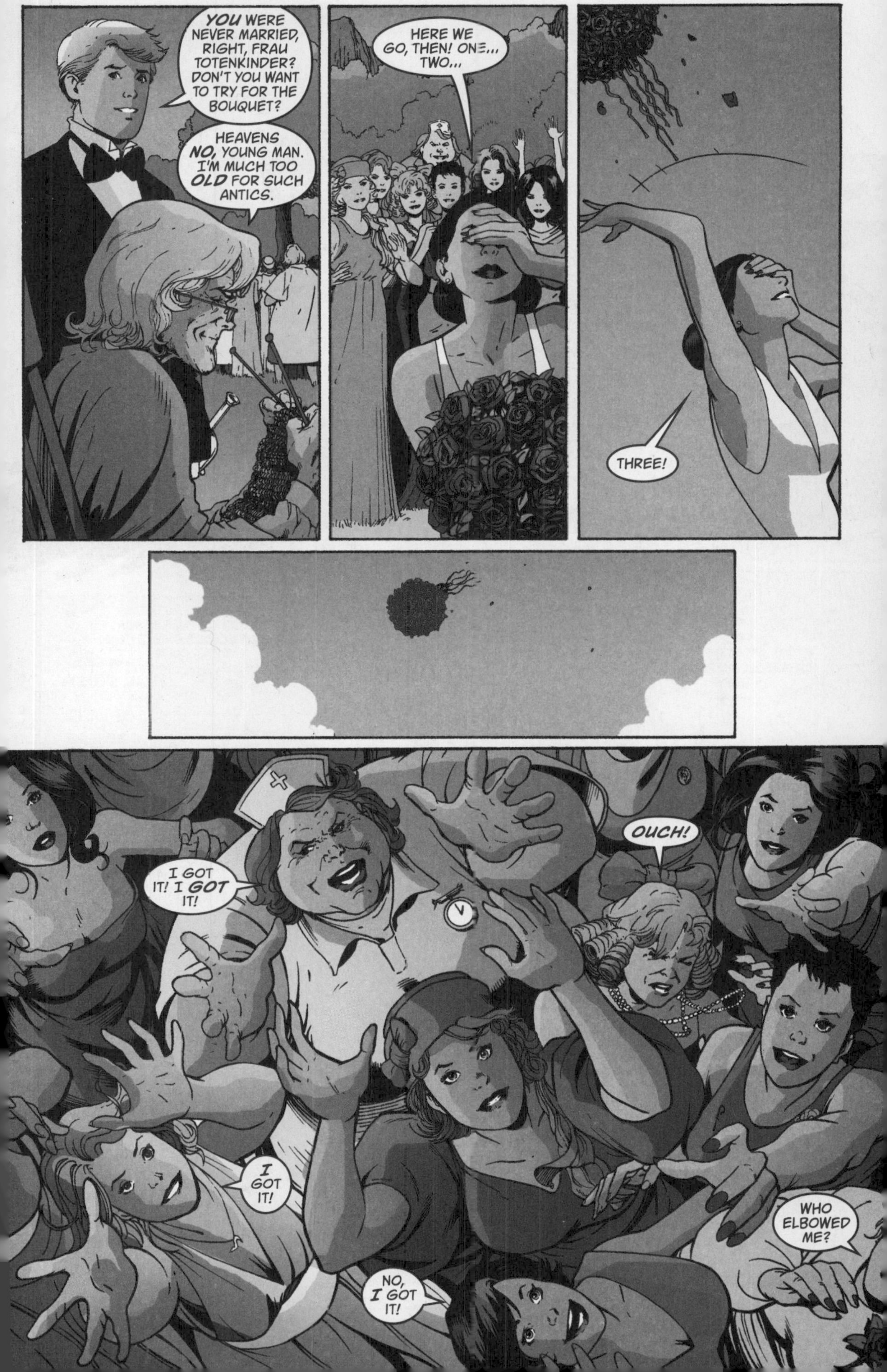
YOU WERE NEVER MARRIED, RIGHT, FRAU TOTENKINDER? DON'T YOU WANT TO TRY FOR THE BOUQUET?
HEAVENS NO, YOUNG MAN. I'M MUCH TOO OLD FOR SUCH ANTICS.
HERE WE GO, THEN! ONE... TWO...
THREE!
OUCH!
I GOT IT! I GOT IT!
I GOT IT!
WHO ELBOWED ME?
NO, I GOT IT!

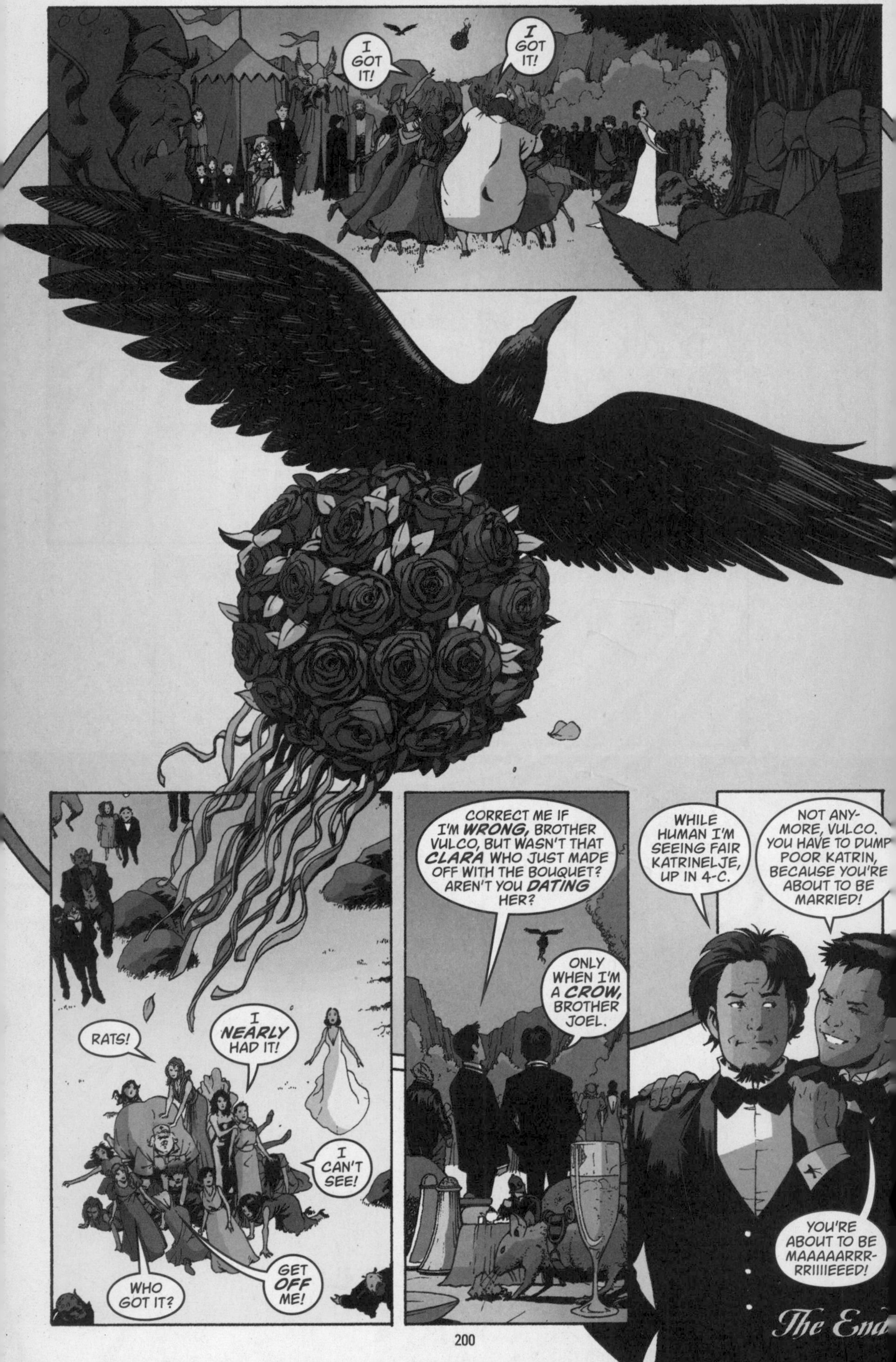
I GOT IT!
I GOT IT!
RATS!
I NEARLY HAD IT!
I CAN'T SEE!
WHO GOT IT?
GET OFF ME!
CORRECT ME IF I'M WRONG, BROTHER VULCO, BUT WASN'T THAT CLARA WHO JUST MADE OFF WITH THE BOUQUET? AREN'T YOU DATING HER?
ONLY WHEN I'M A CROW, BROTHER JOEL.
WHILE HUMAN I'M SEEING FAIR KATRINELJE, UP IN 4-C.
NOT ANY-MORE, VULCO. YOU HAVE TO DUMP POOR KATRIN, BECAUSE YOU'RE ABOUT TO BE MARRIED!
YOU'RE ABOUT TO BE MAAAAARRR-RRIIIIEEED!
The End